Manual 2000

MANUAL 2000

The Ethical Consumer Guide

JOHN ELKINGTON and JULIA HAILES

Adapted for the Canadian market by FRANCIS GILLIS

KEY PORTER BOOKS

First published in 1998 by Hodder & Stoughton, a division of Hodder Headline PLC

Canadian Cataloguing in Publication Data

Elkington, John

Manual 2000 : the ethical consumer guide

ISBN 1-55263-013-7

1. Human ecology. 2. Man—Influence on environment. 3. Environmental protection. 4. Consumption (Economics). I. Hailes, Julia. II. Gillis, Francis B. III. Title.

GF75.E44 1999 304.2 C98-932996-8

THE CANADA COUNCIL FOR THE ARTS SINCE 1957 | LE CONSEIL DES ARTS DU CANADA DEPUIS 1957

The publisher gratefully acknowledges the support of the Canada Council for the Arts and the Ontario Arts Council for its publishing program.

Canada

We acknowledge the financial support of the Government of Canada through the Book Publishing Industry Development Program (BPIDP) for our publishing activities.

Key Porter Books Limited
70 The Esplanade
Toronto, Ontario
Canada M5E 1R2
www.keyporter.com

Electronic formatting: Heidy Lawrance Associates
Design: Peter Maher

Printed and bound in Canada

99 00 01 02 6 5 4 3 2 1

Contents

Part III

Acknowledgements

Adapting *Manual 2000* for Canadians turned out to be a fascinating but mammoth task. I would never have completed it without the flexible schedule kindly allowed me by my colleagues at PDA Partners. I am especially grateful to Pat Delbridge for being the catalyst that brought me and the book's authors together.

I am indebted to many individuals and organizations for sharing information. In particular, I wish to thank Ruth Lotzkar (Environmentally Sound Packaging Coalition of Canada), Olivia Nugent (Pollution Probe), Tina Harrison (Canadians for Ethical Treatment of Food Animals) and Leslie Ballentine (Ontario Farm Animal Council). Dr. David Fraser, professor and research chair in animal welfare at The University of British Columbia, took the time to discuss farming issues in detail and provided me with valuable background information.

Working on *Manual 2000* gave me a true appreciation of the achievement of the book's authors, John Elkington and Julia Hailes. Dealing with them was a pleasure and a privilege. It was also a delight working with Andrea Bock of Key Porter Books, who shared my desire to turn out an excellent resource for Canadians, and with Dianne Broad, who provided thoughtful and intelligent copy editing.

Finally, I wish to thank my family and friends for their encouragement—and their understanding, as time normally spent with them was devoted to this project.

Francis Gillis

Note:
The inclusion of an organization or company in the Citizen 2000 Checklists or in the Directory should not be read as an automatic endorsement. I am familiar with many of these organizations, but not all. I spotlight them as sources of information, products or services. Contact the relevant ones and make up your own mind.

Foreword

Ten years ago, when the *Green Consumer Guide* launched a wave of "green consumerism," public concern for the environment was at an unprecedented high. The last decade has seen a waning of public outrage. It has been replaced by the complacency that comes from the belief that effective governmental and corporate response has made outrage unnecessary.

Green consumerism played an unintended role in mollifying an aroused public, moving it from demanding protection and restoration of our planetary life support system to comparison shopping and recycling. The advent of "easy steps" to save the earth aided and abetted the increasing sense that the world was back in balance. Surely, if the blue box at the curb was full of recyclable material, and our shopping carts had a token number of recycled paper products and biodegradable detergent, the universe was unfolding as it should.

With the advent of *Manual 2000*, it is clear that consumerism *itself* is the problem. We cannot simply shop our way to a sustainable world. We have to change our society's bad habits in a very fundamental way. In short, we have to consume less. And, yes, what we do consume should meet the highest standards of sustainability—not only from the viewpoint of the use of the products, but of the environmental, social justice and human rights aspects of the product's full life cycle.

Given that challenge, perfection is not attainable—unless we take Gandhi literally, and implement the change we want to see in the world by doing as he did: weaving our own cloth, and living in ascetic simplicity.

We can live rich and full lives while avoiding the worst examples of consumerism's collision course with survival. Avoiding aquaculture shrimp, for example, is not a hugely demanding choice. Choosing to take mass transit might be, if home and work are too inconveniently separated. But a commitment to thinking through our choices can consistently reduce what Professor Bill Rees has so eloquently characterized as our "ecological footprint." Right now, Canadians are the "Big Foot" of the planet in terms of our ecological imprint.

Consuming more and living more wastefully reflected a post-war shift in values. North American society moved from Depression-era exhortations of "waste not, want not," to "buy now, pay later." It can be argued that this shift was programmed by an advertising blitz to expand consumer markets. The case for a deliberate manipulation of values is perhaps best made by the following excerpt from the 1960 *Journal of Retailing*, quoting retailing analyst Victor Lebow:

...Our enormously productive economy ... demands that we make consumption our way of life, that we convert the buying and use of goods into rituals, that we seek our spiritual satisfaction, our ego satisfaction, in consumption ... We need things consumed, burned up, worn out, replaced and discarded at an ever increasing rate.

The last decade has seen a steady deterioration of the planet's life-support systems while society's attention was focused elsewhere. *Manual 2000* comes at just the right time in the millennial search for sustainability. Its approach reflects the evolving understanding of the impacts of our decisions, on everything from organic food to fertility options. Developing a more thorough appreciation of the impacts of our decisions on the world around us is critical. So, too, is examining the extent to which we have been brainwashed into believing that happiness is found at the mall.

In the coming wave of public demands for action, we must not be satisfied with mere rhetoric from policy-makers and CEOs. In the next wave of public outrage, we must sustain a demand for fundamental change. This is not a crisis we can solve by shopping.

Elizabeth May
Sierra Club of Canada

How to use *Manual 2000*

Manual 2000 is laid out and cross-referenced to encourage you to flip between sections. The boxes—by simplifying and headlining some of the more complex issues—should also make the text easier to access.

The book is organized in three parts. Part I (Chapters 1 and 2) looks at some of the pressures driving the Citizen 2000 Agenda. Part II (Chapters 3 to 8 and the Directory) focuses on six major areas of our lives, highlighting the issues and providing follow-up contact details in the Citizen 2000 Checklists. Part III (Chapter 9 and the Directory) provides the necessary stepping stones for turning ideas into action.

For a brief summary of the context for *Manual 2000*—and of the Citizen 2000 Agenda—please turn to *2001 and All That* (Introduction, Chapter 1, pages 15–19).

The key global trends that are driving us in this direction are then explained in *The Future We Want* (Chapter 2, pages 20–39).

Then six major chapters review the following inter-linked themes:

Food & Drink (Chapter 3, pages 40–85)
Community & Home (Chapter 4, pages 86–129)
Transport & Travel (Chapter 5, pages 130–162)
Communication & Computers (Chapter 6, pages 163–197)
Money & Investment (Chapter 7, pages 198–223)
Life & Death (Chapter 8, pages 224–279)

At the end of each section in each chapter we provide a Citizen 2000 Checklist. This includes some of the key campaigning organizations, corporate leaders and laggards, and sources of further information. Contact details for all the noncorporate organizations are listed in the Directory, pages 283–296.

Finally Chapter 9, *Action Plan* (pages 281–282), features the Citizen 2000 Action Plan which shows how you can take a stand on key issues—and how to push businesses and government alike towards the changes you want.

Manual 2000 is designed as a tool for thinking, priority-setting and action. We welcome your comments. Please send them to: Citizen 2000, Tintinhull House, Tintinhull, Somerset BA22 8PZ, U.K. or, even better, e-mail us at: Manual2000@tintinhull.demon.co.uk or elkington@sustainability.co.uk.

Part I

1 Introduction: 2001 and all that

The years 2000 and 2001 have long held a peculiar fascination. The new millennium may technically start on January 1, 2001, but most of us will probably stay up on December 31, 1999—and consider the new millennium begun when all the zeroes drop into place somewhere between 00.00 and 00.01 on January 1, 2000. The whole thing may be an accident of Christian dating, but most of the world will still feel that a new era has begun.

We will look back at the 20th century in wonder. But what will we focus on? The way the private car colonized Earth? The way we soared into the skies and then out into space? The way our offices and homes were taken over by successive waves of electronic equipment, including telephones, TVs, faxes and personal computers? Or the almost unimaginable scale of the slaughter in two world wars and many smaller ones?[1] Then we will look forward into the 21st century. And what will we expect? Gene therapy for cancer (page 245)? Digital money on the Internet (page 203)? Animal-grown human transplant organs (page 245)? Self-drive vehicles (page 159)? Orgasmatrons for safe sex? Self-replicating robots? Fetal development outside the womb (page 235)? People on Mars? Or Earth's orbit so bunged up with space junk that we can't even get off the planet (page 178)?

Whether we are optimists or pessimists, it will be an extraordinary, once-in-a-lifetime experience. Many people will attempt not only a list of New Year's resolutions but also a list of new century—even new millennium—resolutions. *Manual 2000* offers some ideas, in the form of the "Citizen 2000 Agenda," on what this list might contain.

In "The Future We Want" (pages 20–39), we look at how some of today's problems may provoke tomorrow's solutions. We'll assess the problems that confront us—and for which solutions must, if we are to survive, evolve in the 21st century. In Part II, we investigate a range of trends, issues and choices that already demand our attention, or soon will. We focus on some of the choices open to us in relation to food and drink (pages 40–85), community and home (pages 86–129), transport and travel (pages 130–162), communication and computers (pages 163–197), money and investment (pages 198–223), and life and death (pages 224–280).

Let's now run quickly through each of the

10 elements of the Citizen 2000 Agenda and begin to make the links with some of the trends, issues and initiatives covered in the rest of the book.

1. Working Out What's Really Important

Time and money are usually in short supply. Few of us can really afford—or want—to become full-time campaigners on the issues that concern us. But most of us still want to help the push toward a better world. The key step here is to decide on our priorities—and then to focus our efforts in these areas, rather than allowing our energies to be frittered away.

If we concentrate on a small number of priority problems and campaigns, we can become much better informed on the issues involved. When we are better informed, we are more effective. You don't have to read *Manual 2000* from cover to cover—you can flip through the sections that interest you. Decide which issues are most important to you. Then work out where you can be most effective. Remember: you will be most effective if the issue is of real interest to you—or links to your local community or work.

2. Making Intelligent Life Choices

Our choices—whether we vote at the ballot box or at the supermarket cash register—can have profound impacts both on the present and on the future. We make choices not only about which products and brands to buy, but also about which lifestyles to adopt. These life choices (about where to live, what career path to follow and what our life purpose is) help to define who we are.

Clearly, our product choices are a key part of all of this. We choose between brand-name products on the basis of their price, quality, safety and, more recently, their environmental performance. Consumer power—wielded by ordinary, green, ethical or conscious consumers—has already provoked major changes in business practice (pages 214–219).

Increasingly, however, people recognize that product choices alone will not change the world. So, growing numbers of individuals and families are making lifestyle choices. Obvious examples would include eating organic (pages 40–51; 84–85), living healthy (pages 263–274), investing ethically (pages 214–219), telecommuting (pages 118–189) and making decisions on how to raise children. The "downshifting" trend is another increasingly popular option (pages 206–213). These lifestyle choices—coupled with even more fundamental life choices—then shape a whole host of lower-order choices, sending powerful market and political signals.

We need to make intelligent choices and recognize the implicit messages we are sending in what we say, buy and do. Among the best sources of information on the various issues are the campaigning organizations listed in our Citizen 2000 Checklists, which are found at the end of each major section in Part II.

3. Acting, as Well as Thinking

Don't just toy with possible priorities and life decisions—get involved! There is an optimism that comes from action that can help to offset the pessimism that so often flows from just thinking—and worrying—about the enormous challenges we face. In any event, who will know what we think if we simply stay at home and fret in front of the TV?

There are many ways to get started, from buying local produce and supporting our local shops, through to using public transport and taking up cycling. In some areas, we may feel that we are sticking our neck out, but that is how all great social changes start. If you are uncomfortable lobbying the manager in your local grocery store, try applying pressure by other means—such as writing letters to the newspapers or choosing to invest ethically (pages 214–219).

There will be times when you may need to go even further on an issue. Don't just grin and bear it. Choose your ground—and take a stand. In some cases, as with the NIMBY (Not In My Back Yard) campaigns against toxic waste sites or other development, others may interpret this as an expression of pure self-interest (pages 103–112); but if we can't protect our own backyard, what can we protect?

As you start to act, keep a careful note of the barriers that make it difficult for you to do the right thing. There is a whole host of problems that can slow us down (pages 112–114). Some are facts of life, but many can be dealt with by politicians and others in authority. Follow the Citizen 2000 Action Plan (pages 281–282) to ensure that they help you do what needs to be done.

4. Using People Power for Positive Change

In today's world, surprisingly, each of us can have an enormous influence. Governments and businesses alike monitor public opinion to see what will—and will not—be acceptable. But even if they didn't, when large numbers of people start to think and act together they can have a huge impact. This is people power.

Think of the people around the globe who paid tribute to Princess Diana after her death—and of the signals they sent. "Diana's Army" powerfully communicated many people's frustration with a world dominated by the Establishment, the status quo, tradition, suits, people-like-us, formality, solemnity, protocol, emotionless behaviour, hypocrisy and (although these are not automatically linked to such problems) male values.[2] Instead, there was a growing desire for a world based on different values: the acknowledgement of feelings, honesty, informality, humour, the personal, diversity, vulnerability, compassion, renewal—and, increasingly, female values.

Such dramatic responses are relatively rare, of course, but they send powerful shock waves when they do happen. And there have been many less dramatic, slower-paced movements that have successfully lobbied for change. Indeed, if enough of us ask for anything, the chances are that it will be offered. We have seen this trend in terms of the calls for healthier foods (pages 40–85), green consumerism and the banning of certain chemicals, such as CFCs (page 21).

Some aspects of the information revolution may even make it easier for individuals to take a stand and have a real say (pages 165–166). Small groups will be able to mount increasingly powerful "virtual campaigns" over the Internet (page 175). But most people will continue to express their opinions and priorities in more conventional ways—including writing letters and joining campaigning groups. In Part III we look at how each of us can use people power (pages 281–282).

5. Fighting for the Right to Know

There are still plenty of people who would like to keep us in the dark. But if we are to make sensible, effective choices, we need up-to-date, reliable information. Read up on the issues before you get involved in the debate. *Manual 2000* will help you get started—and if you want to probe deeper you can contact the organizations featured in our Citizen 2000 Checklists.

Government departments, companies and other business organizations may often feel more comfortable with secrecy and tight information control, but this makes it hard for us to make intelligent, informed choices. So we should all call for less secrecy in society. This applies to many of the "life and death" issues discussed in Chapter 8, as well as to areas like pesticide residues (pages 41–43), animal experiments (pages 243–247) and genetic engineering (pages 59–68).

6. Understanding the Bigger Picture

Paradoxically, as the world shrinks and the pace of events accelerates, we are all having to get our minds around an ever-bigger picture. We need to explore and understand the links between things we do every day and effects that may be felt on the other side of the planet—or even in the distant future.

It is no longer simply a question of the environment. Certainly, we need to be concerned about issues like the thinning of the ozone layer (pages 21–22), which affects our health, and about global warming (page 28), but we also need to be aware, for example, of the working conditions of people in poorer countries, whether they make footballs or running shoes (page 126).

Some people find this challenge baffling, others exciting. But one thing is clear: in the 21st century, we will find our sense of who our neighbours are including, eventually, people living thousands of kilometres away. We may not consciously decide to move in this direction, but increasingly powerful modern communication technologies will ensure that we know about—and are increasingly part of—lives that once would have seemed impossibly remote or exotic (pages 165–167).

7. Expecting the Unexpected

The natural world has long shown itself able to spring all sorts of surprises on us, ranging from earthquakes and tidal waves to pest infestations, plagues and diseases like AIDS (page 267–271). There will undoubtedly be others. The world of technology, too, has sprung unpleasant surprises. These have included the job losses caused by machines and now computers, the Bhopal and Chernobyl disasters caused by the chemical and nuclear industries, and the Millennium Bug—which looks set to become a major plague for businesses and governments (pages 168–170).

At one level, we can prepare ourselves for life's surprises by ensuring that we are flexible—and that our education and training make us employable whatever happens to our current job (pages 211–212). At another level, we can decide to review our lives and ambitions in the light of some of the unexpected developments that may emerge. This is something that major companies are now beginning to do. At the personal level, this could mean saving enough money to get us through hard times (page 205), or even preparing a "DIY obituary" (page 275), to help us make the most of our life while we are still living it.

8. Practising Give and Take

For centuries, through campaigns, revolutions and wars, people have fought for new freedoms and new rights: the rights to liberty, equality and fraternity. The rights to free association and to join a trade union. The right to happiness. The right to vote. The right to the public provision of health-care services. The right to a clean environment. The rights of other species. Human rights. And now, even the rights of future generations.

These hard-won rights are to be treasured, but they often come with responsibilities—which some people have been less inclined to consider and respect. As a result, the 21st century must see the emergence of a new "give-and-take" culture in which there will be a clearer focus on the balance between rights and responsibilities.

This will often require a rebalancing of our relationships with our families (pages 87–96), our communities (pages 96–103), the organizations for which we work, welfare systems (page 87) and—as illustrated by the ethical investment trend—with financial markets (pages 214–219).

9. Knowing Happiness

Most of us assume that if only we had more money or more things, we would be happy. But experience shows that this is far from certain. Since the 1970s, there has been an interesting trend in many of the richer countries, with people simultaneously becoming increasingly better off and increasingly unhappy (pages 96–97). One reason may be that we have focused too much attention on our standard of living—how much we earn or consume—and too little on our quality of life, measured in terms of how we feel (page 208).

Governments, too, use a range of tools to measure wealth creation based on the flows of money, materials and energy. Tools like the Gross National Product tend to be blind to the trends in happiness or well-being (page 208). Among the key contributors to our quality of life are good health, a happy family (pages 87–94), a supportive community (pages 96–102) and a personal sense of mission.

10. Respecting the Living

The 21st century will see and experience the natural world very differently. New satellite, sensor and micro-camera technologies will drive this change. And it seems almost inevitable that the "Gaian" worldview will evolve and spread.

Gaia was the ancient Greek earth goddess, and her name has now been adopted to describe a new branch of science. This views the entire planet as if it were a single living organism. A global ecosystem, in short, where different parts of our natural environment—for example, rainforests and coral reefs—are as vital to the living planet as our hearts, kidneys and other organs are to our own bodies.

If we are to succeed, we need to learn how to pick up the early, weak signals of change and how to respond effectively. Whether the issue focuses on sex changes in wildlife (page 30), a severe reduction in the number of fish caught and in their size (pages 68–79) or smog from burning rainforests, there are always things we can do to signal concern and turn the tide.

2 The future we want

You know those dazzling holograms you get on everything from credit cards to watches? Hold them one way and the face smiles, tilt them and you get a frown. The future is a bit like that. Show the same facts to different people and some react optimistically, others pessimistically. In this chapter, we do something of the same, flipping between problems and solutions—because many of today's problems will inevitably help create tomorrow's solutions. More than ever before, the choice of the future we want is in our own hands. But to make things happen, we must change our own priorities and lifestyles. In the words of Mahatma Gandhi, the unassuming Indian thinker whom future generations will see as one of the 20th-century giants: "You must be the change you want to see in the world."

Manual 2000 sketches out the emerging agenda for action in the Citizen 2000 Checklists, found at the end of each major section of Chapters 3 to 8, while this chapter identifies some of the key trends that will drive innovation in the 21st century—and that will therefore play a powerful role in shaping our future. We focus on six trends, including the need to make life choices.

2.1 One World

Learning to live with six billion neighbours

The phrase "one world, ready or not" perfectly sums up what is happening around us. The impact of financial upheavals on the other side of the planet can now be felt in the space of a few days, even hours (pages 201–203). We are moving toward global markets, global communications, global travel, global culture and even—to some extent—a global language: English. We now have global problems on the environmental front, among them the hole in the ozone layer (page 21) and climate change (page 28). Both of these issues are clearly on a scale unlike anything we have had to deal with in the past, except perhaps nuclear fall-out.

***Humanity is conducting an unintended, uncontrolled, globally pervasive experiment whose ultimate consequences could be second only to a global nuclear war.*[1]**

Globalization is being driven by many factors, but by far the most powerful agents of change are the growing numbers of giant transnational corporations. Companies like Shell, Coca-Cola, McDonald's and Microsoft are individually more powerful than many nation states and look set to grow further.

Although many people in both rich and poor nations are embracing our evolving super-consumer culture, there are also signs of a backlash. There is growing hostility, for example, against what has been dubbed the "McDonaldization" or "Coca-Colonization" of the planet. Such giant companies not only operate by driving local, more diverse suppliers into extinction, but their products also help to reprogram the values and lifestyle expectations of entire societies.

Perhaps most dramatic has been the collision between this western commercial culture and the world of Islam, with many Muslims resisting what they see as the "Westoxification" of their societies. In some cases, the backlash against western values has been taken to extraordinary extremes. Hopefully few other countries will follow Afghanistan's Taliban in forbidding women to appear on the streets, vote or even have the right to an education!

Learning to live with and get along with our six billion neighbours will inevitably involve all sorts of new frictions. So we can "safely" assume that the 21st century will see continuing revolutions, civil wars, even all-out regional or world wars. New weapons will be used (pages 251–252), with the fall-out affecting even those not directly involved. We may wish it otherwise, but human nature does not change overnight.

While many of us may sympathize with the slogan "Stop the world, I want to get off!", the future is coming at us at an ever-increasing rate. And these days there are no new lands to run to. We must learn how to change the world here and now. To do so, we not only need to begin the long haul of changing our lifestyles but also to develop the new forms of government that will enable us to act both locally and globally.

flashpoint: Ozone Holes

- **Towards the end of the 1980s most of us learned for the first time that we had an ozone layer over our heads. And we were warned that this vital protective shield–some 20 to 50 kilometres up–was being destroyed, chiefly by the CFCs (chlorofluorocarbons) used as, among other things, aerosol propellants, refrigerants and insulation materials.**
- **As the ozone layer thinned, an enormous hole–as large as the continental United States–was opening up over Antarctica. The health risks are enormous, with skin cancer and eye cataracts among the problems linked with increased ultraviolet radiation from the sun. In Australia, where ozone thinning is particularly serious, there has been a substantial increase in skin cancer rates. Nor is it simply a question of human health problems: ultraviolet radiation can also damage plants and the plankton on which marine ecosystems depend.**
- **But there is good news, too. The global response to this issue has shown that if the warning signals are clear enough, and the potential impacts large enough, we can react surprisingly fast–and fairly effectively. Yes, there may still be a roaring black market in CFCs made in countries like Russia, but in the more prosperous countries these chemicals have been eliminated from many applications. Increasingly, too, new legislation will require the abandonment of other ozone-eating chemicals, such as methyl bromide (page 42).**

* **And what we have done once, we should be able to do again. Inevitably global initiatives are not easy, but issues like ozone depletion have paved the way for a truly global response to environmental disasters.**

2.2 Growing Appetites

Too many people—or too much greed?

Directly or indirectly, population pressures now drive most serious environmental problems, among them shrinking forests, expanding deserts, dwindling clean water supplies, rising mountains of waste and the thickening blanket of greenhouse gases. But, remember, these problems are caused more by consumption in industrialized countries than by population growth.

Let's begin by looking at the issue of human numbers. When the 20th century dawned there were around 1.6 billion people in the world. In 1950, the figure had grown to around 2.5 billion. It hit the 4 billion mark by 1974 and reached 5 billion by 1987. Already we are approaching the 6 billion mark—and still adding around 87 million people annually, equivalent to about three times the population of Canada, or 10 000 more people every hour of every day of every week.

So much for the bad news. As the 20th century drew to a close, we also began to hear odd bits of good news on the population front. For example, it is predicted that within 20 years two-thirds of the world's population will live in countries with an average birth rate of 2.1 children or less per woman. This is the replacement fertility rate below which populations eventually start to fall.[2] These changes are being achieved by tackling issues such as women's health, sexual equality, and the provision of effective sex education and birth control products and services.

Just as important, however, are the impacts linked to how much each of us consumes. Modern lifestyles, like those enjoyed by ordinary people living in the richer countries, can be very much more damaging to the environment than traditional lifestyles practised by the average African, Indian or Chinese.

Indeed, it's an extraordinary fact that 20 per cent of the world's population now consumes more than 80 per cent of the planet's natural resources. This trend is at its starkest in the United States. With less than 5 per cent of the world population, Americans use nearly 30 per cent of the planet's resources. The average American and Canadian uses 10 times more coal than the average Chinese—and contributes over 50 times more CO_2 to the atmosphere. They also require 4 times as much grain and 227 times as much gasoline as the average Indian.

Another three planets like Earth would be needed if everyone consumed as much as the rich nations do today.[3]

Nor are North Americans alone. Many European and Japanese consumers are catching up, with billions of people worldwide now aspiring to the "American dream." Indeed, for hundreds of millions of people this dream is now becoming reality as we witness the global emergence of "super-consumers."

As our version of the good life spreads around the world like a virus, the impacts on climate change, world agriculture and water availability (see opposite) are phenomenal. By the mid-1990s, for example, China had become a net importer of grain, requiring 16 million tonnes a year—having previously exported 8 million!

The scale of our impacts is also indicated by

the fact that, globally, humans now shift more rock, loam, sand and gravel than all the rivers of the world combined.[4] When Asia recovers from its financial problems, it is almost certain to overtake the West in many categories of consumption. By 1995, for example, Asians bought as many new cars as the whole of Europe and America put together.

As population numbers continue to grow and high-consumption lifestyles continue to spread around the world, the only way to save our environment will be to work out how to do dramatically more with dramatically less. Luckily, as we see below, the environmental revolution of the late 20th century has triggered a wave of innovation that will help to transform the industries and economies of the 21st century.

flashpoint: Water Wars

- **Turn on the tap and clean water flows. Many of us take this modern miracle for granted. But you don't need to be the proverbial rocket scientist to know that our growing thirst will be an increasing problem in the new century.**
- **Each of us needs about 80 litres (23 gallons) of water a day to sustain a reasonable standard of living. But around the world, average consumption ranges from 5.4 litres (just over 6 quarts)–scarcely enough to live on–in drought-stricken areas like the Sahel, through to 500 litres (142 gallons) per person per day in the United States.[5] As an indication of the underlying trends, humanity's thirst for water rose sixfold during the 20th century.**
- **Farming and cities use the most water. Already many great rivers (like America's Colorado) never reach the sea as they once did. And many great African swamplands, once rich with wildlife, are drying out. It is estimated that over a quarter of the world's population faces a struggle to find enough water to drink, grow food and run industry–and that by 2025, as much as two-thirds of the world's population will face "stress conditions."[6]**
- **Unfortunately, waking up to the problem is not the same as solving it. As human numbers increase, drier areas are being farmed. This, in turn, accelerates the destruction of forests and other vegetation. As a result, rainfall decreases. Once the forests have gone and the rains do come, the water sluices straight into the rivers–causing widespread flooding downstream.**
- **As this vicious spiral continues, there is less food, political tension grows and the likelihood of fierce conflicts increases. Already the U.S. government has formed a special task force to watch for impending droughts or other environmental disasters, as an indication of where future international emergencies may erupt.[7] Among the likely flashpoints are the Jordan, whose waters are shared by Israel and its Arab neighbours; the Nile, which flows through Ethiopia, Sudan and Egypt; and the headwaters of the Euphrates and Tigris, shared by Turkey, Syria and Iraq.**
- **Wherever we live it is more than likely that the cost of water will soar. Desalination plants might seem an obvious answer, but they are hugely expensive to build and run–and consume vast amounts of energy. So the pressure will be on in the 21st century to grow food, produce goods and service homes with ever-less water.**

* **But remember the positive side of the coin. The fact that we will all have to learn how to be water misers opens up extraordinary new opportunities for those who can develop new industrial processes, household appliances, garden irrigation systems or crop plants that can do what they have to do with significantly less water. Those with a thirst for profits should take the cactus as their model: able to survive and thrive in a world where water is at least as precious as gold.**

2.3 Less Is More

The big squeeze on technology

One of the central tasks of the 21st century will be to "dematerialize" our economies and societies. In simple terms, we must learn to do dramatically more with dramatically less. Use fewer raw materials, and less water and energy, for example. Happily, some modern technologies are already headed in this direction—although no one denies the scale of the challenge ahead of us.

It is estimated that since 1950 humankind has consumed more natural resources—and produced more pollution and waste—than in all its previous history. The biggest environmental problem associated with our current (mainly rich world) resource consumption is probably global warming, which is linked to a range of climate change issues (page 28). As a result, energy is back on the agenda.

Today, however, we are not only concerned about how much energy is used but also about how it is produced. Table 2.1 illustrates the range of energy alternatives on offer, highlighting some of the environmental problems associated with each option. In each case, in the interests of balance, we look at some of the advantages and disadvantages.

The overall message is clear. However we produce the energy we use, there will be significant economic, environmental and social impacts. We need to increase massively the amount of renewable energy generated—a reality now recognized by major oil giants like BP and Shell, which are racing to build their renewables businesses. But it will be even more important to learn how to use energy (however it is produced) more efficiently.

In the 21st century, we will all need to become energy savers. The real challenge will be to cut down on our energy consumption without materially affecting our quality of life. For this to happen, energy prices will have to rise—and significantly.

But just in case this sounds like doom and gloom, don't despair. We stand on the threshold of an extraordinary new period of innovation, when a combination of new technologies and new lifestyle choices can help us to reduce dramatically the environmental "footprint" each of us imposes on the rest of the world.

Some even forecast an era of "super-innovation," when different technologies spur each other on to create totally unexpected solutions to problems that many people thought were insoluble.[8] The huge potential for improvement is illustrated by the fact that only two per cent of the fuel energy we put into our cars actually results in moving our bodies around. The rest goes on moving the sheer weight of the vehicle—and 75 per cent is wasted as heat.

We need radical new solutions. Perhaps the best example to date of what we are talking about here is the microchip, where the computing power has been doubling—and the size of the chip halving—every 18 months (page 164). The most obvious result is the way personal computers and mobile telephones have

Table 2.1: THE ENERGY MENU

Source	***Energy***	***Advantages***	***Disadvantages***
Coal	Comes in many forms, from soft coals (e.g., lignite) to hard ones (e.g., anthracite).	Hard coals are almost pure carbon, providing intense energy. Coal mines provide much-needed employment. Plentiful supply.	Massive landscape damage, subsidence. Nonrenewable. Highly polluting emissions when burned (worst with soft coals), e.g., smog, acid rain, greenhouse emissions.
Oil	Oil comes in many forms: e.g., heavy oils, light oils, shales, tar sands.	Still in reasonably plentiful supply. Often cleaner to handle than coal. Versatile fuel, packed with energy.	Nonrenewable. Excavation of wilderness areas, e.g., Arctic, North Sea. Highly polluting emissions when burned (worst with heavy oils), e.g., smog, acid rain, greenhouse emissions. Transport hazards (e.g., oil spills and explosions).
Natural gas	Natural gas is usually found with oil.	High-energy punch. Relatively plentiful supplies. Cleanest of the fossil fuels when burned.	Nonrenewable. Hazardous, e.g., gas leaks. Emissions, including methane, contribute to the greenhouse effect, smog.
Nuclear power	Comes in two forms: fission (today's technology) and fusion (tomorrow's technology).	Plentiful supply of uranium raw material. Minimal greenhouse impact. Competitive, if you ignore cost of health, safety and decommissioning. Fusion, if it comes, could be cleaner.	Danger of nuclear accidents, e.g., Three Mile Island, Chernobyl. Radioactive waste disposal, e.g., long-life wastes. Security risks. Massive costs of decommissioning.
Wood	In poorest countries, most energy still comes from fuel wood and charcoal.	Renewable resource. Readily available in many places. Easy to use.	Long trek often necessary to gather fuel wood. Contribution to deforestation and erosion. Emissions, e.g., smoke, soot, smog, acid rain, greenhouse effect.

Table 2.1: THE ENERGY MENU *continued*

Source	***Energy***	***Advantages***	***Disadvantages***
Waste-derived	Fuels produced from waste.	Renewable resource. Uses wastes that would otherwise end up in landfill. Produces both power and potentially useful heat.	Odours, emissions, e.g., dioxin, smog, acid rain, greenhouse effect. Possible disincentive for waste reduction, reuse and recycling schemes.
Biofuels	This term covers everything from wood to oils (e.g., rape-seed).	Renewable resource. Available even in countries with no oil fields.	All the problems associated with intensive monocultures (e.g., pesticides, fertilizers). Large land area required. Emissions similar to diesel. Quality issues (e.g., some biofuels can damage engines if poorly formulated).
Geo-thermal power	Taps heat from deep under-ground.	Huge, renewable resource—or nearly so. Cheaper energy in areas in or near volcanic or geothermal areas.	If the heat is deep under-ground, can require major engineering work. Geothermal fields can be exhausted if overused—and may not be near points of use. Gases and effluents can cause problems.
Wind power	Windmills have been around for centuries, but are now going high-tech.	Huge, renewable resource. Clean, no emissions once in use. Good for remote areas.	Noise problems, bird kills. Potential blot on the landscape. Relatively small amount of energy produced per windmill.
Solar power	Energy from the sun captured as heat or light.	Huge, renewable resource. Clean, no emissions once in use.	Can take a lot of space. Power generation needs large battery capacity for remote applica-tions. Depends on weather (sun). Constructing solar equipment can be an energy-intensive business and costly.

Table 2.1: THE ENERGY MENU *continued*

Source	***Energy***	***Advantages***	***Disadvantages***
Wave power	Driven by the wind, waves store a huge energy punch—if you can harness it.	Huge, renewable resource. Clean, no emissions once in use. Employment for remote regions.	Power of waves: many experimental wave-power collectors have been destroyed, but designs will improve. Visual intrusion in sensitive coastal landscapes. Interference with fishing.
Hydro-electric power	As water moves from the skies to the mountains to the seas, it can be dammed and used to generate power.	Huge, renewable resource. Clean, once the dam has been built. Employment for remote regions.	Flooding of vast areas of land and associated communities. Forced removal of local people. Drowning of wildlife and habitats. Spread of waterborne diseases. Impact on down-stream fisheries and irrigation schemes.
Human power	Muscle power (everything from slave labour to cycling).	Renewable resource. No extra pollution. Can involve good, healthy exercise.	Dwarfed by fossil fuel-powered alternatives. Difficult to convert energy for storage. Tends to be expensive. Human rights issues.

been shrinking while offering ever-increasing services. Next in line is the so-called nanotechnology, with some companies now even beginning to engineer at the atomic level.

Computing power has been doubling–and the size of the chip halving–every 18 months.

Alarmed by the combined impact of population growth and environmental pollution, leading thinkers are now calling for a "factor 4" revolution in our technologies.[9] They argue that, as a minimum, we need to produce four times more from the same amount of raw material or twice as much from half the amount of material. The potential for improvement is illustrated by the extraordinary fact that some 99 per cent of the original materials used in the production of—or contained in—goods made in the U.S. become waste within six weeks of sale![10]

flashpoint: Climate Change

- **If any single environmental factor is going to disrupt lives and threaten survival in the first half of the 21st century, it will probably be climate change. Natural factors like sun-spot cycles certainly play a role, but it is**

now recognized that humans have started a planet-wide experiment with the climate, far beyond natural fluctuations.[11]

- **Normally, the gases in the planet's atmosphere act very much like the glass in a greenhouse. They make the planet liveable. But as we add to these gases with our own emissions, we are increasing the "double-glazing" effect of this process–and accelerating global warming.**
- **Carbon dioxide (CO_2) is the most important greenhouse gas–and is produced by all living things. It also comes from burning fossil fuels, like coal and oil, chiefly for electricity and cars. About half of the six billion tonnes of CO_2 released annually is sponged up by the world's oceans and forests, but we are now producing so much that we are outrunning the ability of such "carbon sinks" to cope.**
- **As a result, it is thought that CO_2 concentrations in the atmosphere have increased by nearly a third since the Industrial Revolution. Other greenhouse gases include methane (produced by sewage and rotting processes) and CFCs (page 117).**
- **Stand by for a hotter world. The 10 warmest years in the last 130 all occurred in the last two decades–and, of these, at least three of the warmest years were recorded in the 1990s (1998 was the hottest year on record). It is possible to imagine that a warmer world climate would be more pleasant, especially in the North. But the Arctic is already warming at three times the global rate–seriously affecting the lives of Inuit people. A drier climate would also increase pressure on water supplies, encourage the spread of pests like cockroaches and extend the reach of deadly tropical diseases such as malaria and yellow fever.**
- **Worse, some scientists believe that the polar ice-caps have already started melting. As a result, whole island chains such as the Maldives could disappear, while low-lying areas of cities like London, Bangkok, New York and Tokyo could eventually be swamped by rising tides.**
- **Meanwhile, we are already seeing more weather extremes, such as the ice-storm that hit parts of Ontario and Quebec in early 1998. Not surprisingly, given that it usually ends up paying for the damage caused, the insurance industry is beginning to get hot under the collar (pages 219–220). For example, when Hurricane Andrew slammed into Florida with winds of 235 km-h (380 mph), flattening 85 000 homes and leaving three million Americans homeless, the bill for the damage reached a record US$25 billion.**
- **Not only insurance companies, but others in the financial sector, too–lenders, stockbrokers and analysts, for example–are recognizing the impact of climate change on their business. The result: they are beginning to exert their very powerful influence on companies to encourage them to come up with effective business and technological solutions.**

2.4 Side-Effects

Today we are all experimental animals

It is often incredibly complicated to work out which health effects are natural and which are not, which diseases are linked to pollution and which to our lifestyle choices. But we can be sure of one thing: chemicals—both old and new—have caused a wide range of worrying side-effects and will remain in the spotlight throughout the 21st century.

In the past 40 years, at least 70 000 new chemicals have been released into the environment. Each one of us has 500 chemicals in our bodies, unknown in our grandparents' time. Trying to work out which of these are harmful is a brain-numbing task. Thousands of scientists toil in laboratories around the world, carrying out huge numbers of animal experiments and other tests to track down problem substances. The trouble is that such tests tend to focus on problems we already know about. The CFC issue (page 117), for example, showed how a family of substances that had been extensively tested for human safety—and had passed with flying colours—nonetheless came back to haunt us.

In the past 40 years, at least 70 000 new chemicals have been released into the environment.

One of the most critical tasks for scientists, governments and industry is to pick up on the warning signs as early as possible. For example, there is now evidence from around the world that frogs—along with other amphibians, such as toads, newts and salamanders—are in dramatic decline. Lacking scales, feathers or fur, and with their eggs floating on top of ponds and other water bodies, frogs are among the most vulnerable animals when it comes to pollution—and a barometer of environmental health, which we ignore at our peril.

There is probably no single, fits-all-cases solution to the mystery of the disappearing amphibians. Among the possible causes are ozone depletion leading to higher levels of radiation; the spread of disease-causing agents; the introduction of exotic predators; and pesticides, fertilizers, acid rain and other forms of chemical contamination. But there can be little doubt that human activity is the root cause. As the world's vanishing frogs are signalling, it is time for us all to wake up and act. Remember: a world fit for frogs will be a world fit for even the most sensitive humans.

It is increasingly clear that intentionally or not, we have changed the chemistry of the atmosphere, of soils, of lakes and rivers, even of the planet's vast blue oceans. The downside for the chemical industry is that the "chemophobia" that really began in the early 1960s will continue into the foreseeable future. Indeed, the ongoing "gender-bender" controversy suggests that many chemicals can have significant effects on our health, even in minuscule quantities (see below).

The upside for the rest of us is that the pressures on this vast global industry will spark radically new cleaner technologies. The world of industrial chemistry will be transformed and many household names will disappear as the companies behind them go to the wall and new ones emerge.

flashpoint: "Gender-Bender" Chemicals

- **More than a generation ago, in her prophetic book *Silent Spring*, Rachel Carson warned that an entire class of chemicals–organochlorines, including the pesticides DDT, chlordane and heptachlor–were polluting the tissues of virtually every person and animal on the planet.**
- **Not only was she right, but we have seen some of the profound effects on human health that she feared would haunt future generations. Her work has been**

followed in recent years by hard-hitting books as *Our Stolen Future*[12] and *The Feminisation of Nature.*[13]

- The subtlety of the biological effects that some chemicals can cause was shown by recent U.K. research carried out on fish close to major sewage works. Downstream of the sewage effluent outfalls, up to 60 per cent of the roach were found to be suffering from severe sex-change symptoms–and some were producing large numbers of eggs in their testes. This was believed to be caused by hormones coming from the contraceptive pill, as well as by chemicals that can act like hormones.[14]
- Human sperm has also been under the spotlight. Studies from some countries suggest that the number of sperm produced by the average man has dropped dramatically over the last 50 years. From an average of over 110 million sperm per millilitre of semen measured in 1940, we have seen a fall to under 70 million today. This trend is not universal; indeed, some studies have found no such trend. But if the pessimistic scientists are right, the number of vigorous "swimmers" among today's sperm is also down.[15]
- All sorts of factors may be involved, such as higher levels of stress, changing diets, even tight underwear. But hormone-disrupting chemicals (also known as "environmental estrogens") have not been ruled out. Even normally cautious scientists admit that something significant is going on with our reproductive systems. The fertility of laboratory animals has been shown to be affected by hormone-disrupting chemicals, and they may well be having the same effect on people.
- The theory is that some chemicals, including organochlorines, can mimic the effects of natural substances (like estrogens) that play a key role in our reproductive systems. These "hormone disrupters" are believed to cause birth defects, falling sperm counts, infertility, other reproductive problems, and cancer, as well as decreasing our resistance to disease by suppressing our immune systems. In some cases, it is even thought they may impair the thinking abilities of our children.
- Over 11 000 different organochlorines are made today, ending up in products ranging from pesticides and plastics through to dental fillings, toothpaste and mouthwash. Phthalates (page 33), a group of plasticizers used to make PVC plastic more flexible, have been among the key suspects.
- Although many people have not yet heard of them, phthalates are used in a wide range of applications, including–most controversially–baby teething rings, where there are fears that the chemicals might leach into the baby's saliva. The industries concerned have vigorously protested that there is no risk, but many people have already decided to play it safe and switch to alternative materials.

2.5 The Moral Maze

Whose commandments?

Whether the issue is globalization, population control, sustainable lifestyles or gender-benders, we increasingly find ourselves moving into the tricky area of ethics. At a time when many traditional religions are in decline, we must

Table 2.2 identifies just a few of the more well-known suspects—and explains their usual haunts. Remember, however, that this "unwanted" list is growing all the time.

Table 2.2: SUSPECTED GENDER-BENDERS

Chemical	***Where Used***	***Comments***
Alkylphenol polyethoxylates	Detergents, paints, cosmetics and, ironically, as spermicidal lubricant in condoms.	Breakdown products of industrial detergents. Most industry associations say they are being removed from products, except in condoms.
Atrazine	Herbicides.	Turns up in drinking water. Possibly being phased out.
Bisphenol A	Coatings inside some tin cans, water pipes, reusable milk bottles (made of polycarbonate plastic) and dental fillings.	Research has shown that humans may be taking in enough Bisphenol A to affect fertility, although the plastics industry denies this.[16] Thirty-five per cent of tins do not have linings, but it is absolutely secret which ones do or do not.
Butylated hydroxyanisole (BHA)	Food antioxidant used to preserve fat in, for example, beef savoury rice and some biscuits.	Also known as E320. Not all that common and its use is declining. Very little is known, but it is listed as a suspected estrogen mimic.
Chlordane	Pesticides.	Among the top 12 "persistent organic pollutants" (POPs) and targeted by the U.N. for global action.
DDT	Pesticides.	Although widely banned, it is still in high demand in developing countries for the control of malaria. One form of DDT is a weak estrogen mimic and another blocks the male hormone.

Table 2.2: SUSPECTED GENDER-BENDERS *continued*

Chemical	***Where Used***	***Comments***
Dieldrin	Pesticides.	Among the top 12 POPs—and widely banned. There are also large obsolete stocks of this chemical leaking into the environment.
Dioxins	Accidental by-product of the chlorine industry (e.g., PVC), the use of chlorine in the pulp and paper industry, and incineration—whenever chlorine is present in the fuels or wastes burned. Metal smelters and municipal waste incinerators are major sources.	The term "dioxins" refers to the class of polychlorinated dibenzodioxins (PCDDs) and polychlorinated dibenzo furans (PCDFs), with between 1 and 8 chlorine atoms. The most toxic dioxin (2,3,7,8 TCDD) has a reputation as one of the most dangerous synthetic substances. Dioxins are produced by many forms of burning. Key concern of many environmentalists.
Furans	Along with dioxins, an accidental by-product of the chlorine industry (e.g., PVC), pulp and paper, and combustion processes.	See dioxins (above).
Heavy metals such as cadmium lead and mercury	In millions of items, from batteries and lightbulbs to plastics and paints.	All heavy metals are suspected hormone-disrupting chemicals.
Hexachlorobenzene (HCB)	Fungicide and by-product of the chlorine industry.	Among the top 12 POPs—and widely banned, so it is unlikely that most people will come into contact with it.
Lindane	As a pesticide in crop cereals, grassland, oilseed rape, cabbages, Brussels sprouts, apples, pears, tomatoes, cucumbers, strawberries, sugar-beet and as a wood preservative.	Although it has been banned in some applications, it is still widely used in agriculture and possible to buy products treated with lindane; it still lingers on in many attics. Possible connection to breast cancer.

Table 2.2: SUSPECTED GENDER-BENDERS *continued*

Chemical	***Where Used***	***Comments***
Methoxychlor	Contact and stomach insecticide.	Organochlorine registered for use on fruit, vegetables, crops and for parasite treatment in beef and dairy cows. Seems to be used mostly in the US.
Pentachlorophenol (PCP)	Wood preservative.	Apparently still used in some U.K. wood preservatives.
Phthalates	Plasticizers in PVC plastics, including cables, vinyl flooring and wallpapers, toys and packaging materials. Also used in some cosmetics.	This is a group of chemicals, some of which are thought to be hormone disrupting. Over three million tonnes of phthalates are consumed every year.[17] At least 95 per cent of DEHP, the most common phthalate, is used in PVC plastic.
Polychlorinated biphenyls (PCBs)	Electrical equipment, flame retardants.	Among the top 12 POPs. Production banned in U.S. in 1977, but still leaking from some old equipment. Banned in the Canada in 1979.
Synthetic pyrethroids	Used in household insecticides and pet flea collars.	Concern over exposure of children in the home. Health effects may include damage to central nervous system, dizziness, headaches, diarrhea and panic attacks. Some countries considering banning these chemicals.
Tributyl tin (TBT)	Anti-fouling paint on boats.	Although it has been banned for use on smaller boats and yachts, it is still used on some ships. Shown to have caused sex changes in dog whelks.

Source: *Friends of the Earth, Greenpeace, PAN, WWF and others.*

learn how to negotiate the growing number of moral mazes, which will be such an inescapable feature of the 21st century.

Given that we all need some form of ethical compass to help guide us, we will no doubt both evolve new ethics and recover old ones, including—perhaps—large elements of the Ten Commandments. One thing we can confidently predict about the future is that our ethics will be tested, often severely. The scale of these challenges may well either spark the revival of existing religions or spur the evolution of new ones (page 98).

Although the media coverage of the latest horrors may sometimes make it seem that we have lost all our morals, the fact is that the ethical agenda is expanding at a breathtaking pace as new technologies create new issues and concerns.

Developments in genetic engineering (pages 59–68) and modern medicine (pages 263–275) raise ethical issues that previously would have appeared only in the most outlandish "sci-fi" thriller. Increasingly, they are an inescapable part of the world we live in—a world that we will hand on to our children and our grandchildren.

Business, meanwhile, faces continuing pressure from "caring," "ethical," "green," "responsible" or—less charitably—"vigilante" consumers. Our own *Green Consumer Guide*, published in 1988, was a key early spur in this direction.

In the process, many forms of pressure are being brought to bear on business, from letters written to directors, through boycotts and demonstrations, to a growing range of non-violent direct actions, as when road protesters tunnel under the proposed route of a new motorway or runway to stop construction work. And growing numbers of businesses are responding. Companies, for example, have almost been lining up to announce new codes of ethical conduct. Environmental and social performance is increasingly reported alongside—or even as part of—the more traditional financial report and accounts.

Putting our ethics into practice can be difficult, however, even when we are crystal-clear about where we stand on particular issues. So, for example, we may find that there are real conflicts between one of our goals (let's say, buying local) and another (let's say, buying organic). In this case, there may be no local source of organic produce.

Luckily, however, new ways are emerging in which we can put our values into action. In the past, for example, it was much easier to buy a mercury-free battery or a phosphate-free detergent than it was to find a pension policy or mortgage supplied by an ethical company. But the market is beginning to respond to the pent-up demand, with ethical investment emerging as a new boom area (pages 214–219). And where the small funds pioneer, some of the larger ones will almost inevitably follow.

flashpoint: Genetic Engineering

- **Japanese biotechnologists have produced mice that glow green–fluorescent green![18] The story may sound like science fiction, but it's science fact. By taking a gene from a jellyfish found in the Pacific and incorporating it in the embryo of a mouse, they have produced the world's first glowing mammal. The green mice will be used in cancer research.**

Japanese biotechnologists have produced mice that glow green.

- **It is hardly surprising that genetic engineering has been one of the most talked-about technologies of the late 20th century. So what is it? In simple terms, it** involves programming living organisms to do new things. In the same way that engineers work with metals, biotechnologists work with natural systems such as plant and animal cells. The difference is that one set of materials is inert, the other living. The ethical issues will clearly be very different.

* Not that biotechnology is completely new. The fermentation processes used in making champagne, wine, beer, cheese or yoghurt are traditional biotechnologies, based on living organisms such as yeast and mould. But these traditional processes have been given a massive boost by new techniques with huge potential for changing our lives and influencing our life choices.
* There were many stepping stones along the way, but the landmark event was the discovery, in 1953, of what one of the scientists involved promptly dubbed the "secret of life."[19] The molecule DNA was found to be the basic building block of life—and the key to understanding the mystery of genes and inheritance.
* In the simplest terms, DNA is like the program (or "software") that runs a computer. Just as the program instructs the machine (or "hardware") on what it should do and show on the screen, so our DNA and genes determine whether we are male or female, tall or short, blue-eyed or brown-eyed, or likely to be fat or thin. They can also shape much subtler elements of our characters, such as our patterns of thoughts—even our tendency to be happy or depressed.
* Some 20 years after the discovery of DNA's structure, scientists also worked out how to remove genetic material—those parts of the code they wanted, in the form of genes or parts of genes—and transfer them to other organisms. At first these organisms were bacteria and yeast, but before long the scientists moved on to the manipulation of plants and animals.
* The first genetically engineered animal really to hit the headlines was the so-called Oncomouse. This mouse was specifically engineered to develop cancer, to assist scientists in their search for cures. In 1988, it became the first living animal to be patented. Not surprisingly, the result has been a heated debate over the ethics of "owning" the design of a life form—in much the same way that a company might own a logo or brand name it has developed.
* Meanwhile, the number of strange animals emerging from these high-tech arks continues to grow. In the mutant tracks of the "Oncomouse" came the "Geep," half-goat, half-sheep. Next came "Mighty Mouse," with muscles three times bigger than normal. Another example of this trend was the transplantation of a gene from a quail into a chicken, with the result that the chicken sang the quail's song. For many people, the resulting "chickquail" illustrated the ways in which these new technologies threaten to transform completely our views on what is natural.
* But most controversial of all, at least to date, was "Dolly," the cloned sheep announced by British scientists in 1997 (page 246). She was named after Dolly Parton, the big-bosomed country singer, because she was grown from a cell taken from a sheep's udder. This latest, astonishing breakthrough raised the real possibility of cloning people (pages 246–248).

- **Down on the farm, too, hormones are being injected into cows to boost milk (page 60). Also in development are pigs with less fat, sheep with better-quality wool, fish that grow faster and larger, and even "furry fermenters." These are animals designed to produce drugs or other valuable substances in their milk or blood. So, for example, a goat might produce a cure for a human lung disease, a sheep a cure for schizophrenia, or cows might start to produce human breast milk.**
- **Nor is the potential of these new technologies restricted to animals. In the pipeline are plants that poison pests without the need for chemical pesticides (pages 41–44), or which shrug off frost damage that would otherwise kill or cripple them. It is quite conceivable that at least some 21st-century crops will make their own fertilizers and produce complex substances that today we can only make in factories.**
- **However devoutly we may wish otherwise, it is too late to stuff the "gene genie" back into the bottle. But we need to be much more alert to the risks it will bring–and the unpleasant surprises it will spring–alongside the undoubted benefits. For just as we once happily sprayed DDT (page 42), squirted CFCs (page 21) and made cows into cannibals (pages 53–54), we will surely make some hideous mistakes with technologies that give us powers once reserved for the gods.**

2.6 Life Choices

How today's decisions shape tomorrow's world

So, we now have the power to shape the future, but what do we do with it? Most of us use this power subconsciously—completely unaware of the wider social and environmental effects of the product, lifestyle and (even broader) life choices we make. Things we do every day of the week—for example, eating meat or driving to work or to the grocery store—can produce ripple effects around the world.

Our lifestyles produce environmental and social footprints felt in countries we may never visit—or may never even have heard of. But what can we do? Perhaps the most critical life choice we can make is to choose to be optimistic rather than pessimistic. Why is this? Because we are most effective when we decide to embrace—rather than fear—the future.

A better future is not ours by right, however. We must work towards it, earn it. And, as Mahatma Gandhi reminded us (page 281), we must make the necessary changes in our own lives and lifestyles if we are to have any hope of seeing them taking effect globally.

Our rights as citizens of the third millennium will come with clear responsibilities for protecting the future. Inevitably, different communities and different cultures will define the nature and extent of those responsibilities in different ways. A globalized world will not be a homogeneous world. But it is no accident that growing numbers of people are talking about looking after the world for their grandchildren and great-grandchildren.

We sense that choices we make today—for example, those that affect biodiversity (pages 38–39)—will significantly shape the choices open to future generations. As a result, we will spend a growing proportion of our resources not only on protecting our own health but also on protecting the health of the young and unborn.

Take childhood asthma as an example. In many countries, including Canada, the number of asthma victims has soared. Parents and doctors alike are increasingly worried. Some doctors tell us that this trend is linked with air pollution. Some claim that children's immune systems are no longer challenged at an early stage by playing in the dirt. Some see the problem as linked to the growing use of antibiotics in childhood, and others believe it is an effect of immunization on immature immune systems. Still others suspect that we are seeing an unexpected side-effect of the huge range of chemicals now found in the average home—a problem made worse as we close up our buildings to make them more energy-efficient.

Who is right? The answer is that we simply don't know—yet. But such complex issues will be typical of the challenges facing us. We must learn how to make the necessary choices in a balanced way, because we simply do not have the resources to waste. At the same time, however, we can be certain that such issues will help drive a number of other trends, including the pressure for cleaner cars (page 155) and for chemicals that are both environment- and people-friendly (pages 112–129).

Later chapters will make it clear that a wide range of new technologies are now in the pipeline, promising new tools for managing our communities, industries, farms, natural resources and, indeed, planet.

Orbiting satellites help us keep an eye on what is happening to our forests, rivers and oceans. New schemes are being developed to sell "negawatts" rather than watts of energy. The idea is that companies get more profits by saving energy rather than selling it. In effect, they are selling energy efficiency, rather than barrels of oil or kilowatts of electricity. And new materials are being developed that mimic natural materials—a field known as biomimetics.

Even more fundamentally, so-called nanotechnologists are now working out how to manipulate atoms, research that could revolutionize many industries within a few decades. If such technologies fulfil their promise, enthusiasts suggest that we might be able to produce materials that could do many jobs at the same time.[20] So, for example, instead of having air conditioning, future buildings might have walls that breathe, sucking out bad air and pushing in fresh air. We might even be able to program our walls to change their shape or colour.

But we know that all new technologies throw shadows, creating unexpected problems. Some of those problems will be environmental, often affecting people indirectly, but others will be social—affecting them directly. People will lose their jobs, for example, or be exposed to new chemicals whose long-term risks are unsuspected.

It may be human nature to be concerned about our own children and grandchildren, but it is interesting that growing numbers of us are also now signalling our concern about the plight of other people—and other people's children. The "fair trade" movement, for example, aims to tackle human rights issues like workers being paid rock-bottom wages that can barely support their families, labourers being poisoned by applying pesticides without proper safety measures, and a growing range of problems related to children and young people.

Increasingly, people are supporting a growing range of "fair trade" (page 79), "organic" (page 49), "free-range" (page 57), "cruelty-free" (page 243) and other more environmental or ethical product options that are now beginning to be offered. And in doing so, we should accept our share of the responsibility for making sure that the right outcomes are achieved. Since we can't do all of this on our own, the main chapters of *Manual 2000* provide a wide range of contacts for those wanting to get started on the journey.

In the process, we should remember this adage: we have not so much inherited the planet from our grandparents as borrowed it from our grandchildren. Some native Indian tribes, it is said, used to ponder the potential impact of their choices and actions on the "seventh generation"—on their great-great-great-great-great-grandchildren. A brain-wrenching task even then, but almost impossible at a time when we are starting to work on such new technologies as genetic engineering (page 59).

Interestingly, however, we increasingly hear talk about "sustainable development" and "sustainability." In the simplest terms, these new words and phrases not only imply taking the interests of future generations into account but also treating our world as if we intended to stay.

Whether in our own lives, in business or in politics, the best way to predict the future is to create it. Let's get to work. The Citizen 2000 Action Plan (page 281) is designed to help us all play our part in the most important transition our species has yet faced.

flashpoint: Disappearing Species

- **With nuclear weapons, humanity now has the power to destroy life on earth. But we don't really need nuclear weapons for this task. We are already doing pretty well–destroying species simply by practising our everyday lifestyles. As a result, when leading politicians meet to discuss world problems, a new word is often on their lips and on the agenda: "biodiversity."**
- **This is shorthand for the extraordinarily rich abundance of life on earth. It is a label both for the unbelievably diverse range of species and for the ecosystems in which they live.[21] It includes everything from slugs to swallows, bacteria to blue whales, pussy willows to giant sequoia trees.**
- **So why is biodiversity so important? Surely we can afford to let a few thousand more species become extinct? After all, we are told, extinction is a natural process. True, but the scale and speed of extinction today is on an unprecedented scale. It is 1000 to 10 000 times faster than the natural rate. And it is forecast that 10 to 20 per cent of the species alive today will become extinct over the next 50 years.**

The speed of extinction today is 1000 to 10 000 times faster than the natural rate–a rate unknown since the time of the dinosaurs.

- **Some ecosystems have almost entirely disappeared. The casualties include the tall-grass prairies that many of the great North American Indians tribes once called home, together with tropical dry forests and rainforests. Forests, which covered 40 per cent of the earth's land surface, now cover just 27 per cent.**
- **This is important for many reasons, but the fact that more species live in the rainforests than in any other habitat is crucial. Each rainforest is a bit like Noah's Ark–which makes it even more extraordinary that we are setting fire to them. Tens of thousands of square kilometres of rainforest are burned every year to make way for agriculture, new communities, roads, mining and other developments. Many other vital ecosystems–among them coral reefs–are under similar pressure.**
- **Sheer human numbers have driven–and will continue to drive–extinction more surely than anything else. One-third to one-half of the world's land surface has**

now been altered by human activity of one sort or another, and that proportion will surely grow in the future. The vast majority of species must therefore exist in a greatly reduced and increasingly fragmented landscape.

- In India, for example, there has been a race to feed the country's soaring population. Where 30 000 varieties of rice used to be grown, representing vast genetic diversity and wealth, just 10 species now cover three-quarters of the land sown. Part of the significance of this trend is that some of the genes found in wild crops have been found to be able to resist deadly plant diseases, which can devastate food crops.
- Whether in our fields, our gardens or in the wild, caring for biodiversity really means protecting the web of life. This has to be one of the most urgent tasks for the 21st century—and a real challenge in terms of defining a new moral code and compass fit for the new millennium. Paradoxically, the genetic engineering industry may help to open our eyes to the extraordinary genetic wealth we are destroying.
- Canada loses 240 acres of wilderness every hour. Canada also has no law to protect species at risk. It is not just a problem in tropical rainforest, but also in the forests of Newfoundland, where that province's pine merten is threatened with extinction, in the northern boreal where the woodland caribou numbers are shrinking, and in Vancouver Island where the marmot is nearly gone. Canada also has an endangered species crisis. Recently, East Coast scientist Dr. Ran Myers realized a species of skate had probably gone extinct before it was even listed as endangered, due to being accidentally caught by dragger fishing.

Part II

3 Food & drink

Additives • Animal welfare • Bananas • BSE • BST • Chemicals • Countryside • Factory farming • Fair trade • Fish farming • Food miles • Free range • Gene foods • Hormones • Irradiation • Labelling • Local varieties • Mad cows • Methyl bromide • Monocultures • Organic produce • Organophosphates • Overfishing • Packaging • Pesticides • Rare breeds • Super-pests • Vegetarianism

To satisfy our needs, one of the world's largest industries grows millions of square kilometres of crops, rears billions of animals, and catches uncountable fish and other sea creatures. It sends armies of combine harvesters droning across prairie landscapes, once home to countless buffalo and to the native peoples who hunted them. Fleets of high-tech factory ships "vacuum" the ocean floor clean in many parts of the world, or trawl the open seas in search of our future fish sticks.

Because of all this activity, much of the planet would not be recognizable to our great-grandparents. No doubt they—like the food industry—would encourage us to be grateful that we no longer suffer from the great waves of starvation that once swept our lands. But they would also mourn many of the things we have lost in the process: the slow, winding rivers; the summer-scented hay meadows; the brilliant stands of wild flowers; the stillness of the traditional countryside.

Nor does the breakneck process of change show much sign of slowing. Every week seems to bring news of a novel food, whether it is a "smart" yoghurt that is designed to ruin your appetite, or a new vegetable containing exotic genes. And happily, there are a growing number of "real," "organic" or "fair trade" products available, too.

What do they all these labels mean—and who should we trust? Below, we ask six simple questions:

- *What's in our food?*
- *Do today's farms guarantee safe food?*
- *Who's playing God with our food?*
- *Wild fish, farmed fish—or no fish?*
- *Are ethics on our shopping list?*
- *How far should our food travel?*

3.1 Eating Impacts

What's in our food?

What we eat and drink has a profound impact on our health and well-being. Indeed, it is an extraordinary fact that 30 to 40 per cent of all cancers worldwide are linked to food.[1] This is often the result of bad diet—too much sugar, salt, fat or alcohol, for example. But there is also growing evidence that the chemical make-up of our food can have profound, unsuspected effects on the way we think and behave, in some cases even triggering violence to ourselves, or to others.

Let's look at some of the ways in which different chemicals get into our food and drink. Some arrive accidentally, for example, as residues from chemicals used on the farm, while others are used deliberately as food additives.

Chemical cocktails

Parents in Britain were shocked recently when the government warned them to peel fruit before giving it to their children. The problem was that some samples of both imported and home-grown apples showed dangerous levels of an organophosphate pesticide (see below). The worst contaminated apples contained up to six times as much pesticide as scientists estimated could be eaten at a sitting, every day of your life, without any risk to health.[2]

Also tested were carrots, imported bananas, imported and home-grown pears, imported nectarines and peaches, imported oranges, and imported and home-grown tomatoes. Nine to 19 per cent of all batches picked at random from fruit and vegetables on sale in shops showed traces of organophosphate and/or carbamate chemicals, although only a small number of apples and peaches contained "higher than desirable" residues.

In the case of bananas, at least five chemicals used on the crop are classified as being "extremely hazardous" by the World Health Organization (WHO). This has frequently resulted in health problems for plantation workers (page 80) and it would be amazing if there were not detectable levels of such chemicals in the fruit we eat.

Canadian produce

Could the British incident of contaminated fruit be repeated in Canada? The experience of Canadian food inspectors, who randomly test thousands of imported and domestic shipments of fresh fruit and vegetables every year, indicates it is highly unlikely. However, the possibility cannot be ruled out that one or more of the many shipments not tested in a given year could be contaminated with unsafe levels of pesticide residues, just as occurred in Britain.

To get a better sense of the chemical cocktails to which we are potentially exposed, let's look at some of the pesticides used on food crops, then switch to chemicals used as additives in food products—and found in packaging. The section "Animal Farms" (page 51) covers chemical residues from the use of hormones, antibiotics and pesticides in farm animals, while fish-related issues are covered in "Fish Dishes" (page 68).

Organophosphates

- **Among the most controversial pesticides in recent years have been organophosphates. Some of their effects are believed to include attacking the nervous system, with early symptoms including headaches, excessive sweating, breathing difficulty, vomiting, blurred vision, slurred speech, slow thinking and loss of memory. Later come convulsions, coma and even–in extreme circumstances–death.[3]**
- **Organophosphates are commonly used on a variety of fruit and vegetables, including bananas, carrots, cabbages and broccoli. For decades they were sprayed on the forests of New Brunswick to combat spruce budworm. They are also commonly used in many household products, such as insecticides for ants, cockroaches, fleas, flies, moths and wasps. There have been recent concerns about their use in de-lousing shampoos,**

which are primarily used on children, and sheep dips, where they are thought to have caused serious illness in farmers. There are also strong suspicions that they may be among the chemicals contributing to "Gulf War Syndrome" that has severely impaired servicemen who fought in the Gulf.

More than 35 000 tonnes of herbicides, insecticides and fungicides are used on Canadian crops each year.[4]

The case for–and against–pesticides

To understand why crop protection chemicals are turning up in our food, we need to understand why farmers use them in the first place.

The case for pesticides is easy to make. Without them, it is thought that some 30 per cent of the world's crops would be lost before they were harvested. They not only help protect crops in the field but also, later, during transport and in storage. They improve hygiene by killing flies and cockroaches, and help fight plagues of locusts, malarial mosquitoes and disease-carrying rodents.[5]

Another way to think of the contribution of pesticides is to imagine how much land we might need to put under the plough without them. Apparently, we manage to produce 40 per cent more food per head than in 1946, with only a small increase in acreage under cultivation. So we need to try to keep things in proportion as we look at the case against pesticides.

The case against, however, is more compelling. Ever since the publication of Rachel Carson's epic book *Silent Spring* in 1962, the world has been increasingly aware of the dangers that such chemicals pose (page 30). But it is clear that her message has not yet fully sunk in—pesticide use in the United States has more than doubled since *Silent Spring* first appeared.

So let's focus in on some of the problems:

Residues: Much of the food that we eat contains measurable quantities of pesticide residues, even though the chemicals have been applied legally. Some imported foods may even contain residues of pesticides banned at home. Given that children are particularly vulnerable, and that we encourage them to eat lots of fruit and vegetables, their potential exposure is a matter of real concern.

Overuse: Some farmers fail to follow the instructions, either spraying too much or at the wrong time—too close to harvesting, for example.

Illegal use: It is strongly suspected that some banned pesticides are still being used. DDT, for example, was banned many years ago in industrialized countries, but its continuing occurrence as a residue suggests illegal use. As well, DDT is legally used in a number of countries, from which Canada imports some produce.

Worker safety: Thousands of people are killed each year by pesticides, particularly in poorer countries, where safety controls are weak or nonexistent. But agricultural workers and farmers are also exposed in Canada. Saskatchewan farmers have an increased risk of cancer, and studies suggest the risk increases with exposure to 2,4-1.

Health effects: Pesticides can damage our immune systems, making us more vulnerable to illness and disease.[6] The immune systems of other animals are also affected. For example, a plague killing dolphins turned out to be caused by a common virus, to which they would normally have been resistant. Blood samples showed that they had high levels of pesticides in their bodies, coupled with major viral infections and weakened immune systems. Other symptoms, in both animals and humans, include fertility problems (page 30). Children living in homes that use pesticides have a six times larger risk of leukemia.

Bird kills: Some bird populations have crashed in the last 25 years—and it is thought that pesticides have been a contributory cause. Insecticides are also killing off insects, an important food source, while herbicides are cutting the number of plants on which insects and birds depend for food.[7]

Food chains: Chemical residues from some pesticides, mainly organochlorine products (page 30), pass up the food chain, building up in the blood, fat and milk of animals and people, often long distances from the original site of use.

Downwind, downstream: As much as 85 to 90 per cent of pesticides used never reach their targets, finding their way instead into air, soil and water—as well as into the bodies of nearby animals and people.

Ozone depletion: Apart from being extremely toxic, methyl bromide is a powerful "ozone-eater" (page 10). Perhaps we should now be looking out for "ozone-friendly" labels on fruit such as strawberries?

With all of these issues simmering away, it is hardly surprising that some of the greener countries are thinking of getting tough with the farming industry. In 1997, for example, the Danish Parliament voted unanimously to set up an independent commission to look at the feasibility of moving away from pesticide use in agriculture.

Meanwhile, the worrying thing is that contaminated fruit and vegetables are still entering the market. It is also worth pointing out that nonorganic gardeners growing their own vegetables may well have worse residue levels because they are more likely to misuse chemicals, by not applying them at the right time or using the right dosage.

Feeding crops

The compounds used as agricultural fertilizers are not usually as toxic as pesticides, but the sheer scale of the applications means that there have been problems.

To begin with, the main focus was on run-off into rivers—where the extra nutrients caused algae to grow faster—and, by stripping oxygen out of the water, as they decompose, suffocating fish and other wildlife. Then the focus began to shift to the risk of nitrates from nitrogen fertilizers gradually working their way down into underground water, with the result that drinking water supplies became contaminated. This is now a major problem in some arable farming regions.

Nitrates are also implicated in such human health problems as stomach cancer in adults and "blue baby" syndrome in newborn infants. And now a new concern is emerging. Some British studies suggest a link between nitrate levels in water and rates of childhood diabetes. We are not aware of any Canadian studies suggesting such a link, but there is no question that more and more Canadian children are being diagnosed with diabetes. Currently, Edmonton, Alberta, has the third-highest rate of Type I diabetes in the world. The cause seems to be environmental. The main theories out there are that cow's milk or something in the diet is making more children susceptible to diabetes.[8]

What's in the packaging?

Even if food is as pure as driven snow, some fear that the packaging used to protect it can be a problem. For example, there was historic concern about the use of materials such as lead in the solder used to make cans. And, more recently, there has been controversy over the effects of phthalates (page 33), which have been widely used as plasticizers in PVC food packaging, such as plastic wrap. Some food manufacturers have reportedly stopped using phthalates. Certainly the packaging industry comes up with some extraordinary items. A quick-chill can appeared in Britain that used a gas that was 1300 times more powerful than carbon dioxide. It was estimated that if the cans won even 10 per cent of the British canned-drinks market, they would wipe out half the proposed cuts in gases the government had promised by 2005. Happily, they have not been allowed as originally designed.

Canada had its short-lived "PETainer," a plastic beer can that contained polyethylene terephthalate (the PET in the PETainer) over which was a layer of PVC, all of it topped by an aluminum lid. Mixing materials in this way makes it very difficult to recycle containers. Indeed, a key packaging issue in Canada and the U.S. is the low rate of recycling. Attempts by the U.S. plastics industry to keep this bad news from the public, while claiming great successes in recycling, has outraged environmental groups.

Another suspect chemical, thought to have an impact on fertility, is bisphenol A. Widely used in lacquer coatings found in the inside of food cans and water pipes, this chemical is also found in dental fillings. A Spanish study found up to 33 micrograms (mcg) of bisphenol A (page 31) in tins of peas, beans, corn and artichokes, when doses as low as 20 mcg per kilogram of body weight have been shown to increase the size of mouse prostate glands.[9] Should we be worried? The truth is that no one really knows.

Overpackaging of food and other products continues to be a problem for many products. Clearly, if less packaging is used, fewer resources will be required and less environmental damage will be incurred. Although packaging plays a crucial role in keeping our food safe and hygienic, we need to keep a close eye on the materials used and how much is really necessary.

What the menu doesn't say

So far, we have looked mainly at chemicals that get into our foods accidentally. But there also are a growing number of issues that relate to substances used intentionally in food processing. Faced with a rising tide of so-called junk food, there has been an increased interest in healthy eating.

Some governments, in fact, are even beginning to warn about the perils of the school lunchbox—provided by parents. In some countries, there have been moves to stop children eating junk food rich in sugar, fat and salt, which are linked with obesity and heart disease. And there is concern that leading fast-food chains are targeting children as young as two years old, making it much less likely that they will grow up eating a healthy, balanced diet.

This is worrying for a number of reasons. One is that research shows that poor nutrition—including too much junk food—is linked with antisocial behaviour, particularly aggression and violence. So, for example, when prisoners were given an improved diet, in terms of vitamins, minerals and fats, violent incidents fell "dramatically."[10]

So let's look at a selection of the vitamins, fats and oils, flavourings, sweeteners, stimulants, emulsifiers, colourings, preservatives and wax coatings found in today's highly processed foods.[11]

Vitamins

There is no question that vitamins are good for us—the real question is which vitamins and in what doses? Overdosing on some vitamins can be just as dangerous as overdosing on some drugs. Yet many of us have taken to consuming vitamins in huge quantities. In the U.S., for example, people are gulping down 10, 50 or even 100 times the daily recommended dose, in the hope of warding off cancer and other diseases.

The U.S. supplements industry, whose sales—partly thanks to these mega-doses—more than doubled between 1990 and 1996,[12] has been shaken by health warnings. There is concern, for example, that too much beta-carotene might not only turn your skin yellow but also increase cancer rates in smokers. Take too much vitamin B_6 and you run the risk of nerve damage—and too much calcium may weaken the kidneys. As the *New York Times* put it in 1997: "Consumers are, in effect, volunteering for a vast and largely unregulated experiment."

The amount of vitamins we take should reflect our age, sex and health. The message is clear: if you plan to take high doses of vitamins, or if you give them to your children, you should consult an expert first.

Fats and oils

These days you seem to need a PhD to understand the fats in your food. A certain amount of fat is essential in anyone's diet, but it can come from a number of sources—and in various forms. Let's look at the different fats and what they do for our health:

Unsaturated fats: Monounsaturated fats, found in olive oil, are the healthiest. But almost as good are polyunsaturated fats, found, for example, in sunflower and corn oils.

Saturated fats: These are the least healthy. They raise blood cholesterol levels and are found in high levels in many fast and junk foods, as well as in many meat and dairy products—including butter, cheese and lard. They are also found in a few plant-derived fats, including coconut and palm oils.

Hydrogenated acids: Also known as "trans-fatty acids," these are often used in semisolid spreads like margarine. This process makes unsaturated fats more like saturated fats—usually to create a consistency more like butter. One of the results of hydrogenating fats is that they make otherwise healthy fats "unhealthy," and capable of raising blood cholesterol levels.

Fish oils: The oils found in deep-water fish (including alpha linoleic acid, or omega-3 series fatty acids) are considered to be extremely healthy. The active ingredient in "oily fish," such as mackerel, tuna and salmon, is EPA (eicosapentaenoic acid), which helps to reduce the blood's tendency to clot, and encourages cardiovascular health. It is possible, however, to get alpha linoleic acid (which is necessary to produce EPA in the body) in your diet without eating fish—it is also found in linseed, canola and soybean oils, as well as in walnuts and vegetable leaves.

Fish liver oils: These are extremely good sources of vitamins A and D, but one area of concern is that traces of toxins like dioxin, PCBs, DDT and Lindane have been found in a range of top-brand products. Although it is apparently possible to exceed acceptable levels of these toxins by using these products, government safety advisers say that normal intakes of such oils are unlikely to cause any problems.[13]

Most basic cooking oils are produced by highly industrialized processes. The raw materials are crushed, heated and pressed, neutralized, bleached and deodorized using a range of chemical solvents, phosphates, alkalis and high temperatures.[14] The aim is to produce an oil that is almost flavourless and will store well. Most of the nutrients, particularly vitamin E, tend to be destroyed in the process. These types of oils are made from crops like corn, grapeseed, groundnut, canola, safflower and sunflower.

Much healthier are cold-pressed oils, which are squeezed in a press and then filtered. Less oil is extracted in this process, which makes the product more expensive, but the vitamins and aromatic ingredients (which give oils their flavours) are maintained. The Mediterranean diet, which is rich in olive and fish oils, is particularly healthy.

Such is our obsession with fat-free or low-fat food that we have taken it too far. Some households buy no whole-milk or full-fat products. And yet full milk, for example, is a vital part of the diet of growing children—particularly for those under two. Furthermore, many "light" or "no-fat" products bear no resemblance to the original food, and have none of the nutritional benefits of whole, natural products; they also often contain a variety of additives to give them flavour and texture.

So what should we do about fats? The best advice for adults is as follows. First, look for cold-pressed oils made from olives, nuts and seeds—but remember to keep them in the fridge, because they can become rancid fairly quickly. Second, include fish oils (fatty fish are best) in your diet. And, third, cut your total fat intake.[15] For children the advice is to eat fewer fried foods—and to include plenty of oily fish and full-fat milk in the diet.

Additives: good, bad and ugly

The last decade has seen huge concern about a range of food ingredients and additives. In particular, the spotlight has focused on a number of substances identified by E-numbers. Considerable progress has been made in understanding the risks, providing information and removing some of the most problematic additives. Below we look at what these additives do and at some of the issues that might still be on our worry list.

Flavourings: Chemicals, used to intensify food flavours, such as monosodium glutamate (MSG or E621), have been shown to overexcite—even kill—brain cells. This ingredient is widely used in "westernized" Asian cooking, but given the potential risks to children, baby-food manufacturers have been forced to stop adding it to their products.

Sugar: Sugars are an essential part of our diet, but too much of any sweetener can be a bad thing. Overconsumption of sugar, for example, causes tooth decay (particularly in children) and may contribute to obesity, which, in turn, is linked to an increased risk of coronary heart disease and diabetes.

Super-sweeteners: Modern sweeteners include saccharin and aspartame (trade-name Nutrasweet). Discovered in a laboratory accident in 1878, saccharin is 500 times sweeter than sugar, but there is some limited evidence that it can cause cancer in animals. Aspartame is a more recent super-sweetener, around 200 times sweeter than sugar. Critics in the U.S. have mounted an intense campaign to have this product banned[16] on the grounds that it may cause serious health problems. But manufacturers have strongly rebutted these claims and campaigns have not been supported by regulatory authorities. What we do know is that aspartame must not be consumed by individuals who have been diagnosed with a condition known as phenylketonuria, since these people must ensure that their phenylalanine intake (a constituent of aspartame) remains as low as possible. One in 10 000 people have this defect (therefore, 3000 people in Canada), and babies are routinely tested (the PKU test) soon after birth, when a blood sample is taken by pricking their foot. So you should already know if your child is affected.

Stimulants: Probably the most widely used legal stimulant is caffeine. It is found in coffee, tea, many soft drinks and colas, headache tablets and other products. It excites the brain both by stimulating the heart and blood circulation, and by increasing the body's output of adrenaline. You would have to be an extraordinarily greedy coffee drinker to risk death: start to worry after your 65th cup of the day! But much lower quantities can cause headaches, digestive upsets, anxiety and depression. This is especially worrying, since it's so easy to get hooked (page 253).

Emulsifiers: Emulsifiers are used to stop mixtures from separating; they are used in growing numbers and quantities, in products such as milk, salad dressings and paint. Synthetic emulsifiers are often used, for example, to combine something fatty, like butter, with something acidic, like lemon. Emulsifiers seem to have a good health record, although it's always worth keeping an eye on the long-term effects of synthetic compounds.

Stabilizers: Some natural stabilizers are still used, including lecithin, which is found in eggs, soybeans, milk, mustard and lanolin.

Colourings: In the public's mind, food colourings have often been linked to health problems. You may have noticed that manufacturers have begun to take note and many foods, such as yoghurts or jams, are less vibrant in colour. There are concerns, however, about the use of canthaxanthin, an orange-red pigment that is used in animal feeds, primarily to colour egg yolks (in some parts of Canada) and the flesh of farmed salmon and trout. Although there is no proof that children or adults will exceed "acceptable daily intakes," this issue does raise the question of whether consumers really do want very yellow egg yolks and very pink salmon flesh, requiring the use of synthetic or even naturally based colourings. Even people eating eggs from home-reared chickens may not be able to avoid such colouring because chicken feed may contain them.

Preservatives: Most foods go off fairly rapidly, particularly in hot weather, unless they are preserved in some way. Basic food preservatives include salt, vinegar and sugar, none of which is completely safe. However, given that some preservatives can prevent such potentially deadly diseases as botulism, they clearly play an important role in protecting our health.

Wax coatings: This is an odd one. The skins of some apples, lemons, melons, oranges and pineapples are waxed with animal products, of a sort.[17] Shellac, an insect secretion, and beeswax are often used, which could prove unacceptable for some vegetarians. Oranges and lemons may be labelled as "unwaxed," but this is not the case for the other fruits.

Irradiated food

Throughout history it has been crucially important to find ways of treating foods to reduce or destroy naturally occurring contaminants, including insects, pests and bacteria. The importance of tackling contamination is illustrated by the fact that an estimated 60 per cent of chicken sold in the U.S. is infected with salmonella, and the figure is more like 75 per cent in Europe.[18] In Canada, the figure is lower, but it is still significant—around 20 per cent. Among the food preservation methods used have been drying, fermentation, pickling, salting, smoking and—most recently—irradiation.

An estimated one in five domestically produced chickens sold in Canada is infected with salmonella.

Irradiation is a controversial new technology, which involves exposing food to high doses of radiation. Done in the right way, it should not make the food radioactive. Among its potential advantages, irradiation can:

- kill insects and pests that infest food;
- reduce levels of dangerous bacteria, such as salmonella, listeria and campylobacter;
- delay ripening and decay, so foods can be kept longer; and
- completely sterilize food, making it fit for vulnerable patients in hospital.

But among its possible disadvantages,[19] irradiation:

- is not suitable for meats and dairy foods;
- is relatively expensive;
- can substantially reduce nutrient levels (including vitamins, minerals and phytonutrients) and therefore the nutritional value of the food (up to 90 per cent of the vitamins are potentially lost);
- may leave some active bacteria, which can reproduce rapidly;
- is likely to kill off "healthy" bacteria as well as the bad ones;
- is ineffective against viruses;
- could enable dishonest traders to disguise food that is unfit for human consumption; and
- could also bring new risks that are as yet not understood.[20]

Consumer resistance has slowed down the introduction of food irradiation. When it does appear, foods should be labelled as "irradiated" or "treated with ionizing radiation." However, there is no such requirement in Canada. Furthermore, this labelling requirement does not apply to ingredients that comprise less than 25 per cent of a labelled product.

Food hygiene

Food poisoning has increased tenfold over the last 15 years,[21] for a number of reasons. These include the increased use of antibiotics in farming; animals being transported longer distances to abattoirs, causing them to collect bacteria in transit; fast production lines in abattoirs; spread of slaughterhouse waste on grazing fields; lack of training of meat handlers; insufficient inspections of premises; an increase in the number of people eating out; and more fast food, such as hamburgers, on our menus.

But we should not forget about hygiene in our own kitchens. There is a growing obsession with fashionable antibacterial sprays and germ-killing chopping boards, but this is not the real solution. Indeed, it can be a real problem, potentially killing off good germs and enabling dangerous germs to develop resistance.

The important things to remember are to put uncooked meats at the bottom of the fridge, where it is coldest; use different knives and boards for uncooked meats and raw vegetables; wash your hands after handling different foods; change or bleach dish-clothes regularly; and don't wash your own dishes along with those used by your pets (unless you use a dishwasher, which washes at a high enough temperature to destroy bacteria).

Eating Impacts

✔ Citizen 2000 Checklist

1. Choose a Healthy Diet

Most of us know that a healthy diet will include plenty of fresh vegetables, fruit and fibre. We also know that certain food ingredients–including salt, sugar and certain fats–should be eaten in moderation. That said, the advice on which foods are and are not healthy tends to change fairly frequently. To keep track of the latest information, it makes sense to subscribe to the **Centre for Science in the Public Interest**, which campaigns across the food agenda in Canada and the United States and publishes *Nutrition Action Healthletter.* This publication is not shy about naming names in rating supermarket or fast-food offerings as good or bad for your health.

For consumers who want to read about the latest findings in a little more depth, the **National Institute of Nutrition** publishes *RAPPORT* four times a year. Each issue also includes the latest *Health Bites*, a consumer-friendly series of fact sheets on a variety of nutrition topics.

A useful book on food issues is Joanna Blythman's *The Food We Eat* (Penguin Books, 1998). And anyone wanting the inside story on the fast-food industry should read John Vidal's *McLibel: Burger Culture on Trial* (New Press, 1997). Liz Pearson's *When in Doubt, Eat Broccoli* (Penguin Books, 1998) is a well-written guide through the sometimes confusing field of nutrition.

2. Encourage Reduced Pesticide Use

Two excellent sources of information on pesticides are the **Sierra Club of Canada** and the **World Wildlife Fund**. They are among the leaders of the **Campaign for Pesticide Reduction (CPR!)**, a coalition of over 100 groups across Canada concerned with the environmental and health risks of pesticide use. Copies of **World Wildlife Fund**'s new booklet *Reducing Your Risks from Pesticides* are available from that organization. Copies of *Pesticides and Your Child: An Overview of Exposures and Risks* are available from **CPR!**. Other recommended reading: *Silent Spring*, by Rachel Carson (Fawcett World Library, 1962–a classic, still relevant today); *Pesticides and You*, the journal of the **National Coalition Against the Misuse of Pesticides** (Washington, DC); and *How To Get Your Lawn and Garden Off Drugs*, by Carole Rubin, **Friends of the Earth** (Cavendish Books, 1989).

Given that we import much of our food from the United States, Mexico and elsewhere, you may also want information on what is happening in other countries. **Pesticide Action Network North America (PANNA)** gives citizens access to information about pesticide hazards and alternatives through the PANUPS news service and their quarterly periodical, *The Global Pesticide Campaigner.*

The **Crop Protection Institute**, while it represents the interests of the pesticide industry in Canada, does provide useful information on "integrated pest management" (IPM), an approach to crop growing that actually dates back to the beginning of this century. IPM reduces the need for pesticides by integrating their use with such methods as crop rotation and mechanical weed control. However, the use of crop protection chemicals continues to develop pesticide-resistant pests. More recently, IPM has included biotechnology, which raises serious concerns in its own right (see page 34).

3. Support Organic Agriculture

Organic food is produced without the use of synthetic or artificial fertilizers, pesticides, herbicides, growth regulators, antibiotics, preservatives, dyes, additives, chemical coatings or irradiation. It includes not only fruit and vegetable products, but also dairy products, meat and poultry. In contrast to intensive or factory farming (see the following section on Animal Farms), organic farming entails more humane treatment of animals throughout their lives.

In at least some of their stores, supermarket chains such as **Loblaw**, **Super Valu** and **Sobeys** are beginning to devote space for organic dairy products and a whole range of organic produce.[22] The more people who ask store managers for organic products, the sooner they will become part of the standard fare on supermarket shelves. In the meantime, organic products are available in health and natural food stores in many centres across Canada. The key organization in this area is **Canadian Organic Growers (COG)**, the national information network for organic gardeners, farmers and consumers, with links to local and provincial organizations. **COG** publishes a quarterly newsletter and the *Organic Resource Guide*, a national directory of organic retailers, farmers and other useful contacts. The Directory (pages 283–296) at the end of this book lists **COG** chapters and other local organizations that provide information on organic agriculture and where to buy organic food. Directories of organic sources are also available on the websites of some provincial governments.

In addition to dozens of tasty recipes from some of Canada's top chefs, *The Organic Gourmet* (Robert Rose, 1998) includes a very useful list of organic sources: websites, organizations and retail outlets across the country. The cookbook is available from **Knives and Forks, Advocates for Organic Agriculture**, which organizes the annual Feast of Fields event in Southern Ontario.

But how do we know a product is organic just because the label says so? At this point, there are 43 organic certification bodies in Canada. These bodies, and the organic industry as a whole, have recognized the need for a single, national organic standard under federal legislation. The **Canadian Organic Advisory Board (COAB)** is very close to reaching consensus on a *National Standard for Organic Agriculture*, which will define the meaning of "organic" in Canadian agri-food products. The COAB board of directors represents organic producers as well as the diverse interests of the organic processing, wholesale, retail, government, research, consumer and environmental communities. To keep up-to-date with developments, contact **Canadian Organic Growers**. As well, the **COAB** produces a bulletin and runs a website for board members and other interested parties.

Worldwide, the **International Federation of Organic Agricultural Movements (IFOAM)** aims to unite the organic movement in setting standards and lobbying governments.

4. Care for the Wilderness and Wildlife

Food producers and retailers have a responsibility not only for the quality of the food we eat, but also for the state of the land where most of the food is grown. They should set standards for their suppliers to ensure that they are not destroying trees, wetlands and wildlife habitats in favour of vast fields of single-species crops, with frequent applications of chemical fertilizers, herbicides and pesticides. **Ducks Unlimited Canada**, one of the key organizations active in this area, emphasizes that responsibility for wildlife habitat must be shared between the landowner and the public at large. Their literature puts it this way: "Urban folk say it's important to see birds and animals in the wild. Farmers say, 'Yes, we *do* appreciate wildlife and its role in our world. But we're trying to run a business and make a living. If society truly believes wildlife is important, they'll have to share the responsibility so we can afford to protect the habitat.'"

Ducks Unlimited allows society to share the cost of wildlife habitat protection by delivering two programs: Prairie CARE (Conservation of Agriculture, Resources and Environment) and Ontario Land CARE. Financial incentives and technical assistance help farmers conserve their soil and water resources while improving the environment for wildlife and for people. In some instances, restoring or improving habitats is in itself profitable for farmers. Managing woodlands to provide habitat as well as saleable timber is a common example of such a win-win situation.

Assistance and financial incentives to farmers for such initiatives as Environmental Farm Plans are also available through **Agriculture and Agri-Food Canada**, in partnership with provincial agriculture departments and farm organizations.

Other organizations have long been active in such areas as advocacy, educational campaigns, technical assistance and land purchase programs. Among national organizations are the **Nature Conservancy of Canada**, **Fly Fishing Canada**, **World Wildlife Fund** and **Wildlife Habitat Canada**. Contact them to learn more, or to find out about local and provincial organizations.

3.2 *Animal Farms*

Do today's farms guarantee safe food?

In the past, supermarkets did not encourage consumers to look up and down the food chain. However, issues like pesticide contamination and animal welfare have encouraged us to take a much greater interest in how our food is grown or produced. And few issues did more to push things in this direction than the "mad cow" controversy (page 53).

Whether you are an animal welfare activist, or simply interested in the safety and quality of the food you eat, modern farming methods raise worrying health, animal welfare and environmental concerns. Think of water pollution, for a moment. Silage effluents are some 200 times more polluting than raw human sewage and, along with animal manures, they are highly damaging when they get into rivers. But who thinks of this when drinking milk or eating beef?

Silage effluent is 200 times more polluting than raw human sewage.

In this section we focus on three big issues. The first is whether to eat animals at all. The second is how we should treat animals. And the third is how chemicals are used in rearing animals and what effect they may have on our health.

The vegetarian option

Vegetarianism is on the rise across the western world.[23] Most people who choose vegetarianism do so for religious or health reasons, taste, or objections to cruelty or killing animals. Also, a growing number of people are now opting for vegetarianism or eating more plants because they recognize that less land is needed to satisfy our appetites with fruits and vegetables than with food animals.

More positively, one key benefit of animal farming is that we no longer need to hunt wild animals for food. With the number of meat-eaters and the ever-more sophisticated weaponry available, this would inevitably mean pursuing the last remaining wild animals to extinction. Also, most pesticide residues in the diet are from meat, not vegetables.

So let's look at the case for vegetarianism:

Ecology: There is a strong case for eating low on the food chain. For example, it takes 7 kilograms (nearly 16 pounds) of soybeans or grains, plus 22 litres (about 6 gallons) of water, to produce a kilo of beef. Since four-fifths of the world's agricultural land is used to feed animals, the meat industry is a massive contributor to the destruction of such endangered resources as tropical forests.

Ethics: Many people feel it is wrong to cause animal suffering. But different people draw the line in different places. Vegans eat no animal products at all. Lacto-vegetarians supplement the vegan diet with dairy products, including milk, yoghurt, cream, butter and cheese. Lacto-ovo-vegetarians eat eggs, too. It should be pointed out, however, that large numbers of animals are killed to produce both milk and eggs—male calves and male chicks are often killed soon after birth. One day, for better or worse, genetic engineers will probably work out how to produce only females (page 230). Would this be preferable?

Diet: It is obviously easier for lacto-ovo-vegetarians to create a nutritionally balanced diet than it is for vegans. But vegetarians of every description can enjoy a healthy diet if they plan their menus reasonably carefully. It is important, for example, to ensure that such diets include enough protein, iron, zinc and vitamins (especially B_{12}). Because plant proteins do not contain all the nine essential amino acids, it is necessary to eat the right combinations and get a healthy balance.

Health: Even orthodox governmental bodies are suggesting that a plant-based diet can be healthier for you—potentially even lessening the likelihood of developing cancer. They recommend limiting red meat in our diets[24], largely because of its high concentration of saturated fat. Because vegetarian diets are lower in cholesterol and other animal fats, and richer in complex carbohydrates, vegetable fibre and roughage, vegetarians are also less prone to coronary heart disease, high blood pressure, diabetes, obesity, arthritis, rheumatism, constipation and kidney disorders.

Money: Given that meat, poultry and fish tend to be expensive, it is hardly surprising that even a fairly luxurious vegetarian diet can work out cheaper.

Eating meat makes a giant ecological footprint!

Welfare on the farm

So what's it like down on the factory farm? Let's look at some animal welfare issues raised by the intensive farming of dairy cattle, veal calves, pigs and chickens. We will also look at how once-wild animals such as deer and ostriches are increasingly being raised for the table.

How now brown cow?

These days, a dairy cow's lot is rarely a happy one. Many cows now have udders so large that there is a risk of trampled teats. They may even be deprived of the chance to wander in a pasture. Most dairy farmers build modern barns, with temperature and air-flow controls, but some decide they can therefore keep their cows inside throughout the year. The resulting lack of exercise often leads to lameness. Sadly, the pressure to produce more and more milk per cow seems to be leading Canada in the direction of dairy practices in Europe where, in any given year, a quarter of the EU dairy herd suffer from lameness—and over a third suffer from mastitis, a painful inflammation of the udder. In some cases, cows' udders are actually crushed when the animals lie down.[25]

On the meat front, few methods of production stir quite as much emotion as veal farming. Veal calves have traditionally been separated from their mothers when just a few days old. They are then reared in very narrow crates—often in the dark. Although some people challenge whether veal in any form is acceptable, work is under way to improve rearing conditions. In Europe, group housing for veal calves is widely used, which means less restriction on behaviour and more social contact between the animals. In the future, group housing, with lots of room for the calves to move around, may become a requirement in Europe and the United Kingdom.

In Canada, there is a voluntary veal code (currently undergoing revision) that calls for individual stalls to be large enough for resting postures and for the calf to get up and lie down without difficulty.[26] The extent to which veal producers comply with even this minimum standard is unknown. The code also encourages producers to "monitor" developments in group housing for veal calves, though it is less than enthusiastic, complaining that group housing "requires a greater degree of husbandry to ensure health and well-being."[27]

The veal code is one of a set of voluntary codes that cover all of the common farm animals. The codes, put together by producer groups and the Canadian Federation of Humane Societies, seek to set standards for existing systems rather than advocating radical changes or improvements.[28] Clearly, public pressure is needed to move Canadian practices toward the much higher standards being set by the Europeans. In the meantime, the voluntary codes are better than having no accepted standards at all.

If you are a meat-eater, free-range beef provides an excellent way of turning grass into human food. But the closer we get to intensive feed-lot beef farming, the more cause there is for concern about issues such as the use of hormones (page 57) and other growth promoters. In Britain, if not in other countries, even committed meat-eaters began to look at the beef on their plate in a rather different way after the "mad cow" scandal surfaced (see below).

The "Mad Cow" Saga

- ***What is it?*** **A deadly disease of cattle and, potentially, people. The media called it "mad cow" disease, scientists "BSE"–which stands for bovine spongiform encephalopathy.**
- ***What is the cause?*** **We now know that cows were fed with waste products from dead sheep, some suffering from a disease called "scrapie." It is still not certain that this was the cause of BSE, but it seems likely. Another route, also through feed, may have been from wild African animals made into bone-meal and imported to the United Kingdom in the 1970s. A third theory, gaining credence, is that the real culprits were organophosphates (page 41) used to eradicate warble fly in cattle. Supporters of this theory believe these chemicals either helped trigger BSE directly or by suppressing the animals' immune systems, hence making them more vulnerable to disease. One strong piece of circumstantial evidence is that, after the U.K., Switzerland has the highest incidence of BSE–and also happens to use high doses of these chemicals.**
- ***What is the issue?*** **It became clear that the BSE infection in cows could pass both to calves and–in the form of Creutzfeldt Jakob Disease (CJD)–to people eating contaminated meat.**
- ***Why was this a surprise?*** **It shouldn't have been. Experts had warned of the dangers for years–one expert had even called for the slaughter of six million cows years earlier, arguing that anyone under the age of 50 should avoid eating beef. He was attacked in articles based on government briefings, excluded from expert panels and denied research funding.[29]**

- *What action was taken?* When BSE first surfaced, in 1986, the U.K. government decided to ensure that no more cattle feed was contaminated with animal proteins. If their ban had been properly enforced, the problem might have disappeared. But it wasn't.[30]
- *How serious is it?* CJD is potentially fatal in humans. Commercially, too, BSE has been devastating. Across the European Union, beef consumption initially dropped by 30 per cent. And farmers suffered terrible losses.
- *Just a U.K. problem?* No. The problem hit the U.K. hardest, but the disease is also found in other countries. And even gorier stories surfaced in the wake of the BSE scandal. It transpired, for example, that in Switzerland thousands of human placentas from hospitals had been used since the 1960s to make animal feed!
- *BSE in Canada?* Canada has recorded only one case of mad cow disease, and that was from a cow imported from Britain in 1993. The cow, her offspring and all other animals in the Alberta herd were destroyed.[31] However, there may be other routes of infection. As noted above, BSE in the U.K. was likely caused by mixing animal proteins–basically a rendering of the intestines, other innards and the trimmings from slaughtered animals–in cattle feed. In North America, rendered sheep and cattle offal have been used for years to enrich the protein content of cattle feed to boost growth and weight. After the mad cow story hit the headlines in the United States, news of this practice reached a wide public, many of whom were appalled at the thought of cows eating other cows. The media described it as turning herbivores into carnivores.[32]
- *Foot dragging in Canada.* When you consider that scrapie–a disease rather similar to BSE–is found from time to time in Canadian sheep herds, it is not far-fetched to suggest the disease could get into the food chain via cattle feed contaminated with animal products. What is disturbing is the slowness of the Canadian government in responding to this issue. By March 29, 1996, the U.S. Department of Agriculture had announced they were expediting regulations prohibiting ruminant protein in ruminant feed–cud-chewing animals are not to be fed to other cud-chewing animals. Several days later, the World Health Organization called for a similar ban globally. Here at home, aside from statements that they are consulting with industry groups and reassurances about the safety of Canadian meat, officials at Agriculture and Agri-Food Canada have been silent on the issue.[33]
- *British beef in Canada.* There is also the possibility of British beef, banned in Canada since 1990, entering the country illegally. In early 1998, federal food inspectors seized British meat products from half a dozen stores in Calgary, Halifax, Richmond, B.C., and Toronto.[34] The Canadian Food Inspection Agency advises consumers to check labels of meat products and, if they are made in Britain, to view them with suspicion. If they do not have bilingual labels, they are more than likely illegally imported and should not be eaten.[35]
- *Key message?* As one farmer put it: "If the first priority of consumers is cheap food, it may not be entirely coincidental

that the same objective is adopted all the way up the food chain."[36]

- ***What can we do?* There are a number of options. Become a vegetarian (page 51). Eat organic or "real" meat (page 57). Or simply hope that governments and farmers have learned from this disaster.**

The pig's tale

In the wild, pigs forage and dig in woods and forests. They are naturally both intelligent and clean. But conditions on the farm are usually very different. Most controversially, the reduction in farm workers has been a key factor leading to the use of "farrowing crates" for pregnant pigs.[37] These narrow, metal crates confine the sow, usually from up to a week before she gives birth until the piglets are weaned, some three to four weeks later.

In Canada, most of the breeding herd—which is housed indoors for both climatic and efficiency reasons—give birth in farrowing crates. Often, little or no straw is provided, so the animals cannot express their natural nesting instincts. The result can be high levels of stress and frustration. One side-effect of this is thought to be prolonged and more difficult labour—and a lower-quality taste. To make matters worse, most big producers confine sows in narrow stalls for two to three months as a labour-saving way to prevent overfeeding.

Chickens and eggs

Watch farmyard hens scratching and pecking in the soil: this is not so far removed from conditions familiar to the wild jungle fowl from which they are descended. Battery farms, introduced earlier in the 20th century to provide cheap eggs for consumers, are another world altogether. The chickens stand on a wire mesh—and can do little more than eat, drink, defecate, lay eggs (page 57) and peck at their neighbours. Their pecking instinct is a hangover from the wild and is controlled by de-beaking, usually done with a red-hot guillotine.

Proposals have been made to phase out conventional battery cages for egg-laying hens across Europe.[38] In the meantime, it has been suggested that the cage space for each bird should increase to nearly the size of a tabloid newspaper page, and that breeding companies should pursue genetic selection for birds less prone to feather-pecking and cannibalism. Among conventional egg farmers in Canada, there has been little or no discussion of phasing out battery cages, but the voluntary codes of practice call for increasing cage space per bird from the current standard of 387 to 450 centimetres^2 (or 62 to 72 inches^2). This still works out to four hens being permanently confined in cages measuring 40 by 45 centimetres (16 by 18 inches), analogous to four people living inside an elevator.

Conditions for broiler chickens destined for the Sunday roast have been described by one professor, who has studied the industry, as "the single most severe, systematic example of man's inhumanity to another sentient animal."[39] Indeed, chickens have a lot to complain about. They are often shipped to the slaughterhouse in overcrowded trucks, tied upside down by their feet and electrically stunned—before having their necks cut, being immersed in boiling water and plucked.

Pressures on the Family Farm

- ***Canadian farming: a family business.* In the 1950s, farm labour was hard to find, which helped to usher in a shift toward a high-tech, assembly-line approach to the raising of animals for food. In addition, for several decades there has been a trend in Canadian agriculture toward fewer and larger farms. Yet, more than**

98 per cent of Canadian farms and ranches are still family owned and operated.[40] Most cases of corporate ownership involve religious communities, such as the Hutterites, or families who own more than one farm.[41] Certainly there is nothing in Canada to compare with the 30 000 sow units or 10 000 dairy-cow units now common in the United States. On family-owned farms, decisions are made by people in contact with the animals, and Canadian farmers still see themselves as caring for rather than exploiting animals. However, they use essentially the same technology as their much larger counterparts.

- ***The marketplace vs. animal welfare.*** **A pig farmer once told an agriculture professor that he could solve the animal welfare problems on his farm for $30 000. His point was that he wanted to improve conditions for his animals, but that he could not afford to do so because his profits were too slight. In his view, economic competition among producers had driven the price of pork too low for him to raise pigs in the way he wanted.[42] This, in a nutshell, is the dilemma facing all Canadian farmers who care about their animals. Under Canada's supply-management system, which limits the amount of competing products in milk, eggs and poultry, farmers in these three areas enjoy a more predictable profit level and have more discretion to maintain a higher standard of animal care. Indeed, this quota system has been a major factor in keeping smaller, family-sized farms economically viable.[43]**
- ***The cost of kindness.*** **One way to improve conditions for farm animals would be a kind of animal welfare contract between consumers and farmers. Consumers would agree to pay slightly more for food products, with the extra amount being applied back to housing and management of food animals. One expert says that such a contract would solve an enormous amount of the animal welfare problem, and estimates the surcharge needed would be in the order of 10 per cent.[44]**

Wild animals

Beef, lamb, pork and chicken may not be the only thing on offer at your local butcher. Increasingly, wild or semiwild animals—including crocodile, buffalo, deer, kangaroo, ostrich, peacock and even locust—may be on the menu.

The concern here is whether the conditions of modern, high-tech farming cause too much stress and suffering for once-wild animals? Take ostriches. Although they have been farmed for about 100 years in Africa, they are still relatively wild—and some critics argue that they are "fundamentally unsuitable for farming."[45] These birds can grow up to 3.3 metres (9 feet) tall and are adapted to run across the African plains at 64 km-h (40 mph). They can live for over 70 years, although farm breeding stock will be killed off at 30 years and birds reared for meat at little more than one year old.

South Africa slaughters around 150 000 birds a year—and the number of ostrich farms in countries such as the U.K. has boomed. Ostriches each produce around 44 kilograms (100 pounds) of edible meat, known as "Volaise." They are so valuable that they may need to be tagged with microchips to prevent rustling.

Another concern is where meat, such as crocodile, is sourced from the wild and may therefore contravene wildlife protection regulations. Companies selling these meats need to check that they are approved by the appropriate controlling body.

Otherwise, unless wild or exotic meats are poached from the wild, the issues are no different than for other meats. A plus point is that the relatively small-scale nature of most businesses rearing exotic meats here means that they are generally free-range. Some organic farmers raise wild animals as an alternative to the large-scale farming of domestic animals. In the Ottawa Valley, for example, some unconventional farmers raise free-range emu, quail and wild boar.[47]

Free Range and Organic

- **Here are some of the options available if you want to promote better welfare conditions for animals–and better-quality food products. Although prices for non-factory-farmed products are often much higher, recent research suggests that the gap would close automatically if best-practice methods were adopted everywhere.[46]**
- **Free-range eggs and poultry: While almost all the eggs sold in mainstream supermarkets in Canada are laid by battery hens, free-range eggs are sold by organic food retailers and are beginning to appear in some chain stores.**
- **Organic meat: Whereas most conventional meat suppliers are only concerned with price, uniformity and supply, organic meat suppliers put animal welfare first–also banning growth promoters and the pre-emptive use of drugs such as antibiotics.**
- **Organic meat and poultry: Organic meat, poultry or eggs should be from a certified supplier to ensure that the meat is free range and that no antibiotics are used. Currently, 43 organic certification bodies are active in Canada. Fortunately, the Canadian Organic Advisory Board (COAB) is very close to reaching consensus on a national standard for organic agriculture.**

Antibiotics and hormones

Although factory farming is unlikely to disappear in the near future, some aspects of it may be vulnerable. Much of the intensive livestock industry is keen to use hormones, which may in turn require greater use of antibiotics. When mismanaged, both hormones and antibiotics can have an adverse impact on human health (see below).

Stress up, antibiotics up

Common sense suggests that cramming large numbers of animals into a small space will result in stress. This, in turn, will lower the animals' immune defences, making them more vulnerable to bacterial and viral diseases. These conditions may have contributed to recent outbreaks of such infections as salmonella and E-coli.

To deal with overcrowding, the farming industry uses growing quantities of antibiotics. These have a dual use: they protect animals against disease and also make them grow faster. As a result, the vast majority of pigs and poultry are routinely given antibiotics in their feed or water.

Worryingly, the overuse of antibiotics can promote the development and spread of antibiotic resistance, which could mean that some of the antibiotics used in human medicine become less effective or, in extreme cases, useless. For example, in the U.S., one of the best drugs for treating typhoid had to be banned for use in animal husbandry over a decade ago because its overuse had increased the resistance of typhoid bacteria.

Growth-promoting hormones

Recent years have seen a raging row between Europe on one side and the U.S. and Canada on the other on the question of whether beef animals should be treated with certain hormones, used as growth promoters. In May 1997, a World Trade Organization panel ruled that the European Union's ban on Canadian hormone-treated beef violated global trade rules, because the EU's health concerns were not scientifically supported. However, the EU has continued to stall on lifting the ban, much to the frustration of Canadian beef exporters.

Among the substances in the spotlight have been the anabolic hormones, of which there are five main types: testosterone (naturally occurring male hormone), estradiol (naturally occurring female hormone), progesterone (naturally occurring female hormone), trenbolone (synthetic male hormone) and zeranol (synthetic female hormone).

Research results vary, with a recent scientific conference concluding that "the effects of hormones on animals in terms of incidence of disease, performance, general mobility and meat-producing efficiency are either unchanged or improved." Yet, there have also been studies suggesting that at least some of these substances may be linked with fertility loss, higher risk of miscarriage, liver abnormalities, accelerated tumour growth and cysts in treated animals.[48] Debate also rages about whether the earlier average age of puberty in North American girls is also due to such hormones.

The use of these hormones for growth promotion in food animals was banned in the EU in 1988, following consumer concerns about possible health effects. No such ban was implemented in the U.S., where the EU ban was recently said to be costing cattle growers US$100 million a year in lost exports. Not surprisingly, the U.S. put huge pressure on the World Trade Organization (WTO) to overturn the EU ban. Just as controversial have been the attempts to introduce genetically engineered bovine growth hormone (known as BGH or BST) to the dairy industry in Europe and the U.S. (page 60). Canada rejected BGH in January 1999.

Beta-agonists

Another controversial group of chemicals used to promote animal growth are the beta-agonists, including clenbuterol, or "Angel Dust." These substances can have dramatic effects on the way animals produce fat and muscle. The result is usually a leaner, more heavily muscled animal.

No beta-agonists have yet been approved as growth promoters in farm animals, largely because of the risk to human health from residues—but there is widespread evidence of misuse. These chemicals are highly active even in extremely low doses, potentially resulting in bronchial dilation, increased heart rate and heart tremors.[49]

Regardless of the concerns of U.S. beef farmers, this is an area that needs to be kept under close scrutiny to ensure that the health of meat-eaters is protected. And the list of drugs used on intensively farmed animals can only grow in the future.

Animal Farms

✔Citizen 2000 Checklist

1. WORK OUT WHERE YOU STAND ON ANIMAL PRODUCTS

One of the biggest dietary choices is whether to eat meat or meat products. Vegetarian societies across Canada (listed and cross-referenced in the Directory at the end of this book) provide support and information for people intent on dropping animal products. Most of these organizations are affiliated with the **North American Vegetarian**

Society (NAVS), which works in a variety of ways to promote the health, nutritional, environmental and compassionate benefits of a meatless diet. But remember that as a meat-eater, you can also choose organic or free-range options.

2. Support High Animal Welfare Standards

The Council (also known as **CLAW: Creatures of Land, Air & Water**) has developed the *Wholesome & Humane Program 2000*. Based loosely on the *Freedom Foods* program in the U.K., the Canadian program is taking a two-phase approach. First, it seeks legislation at the provincial and federal levels, including steps to abolish factory-farming practices and to institute labelling of genetically altered foods. Second, a plan has been submitted to the head offices of grocery stores, wherein grocery stores that agree to take steps to ensure improved consumer and animal welfare will be accredited to display the *Wholesome & Humane Program 2000 Member* emblem. Contact **The Council** for a progress report.

Canadians for Ethical Treatment of Food Animals (CETFA) investigates and speaks out against factory-farm practices, and campaigns for enforced humane protection. It publishes informative newsletters and bulletins, and has links with other animal welfare organizations across the country.

Compassion in World Farming (CIWF), which campaigns on animal welfare issues at the international level, has produced a wide range of excellent publications, including *Factory Farming and Human Health* (1997).

The less attractive side of the fast-food industry, including animal welfare issues, was thrust into the limelight in the "McLibel" case between **McDonald's** and two U.K. activists. None of the fast-food chains–including **Kentucky Fried Chicken (KFC)**, and **Burger King**–offer "free-range" or "organic" options. Clearly, if you go for cheap meat, in whatever form, you will be much less likely to be able to choose higher welfare alternatives.

3. Buy Organic Meat and Dairy Products

Canadian Organic Growers (COG) is the main campaigning body for organic farming. This is an area where standards are very important. The **Canadian Organic Advisory Board (COAB)** is developing a single, national standard for organic Canadian agri-food products. In the meantime, the Directory at the back of this book lists **COG** chapters and other relevant organizations.

Almost all eggs sold in grocery-store chains across Canada are battery eggs, despite such potentially misleading names as "farm fresh" or "country fresh." Whenever eggs are advertised as "free range" or "free run," the market manager should provide details about the supplier, so consumers can follow up to ensure authenticity. While free-range eggs do not necessarily meet all the criteria to be called "organic," organic organizations in your area would tend to view them as a step in the right direction and are probably good sources of information as to whether a given brand is truly free range.

3.3 Genes on the Menu

Who's playing God with our food?

Sometimes genetic engineers try to change the way genes work in a given plant or animal, and sometimes they try to make genes work in totally different species. Their work opens up the prospect of tomatoes containing fish genes (flounder genes, to be precise, designed to protect tomatoes against frost damage[50]), pork with human genes (to produce leaner meat), medicinal bananas, and even lentils that don't cause flatulence.

Many people in the food industry welcome these developments as opening the way to an exciting array of safer, healthier and more affordable products. But some critics argue that consumers are being used as unwitting guinea-pigs for what they call "Frankenfoods."[51] Who is right?

Gene foods

Anyone who has seen prize-winning bulls, with their bulging, over-sized muscles, will know that you don't have to be a genetic engineer to breed grotesquely deformed animals and plants. But it helps. To get a better idea of what all this means in practice, let's look at one example each of switching a gene on, switching a gene off, and moving a gene from one organism to another.

BST and milk

First, switching a gene on. Think of the milk you put in your coffee—or pour over your breakfast cereal. Dairy cows produce milk partly thanks to the BST (or bovine somatotropin) hormone naturally produced by their bodies. Normally, they produce just enough milk to satisfy their calves. The challenge for modern farmers has been to find a way of boosting the amount of milk produced by each cow. Now genetic engineers have programmed bacteria with the same gene, so that they churn out lots of the hormone—which is then injected into cows to encourage them to produce more milk. Research into this gene technology has been led by several big American companies.

It is easy to see the attraction for dairy farmers. Injecting BST into their herds can boost milk production by up to 20 per cent. In the U.S., the hormone has been legally used since 1994. It is banned in Europe. Canada had kept BGH (or bovine growth hormone) under review for nine years and recently resisted strong pressure from Monsanto, the manufacturer, and rejected registration of BGH. Monsanto plans to appeal the refusal to register BGH. In 1998, six scientists at the Canadian Health Protection Branch claimed that senior officials had attempted to prevent them from publicizing their concerns about the safety of BST. Across the Atlantic, the EU-wide ban is up for review in 2000 and the U.S. industry is again lobbying hard to overturn it.

Injecting BST into cows can boost milk production by up to 20 per cent.

It is hardly surprising that there are critics who attack the use of BST. Some farmers using the drug are finding that the levels of disease are rising in their herds. Among the problems: more cases of mastitis; a distressing udder inflammation; falling rates of conception; inflammation due to repeated injections; lameness, often because of the difficulty of walking with milk-swollen udders; and heat stress.

Critics of BST also point out that since the 1960s the milk-yield of the average dairy cow has doubled, while her life span has halved. BST is not the main culprit, of course, but vets say that the use of the hormone can mean that a cow's body is pushed to the point where her metabolism is exhausted, making her prone to disease. One of the concerns is that this means a greater use of antibiotics, which could leave residues in the milk.

Not surprisingly, there are counter-arguments. On the environmental front, for example, companies like Monsanto have insisted that BST helps cows make better use of their feed—cutting down on the methane they release into the atmosphere. The result: global warming is slowed! True, perhaps, but the other side of this equation is that the economic impact of the wide use of BST would be felt by thousands of smaller farms, closing many and hurting both the communities and landscapes that depend on them. And all of this at a time when Europe is already awash in milk and most countries have a surplus.

The Flavr Savr tomato

Next, let's switch a gene off. Think of tomatoes. Nature sees such fruit and vegetables as carriers of seed, programming them to ripen and rot. In turn, the process of rotting ensures that the plant spreads its seed and speeds germination.

For the food industry, on the other hand, rotting is a problem. Valuable crops are lost and the quality of the final product can be severely affected. Who hasn't picked up some fruit only to find it brown and mouldy on the other side? Not surprisingly, scientists wanted to find out why rotting happens. Often, the answer is ethylene, a gas produced by the plants themselves.

So the next step was to find which gene was responsible for producing the ethylene—and to switch it off. Fruit such as avocados, bananas, cantaloupe and melons, strawberries and tomatoes have all now been experimentally engineered to slow rotting—and retain taste—by cutting their production of ethylene. The delayed ripening means better flavour (because the fruit can stay longer on the vine) and higher yields (with less fruit rotting).

Monsanto has also perfected "terminator crops," which do not produce seed capable of natural reproduction. This is so the company can protect its patented bioengineered "advantage." But environmentalists worry that if "terminator" varieties contaminate natural crops, Monsanto could switch off more than a gene.

In another process, the pectin levels of tomatoes have been altered by genetic engineering to produce denser fruit for use in tomato purée. This makes a thicker paste—and requires less energy for processing. This, in turn, should make the product cheaper, and some grocery stores have not only labelled their purées and pastes to say they contain genetically engineered ingredients, but also passed on the cost savings to consumers. The result has been that many consumers have happily bought the products.

On the other hand, there is concern that introducing these products is simply the thin end of the wedge. Scientists have also now come up with a tomato that contains high levels of lycopene, which can prevent prostate cancer and—possibly—prolong men's active sex life.[52] Will we see a "virility" tomato next?

Insect-proof corn

Finally, let's focus on moving a gene between species. Think of corn, a crop that many insects love to eat while it is still standing in the field. Farmers have to use large quantities of insecticides to control pest damage, but what if the corn plants could be persuaded to fight off the insects themselves?

One way to do this is to exploit a bug found in the soil that has been shown to kill more than 50 species of moth and butterfly and their caterpillars. Scientists studying the bug identified the Bt *(Bacillus thuringiensis)* gene as the source of the relevant insecticidal protein—and have since been working hard to transfer it into a range of crop plants.

The number of insect-proof crops is growing all the time. Bt-corn is designed to resist the European corn borer, the Bt-potato to ward off the pink bollworm and Bt-cotton to repel the cotton bollworm (as well as the pink one). All three of these crop plants are being grown in America, with trials also under way on tomatoes, aubergines, oilseed rape, rice, apples, cranberries and walnuts.

Great, if the result is to cut the need for the spraying of deadly pesticides. But the use of the Bt gene also raises the threat of resistance. The more insects, including caterpillars, are exposed to a given chemical, natural or synthetic, the more likely they are to develop resistance. If they do, organic farmers (who have long used non-genetically engineered Bt pesticides) will find a key biological pesticide becomes useless, while mainstream farmers will simply switch back to chemicals.

Varieties of grain are also being bioengineered to be resistant to herbicides, allowing weed-killers to be used around a crop without killing it with the "weeds"; Canada has thousands of hectares of "Round-up Ready Canolas" and soy products.

For and against

We are told that, used wisely, these new genetic tools have the potential to ease the strains of feeding a world of 10 billion people. In the pipeline are higher-protein foods, modified-fat foods, longer-lasting produce, and crop plants that resist drought, shrug off frost and fix their own nitrogen—cutting the need for artificial fertilizers. So are the critics of genetic engineering mad? Were the hundreds of thousands of Austrians who voted for a "gene-technology-free Austria" trying to commit economic suicide? Were the 59 per cent of Europeans who opposed gene foods in a recent MORI poll worrying too much? Maybe, and perhaps some critics *are* too vehement, but they are also right to warn about the risks.

No new technology, be it fire, the internal combustion engine or nuclear electricity, has been developed without causing major economic, social and environmental impacts along the way. Biotechnology, too, will almost certainly bring major disasters and tragedies, alongside the undoubted benefits.

Over 80 per cent of Canadians support labelling of genetically engineered foods,[53] for the most part because they want to avoid it.

Let's look at a few of the issues these new technologies raise in relation to food:

Allergies: The logic is simple. The number of people suffering from allergies is growing continually. Allergies are often caused by proteins—and genetic engineering results in new proteins in food products. It is at least possible that some "gene foods" will trigger allergic reactions in some people. These could range from minor irritations to extreme cases where the victim dies.

Antibiotic resistance: Another concern focuses on the "marker" genes used by scientists to see whether a desired gene has been incorporated into an organism. The Flavr Savr tomato, for example, can survive otherwise lethal doses of antibiotics. Fine for plants, perhaps, but what if antibiotic resistance spreads into other species (page 264)? In theory, at least, this may already be possible, via the intestines of animals fed unprocessed genetically engineered corn. Companies have been made aware of this problem and have agreed to use alternatives in the future.

Toxicity: Many plants, as our ancestors found to their cost, already produce a range of toxic compounds in self-defence. Some of these substances are already present in today's food at levels that are apparently safe. But what might happen if genetic engineering accidentally raised their levels? Or produced new toxins? We would have to hope that the regulatory authorities would detect this before we did.

Nutritional content: Ever since our ancestors were hunter-gatherers on the plains of Africa, we have relied on the look and taste of fruit and vegetables to check whether they were safe and nutritious to eat. Genetic engineering could result in food that looks both tasty and nutritious, but does not provide the nutrients we need—or gives us more than we bargained for.

Super-weeds: Over half of the genetically engineered crops currently under development are designed to resist commonly used herbicides. One worrying possibility: a gene for herbicide resistance might be acquired by related plant species, with the result that farmers face new strains of pesticide-resistant super-weed.

Biodiversity: Traditional farming grows crops that suit the local environment and climate. This helps preserve at least some biodiversity. However, genetically engineered crops may be developed to survive in a wide range of circumstances, pushing us closer to global monocultures. Equally, there might be problems with "genetic pollution." To date, we have little experience with the potential long-term consequences of gene transfers in the wild.

Surprises: Some of the effects of gene transfer may be unpredictable, others undetectable—until it is too late. Putting a human growth gene into mice produces giant mice, yet the same gene inserted into pigs can produce animals that are skinny, cross-eyed and suffer from arthritis.

Ethical concerns: Genetic engineering has already caused a number of extraordinary controversies. For one thing, vegetarians would prefer not to eat vegetables containing animal genes. But without full labelling they would have no choice in the matter. Even nonvegetarians might prefer not to become—effectively—cannibals, once human genes are used in our foods (something that is still perfectly legal!).

Third World impacts: Biotechnology could increase food production and would therefore be a blessing for many developing countries. So far, however, the technology has mainly been used for the benefit of the richer countries. More worryingly, it could devastate some Third World economies by coming up with genetically engineered substitutes for products such as coffee, sugar or palm oil, which can then be produced in other parts of the world. Feeding the world's people would be possible today if we fed people, not livestock.

Untested: No one can yet say with certainty that gene foods are safe to grow or eat. The reason: these products have not been thoroughly tested for their long-term effects. Worryingly, too, many safety assessments are carried out on a case-by-case basis, rather than considering the likely overall impact of a series of new developments.

Side-effects: Picture a simple chain of events. The use of BST (page 60) boosts milk production, but requires greater use of antibiotics to control the resulting increase in mastitis. As a result, antibiotic contamination of milk goes up. Sadly, experience shows that such unexpected side-effects are more or less guaranteed.

Super-predators: Most genetically engineered animal organisms are likely to be weaker in the wild than the natural version, but what if we managed to produce a super-pest? This is less likely to be a new version of T-Rex than a particularly virulent mosquito.

Who benefits? In medicine, the patient usually benefits alongside the doctor, hospital and drugmaker. But with some bioproducts currently on offer in the food area, the benefits go to farmers and the biotechnology companies—while many of the risks are borne by consumers.

Table 3.1 shows some of the current applications of genetic engineering used in our food—and the types of food they may be used for.

Looking for labels

Like the chemical and nuclear industries before it, the genetic engineering industry has often shown a worrying taste for secrecy. Offered the choice, it would prefer not to label products as "genetically modified." If they were totally safe, this would perhaps be acceptable, but there are real reasons for concern. Take the case of L-tryptophan used as a treatment for depression and premenstrual syndrome (PMS). It was linked to a new and painful disease that caused 1500 illnesses and 31 deaths in the U.S. before the product was withdrawn from the market.

The batch of the drug believed to have been responsible had been produced by a new strain of genetically engineered bacteria.

Whether or not the product—or the process—was responsible, the government regulatory body tried to cover up, fearful of a backlash. Apparently, it was trying to protect the bio-industry. But the long-term effect of such moves is to undermine public confidence, not build it.

So labels and other forms of product and process information are essential. The issue of labelling genetically altered foods in Canada is a current example of where industry is unable—or unwilling—to help customers and consumers to make informed choices.

The Labelling Debate in Canada

- **The debate in Canada has persisted for about three years, when the first genetically engineered Newleaf potato appeared in grocery stores in Eastern Canada. To date, the Canadian Food Inspection Agency has approved 34 genetically altered vegetables and grains for use. They include thirteen varieties of canolas, twelve of corn, three of tomatoes, three of cottons, two of potatoes and a soybean. For the most part, these are "single-trait" crops where one gene from among 750 000 has been altered to achieve a certain purpose, such as herbicide resistance.**
- **But experts say there are many more genetically altered foods on Canadian store shelves than the 34 approved commodities. Taking into account mixed and processed foods, they estimate 70 per cent of products on our store shelves include genetically altered components. Soybean, for example, which is engineered to be resistant to pesticides, is a component in products ranging from ice cream to breakfast cereals.**
- **Calling for labelling of genetically altered foods are consumer groups, organic growers, and retailers and organizations such as Greenpeace, Sierra Club and the Council of Canadians. Surveys indicate that most Canadians support them on this issue. All base their arguments on the consumer's right to know in order to make an informed choice.**
- **The biotechnology and agriculture industries and the federal government take the position that a labelling system would be costly and cumbersome, and is not necessary because genetically altered foods have been thoroughly tested and found safe, and are substantially similar to their nonmodified counterparts. In short, "you don't need to know." Consumers suspect industry doesn't want genetic labelling because they are worried that sales of these products would plummet.**
- **Critics question the safety of genetically altered foods, saying they may produce**

Table 3.1: SOME FOOD APPLICATIONS OF GENETIC ENGINEERING

Objective	***Applications***	***Issues***
Herbicide tolerance	Beetroot; corn; canola (for oils used for deep-fat frying, confectionery and margarines, as well as pharmaceuticals, toiletries, soaps and detergents). Soya (used in 70 per cent of processed foods, including baby foods, biscuits, cakes, margarines, chocolate and processed meat)	Biodiversity; environmental concerns (e.g., super-weeds); continued use of chemicals. Monsanto introduced "Round-up Ready Canolas" in Canada. Unlike in Europe or India, no one ripped up their fields.
Increased production	Milk (page 60)	Animal welfare; antibiotic use; health concerns, breast and prostate cancer
Insect resistance	Corn; canola	Biodiversity; super-predator; environmental concerns; resistance
Marker genes	Corn, tomatoes	Antibiotic resistance
Quality traits (e.g., longer ripening)	Apples (stop browning); eggs (cholesterol-free); lentils (won't cause flatulence); oranges (easy to peel); pork (leaner meat); potatoes (absorb less fat, using genes from bacteria in animal and human gut); raspberries (slow ripening); salmon (speed up growth); tomatoes (slow ripening, reduce freezer damage, longer shelf life, less bruising); vegetables (more vitamins)	Animal welfare (in some cases); nutritional content; ethical concerns
Virus resistance	Corn (used in or part of: sweetcorn, corn flour, oil, starch, sweet syrups, margarine, snack foods, soft drinks and animal feed)	Resistance; biodiversity

unexpected allergic reactions or they may be toxic or reduced in nutritional value.

- **The irony is that, once they became more familiar with the whole area of genetic alteration of foods, many if not most consumers would probably be quite happy to accept many modified foods, as long as they knew what they were eating. The instinctive secrecy of the biotech industry and food companies in this area seems certain to backfire.**

(Source: Includes material compiled from *The Globe and Mail*, *The London Free Press* and *Winnipeg Free Press*.)

What's in store?

So what are the genetic engineers going to do to a range of products that we currently take for granted? Table 3.1 lists some of the changes in the pipeline. And there are many projects not covered there. In Germany, for example, genetic engineers accidentally created the world's largest potato, weighing in at 3.2 kilos (just over 7 pounds). They managed the feat by putting a yeast gene into the potato plants.[54]

One thing we can be sure of is that a growing array of gene foods will sweep out from laboratories and trial-plots to the world's farmlands, the production lines of food manufacturers, grocery-store shelves and, eventually, our kitchens and plates.

The 21st century seems certain to see the launch of a whole series of new fruit and vegetables, either bred or engineered to contain not only extra nutrients but also medicinal compounds. These are likely to include chemical compounds known to help in the fight against cancer, diabetes and heart disease.[55]

Already on offer are: an onion designed to prevent stomach cancer, and green peppers with extra vitamin C and beta-carotene. Other projects include onions rich in chemicals that inhibit strokes and beetroot loaded with folic acid, which helps prevent birth defects when taken during pregnancy.

Children have not been enthusiastic about chocolate-flavoured carrots and pizza-flavoured sweetcorn, launched in an attempt to make them eat up their vegetables.[56] So for those unfortunate people who do not like vegetables, one obvious benefit would be that anyone wanting to get his or her daily vitamins would only need to eat half a carrot, rather than three!

Genes on the Menu

✓Citizen 2000 Checklist

1. Take Time to Understand Food Gene Issues

The **Canadian Institute for Environmental Law and Policy (CIELAP)** has published *The Citizen's Guide to Biotechnology*, which provides some basic science and discusses ethical and environmental concerns about genetic engineering. **Greenpeace** campaigns in Europe and North America on issues relating to genetically modified foods–and led the European protests against genetically modified soybeans. They also produced a report entitled *Genetic Engineering: Too Good to Go Wrong?*, which contains studies of 10 cases where it has gone wrong.

Greenpeace USA has produced a series of reports on genetic engineering issues. The **Campaign for Food Safety** (formerly the **Pure Food Campaign**), a U.S.-based organization of organic farmers, retailers and consumers, carries information on genetically engineered foods and other issues in its free electronic newsletter, *Food Bytes*. Their website also lists recent news and in-depth articles from a wide range of publications on genetically engineered foods. The **Council for Responsible Genetics (CRG)** is a U.S. nonprofit organization of scientists, public health advocates and others that promotes a comprehensive public interest agenda for biotechnology. They produce and distribute educational materials that raise awareness about the social and environmental effects of new genetic technologies.

The **Sierra Club of Canada** has produced a backgrounder on bovine growth hormone (BGH), also known as recombinant bovine somatotropin (BST), the controversial genetically engineered hormone that is injected into dairy cows to increase milk production (see page 60). They also report on the considerable industry pressure being put on the federal government to approve BST for use in Canada. The **Sierra Club** worked with the **National Farmers Union** and the **Council of Canadians** to keep BST out of Canada. They were successful in January 1999, when Allan Rock announced that BST would not be registered in Canada.

2. Insist on Labelling and Openness

Many environmental and consumer groups around the world are calling for labelling of genetically engineered foods, on the principle that consumers have a right to know what is in their food and how it is produced. Among these are the **Council of Canadians**, **Greenpeace** in Europe and North America and **Consumers International**, which brings together 230 organizations in more than 100 countries.

The **Consumers Association of Canada (CAC)** supports labelling on the principle of the consumer's right to know and choose. The **CAC** maintains, however, that mandatory labelling is not as simple as it sounds, given the many stages that a food product, especially a mixed product, goes through between the farm gate and the grocer's shelf. As an alternative to jamming more information onto already crowded food labels, the **CAC** supports making available information about genetically engineered foods in stores, on computer websites or through toll-free numbers. A spokesperson says such information would have to be based on "scientific fact" so consumers could trust it, and could include everything from how the food was produced to benefits and potential side-effects.[57]

Experience in the U.K. suggests that labelling of gene foods is feasible. Several major grocery-store chains there recently carried out promising marketing trials of well-labelled genetically engineered tomato paste, and they passed on the cost benefits to consumers. The British Retail Consortium has called for less secrecy and the segregation of gene foods.

A worrisome development in the U.S. is that some companies have fallen foul of the law by labelling dairy products as "BST-free." **Monsanto** successfully argued that since BST was not dangerous for consumers, this implied a false claim of safety. But **Ben & Jerry's**, the U.S. ice-cream maker, has been paying a premium to farmers who do not use BST hormones in their cows.

In the U.S., the **Campaign for Food Safety** (through its **Organic Consumers Action** campaign) and **Greenpeace**, among others, have organized a mass movement at the grassroots level to prevent the **United States Department of Agriculture (USDA)** from including genetically modified organisms (GMOs) in their National Organic Standards. For the sake of Canadians who buy organic labelled food products imported from south of the border, the **Council of Canadians**, the **Sierra Club of Canada** and other groups are organizing Canadian support for the U.S. groups in this endeavour.

3. Encourage the Intelligent Introduction of Gene Food

Greenpeace International is one of the leading

organizations campaigning against the over-hasty introduction of genetic engineering. The group calls for the application of the "precautionary principle" to this area. The precautionary principle holds that: 1) the burden of proof of safety rests with the proponent of a new technology, not the public; and 2) where there are threats of serious or irreversible damage, lack of science should not be used as an excuse for postponing measures to prevent environmental degradation.

Thousands of companies are now involved in genetic engineering research worldwide, but a few names keep popping up. **Monsanto** has most consistently stirred controversy. This U.S. company stands behind the dairy hormone BST (page 60) and "Round-up Ready" soya and canola. Other companies actively involved in the genetically modified foods sector include **Ciba-Geigy** (now part of **Novartis**), **Zeneca** (once part of **ICI**) and **Eli Lilly**.

4. Take a Stand Against Animal Machines

The current trend is very much toward turning animals into machines. **The Council** and **Canadians for Ethical Treatment of Food Animals (CETFA)** oppose the genetic engineering of animals. Vegetarian societies across Canada (listed in the Directory at the back of this book) are concerned about the use of animal genes in plants and other vegetarian produce. Ironically, the first gene food introduced in the U.K. was a "vegetarian cheese," curdled using rennet produced by genetically engineered bacteria–instead of being extracted from the stomachs of calves.

3.4 Fish Dishes

Wild fish, farmed fish—or no fish?

Fish is an excellent, healthy food. But, we should ask: have the world's fish had their chips? It often seems so. Below, we look at marine fisheries, industrial fishing and fish farming, before considering the prospects for some of the fish that most often end up on our plates.

Sea fishing

The overfishing of the world's oceans and seas has reached alarming proportions. As a result, "fish wars" are now almost commonplace. In 1995, Canadian patrol vessels seized a Spanish trawler for suspected illegal turbot fishing in international waters off Newfoundland. In 1997, B.C. fishermen blockaded an Alaskan ferry in retaliation for American fishing of sockeye salmon headed for the Fraser River to spawn. We can expect more such wars on fishing grounds around the world. Nor is this surprising. At least 60 per cent of the world's 200 most valuable fish species are either overfished or fished to the limit, with 35 per cent experiencing declining yields.[58]

And, although the grocery-store fish counter may still look well stocked, the uncomfortable truth is that the availability of fish products per head started to fall in 1970—and continues to decline rapidly.

A full 70 per cent of the world's commercially important marine fish stocks are completely fished, overexploited, depleted or slowly recovering.[59]

Before looking at some of the issues associated with specific fish dishes, let's briefly flip through a few key facts that may not be foremost in our minds as we search through the deep freeze for the week's fish-fingers or shrimps.

Warning signs: Marine fish are under intense pressure. The cause is clear: the advances in fishing technology have outstripped the fisheries' ability to rebound. We are now ruthlessly hunting once-bountiful fisheries to extinction. Globally, the fish catch has increased nearly fivefold since 1950, but the warning signs of major future problems are increasingly difficult to ignore. The world fishing fleet is now thought to be twice as big as it needs to be to catch the available fish. Much of this overcapacity is due to well-intentioned but disastrous government subsidies.

Wastage: There is staggering waste in the fishing industry. Annually, 18 to 40 million tonnes of "nontarget" fish or wildlife, such as sea birds or turtles, are caught and simply dumped back into the sea, dead or dying. Recently, the barn door skate off Canada's East Coast was identified as extinct or near-extinct due to such killing, called "by-catch." This loss is equal to more than a quarter of the entire catch, with over a third of the waste occurring during trawling for shrimps (page 74).[60]

Cyanide fishing: The trade in live fish to satisfy the demand of restaurants in China and Hong Kong and for North Americans' tropical fish in pet store is estimated to be worth over HK$1 billion a year, but is causing major ecological problems. Many of the fish are caught in the seas around countries like the Philippines using deadly cyanide. The toxin stuns many fish, so that they can be revived later, but in the process kills huge numbers of fish and other reef organisms. In the Philippines alone there are thought to be more than 4000 cyanide fishermen, squirting some 150 000 kilos (330 000 pounds) of cyanide solution onto over 30 million coral heads each year. (OceanVoice International, based in Canada, works on this issue.)

Other wildlife issues: Untold numbers of marine mammals (such as dolphins and whales), turtles, sea birds and other marine wildlife are caught and killed in fishing gear. Tens of thousands of turtles are killed each year, as well as up to 10 per cent of the world population of wandering albatross.

Lost Fish of Canada

- **With the world's largest coastline–which would circle the earth more than six times–Canada has always been known for the teeming abundance of its fishing grounds. The myth of the inexhaustible bounty of nature has been badly shaken, however, with the collapse of the cod fishery off Newfoundland and plummeting salmon stocks off British Columbia. The full measure of what has been lost, in human and environmental terms, is illustrated by the following facts:**
- **A contemporary report of John Cabot's voyage to North America in 1497 describes a wealth of cod: "The Sea there is swarming with fish which can be taken not only with the net but in baskets let down with a stone." We do not know whether Cabot's men caught cod simply by dropping weighted baskets, but subsequent accounts of schools of a density never before seen by Europeans suggest it may well have been possible.[61]**
- **In the centuries after Cabot there are persistent North American accounts of "codfish as big as a man."[62]**
- **In 1838, an 81-kilogram (180-pound) codfish was caught on Georges Bank, off Newfoundland.[63]**
- **Canadians (with foreign assistance) have extirpated or driven to outright extinction many marine species, including sea otters and many toothed whales.[64]**
- **Along with the Atlantic cod, American plaice, redfish, flounder, capelin and salmon fisheries on the east coast have also collapsed.[65]**

- **The salmon is in trouble in B.C., where abalone, coho, chinook, and steelhead stocks have plummeted.[66]**
- **Once-plentiful fishes like rockfish and lingcod, and some marine mammals, have slid into serious decline from their traditional abundance.[67]**
- **The collapse of the East Coast cod stocks in 1992 threw nearly 40 000 Atlantic Canadians and Quebecers out of work[68] and may have brought to an end an industry that began before Shakespeare was born.**
- **As the salmon disappears off the West Coast, so does a way of life in over 100 B.C. communities built around fishing wharves.[69]**

There is hope, however, that we may have learned something from these dire events. On the East Coast, we know that, unless the number and size of fishing boats is reduced, and some gear types such as huge, mobile drag nets are banned, there will be no cod in Atlantic Canada in a very short time. The federal government has a lot to answer for in mismanagement of the fisheries on both coasts. But, so far at least, the Department of Fisheries and Oceans (DFO) is doing the right thing in maintaining the moratorium on most of the cod fishery in the east and drastically reducing the salmon fishery in the west. As well, there are grassroots efforts on both coasts to protect fish habitat (see page 68).

Nor is the picture completely bleak on the international scene. Remember the massive "wall of death" drift nets used in the Mediterranean and the Pacific, which often broke loose and became "ghost nets," killing fish, sea birds and dolphins as they drifted through the seas? The (reasonably) good news is that the legal size of drift nets has been cut from over 80 kilometres (48 miles) long to 2.5 kilometres (1.5 miles).

The high-profile tuna-fishing campaign has also been fairly successful. Yellowfin tuna, sold in cans and for sandwiches, tend to swim alongside dolphins. Tuna fishers caught—and killed—millions of dolphins in their nets and threw them back into the sea. Environmental campaigning groups successfully organized a boycott of tuna, unless it could be identified as "dolphin-friendly."

The number of dolphins killed in the Eastern Tropical Pacific as a result of tuna fishing has fallen from 350 000 ten years ago to less than 4000 today.

Unfortunately, these issues are never simple. The most effective alternative to netting tuna with dolphins is to attract the tuna by throwing fish waste into the water. Instead of dolphin, a whole range of other sea creatures then get caught in the nets. So campaigners have agreed to compromise on this issue. Countries such as Mexico and Venezuela, which complained that they could not meet the "dolphin-safe" criteria, have been permitted to catch the dolphins, as long as they throw them back. But some environmentalists are still at loggerheads over this issue, saying that no compromise should have been made.

The dolphin issue does not affect all tuna. Albacore—better known in the form of "chunk white tuna"—do not swim alongside dolphins and are frequently caught on a line anyway. The pole-and-line approach has social advantages, as well as environmental ones, because of its small-scale approach and the fact that more people are employed. Campaigns are also under way to protect sea turtles, with demands for "turtle-safe" shrimp.

Bluefin tuna are another kettle of fish. They are hugely endangered. The main market for this exorbitantly priced tuna is for sashimi in Japan. Few of these fish are left in the North Sea and about 10 per cent of 1970 levels remain in the North Atlantic. The Gulf of Mexico, an important spawning ground, is closed for bluefin fishing, although many are caught incidentally. Meanwhile, the sky-high prices in Tokyo have precipitated a "gold rush"—fishers use spotter planes to find them and may take two weeks to track down a single fish.

Industrial fishing

Some 30 per cent of the world's catch is taken by the so-called industrial fishing fleet. These vessels target small, unpalatable fish species (such as sand eels, pout or capelin) for conversion into fishmeal to feed poultry, pigs and farmed fish—or into fish oil for use in a wide range of processed-food products, such as biscuits, margarine and pet foods. Anchovies, too, are caught this way.[70]

If these fish were left in the sea, they would form part of the food chain for bigger fish, such as cod, quite apart from the fact that they are crucial to the survival of many sea birds, including puffins, and of marine mammals, such as seals and whales. The Barents Sea cod population collapsed when there was a crash in the capelin on which they fed, suggesting that industrial fishing could easily have a similar impact in other parts of the world.

Some fish oil used in food products, however, may come from waste from fish-processing plants—obviously a sensible use of a resource that would otherwise be wasted.

Fortunately, a number of North Sea countries have finally agreed to limit "industrial" fishing and trawling, at least from sensitive areas. Particularly welcome was the decision to limit the activities of Danish "vacuum" trawlers, which catch sand eels within sight of salmon rivers and bird colonies. Shockingly, until recently, the Danes burned vast quantities of these fish as a power-station fuel!

Caviar

- **Pity the poor sturgeon, whose roe are used to make caviar. The roe's scarcity makes it extremely expensive–and increases the pressure on these long-living, slow-breeding fish. Sadly, in the chaos of postcommunist Russia, warnings that overfishing has already put sturgeon on the endangered list have gone largely unheeded.**
- **An entire subeconomy has grown up dedicated to poaching the fish and smuggling the resulting caviar.[71] Following an attempt to crack down on the local caviar mafia, Russian border guards were killed in a single bomb attack. Nor is it difficult to see why this should be so. A poacher can expect to sell a day's catch for the equivalent of $75 a kilo ($34 a pound), more than a month's salary for most citizens in Astrakhan.**
- **By the time the caviar has worked its way to Moscow, the price has doubled to $150 ($68 per pound)–and by the time it arrives in a city like London or Montreal, the cheapest caviar on the market sells for perhaps 10 times more.**
- **The United States and Canada account for about 30 per cent of the world caviar market. About 70 per cent of our caviar comes from Russia. Given that over half the world trade in caviar is illegal, we must assume that much of the caviar sold here has been repacked and falsely labelled; consequently, many consumers are unwittingly contributing to the demise of the sturgeon.**
- **"Ten years ago, our nets were full of sturgeon," one veteran at a state fish farm explained. "Now I would not even qualify what we do as fishing. We are**

lucky to land three or four sturgeon. They are being killed off by man's greed and the Mafia." This gloomy view is reflected in the numbers. It is estimated that the number of adult fish in the Caspian has fallen from 142 million in 1978 to some 40 million today. It is predicted that the Caspian sturgeon could be extinct in 20 years–in waters where it has lived largely unaltered for 250 million years.

Fish farming

Fish farming is generally more energy efficient than growing animals—1.5 tonnes of fish-food can result in 1 tonne of farmed fish. But many barriers need to be overcome for this to be a sound solution to the problem of overfishing. For a start, farmed salmon are often fed on fish-meal made from industrially fished sand eels!

The fish-farming industry is exploding. During the 1980s alone, there was a doubling in the production of tilapia, which originates from Africa and is sometimes described as "aquatic chicken." Meanwhile, production of farmed salmon shot up from 23 million pounds a year to 540 million pounds.[72] Today, nearly 200 species of fish and shellfish are cultivated in ponds or coastal tanks and pens. Fish farming—or aquaculture—produces more than half of all the freshwater fish (such as carp, catfish and tilapia) eaten around the world, a third of all the world's salmon and a quarter of the shrimps. Not surprisingly, this burgeoning new industry is now causing fairly considerable environmental headaches of its own.

Let's focus on salmon as an example of some of the issues raised by fish farming.

The salmon's shadow

Salmon, once the "king of fish," is becoming one of the most popular fish dishes. Indeed, it is even appearing on the menu in fish-and-chip shops (although it is not the same as rock salmon—see below). Its leap in popularity is almost entirely a reflection of the success of fish farming, which has made it more affordable. At the same time, the stocks of traditional fish, such as cod and haddock, are crashing and their prices rocketing.[73]

Among the benefits of salmon are its versatility and health benefits. It can be poached, baked or grilled—and can be cooked in 10 minutes. It's low in saturated fat, low in calories and rich in fatty acids (page 45), which help reduce cholesterol. Unfortunately, the salmon farming industry also brings a range of problems.

Landscapes: Fish farms tend to be found in otherwise unspoiled landscapes, both because this is where fish do best—and also because regional grants are often available because of the employment opportunities. There are real concerns in these areas that obtrusive and unsightly fish farms will put off tourists.

Wildlife: It is estimated that for every marine mammal killed by B.C. salmon farmers under legal permit from the Department of Fisheries and Oceans (DFO), about three are killed illegally. A threatened expansion of the netcage industry in that province would bring increased attention to predator control and more killings of seals, Stellar sea lions (currently listed as endangered), otters and other marine mammals and sea birds.[74] In the U.K., it was estimated that, in the 1980s, fish farmers illegally shot more than a 1000 seals, 2000 cormorants and between 3600 and 5600 herons. Another method of protecting fish from predators, underwater acoustics, is causing serious problems of its own. Research in British Columbia showed negative impacts on porpoises, whales and other cetaceans.[75] 'Worse, as the marine life gets used to the sounds, the noise is increased—and it is not certain what further effects this may be having.

Wastes: Often thought of as a clean new industry, fish farming can actually be highly polluting. Waste food and fish feces from the moored cages fall through the cages into the lochs or sea. The scale of this problem is suggested by the fact that for every tonne of salmon grown, half a tonne of waste material can settle on the seabed near the cages. One suggestion is that feeding by hand rather than using automatic feeders might reduce the problem. Another idea is to put the fish cages in "diapers" to catch the waste!

Fish feed: There is a link here to industrial fishing, since feed for fish farms is often made from industrial fishing catches. The feed also often contains chemicals designed to control diseases and pests. And questions have been raised about canthaxanthin, the red pigment added to make the flesh of farmed fish as pink as that of their wild cousins. Government bodies, however, saw no reason to take action.

Antifouling: Fouling is often a problem with boats and offshore structures. As a result, fish cages and nets are treated with such compounds as copper and zinc, which are both potential pollutants.

Sea lice: The range of chemicals used to protect farmed salmon against the sea-lice scourge is the cause of continuing concern. The louse starts off eating the slime coating the fish—then pretty much eats the fish alive. One controversial chemical used has been Ivermectin, which kills sea lice and other insect-like creatures by attacking their nervous systems. This product may also be damaging other sea life. Worryingly, too, other chemicals that have been approved for use against sea lice include organophosphates (page 41).

In the U.K., at least, there are strict regulations on the use of such chemicals, but this has not stopped shell-fish farmers, whose produce is particularly sensitive to pollution, protesting about the practices of the salmon farmers. Work is under way to develop a sea lice vaccine, but this is unlikely to emerge for a number of years. Another treatment that seems to work well is cypermethrin, but this is no panacea as it is extremely toxic to invertebrates.[76]

Escaped fish: Another concern focuses on escaped farm fish, given that they can spread diseases, parasites and potentially debilitating genes to wild salmon populations. This risk is likely to grow in future as genetic engineering begins to be used to boost the growth of the farmed fish—and to promote other characteristics that may be of interest to the salmon farm. If transferred, however, these could end up damaging a wild fish's survival prospects. Escaped fish, like the Atlantic salmon farmed in America's Pacific northwest, upset the natural balance and threaten to oust the wild fish populations. Recently, the first documented use of interbreeding of a fish-farm Atlantic salmon with a B.C. wild salmon occurred in B.C., increasing calls to end fish farming with Atlantic salmon.

Disease: Farmed fish are more prone to disease because of the conditions they are kept in. Fish farms that are poorly sited or do not operate to high standards tend to have a higher incidence of disease, and therefore require treatment. This can be a vicious cycle, because the fish then become immune to one remedy, so that another —perhaps more powerful one—needs to be used.

Antibiotics: With humans and farm animals it is at least possible to treat on an individual basis, whereas farmed fish tend to be treated en masse. The routine use of antibiotics in fish farming is causing concern, since it may be yet another way in which we are undermining the effectiveness of our medicines. It is thought that antibiotic resistance may be transferred to wild fish and, at least theoretically, through the food chain to humans (page 264).

Free-range lobsters

Sometimes, fish farming can involve releasing fish or other creatures into the sea—and then catching them when they have grown to maturity. This has been tried with fish like salmon, although not very successfully. Now, if current plans come to fruition, lobster—the ultimate in luxury foods—could become more plentiful and, as a result, cheaper. Lobster-ranching projects are already under way in Australia, Malaysia and the U.K.[77]

The approach works like this. Thousands of young blue lobsters, reared in tanks from eggs collected from the wild population, are released offshore when they are three months old—and just under 4 centimetres (1.5 inches) long. They are then left to their own devices until caught for the table, at between four and six years of age.

Research has shown that, if the water is not polluted and the young lobsters can evade predators, the recapture rates can average 50 per cent. This is one area where the resulting catch should be indistinguishable from the truly wild harvest.

Future fish

As our population numbers grow, and as the shift from red meat to fish accelerates, the pressure on fish resources will intensify. The current status of a number of key fish species is shown in Table 3.2. Even if the fish-hunting industries can learn to cut back dramatically on wastage, as they must do if they are to survive, they simply will not be able to keep pace with demand.

So, unquestionably, fish farming is a key industry of the future. Over the centuries, we must hope, it will help us match our growing appetites for seafood with the need to keep marine ecosystems healthy. But it must also move beyond the "cowboy" stage, investing huge efforts to ensure that it does not cause impacts almost on the scale of the fish-hunting industries it is meant to replace. The scale of the challenge we face is perhaps best illustrated by what has happened to the shrimp fishing and farming industries.

Shrimps—Fished or Farmed?

- **Few seafoods are as controversial at the moment as the humble shrimp. Over the past 20 years, the price of the once-exotic shrimp has sunk—and the associated environmental costs have soared.[78]**
- **When taken from the open sea, the main problem with shrimp fishing is the extraordinary devastation of other marine life caused in the process. For every kilo of shrimps, an average of over 5 kg (11 lb) of other fish and creatures are caught, die and are dumped back into the sea. In Trinidad, one report suggested that the figure was closer to 7.5 kg (17 lb) of waste to every kilogram of shrimps!**
- **Shrimp fishing accounts for around a third of the total world by-catch of "nontarget" fish. And a significant proportion of the fish wasted are species normally caught for food, among them red snappers, croakers and sea trout. Young finfish are also victims, undermining the ability of**

Table 3.2: HOW'S YOUR FISH?

Fish	***Current Position***
Caviar	Overfishing of sturgeon is pushing them into extinction. Already extinct in the Adriatic—and could soon disappear from the Caspian Sea. Consumer demand and the collapse of Russian law enforcement have caused a boom in illegal poaching.
Cod	Cod have been severely overfished and are at risk of stock collapse in the North Sea.[79] Cod fisheries off Newfoundland and New England collapsed in the early 1990s but are starting to recover in New England. Large-scale recovery of the Newfoundland stocks remains iffy.
Flounder	Virtually all flounder in the Atlantic are overfished and winter flounder (also known as lemon sole) are particularly at risk. Restrictions on fishing have been imposed, but stricter measures may well be needed to restore the species.
Grouper	Most often taken at a critical point in their lifecycle, when they gather by the thousands to spawn. In some places, fishers have wiped out nearly an entire generation of reproducing adults in just a few seasons.[80]
Haddock	Have suffered the same problems as cod.
Hake	At risk of stock collapse in the North Sea.[81]
Herring	At risk of stock collapse in the North Sea.[82]
Lobster	Native lobsters are under pressure, but lobster ranches could help.
Mackerel	Under huge pressure from Russian factory ships. Risk of stock collapse in the North Sea.[83]
Monkfish	As other species have been depleted, fishers have turned to monkfish—which, in turn, is now being overfished. A management plan for the species is being developed.
Mussels	PEI-cultivated mussels have traditionally been a good choice, grown on ropes in the open bays near the coast. Overcrowding of mussels is now causing some problems, forcing out other fish.
Orange roughy	Orange roughy, especially popular with U.S. chefs, is a mild-tasting, white-fleshed fish. It lives in the deep ocean and grows extremely slowly, not reaching sexual maturity for at least 25 years—and with a lifespan of over 100 years. Some current specimens are thought to have been alive when Queen Victoria ruled![84] As it takes so long to replenish stocks, it should not be fished at all.

Table 3.2: HOW'S YOUR FISH? *continued*

Fish	***Current Position***
Plaice	At risk of stock collapse in the North Sea.[85] American Plaice collapsed off Canada's East Coast.
Shrimp	Both trawled and farmed shrimp have an enormous negative impact on the environment. There are some examples of responsible shrimp farming, but they are few and far between.
Red Snapper	Large quantities of red snapper are wasted by being caught in shrimp nets and discarded; under pressure; stricter controls required.
Rock salmon	Essentially "dog fish," a type of shark. It used to be caught while fishing for cod and haddock, but, as these species have become threatened, it is now targeted and used in fish-and-chip shops. Slow to reproduce and vulnerable to overfishing.
Salmon	Alaskan salmon have been thriving recently, but Scottish salmon have not. Salmon farming is expanding rapidly, increasing availability. Pacific and Atlantic wild salmon, on the other hand, are being threatened by overfishing and by damage from logging, dams and pollution in the rivers and streams where the salmon spawn.
Scallops	Dredges used to harvest sea scallops can disrupt crucial habitat. In some areas, scallops are over-fished and need time to recover.
Shark	In some parts of the world, sharks are taken out of the water, have their fins cut off and are thrown back into sea alive, maimed and dying—a practice known as "finning." Fins are used to make shark fin soup, where they are prized essentially for their texture, rather than taste.
Shell-fish	Shell-fish are filter feeders, so are particularly sensitive to pollution. Shell-fish farmers often campaign vigorously for cleaner waters.
Sole (see flounder)	Dutch scientists have shown that for every kilo of marketable sole, North Sea trawlers kill over 14 kg (31 lb) of under-sized fish and bottom-living animals.
Swordfish	This predatory fish is being wiped out throughout the Atlantic and the Mediterranean, and pressure is also mounting in the Pacific. In the 1960s, the average size of swordfish was almost 135 kg (300 lb). Today it is down to 50 kg (110 lb). We are catching juveniles that have not yet had time to reproduce.
Trout	Fish farms producing trout suffer from many of the same problems as salmon, but tend to use even greater quantities of antibiotics.

Table 3.2: HOW'S YOUR FISH? *continued*

Fish	***Current Position***
Tuna	World tuna catches doubled over the past 11 years. Eastern yellowfin tuna are still abundant, but there are concerns that, if fishing continues without limits, there will be a collapse. Americans eat more than 400 000 metric tonnes of canned tuna a year, or 1.6 kg (3–4 lb) per person. Northern bluefin tuna is endangered and there has been a dramatic decline in the western Atlantic (pages 70–71).[86]
Whiting	At risk of stock collapse in the North Sea.[87]

Sources: *Greenpeace/WWF/Time Magazine*

other ravaged fish populations to recover.

For every kilo of shrimps caught, over 5 kilos (11 pounds) of other fish and sea creatures are caught and dumped back into the sea, dead or dying.

- **This is an outlandish situation, given that many of the solutions are already known. Consider sea turtles, for example. In 1995 alone, some 124 000 sea turtles were killed by shrimp nets, even though there already exists a simple device (the "Turtle Excluder Device"), which is 97 per cent effective at releasing turtles from nets. But the fishers saythe device is too expensive and complain that it marginally reduces their shrimp catch.**
- **So is shrimp farming better? No, it brings its own very real environmental and social problems. For example, the world has lost half its mangrove forests, and shrimp farms have caused up to half this loss. This is extremely worrying, given that mangroves play such a vital role in marine ecology, providing fertile breeding grounds for fish and protecting coastal land from erosion.**
- **One study found that for every acre of mangrove lost, the marine harvest offshore dropped by almost 310 kg (700 lb) a year. As a result, shrimp farms have been described as a "rape-and-run" industry. In some countries, like Bangladesh, Thailand and Ecuador, there has been the equivalent of a gold rush, with "shrimp pirates" and dozens of killings of people protesting about the spread of the shrimp farms.**
- **Often the shrimp farmers move on after a few years, having exhausted a particular site. Not surprisingly, local communities fear that their agricultural land will have become unproductive, because of salt contamination. Matters are made even worse because the shrimp farms put very little, if any, of their profit back into the local economies.**
- **Because the farms are simple ecosystems, with a single species crowded together, viruses and other disease agents can spread like wildfire. These**

problems, in turn, require the use of a wide range of chemicals. So when the ponds are discharged, the effluents are usually contaminated with antibiotics and pesticides.

- **Most of these problems are not insoluble, but real pressure now needs to be put on both the fish-hunting and fish-farming industries. There is a good chance that labelling schemes (page 64) will play a crucial role in raising standards. They need our support if they are to have any chance of succeeding.**

Fish Dishes

✓Citizen 2000 Checklist

1. Get Informed

For background reading, start with Mark Kurlansky's fascinating book, *Cod: A Biography of the Fish that Changed the World* (Walker and Company, 1997). Then move on to Michael Harris's *Lament for an Ocean: The Collapse of the Atlantic Cod Fishery–A True Crime Story* (McClelland & Stewart, 1998). According to Harris, the criminal here is the Canadian government for virtually directing what could turn out to be the extinction of the greatest fishing ground in recorded history. *When the Fish Are Gone: Ecological Disaster and Fishers in Northwest Newfoundland* by Peter R. Sinclair and Greg Palmer (Fernwood Publishing, 1997) describes how a sustainable way of life, where cod was fished with small boats and stationary nets, was undermined by huge factory fleets using long tapered nets dragged along the ocean floor. The factory ships, which were able to take unprecedented quantities of fish because they had on-board freezers, may have been responsible for the two-thirds decline in Newfoundland's inshore cod stocks between 1956 and 1977.

Dead Reckoning: Confronting the Crisis in Pacific Fisheries, published in 1997, is available through **The David Suzuki Foundation**. "Salmon's Sea Change," an article that appeared in the Focus and Books section of *The Globe and Mail* (July 18, 1998), is an absorbing analysis that connects the fate of the salmon with "galloping climate change." **The Sierra Club of Canada** has a number of publications on the problems of shrimp aquaculture.

2. Support Good Fishing Practice

In the Atlantic provinces, communities are coming together to support fish conservation. **The Partnership on Sustainable Coastal Communities and Marine Ecosystems in Newfoundland and Labrador**, a project of the National Round Table and its provincial counterpart, calls for the application of the "precautionary principle." This includes an environmental assessment of the different gear technologies (e.g., stationary nets vs. dragger nets) to avoid repeating the disastrous mistakes of the past. They are also calling for better enforcement of fishing bans. In 1998, raids by the **Department of Fisheries and Oceans (DFO)** indicated that as much as 10 000 metric tons of endangered cod was being illegally fished.[88]

The **Coastal Communities Network of Nova Scotia** brings together community economic development agencies, fishers, fish processors, municipal leaders, church and community groups, unions and universities. Through workshops and other means, the **Network** supports development of fishing communities that is economically, socially and environmentally sustainable.

On the West Coast, the **Pacific Salmon Alliance** unites more than 40 individuals and groups around a common concern for the B.C. salmon fishery. The **Alliance** represents First Nations, academic, industry, labour, environmental and community groups. What brought these diverse interests together was a shared dissatisfaction with the management of the fishery by the **Department of Fisheries and Oceans (DFO)**, and a belief that "the only way to effect change and stop the privatization of Canada's common-property salmon resource was for groups to put aside their political differences and work together to build a consensus on how to save the salmon."

Greenpeace and the **Sierra Club** are very active in British Columbia and at the international level in campaigning to promote improved conservation of fish. They emphasize the importance of good forestry practices in protecting fish habitats.

One exciting initiative in the U.K. is the **Marine Stewardship Council (MSC)**, a partnership between the food giant **Unilever** and the **World Wide Fund for Nature (WWF)**. **Unilever** decided that its own best interests would be served by ensuring that there were adequate fish stocks to supply its food business, while **WWF** wanted to promote sustainable fishing in ways other than lobbying government.

3. Avoid Problem Species

Avoid flounder, Atlantic halibut, red snapper, Chilean sea bass, North Atlantic swordfish and Atlantic sea scallops–varieties that are being over-fished, according to the **U.S. National Marine Fisheries Service**. Avoid shrimp from Thailand and Ecuador (the main sources of shrimp in Canadian restaurants and grocery stores) and also the more exotic varieties of such as orange roughy and caviar from sturgeon, until you can be sure they are being caught in a sustainable way. Challenge your fish seller on these issues. Only buy tuna that is labelled "dolphin safe" or "caught on a line." And if you are in Japan, avoid sashimi made with bluefin tuna, even if you can afford it!

4. Press for Responsible Fish Farming

The **Georgia Strait Alliance (GSA)** works to protect, preserve and restore the marine environment and ecological well-being of Georgia Strait, a 240-kilometre-long inland sea located between Vancouver Island and the coastal mainland in southwest British Columbia, and adjoining Washington State's Puget Sound and the Strait of Juan de Fuca. The **GSA** is advocating that the current moratorium on expansion of aquaculture in B.C. be retained until conversion of the entire industry to closed-loop containment technology. As well, they are calling for an immediate ban on importation of Atlantic eggs and cultivation of Atlantic salmon in the province. The concern is that human error and storms will undoubtedly continue to result in escapes from netcages, resulting in disease outbreaks, colonization and displacement of wild Pacific stocks by feral Atlantic salmon. They are also calling for immediate bans on acoustic deterrents and night lighting (popularly known as "pit-lamping") because of their impacts on wildlife.

As well as supporting or taking an active role in such groups as the **Georgia Strait Alliance**, you can ask your grocery store what they are doing to ensure that fish farms are being run responsibly.

3.5 Fair Trade

Are ethics on our shopping list?

The Third World workers who grow our coffee and tea and other produce rarely get a fair share of the returns (page 80). As a result, there is a growing interest in and demand for fairly traded products. Let's look at a small selection: bananas, dried fruit, coffee, tea and chocolate.

Going bananas

How do you like your banana? Apparently most of us prefer a spotless, yellow fruit of uniform shape and taste, and we want it to be available all year round.[89] These seemingly simple tastes and priorities produce effects that are felt around the world.

North Americans and Europeans are the biggest consumers of bananas. The average Canadian eats more than 13 kg (29 lb) of bananas a year. As a result of increased demand, forests have been felled to make way for plantations and soil erosion has increased, causing pesticides to run off the land and poison the rivers and seas. In Costa Rica, the country's coral reefs have been irreparably damaged.

There are two main types of bananas: "dollar" bananas and "Caribbean" bananas. Dollar bananas are grown mainly on large plantations in Central America, covering huge areas with a single banana species and making the crops more vulnerable to pests.

This means that they tend to use large quantities of pesticides, including organophosphates (page 41), some of which are banned for use in the countries that consume them. Banana plantations account for the fact that, per head of population, Costa Rica is the largest consumer of agrochemicals in the world. Low-paid plantation workers frequently work in appalling conditions and there have been numerous cases of them being poisoned by the toxic chemicals they apply to the plants.

Caribbean bananas are smaller and sweeter. They are produced in the Windward Islands on small and medium-size plantations, and in Jamaica on small farms and larger plantations. Smaller quantities of the chemicals are used, other plants are grown among the bananas for subsistence food, and the fruit provides an income for farmers who rely on this crop for their living. Not surprisingly, these are the bananas that are promoted by fair trade organizations.

Dried fruit

Some countries that do not produce bottles or cans have turned to solar drying to preserve their fruit and vegetables. Where the raisin once reigned supreme, dried fruit such as pineapple, papaya and mango are now turning up in our kitchens.[90]

So what does fair trade mean in this sector? Some farmers who deal with fair trade suppliers are getting good, guaranteed prices for their produce, and free or subsidized training in solar drying and business management, as well as a growing market for their products.

In addition, in some land-locked African countries, farmers cannot afford agrochemicals, which means that their products are necessarily organic. Getting a Fair Trademark (page 81) might further boost their sales.

Chocolate

By way of background, a word or two on how cocoa is grown: in countries like Brazil, Indonesia and Malaysia, cocoa is grown on large plantations, where worker conditions can be pretty grim. In part, this is because the economics of the cocoa trade are stacked against developing countries. The real money is made through processing the cocoa into chocolate, and this is done in the industrialized world. Some years back, Nigeria tried to ban the export of unprocessed cocoa, but failed because it did not have enough processing capacity.

Whereas conventional cocoa plantations tend to include nothing but cocoa trees, the cocoa beans used for fairly traded cocoa are grown in the shade of other trees and on organic principles—assuming that "what is good for the planet has to be better for the people involved in production." Where fair trade practices are operating, fair prices, no middlemen and long-term contracts have improved security for growers and their families. Indeed, some farmers who had been forced to leave their homes through financial hardship have been able to come back ome.

Coffee and tea

Coffee is one of the world's most valuable crops. Almost all of it is grown in the developing world, because it requires tropical conditions to flourish. And, once again, working conditions in the industry have been notoriously bad. Until

1989, the international coffee trade was regulated by the International Coffee Agreement, but this collapsed and prices plummeted, leaving millions of farmers destitute. Later, frost and drought in Brazil led to a temporary price boom, but this was short-lived and the outlook for coffee growers remains uncertain.

Against this backdrop, it is easy to see why fair trade initiatives have an appeal to coffee growers. Small family farms of just a few hectares where coffee is grown alongside other crops, such as corn and plantain, are favoured. And by working together in cooperatives, the farmers are often able to export their own coffee, cutting out local middlemen.

Unlike coffee, most tea is grown on vast estates. The concern here is for workers employed on tea plantations, with the focus on fair wages and decent working conditions. Luckily, it is possible to find fair trade brands that are also organic.

Fair Trade

✔ Citizen 2000 Checklist

1. SUPPORT FAIR TRADE INITIATIES

TransFair International was set up by a worldwide network of churches, social justice groups, unions, co-ops, businesses, ATOs (alternative trading organizations) and nongovernment aid and development organizations (such as Oxfam), as well as producers and consumers. **Transfair** sets criteria and standards for a "people-friendly" stamp of approval–the Fairtrade Mark–which include the following: decent wages, adequate housing (where provided), democratic systems, fair prices, fair credit terms, and effective health, safety and environmental protection.

Launched in 1996, **Fair TradeMark Canada** is the Canadian member of **Transfair International**. The Canadian organization has focused first on coffee, one of the most highly traded commodities in the world, involving 25 million producers in more than 70 countries. Under the current system of trade–which is dominated by four multinational companies–very little of what consumers pay for coffee, often less than 10 per cent, reaches the farmer who grows the beans. The **Fair TradeMark** label ensures that the product meets **Transfair International** standards. It is an independently monitored guarantee that fair trade conditions are being met and that the label is not just marketing hype. **Fair TradeMark Canada** recognizes, however, that while a growing minority of consumers may be willing to pay extra to ensure fair prices for products, they demand easy availability and no compromise in product quality.

Both **Fair TradeMark Canada** and **Oxfam** offer background resources and action kits for starting a small fair trade committee (two to six persons or more) in your neighbourhood. The kits provide guidance on how to take a positive approach to lobbying local cafés, supermarket managers and institutional coffee buyers, and how to get local media attention.

2. BUY FAIR TRADE PRODUCE

Fairly traded foods can be found in many health food shops across Canada. Fairly traded coffee is available through direct mail from **Bean North Coffee Roasting Company**.

Oxfam-Canada Bridgehead sells ethically traded high-quality food products and handcrafts through a direct mail catalogue, retail stores (in Toronto, Ottawa and Vancouver) and a wholesale division that ships directly to customers in Canada.

3. CHALLENGE COMPANIES TO INTRODUCE FAIR TRADE POLICIES

The **Fair TradeMark Canada** action kit provides guidance on how to organize letter-writing campaigns targeting national coffee companies.

3.6 Local Varieties

How far should our food travel?

The effects of globalization, both positive and

negative, can be seen wherever you go. In Mongolia, a country that has survived on local milk products for thousands of years, you find mainly German butter in the shops. In Kenya, butter from Holland is half the price of local butter. In Spain, the dairy products are mainly Danish. In England, butter from New Zealand is usually considerably cheaper, even though it has been shipped from the other side of the world! And the Canadian shopper is as likely to find Californian lettuce, South African fruit and Mexican asparagus.

Whether it is a question of butter and lamb from New Zealand, cut flowers from Guatemala, peas from East Africa or strawberries from Spain, it seems absurd that people are becoming increasingly dependent for their everyday "needs" on products that have travelled thousands of kilometres (see opposite). At the same time, making matters worse, many poorer countries are using their best agricultural land to grow crops for the rich, rather than food for local people who may even be starving (page 84). Poor labour standards mean that flowers grown in Colombian greenhouses for the Canadian market allow women to be exposed to unacceptable levels of toxic pesticides. That lovely hot-house flower isn't so lovely after all. The trend started long ago, with trade in products such as tin, sugar and cotton. Today, it has widened to include oil, microchips and genetically modified foods. And the process has only just begun to hit its stride.

Summer, autumn, winter or spring, there is often little difference in what is available on the grocery-store shelves. Apples may not be ripe locally—so we simply fly them in from South Africa. Avocados may not grow in this country, but we can ship them halfway around the world. Similarly, we import bananas from Costa Rica, flowers from Guatemala, grapes from Chile or orange juice from Brazil. So we see a new focus on "food miles."

Food miles

Food, quite simply, is travelling further to get to our tables—oranges from Florida, bananas from Ecuador, mangoes from Brazil, canned mushrooms from China. Canadian imports of fruit have doubled since 1985. In 1995, Canada purchased 60 per cent of its fruit from the U.S., and the remaining 40 per cent from countries in the Southern Hemisphere—primarily in Latin America. Even within countries, food is travelling further. A chicken sold in the United States, for example, will typically have travelled 3600 kilometres before it reaches the dinner plate of the purchaser.[91]

Canadian imports of fruit have doubled since 1985.

All this transport uses a great deal of fuel. Flying commodities by air, for example, is now commonplace, even though air transport (page 141) uses 37 times more fuel per tonne of food transported than does sea transport—all affecting climate change! The real problem is that fuel prices are so cheap—with the airlines even being given tax breaks on fuel.

A chicken sold in the United States will typically have travelled 3600 kilometres before it reaches the dinner plate of the purchaser.

Nor is it just human food that travels. Brazil, for example, is a major supplier of soybeans for European animal feed. To produce these soybeans it has cleared its Cerrada plateau forest—about five million hectares (twelve million acres). These have been dubbed "ghost acres" because—although they are not immediately visible—they are nonetheless used to support our diets and farm animals.

There can also be problems at the other end of the chain. In the Netherlands, there is an estimated 40-million-tonne "manure mountain" produced by Dutch farm animals. Because they don't have the land space to spread the muck, they have even been thinking of shipping it overseas.[92]

Vanishing varieties

Another key change has affected the types and varieties of produce we eat. These days, we expect to be able to buy fruits such as bananas, kiwi fruit, mangoes and avocado pears whenever we want, even though they are tropical produce. Surprisingly, however, this expanding range of choices is often achieved at the expense of a considerable narrowing of the varieties of any particular fruit or vegetable available in the supermarket.

In the U.S. and Canada, two-thirds of the nearly 5000 nonhybrid vegetable varieties that were offered in 1984 catalogues had been dropped by 1994.[93]

Increasingly, crop varieties have been chosen for their size, ability to travel long distances and for their shelf-life, rather than for their taste. Paradoxically, the relatively low price of this fruit often means that it is more expensive to buy local varieties than to buy produce shipped around the planet. Consumers then acquire a taste for big-brand produce, such as Granny Smith or Golden Delicious apples, and the market for local varieties disintegrates.

Looking at the number of vegetable varieties listed in seed catalogues is a good illustration of the dramatic decline in what is available. In 1885, the leading seed catalogue[94] offered 25 varieties of carrot, 53 onions, 58 turnips, 66 potatoes and 120 different types of garden pea. The current Suttons catalogue contains just 11 varieties of carrot, 13 onions, 4 turnips, 10 potatoes and 16 different types of pea.

Should we be worried?

The combination of the "food miles" issue and the loss of diversity constitutes one of the most complex challenges for anyone interested in ensuring that our food and drink are produced sustainably. Indeed, it is possible to raise a virtual A-to-Z of issues in this area:

Animal welfare: The farther you have to ship animals to market, the more they are likely to suffer. At the same time, animals may be sent to countries where welfare standards are lower, as when the U.K. exports lambs, sheep and calves to continental Europe or Australia exports animals to Asia.

Biodiversity: Issues such as appearance, uniformity and shelf-life have become paramount in the supermarkets, which means that local crop varieties have given way to a few commercial varieties. A decrease in crop variety increases vulnerability to pests and disease, which in turn can mean that more pesticides are required. So, too, are species of livestock going extinct.

Wildlife habitat: As farmers have to compete on world markets, they are forced to focus on keeping costs down. In Canada, draining of wetland to make bigger fields has been one of the most obvious results of this trend. This means less habitat for wildlife, including birds and other natural predators, and again a greater need for pesticides.

Developing world: Paradoxically, the ability of developing countries to feed themselves may be compromised as they start to grow more food for export to rich countries. The result can be that food grown locally is not available for local consumption, or is too expensive for local budgets—so that people become malnourished or, in extreme cases, starve.

Energy: Apart from the fuels needed for transport, a great deal of energy is used by the greenhouses, cold storage facilities and other elements of the food chain that bring us food out of season.

Farming patterns: The landscapes and wildlife diversity we appreciate in the countryside often reflect long-established patterns of farming. Now, as factory farming becomes the norm and foods are flown halfway around the world, the pressures on smaller and more traditional farms are intensifying. Tens of thousands of farming jobs have been lost, with farmers leaving the land in droves.

Local economies: Cheap imported food is bought at grocery stores, with the result that any local stores sourcing food locally simply cannot compete. This is a double loss, in terms of activity and income. Money spent on local produce tends to stay in the area, to be spent on other local goods and services, whereas 80 to 90 per cent of money spent in grocery stores may be "sucked" out of the area to distant shareholders.

Packaging: More packaging is needed to protect produce that travels. It is easy to forget that as consumers we do not see a lot of the packaging used, because its purpose is to protect produce in transit. Up to two-thirds of North American packaging is used for food and drink, although increasingly returnable crates are replacing disposable packaging.

Pollution: Transport is one of the biggest contributors to air pollution (page 146). Cutting down on unnecessary journeys and using less damaging forms of transport can make a real difference.

Soil erosion: Monocultures (single crop species) have meant that soils have become more vulnerable to erosion—and crops to wind damage. Intensive production of soybeans in Brazil has led to soil loss up to 80 times higher than in natural vegetated areas.

Toxins: Much produce needs to be treated with pesticides to help preserve it during long-haul travel to prevent damage and to extend its shelf-life. Examples include citrus fruits, which are often waxed (page 47) or treated with fungicides. Some produce also requires treatment to stop pests hopping on board for the ride and causing problems in the importing country.

Clearly, none of us can hope to address all of these issues. Working out the complexities would probably be a full-time job in its own right. But asking for local, seasonal food and drink sends powerful signals through the markets that these issues are important to us—and that we want the food chain and supermarkets to tackle them seriously.

Local Varieties

✔Citizen 2000 Checklist

1. Grow Your Own Organic

There are lots of reasons to grow your own organic fruit and vegetables. Home-grown produce is usually more nutritious, partly because it is freshly picked. It also often has more flavour–and you know that it is grown without pesticides. Moreover, it is cheaper than buying organic produce and does not need to travel far. **Canadian Organic Growers (COG)** and its local chapters (see the Directory at the back of this book) can provide information and advice on organic growing "in the back yard or the back forty." City gardeners will also want to link up with **City Farmer: Canada's Office of Urban Agriculture**, a nonprofit society promoting urban food production and environmental conservation. Their continuously growing on-line library provides resources on subjects ranging from roof-top gardens to composting to community development.

Among organic seed suppliers are **Seeds of Diversity Canada** and **Seeds of Change** (see No. 3 below) and **Johnny's Selected Seeds**, who operate a certified organic trial and research farm in Albion, Maine. **Shepherd's Garden Seeds** purchase seed from companies throughout the world. They make every attempt to carry untreated seed. If customers request "untreated seed only," they will receive no treated varieties.

2. Buy Local and Seasonal Produce

A wide range of campaigning groups promote local or seasonal produce, for example, through local or regional food festivals from coast to coast. **FarmFolk/CityFolk**, a not-for-profit registered charity in Vancouver, strives to reduce the distance between field and table, and to develop and maintain a just and sustainable food system. Among other activities, they organize the Feast of Fields in Vancouver. **Earth to Table**, a Calgary-based coalition of chefs, growers, distributors and consumers, promotes the use of fresh local foods and strengthening the bond between earth and table. **Knives & Forks, Advocates for Organic Agriculture**, organize the annual Feast of Fields event in Southern Ontario.

Organic retailers (see list under **Canadian Organic Growers** in the Directory) tend to emphasize local and seasonal produce.

3. Support Biodiversity Initiatives

Seeds of Diversity Canada maintains over 1200 distinct varieties of heirloom and endangered vegetables, fruits, grains, herbs and flowers, many of which would now be extinct were it not for this growers' network. The group maintains preservation collections of cereals, potatoes, garlic and other crops, and liaises with other groups around the world to share information and plant materials. You don't have to be a grower to join **Seeds of Diversity**. Members receive three issues of *Seeds of Diversity* magazine each year and an annual seed listing. **Rare Breeds Canada** promotes and preserves rare farm livestock and poultry. **Seeds of Change** in Santa Fe, New Mexico, owns and operates a seed bank with more than 1000 varieties.

4. Encourage Your Favourite Shops to Play Their Part

Overall, progress in this area will remain slow until the big grocery-store chains see significant demand for local produce. Part of the problem is our buying habits–every time we specify a national or international brand-name, rather than trying an unbranded product from closer to home.

4 Community & home

Adolescence • Barriers to greening • Buildings • Childhood • Coca-colonization • Communities • Corporal punishment • Crime • Cults • Diapers • Divorce • Energy efficiency • Fashion • Flirting • Gated communities • Greenfield sites • Green homes • Happy families • Homosexuality • Light pollution • Midlife crisis • Neighbours • Nimbys • Noise • Old age • Parenting • Recycling • Relationships • Religion • Role of men • Sex roles • Sexual abuse • Toxics • Vigilantes • Water • Zero tolerance

It's all too easy to take the most crucial things in life for granted: air, water, family, community. Often we only notice them when they are gone—or under threat. If we are drowning, air becomes the most important thing in the world; if thirsty, water shoots to the top of the list. In the same way, if our families and communities start to collapse, we pay more attention to our relationships with friends and neighbours. It is vital that we do, since they are critical foundation stones for a civilized life.

No one on their deathbed wishes they had spent more time at the office.

In this chapter, we will spotlight the growing pressures not only on families and communities in general, but also on the individuals—particularly the young and old—who depend on them. We zero in on some of the causes of change, such as the impact of more women entering the workplace and other traditional male preserves, the increase in single mothers and the often-embattled position of modern fathers. We look at the tensions and conflicts between the rich and poor, between different races and different religions. And we focus on some of the ways in which big business affects our lives and communities.

We challenge the assumption that "NIMBY" protests are simply about self-interest. The pace of modern development often forces us to decide how much countryside we are prepared to lose, how many local stores we are prepared to see replaced by megastores, how much waste we are willing to accept in our neighbourhood. If we can't show our concern locally, where can we show it?

Finally, we look at ways of reducing our environmental impacts at home—and show how we can speed up the process of greening. We explain how a number of key barriers can stop us from acting—and how we can remove them. In summary, this chapter asks four main questions—and then looks at some of the practical issues arising from them:

- *Is there a recipe for happy families?*
- *Can the modern world find its heart?*
- *Is it wrong to fight for the places we love?*
- *Can we pull out all the stops?*

4.1 Family Values

Is there a recipe for happy families?

Reading the press, you could be forgiven for believing that the family is almost extinct. Hardly, but recent decades have seen the traditional family under growing pressure. In 1951, in Canada, for example, 24 couples married for every one couple that divorced. By 1987, there were only two marriages for each divorce.[1] Twenty per cent of all Canadian families with children are led by one parent alone, the vast majority of them women.[2] As a result, the familiar version of the family—a mother and father, with children—is becoming a minority way of life.

Not all of this is bad, of course. Society is adapting to a changing world, just as it always has. The family will survive; indeed, it may even emerge stronger in some key respects. But the real problem is the sheer speed of change—coupled with our sense that we have little or no control over the process. So let's look at some of the ways in which families are being transformed and at some of the implications. If we are to build a future that works it will depend on families and communities that work too.

Changing sex roles

Open your passport. One of the key pieces of information it gives is your sex. Normally, just about the first thing we notice about other people—often without even being conscious of the fact—is whether they are male or female. Once we have this information, we feel we know better how to deal with them.[3]

Few trends are having as great an impact on our family lives as the sexual revolution. This has not simply involved changes in what we can and cannot do (for example, sleep together before marriage), but also in the ways the sexes view and value each other. Every culture in history has distinguished between men and women, seeing them as different both physically and psychologically, but we appear to be moving toward a world where our sexual identities are increasingly blurred because they are more complex.

Will there be a role for men?

Women's liberation unsettles people—particularly men—for a number of reasons. Most fundamentally, it challenges men's traditional role as breadwinners. In recent years, more and more women have been moving into the world of paid work, with dramatic effects. One key reason for this has been a worldwide shift away from manufacturing (page 186), where many of the heavy and often dangerous jobs were done by men, to service businesses—where women are often better qualified to succeed.

Frequently, welfare systems unintentionally pile on the pressure. In some countries, single mothers have been targeted for assistance with housing, benefits and other forms of social support—to such an extent that they can get a better deal without help from the father of their children. Where men find they have no major role to play in supporting their families, it is perhaps not surprising that the results include increased male depression, aggression, violence and crime.

So do these trends mean that males will soon only be found in glass cases at the museum, alongside the dodo? Of course not, although with the introduction of artificial insemination (page 232), and now even a pill to induce female orgasm, some men are beginning to get seriously worried.

This is not simply a struggle about who controls the home, the family or, ultimately, the world. It is also about who takes responsibility for what, about where boundaries are drawn between the worlds of family and work, and—in the final analysis—about the sort of society and future we want.

Interestingly, research on fathers and fatherhood shows that the overwhelming majority of men who have children are employed, have higher rates of employment than men who are not fathers, and tend to be in full-time employment. But they are less likely these days to be the sole breadwinner. In Canada, for example, in nearly two-thirds of all two-parent families, both parents hold paying jobs.[4] But mothers in dual-earner families are much more likely to be working part-time: women (married and unmarried) occupy almost 70 per cent of all part-time jobs.[5]

Changing to a world where men and women will increasingly trade places, jobs and roles will almost inevitably lead to a certain amount of friction as we adapt to the new order. One interesting trend, for example, involves increasing numbers of men suing their higher-earning former wives for support rather than the other way round.

Men and women will increasingly trade places, jobs and roles.

Can women have it all?

It's a question often asked. In doing so, we often forget just how much things have already changed. Although there are still "glass ceilings" in many organizations, effectively preventing women getting into top management positions, the battle for equality in the workplace is beginning to turn in their favour.

American and Canadian women now occupy more than 40 per cent of managerial jobs; they are far ahead of most countries. But they still have a fair way to go. A recent survey showed that in the top 500 companies, women held less than three per cent of the top managerial jobs.[6] As women move up the hierarchy, men are learning to behave differently, although for many the process is proving highly confusing. Traditional sexual etiquette is being thrown out the window and new "politically correct" rules and expectations are taking their place. In offices, it is said, men and women are even becoming frightened to flirt.[7]

Consider the many controversies over sexual harassment. Actual violence against women is relatively rare in the working environment, but sexual harassment can sometimes be rampant. There are many other forms of harassment, with a majority of women surveyed saying that they have suffered such harassment at some time in their careers.

Once it was largely a case of women complaining that male colleagues, usually their superiors, were taking advantage of them. But an indication of just how far things have gone is that some men are now claiming that they have been sexually harassed by their female superiors.

The trends in favour of increased female employment are very powerful. With a rapidly growing service sector, providing more jobs suited to women and with greater numbers of women in senior roles gradually feminizing the workplace, it may become increasingly hard for ultratraditional males to fit in. The eventual outcome of this extraordinary shift in sex roles may have to be some form of positive discrimination in favour of men in the workplace.

Quite apart from the added stress for men, this role reversal may also cause problems for women. Those who choose to stay at home may feel that their high-achieving friends are looking down on them and that their home-bound roles are undervalued. On the other hand, while the high-powered workers may have a strong sense of achievement, they may also be exposed to at least as much stress as their male counterparts. Indeed, it has been reported that, presumably as a result, some women now have increased levels of the male hormone testosterone—and have even begun losing their hair in the same way that many men do!

In parallel, there can be growing frictions within the family. The rebalancing of sex roles brings new reasons to argue—and often older relatives are unsympathetic, because they have little experience of these new problems.

The necessary dependence on nannies and other forms of external child care brings problems of its own. Quite apart from the difficulty of finding good-quality child-care workers and paying for them, some women must deal with emotional conflicts. They feel guilty about not giving more time to their children—or worry about losing their affection. These feelings can be compounded by a growing body of opinion that working mothers are selfishly pursuing their own goals at the expense of their children—and perhaps should choose one or the other. So, can women really have it all?

A recent survey of 6000 European and American women asked whether they thought they were happier than their mothers.[8] The results: 51 per cent said they were happier and 27 per cent equally happy. Only 14 per cent thought they were less happy. Most felt that the combination of contraception and new domestic appliances had improved their quality of life, as had better educational and job opportunities. Their main concerns were in such areas as health care, job losses and crime.

Whatever the answer turns out to be, there will continue to be those who advocate a return to traditional family values. But they are very unlikely to reverse the trend of more women moving into the workplace—and the linked changes in family structures and roles. The other side of this coin is the possibility that there will be a growing number of men who spend more time at home—either for negative reasons, such as unemployment, or for more positive reasons, like teleworking (page 188).

Where once women had authority at home and men were "top dogs" in society, the lines are being redrawn. The challenge for families will be in learning to accept and adapt. It remains to be seen whether men and women can move closer together and work in partnership, sharing control and responsibilities. The lesson of history, however, is that if the pressures are strong enough we can make extraordinary changes in the ways in which we live.

Family affairs

All of this matters not simply because our families are crucially important to our own lives, but also because the family is still the basic building block of our communities. In a very real sense, our family relationships provide the glue that holds our communities and societies together. They provide the love and other support that children need to develop fully—and which we all need for our long-term emotional health. But, like communities, families depend on us being prepared to give, not simply to take.

Recent decades have seen dramatic changes in some aspects of family life. The sixties brought more liberal, open attitudes to sex before marriage, as well as a growing pursuit of personal happiness, even at the expense of more traditional family duties. But these changes seem to have gone into overdrive on the cusp of the new millennium.

One interesting influence on how families work, or fail to, is the impact of changing communication technologies on succeeding generations of people. The radio generations, for example, behaved and even thought differently from the first TV generation, the "baby boomers." The generations that followed had access to an early form of interactive TV, via video recorders, so that programming was increasingly under their control. And now we have the Internet, the fastest-growing communication channel in human history—and potentially the most revolutionary (pages 165).[9]

In the process, the family world has been transformed. The TV generation, for example, developed a more immediate, emotional response to what was happening in other parts of the world, as in Vietnam, which most of their parents did not have.

When the video came along, many parents suddenly found themselves—for the first time in history—having to learn about a new technology from their children. Now, again, with the Internet, the old are learning from the young[10]—even schoolchildren are coming up with viable business ideas and in some cases businesses. The old order is being turned on its head.

Against this backdrop, let's focus on three different aspects of the modern family: new definitions of the family, the increasing rate of family break-ups, and emerging ideas about the role of parents and of parenting.

Partners for life?

Most of us assume that the normal family is made up of a man (often a father), a woman (often a mother) and a number of children, (usually produced by the same father and mother). Now, growing numbers of people live with several partners during their lives, in the form of serial relationships and/or marriages. As a result, many children are raised in families made up of past, present and possibly even future families.

One of the more prominent trends of the second half of the 20th century has been the rise in the number of break-ups and divorces. The causes are many and various, but they include: the stresses and strains of modern life; changing sex roles in the home and at work; the removal of religious, legal and other barriers to divorce; rising expectations because of greater choice; and perhaps even the fact that our experience with consumer choice means that more people are less prepared to put up with unhappy marriages. Past generations may not have expected to love—even to like—their spouses, but today's generations are looking for something deeper in their relationships.

Half of today's marriages are predicted to end in divorce.

Inevitably, divorce has a dramatic impact on family structures. Many children find it particularly hard being torn between two fractious parties—and subsequent relationships with step-relatives can often be particularly fraught. Second families, too, can lose out where fathers must support children from a previous relationship.

For society, if not for lawyers, divorce has also been damaging. One-parent families tend to need more welfare support. And sadly, truancy, vandalism and crime are more common in children without a father to provide discipline. On the environmental front, too, there are problems. Divorce means a need for more homes—helping to boost the demand for development of the countryside (page 107).

But as traditional families fall apart, so new types of families are being formed. Gay and lesbian families are becoming more common. It is too early to say how they will fare, either in terms of sticking together or of providing love and support for the partners and any children. Society needs to decide whether those in such relationships should be given the same level of recognition and support as heterosexual couples. It is a measure of how far things have changed, however, that it is now almost impossible to imagine society turning back the clock.

Good parenting

The importance of good parenting can hardly be overemphasized. Apart from the ability to provide the basic requirements such as food, clothing and a home, this entails being able to give love and care to another human being through different—and often difficult—life stages. Such trends as divorce and the move of more women into work all put pressure on those responsible for parenting.

Harassed parents may talk in terms of giving "quality time" to their children, yet they have an uneasy feeling that this is not enough. They fear that they will not be around when a crisis arises or when their child makes an exciting discovery.

Another pressure on parents, whether in Europe, North America or Asia, is the steadily growing level of competition in schools and afterwards. Many parents feel the need to push their children to succeed at ever-younger ages as they try to ensure that their children have the best educational opportunities. In Canada, where the long summer holiday used to be sacrosanct, more and more children are spending a good part of the summer taking courses. These are bright children seeking an edge in the competition for university spaces. But there are real concerns about the risks of putting children in "hot-house" environments to speed up their learning and development, squeezing the time available for them to relax, play and generally enjoy childhood.

In such countries as Japan, where competition in the educational sector is intense, the strains have been shown through widespread misery, stress-related disease and, inevitably, suicide.

Another issue that has fiercely polarized opinion has been the question of whether (and how) children should be disciplined. More specifically, whether—and in what circumstances—they should be spanked or beaten. There are those who are fiercely opposed not just to spanking their own children but also to other people doing so. The Canadian Foundation for Children, Youth and the Law recently took the federal government to court to establish that corporal punishment of children is unconstitutional.

Whatever happens within the family, there is little support these days for schools that use physical punishment. Few people would argue that some young people benefit from physical discipline, but the system is too open to abuse. Overall, however, it does seem logical that parents should be able to decide for themselves on how to discipline their own children—so long as they do not cross the line into abuse or child battering. And schools and teachers are going to need more help in civilizing problem youngsters.

Wherever in the world we live, the new century is likely to see even greater interest in how children are raised, trained and educated. Child-rearing and parenting skills will be in the spotlight as never before. In the process, we must learn to place a much greater value on those people involved in these tasks, whether they be parents, caregivers or teachers.

The formative years

The big question is whether we are most shaped by our genes (shorthand: nature) or our childhood environment (nurture). Although genes have been shown to have a strong influence on what we are like, our upbringing is also crucial.

"Give me a boy until he is seven and I will show you the man," a Jesuit thinker once put it. Here the view is that our adult lives are powerfully shaped by what we learn—and by what happens to us—when we are young. This notion was enormously boosted by the theories of Freud, who believed that the roots of most psychiatric problems plaguing adults could be tracked back to events that happened during childhood.

Most children can cope with enormous stresses and strains so long as they feel loved and wanted. That said, childhood itself is a relatively modern—and largely western—phenomenon.

Traditionally, children moved straight from a fairly lengthy infancy into working roles in the community. As recently as the last century, some children would leave home at the age of seven or eight to work as domestic help or become apprentices, many never seeing their parents again. Today, thankfully, child labour is illegal in developed countries, but remains a significant problem in some parts of the Third World.

Such problems range from young people being used to make everything from carpets, soccer balls and track shoes through to others being forced onto the streets to beg. No one doubts that most—and many of their parents—have little choice in the matter. But the resulting cycle of poverty means that working children miss a proper education and are condemned to poverty for life. Equally, because they are illiterate, desperate and poor, such people tend to have no political voice. However, with campaigners now on the case and the world media engaged, real change for the better now seems possible.

Sexual abuse

As the richer countries have become more industrialized, they have also tended to become more child-centred. In part, this is because there are longer periods of education and training, which in turn means that employment is delayed for longer. In many ways this has provided benefits for children that would have been unimaginable just a few generations ago. But, unfortunately, a child-centred world is not necessarily a world where every child is loved—nor, indeed, one in which even most children enjoy greater freedom.

As the world becomes more open, we have learned of problems that would once have been kept largely behind closed doors. One issue that has attracted huge publicity is the sexual abuse of children. With the power of the media to magnify events out of all proportion, it is often very difficult to assess the full extent of this abuse. So, for example, has there been a real historical increase in the number of abuses—or, instead, just in the number of cases detected and publicized?

What is clear is that most cases of abuse take place within families, not outside them. It also seems that the move toward multiple partners and more casual live-in relationships potentially opens up opportunities for abuse. While greater awareness may well prevent some cases, increasing the likelihood of timely support, there can also be negative repercussions. The sensitivity of these issues—coupled with the intense publicity such cases typically attract—can breed new forms of injustice. On occasion, overzealous authorities have threatened to remove children from their families for behaviour that illustrates more a lack of modesty on the part of adults than any sort of abuse.

Some abusers were themselves abused as children, which suggests this is a problem that could grow more serious over time. And given that the consequences for the accused can be so devastating, with the possible loss of family and friends, this is an area sown with powerful emotional landmines. Clearly, given the terrible impact of real abuse, none of this is an argument for inaction or lack of concern, but rather for greater sensitivity to ensure that those targeted are not innocently caught up in a modern variant of the medieval witch-hunt.

Another result of this heightened awareness of the abuse of—and violent crimes against—young people is that growing numbers of parents are unwilling to let their children out of the house unsupervised. The freedom to roam, taken to its extreme in fiction by *Tom Sawyer* and *Huckleberry Finn*, is being radically restricted. By keeping children indoors, either watching television or otherwise at a loose end, are we in a sense stealing their childhoods?

Teenage blues

The gradual extension of the time we spend at school or university, coupled with new laws designed to protect us through our teenage years, have been among the factors driving the evolution of a distinct teen culture. Teenagers inhabit an "in-between" world, wanting to be adults, yet often treated in law as children. At the same time, teenagers now represent a massive market around the world, with the result that they are the focus of intense advertising, media interest and peer pressure.

Perhaps this is why it is often so difficult to be a teenager in the richer countries. The biological changes that we go through at puberty are pretty much universal, yet it appears that the process can be less turbulent and uncertain in more traditional cultures. Indeed, it seems that our very approach to childhood makes the transition to adulthood an even greater gap to be bridged. In "less sophisticated" cultures, young people usually have less to "unlearn" because they have been working alongside adults for some time.

In contrast to societies that put their young people through initiation ceremonies to mark clearly the transition from adolescence to adulthood, it often seems that the best the modern world can offer is the driving test. Is it coincidental that so many teen cultures revolve around the scooter, motorcycle or car, each of which offers freedom from parental supervision?

Different societies have very different ideas about the age at which teenagers become adults. One of the most controversial ongoing debates revolves around questions about the age at which teenagers should be allowed to smoke, take drugs, have sex or practise homosexuality. On the one hand, there are sensible concerns that teenagers are too young to take responsibility for making these important decisions. On the other hand, if young people are not given a degree of flexibility and real responsibility, they will be much less likely to learn how to take control of their own lives.

This whole area is further complicated by the fact that the natural desire of parents to care for their children often collides head-on with the young's desire to experiment. You don't have to be a fortuneteller to predict that this debate will not run out of steam any time soon.

Indeed, the future is likely to see the period of experimentation extending well into the "twenties" as young people take "time out" to travel and explore the expanding range of lifestyle, sexual, political and religious options open to them. In the process, they will be increasingly free to build their own networks and, in a sense, choose their own extended families.

The adult years

With people living longer and changing their jobs more frequently, we no longer have the security of having our lives mapped out for us. A considerable number of people reach middle age having spent the "best years" of their lives working flat-out to raise their children. So they hit the so-called midlife crisis worrying that they have squandered their opportunities—and concerned that they no longer have any social value. Although the time before old age really kicks in can genuinely be the "golden years," many find it is a time when their income is severely squeezed and their health is deteriorating.

Some of these problems are simply unavoidable, unless we make a miracle breakthrough and find a cure for aging. But harnessing—and developing—the resource that older people represent will be a key challenge for the next century.

In Berlin, for example, overstretched working mothers have found a way to get around the fact that childcare is scarce and expensive: they rent "grannies." The so-called Grandparents Service matches families with elderly women or couples, who often form lasting relationships with both children and parents.[11] Apparently, the only problem is that existing grandparents can feel jealous of their "rented" replacements!

In Berlin, they have set up a rent-a-granny agency.

Traditional respect for the elderly has been greatly eroded in modern times. The speed of change has meant that many older people are increasingly viewed as "out of touch." However, it will be important for a stable society to make sure that the old and the young are mixed—and that each generation does not end up walled off in its own ghetto.

More positively, the early years of the 21st century may well see older people playing a much more active role. People over 50, for example, now have more expendable wealth, more time and a greater thirst for knowledge than ever before.[12] The result is that there is a new interest in "grey education," and we are seeing the movement of millions of senior citizens across the world. In Canada, for example, 1.5 million "snowbirds" (the vast majority of them over 55) escape the winter each year by spending up to six months in a warmer climate. Many of these people take additional short-term trips throughout the year.

These people will increasingly demand a voice—and not just on pension rights. Indeed, some people even forecast that so many older people will live beyond their allotted "three-score-and-ten" years without adequate pensions (page 219) to sustain them that the street riots of the 21st century will be led by senior citizens rather than student activists!

In the end, we all have different needs, but some things never change. We all need to feel that we are wanted, respected and loved. Rather than steering the members of our families toward particular destinations, we need to give them the support they need on whatever course they choose. Most of us will only be able to cope with the increasingly furious pace of change in the modern world by feeling comfortable with who we are and what we are doing, enabling us to be flexible and adapt to new situations.

Family Values

✔Citizen 2000 Checklist

1. VALUE FAMILY LIFE

The value of family life needs to be recognized by individuals, communities, employers and governments. Indeed, it is no accident that books with such titles as *The Little Book of Calm* have become bestsellers: as stress levels build, we all need to be able to step back regularly and catch up with ourselves, and to invest more time in our families and friends. Some employers are beginning to develop family- and child-friendly policies. Consulting firms such as **Work-Life Harmony Enterprises**, **Working Well CHC** and **WFD Canada** provide such services as employee assistance programs, employee counselling and development of workplace arrangements that make for better integration of work and family life. The **Shorter Work Time Network of Canada** promotes a 32-hour work week as a way to allow working people more time to pursue family, personal and community life, while addressing unemployment due to corporate downsizing.

The **Child Care Advocacy Association of Canada (CCAAC)** advocates for accessible, affordable, high-quality, comprehensive, not-for-profit child care for every Canadian. The **YMCA** is the largest provider of quality, not-for-profit child care in Canada, serving over 24 000 children and their families. Subsidies are available for those who can't afford the service. The **Canadian Day Care Registry** provides, through the Internet, a list of available day-care providers (profit and not-for-profit) organized by province and city.

2. Take Parenting Seriously

Being a parent is probably the most important role any of us plays in life. But many of us are ill-prepared for the task. There is a wide range of organizations dedicated to helping and advising parents. **The Vanier Institute of the Family** is perhaps Canada's best-known source of information about trends affecting contemporary family life. The Institute is particularly good at interpreting government and academic material for the general public. Recent issues of its quarterly newsletter, *Transition*, have focused on such topics as family violence, family housing and adolescence. The **National Foundation for Family Research and Education (NFFRE)** aims to provide insightful information about families to families.

There are a number of inspiring and informative publications that parents, would-be parents and anyone interested in parenting issues can turn to. Since 1978, *Empathic Parenting*, the journal of the **Canadian Society for the Prevention of Cruelty to Children**, has focused on the nurturing of children under the age of three. On-line resources for parents include **Child and Family Canada**, presented through the cooperation of 41 nonprofit organizations, and **Today's Parent Online**. *Today's Parent Magazine* is available by subscription and at newsstands.

For single parents, a key support organization is **One-Parent Families Association of Canada**, which provides a comprehensive program of family and adult activities. As of this writing, there are chapters in Alberta, Ontario and Quebec, but chapters can be started wherever there are single parents. **Fathers' Resources International** works with the "Fathering Community" locally, nationally and internationally to provide mutual support as well as conflict-resolution tools and strategies for divorced families. This organization partners with the **National Shared Parenting Association**, which promotes shared custody of children of divorced parents.

3. Don't Be Afraid to Ask for Help

We are able to ask for advice before we commit to a relationship, while it is going on and, if things go badly wrong, when it is over. Religious institutions as well as community and social service agencies can help in all of these situations. **Marriage Encounter Weekends**, offered by several Christian denominations, can help to improve communications and make good marriages even better. There are Baptist, Roman Catholic, United Church and other faith expressions of **Marriage Encounter**, but couples do not have to belong to a particular church to participate.

For those feeling overwhelmed by the challenges of child rearing, there are parent support groups across Canada. A national group referral service is provided by **The Association of Parent Support Groups in Ontario**, which provides 24-hour support for parents. They stress self-help and mutual support, and hold weekly parenting strategy meetings. (See also "other parent support contacts" on page 283 of the Directory.)

For children and youth needing assistance, **Kids Help Phone** provides a toll-free, national telephone counselling service. Parents, teachers and any other concerned adults are also welcome to call for information and referral services at any time. **Parents and Friends of Lesbians and Gays (PFLAG)**, with chapters across Canada, provides support groups for family members who recently had a child "come out" and declare they are gay, lesbian or bisexual.

With the aging of the Canadian population, elder care has become a major part of life for many families. **Caregiver Network Inc.** provides information on the Internet, educational seminars, and personal contacts and support through the *Caregiver Club/newsletter*. Their new *Canadian Aging and Caregiving Resource Guide* lists federal, provincial and local agencies and services. **The Canadian Senior**

Citizens Information and Services Center provides older Canadians and their families with easy access to valuable information on programs, services, events and so on available to senior citizens. They cover everything from health issues to retirement residences to recreational and travel information. The **Canadian Association of Retired Persons** helps people over 50 (retirees are getting younger and younger!) get the most out of life, and also advocates on behalf of retired Canadians and senior citizens.

4.2 Community Spirit

Can the modern world find its heart?

Until surprisingly recently, most of us lived in villages and other rural communities. Some of these still survive, but today the vast majority of the world's people live in urban areas and in the world's growing number of cities and "mega-cities." These huge concentrations of humanity often have populations of over 10 million and some are expanding outwards at a pace of several kilometres a year.

Friends and neighbours

You don't need to be a hermit to feel sometimes that there are too many people. But there is a positive side to the equation. From cradle to grave, we depend on others for protection, housing, water, electricity, hospitals, waste removal and many other things. Without these facilities, and the people to provide them, life as we know it would be impossible.

Nor is it simply a question of the services provided by our communities. Human beings are the ultimate social animals and, like other primates, most of us need—indeed thrive on—social contact. We need other people to define our sense of personal identity and worth.

The evidence suggests that although we may no longer identify with the people who live next door, new types of communities are forming, often based on common interests. Anglers meeting on the riverbank or golfers at the club house —people are linking up, often in totally new ways. The combination of cars, trains and planes (page 136) and modern-day technology (page 165) means that we can share interests and enthusiasms with people kilometres away from where we live.

In the past, we had a wide range of self-help institutions, from clubs through to friendly societies, cooperatives and social welfare organizations. Many of these have been under pressure in recent years, but the closing years of the 20th century have seen a new interest in innovative give-and-take networks, some evolving over the Internet. And the 21st century will very likely see these seeds blooming in unexpected ways.

Who's Happiest?

- **One of the biggest tensions in the modern world is between the contrasting lifestyles of the richer and poorer nations. North Americans, Europeans and the Japanese, to name only the key culprits, roar around in fast, gas-guzzling cars and live surrounded by TVs, washing machines and fridges. Meanwhile, huge numbers of people in Africa, Asia and South America make a living through subsistence agriculture–and count themselves remarkably fortunate when they get access to clean water, let alone electricity and the telephone.**
- **But who is actually better off? On the surface, the answer has to be the richer nations–largely because we measure a country's well-being in terms of its economic activity and standard of living**

(page 208). Indeed, almost all the measures used by governments reinforce this view. Surely, however, we need to find ways of measuring our contentment that are not linked to financial status?

- **Paradoxically, many countries and communities that would be judged among the poorest seem to be among the most content. Often they enjoy stronger family support networks, with children, parents, grandparents and even great-grandparents either living under the same roof or close by.**
- **If something needs to be done–a new building erected or harvest brought in–people will often help each other out as a matter of course. Indeed, what the richer countries (which are more focused on the individual) would view as "nepotism" or corruption is often seen as the virtuous path in poorer countries.**
- **The downside is that life expectancy is dramatically lower than in the richer countries. There is more disease, less medicine and fewer doctors and hospitals. As a result, few people with a real choice would abandon the richer lifestyle for the poorer. But some people do–and their experience suggests that there are many things we could learn from those communities we tend to view as less sophisticated.**

Leaving home

Communities in the developing world are being undermined by a multitude of pressures that are forcing people to leave home, usually moving from the small rural communities in which they were brought up to urban areas. The combination of local job shortages and the lure of the cities can prove irresistible, particularly for the young.

Many migrants, to be fair, do indeed find a better life. But many do not, living in pitiful conditions and with fierce competition for jobs. And the communities they have left behind may begin to collapse as the structure of the population skews to the young and the old.

Nor is this simply a problem for the developing countries. Many of the migrants leave not just their original communities, but also their countries. The constant stream of Mexican migrants moving northwards toward California and beyond is one current example of the trend.

Some of the richer countries are struggling to cope with—or rebuff—foreign migrants moving in search of jobs or better lifestyles. Even countries with a humane history of taking in political refugees are finding their tolerance stretched to the limit. And now we also see the number of "environmental refugees" on the rise. These are people who have been displaced through natural disasters or environmental degradation, driven by population pressures or climate change. As a result, immigration laws and services are being strained to the limit and, in many countries, racial tensions are growing as different ethnic groups try to live alongside one another. Quite apart from ethnic issues, those already living in a country often resent having to support new arrivals on welfare—and are deeply uncomfortable with the intensifying economic competition for jobs. These are social powder kegs in the making.

Living together

For many westerners, traditional religion is a thing of the past. This brings both benefits and problems. In the past, communities around the world were bound together by Christianity, Islam or other religions. Communism, for some, was equivalent to a religion—and that, too, has experienced a massive collapse. Capitalism and consumerism may be more attractive in some ways, but they fail to satisfy some of the needs that religions met in the past.

The God spot

So we would be wrong to assume that the future will be religion-free. Our beliefs may change, but our need to believe will not. Indeed, some scientists now argue that humans are genetically programmed to believe in God, possibly as an evolutionary way of imposing order and stability in society. They think they have found evidence of what they call a "God spot" in the brain.

True or not, the styles in which we choose to express our spiritual and religious impulses may well be rather different. For several decades, westerners have been increasingly interested in Eastern religions, for example. And, at the same time, we have seen new "religions" emerging. Take the so-called Moonies. The world's strangest (and largest-ever) wedding service was conducted by Sun Myung Moon in South Korea in 1995: he simultaneously married no less than 35 000 couples in the Olympic Stadium—and 325 000 other couples around the planet who were linked in by satellite.

Some of the more traditional religions may well enjoy a new lease on life. The Vatican, for example, is exploiting modern technologies, with its own website and work under way to build a powerful astronomical laboratory to find the "fingerprints of God" amid the chaos of the cosmos. But we are also likely to see a huge rise in the number and membership of new cults. Whether or not we welcome the trend, they fill —or at least promise to fill—an aching gap in some people's lives. Unfortunately, we suspect that a 21st-century rule of thumb would be that "the higher the rate of new cult formation, the worse the health of the host societies is likely to be." The proliferation of cults can be both a symptom and a cause of wider social ills.

It is hard to anticipate what might replace traditional religions in terms of giving us common moral certainties for the future. But it is not impossible that this might be a profound feeling for the global environment—particularly the concept of Gaia (page 1), the "living earth"—and a linked desire to preserve it for future generations. The traditional religions may succeed in capturing this new mood, but the interest of most religions in the "next world" rather than this one remains a major obstacle to progress in this area.

Alternatively, this focus on different beliefs that has characterized so much of the "new age" movement may encourage the development of a completely new religion—or "world view." New belief systems emerge all the time, of course, though most do not make it to full world religion status. Our changing circumstances may, however, open the door for a new ideology—one that suits our current situation or ever-changing needs. It may take a massive catastrophe or an amazingly persuasive prophet to inspire change and allow a new or "Gaian" world view to flourish. But neither possibility can be ruled out.

Caring communities

A key part of most people's environment is other people: family, friends, workmates and so on. So, how many of us these days are aware of—let alone care for—even our nearest neighbours? It often seems that the real community spirits are fighting against the tide. In many communities, there is diminishing contact between neighbours —with most people preferring to stay indoors and watch television. When they do emerge, many take the car to work or to the mall, insulated from both the risks and benefits of community.

Despite modern telecommunications, it can be difficult for people to maintain the range of local contacts they would once have had. As hospitals, schools and other facilities become more centralized, there is a risk that the people-centred approach is sacrificed to improved economics, time-saving and efficiency. No surprise, then, that people are increasingly voicing their discontent with this approach. It may work well on paper, they say, but its real life effects can be devastating.

The very heart of some communities has been torn out as those in power remove the local school or close down the hospital. We are likely to see more people challenging this centralizing trend and trying to make sure, for example, that they can give birth (page 237) or die (page 276) at home if they choose to.

Even locking up the mentally ill in centralized institutions has been shown to be a flawed approach. While those prone to commit murders or other offences certainly need to be kept out of the community, it turns out that those who are not such a threat have a significantly greater chance of recovery or rehabilitation if they are able to mix with other people.

An even larger problem, and one that is growing in most societies, is that of caring for the elderly. Many old people live on their own, and are intensely lonely. Others may have moved into institutions, where there are many other elderly people, but here too they can suffer from boredom and a loss of dignity. They are dependent on the government in the same way that they were once dependent on their parents, but with a very different relationship to those now providing care. With more people living longer and many families breaking up, this is an issue that will require some highly creative thinking.

The curse of crime

And then there is the crime rate. From the common or "garden" mugger or house-breaker to the Mafia chief, criminals are like termites in a timber-frame house. For a long time the building may seem unaffected by the damage being done, but if the attacks are allowed to go on for long enough the roof falls in.

Our towns and cities are among our most wonderful inventions for ensuring a community life, but growing concerns about crime and general security are often making them less attractive places to live in. It is no accident that we have seen a boom in companies making burglar alarms, car security systems, closed-circuit TV and electronic fences.

Like cults, crime and criminals tend to thrive when society is in relatively poor health. For one thing, criminal behaviour often reflects wider social pressures and problems. However, this fact has led to some abuse of the system as poverty, family breakdown and other pressures are used as excuses by those trying to escape punishment. Criminals are often presented as victims, or are fêted by the media as they sell their stories for huge sums. Their victims, meanwhile, suffer twice over.

The causes of crime are complex and diverse, ranging from deviant personalities, the use of intoxicating drugs, greed, boredom and rebellion. The trend is also spurred by the ways in which people have been removed from areas that used to be staffed. Video cameras are no substitute for people when it comes to deterring vandalism or giving ordinary people a real sense of security.

Meanwhile, the legal system struggles to deal with crimes once committed as well as trying to prevent crime from happening in the first place. Clearly, few people would complain if we could really get at the causes of crime and thereby the number of offences. But how do we achieve this? Part of the answer is to stop criminals from reoffending once they have been caught. But this focus can encourage us to forget that there are other important objectives in punishment.

If someone has committed a serious crime, at least four main objectives need to be considered. First, we need to show them—and the rest of society—that they have done wrong and that they are being punished for this. Second, we may need to remove the opportunity for them to reoffend, either by imprisonment or some form of tagging or probation. Third, we want a system that enables criminals to reform so they do not reoffend. Fourth, and an objective that is often ignored, the victims and society need to be convinced that justice has been done.

Few approaches manage to achieve all these objectives, with the result that in many communities there is a deep—and often growing—unease about the justice system. New approaches are being tried by some police forces, based on "zero tolerance." They rely on a much tougher approach to even the smallest of crimes, sending a powerful message to the wider criminal community that crime does not pay.

Allowing small crimes to go unpunished, it is argued, is like leaving one broken window in a building: soon all the windows will be smashed. Once all the windows are broken, a sense of lawlessness spreads, encouraging growing numbers of criminal acts. Instead, cities like New York have concluded, the tide can be reversed—and the best place to start is by dealing with all the petty crimes that can make urban life such a nightmare.

If, for whatever reason, crime is not kept under control, then there is a very real danger that the victims and other members of the public may start taking the law into their own hands. So we have seen new initiatives designed to fill the gap between traditional policing and what people believe it takes to make a safe society.

At the community level, there have been such initiatives as Neighbourhood Watch schemes, set up in cooperation with the police. But, in some areas, vigilante gangs have also sprung up, together with private police forces, and there are real fears that this approach could spiral out of control. Vigilante activities are almost unheard of in Canada, though in the early 1980s, the Guardian Angels patrolled the streets of some Toronto neighbourhoods. The group was a U.S. phenomenon and did not find a lasting niche on this side of the border.

In the United States, faced with ever-escalating levels of violence, growing numbers of Americans have taken a different approach—retreating into "gated communities." There are now some 30 000 of these fortified communities across the country, providing homes for an estimated eight million people. They are increasingly seen as a safe haven for people wanting to live among their own kind in a compound sealed against outsiders.

We like to think of gated communities as rare in Canada, but critics argue that we have many communities with invisible gates. The "new-urbanism" developments, which plant old-fashioned neighbourhoods amid the suburban sprawl, may be putting up economic walls against the kind of ethnic and lifestyle diversity you'll find in the city centres.[13] Others see invisible gates around the ethnic enclaves in our large cities, but with the suggestion that they are part of what makes our multicultural society work so well.[14] Communities with actual locked gates are being developed for elderly Canadians, who are attracted to the safety they offer. Since the early 1980s, Canadian Adult Communities has built a dozen gated villages in Western Canada. Ten of these communities are located in Kelowna, B.C., which has become something of a regional capital for the exclusive developments.[15]

Since the early 1980s, Canadian Adult Communities has built a dozen gated villages in Western Canada.

In the long term, however, gated communities are no real solution to the problem. In fact, they could even be the first step toward a patchwork of elitist fiefdoms, each virtually "at war" with those on the outside.

Clearly, traditional forms of community are no longer delivering what many of the residents of these places want. When free citizens choose to hide themselves behind walls, gates and armed guards, the usual trappings of a prison, they are signalling that something is seriously wrong with the world. We need to find solutions that work and help to rebuild the sense of community and shared interest that is vital to the long-term health of any society.

The give-and-take society

The global economy forces businesses to cut jobs, reduce costs and reorganize their operations in fewer, often distant sites—or risk going out of business. Giant companies are quite literally operating in a different world. Jet travel, satellite telecommunications and super freighters mean that their operations straddle the world in ways that would have been unthinkable even a few decades ago.

A modern paradox

In the process, many companies are losing what limited contacts they already had with local communities. Once, gas stations were garages run by locals who could help fix your car and give you directions. Today, they are concrete islands with a fast turnover of employees who don't know (or care) where they are—and, in any event, are frequently barricaded behind thick glass windows to protect them from attack.

Big grocery-store chains buy all their produce centrally and truck it around the country, in giant vehicles using vast quantities of fuel (page 82). They rarely stock local produce. Indeed, if they do, it may well have travelled to a central depot before being returned to the store.

Furthermore, most superstores no longer know their customers personally, except through "loyalty schemes," as names and data on computer systems (page 191).

Grocery stores are popular because they are both cheap and convenient, at least for those with a car. We vote for them with our feet and wheels. But we don't always like what happens as a result, even if we fail to spot the link between cause and effect. As the size and number of these giant operations grow, together with their ability to cut prices, they force millions of small businesses over the edge. In some towns the result is that the main shopping streets are empty, their shop-fronts boarded up, while the parking lots of suburban malls are spilling over.

So here's the paradox. At the same time that business is seen as the source of such problems, the world is also waking up to the fact that that business is a crucial element in any community. The big, footloose companies that open and close plants without a thought for the social impacts are only part of the story. There are also many companies that can see real value in building reputations as good "corporate citizens." They see that if they support their local communities, employees and other interested parties, the company itself will benefit both directly and indirectly.

This simple idea—that if you give something you generally get something back—is also being recognized, and encouraged, by some governments. As citizens we need to acknowledge the fact that if we are to have "rights" in society, we must also accept responsibilities. Most of us do not want to be dictated to by our families or communities, but growing numbers of us recognize that if we are to exercise real choice we need other people's support in the process.

As the power of governments grew, this balanced relationship between rights and responsibilities got squeezed out—but now it's coming back again.[16]

Community Spirit

✓Citizen 2000 Checklist

1. Play an Active Part in Your Community

If our communities are healthy, we all benefit. It makes sense to do everything in our power to ensure that our local community flourishes.

There are many ways in which we can do this. We can give money–or we can give time, which can often be at least as valuable. We can join local associations and groups, or volunteer to help with fairs, festivals and community clean-up projects. One organization, dedicated to the prevention of crime–and now operating all over the country–is **Neighbourhood Watch**. Contact your local police community relations officer or **Neighbourhood Watch** (in Ottawa) for details.

Volunteer Canada: The Canadian Association of Volunteer Bureaux and Centres is mandated to promote the growth of volunteerism and community participation in Canada. They can refer you to provincial volunteer associations, which can provide information on volunteering opportunities in your area. For parents, a key contribution is to actively support local parent-teacher associations.

2. Encourage Businesses to Put Something Back

Business is beginning to recognize a wider range of social responsibilities. Many companies and other business organizations now acknowledge that they must invest in their local communities. This is not simply for altruistic reasons, but also because of direct self-interest. Healthy communities, they accept, make for healthier businesses. **The Body Shop**, for example, is developing a range of trading relationships with "communities in need" to encourage positive social and environmental change where it is most needed. As well, each shop allows its employees time to volunteer in a community project of the staff's choice. Another example is **The Canada Trust–Friends of the Environment Foundation**, which supports local and national environmental initiatives.

The Canadian Centre for Business in the Community (CCBC), an independent centre at the **Conference Board of Canada**, promotes corporate responsibility in ways that help to achieve business and community goals. The centre provides counselling, information, seminars and research in corporate community investment and community economic development. **The Canadian Centre for Philanthropy/IMAGINE** works to strengthen charitable, voluntary and non-profit organizations through advocacy, research and information sharing. The **Canadian Community Investment Web Site** supports and nurtures the growing movement to find local solutions to the problem of financing small and community-based businesses. The **Council for Business and the Arts in Canada (CBAC)** is the national association of businesses that support the arts through community investments. (**CBAC** itself does not make grants.)

3. Accept—and Celebrate—Human Differences

For interesting reading on diversity issues, you can turn to the **Media Awareness Network**, which examines the portrayal of diversity in the media, and to the **Canadian Centre for Multicultural Development and Documentation**, which explores multiculturalism in both Canadian and world contexts.

The **Canadian Council for Multicultural and Intercultural Education (CCMIE)** brings together provincial and territorial organizations to encourage public participation and respect for cultural diversity. The **Canadian Council of**

Christians and Jews (CCCJ) is a nonreligious organization dedicated to promoting cultural, racial and religious harmony among the people of Canada. The unique bridging role of the **CCCJ** is to represent the interests of all groups rather than any one segment of society. The **Canadian Ethnocultural Council** represents a cross-section of ethnocultural groups across Canada. Among its objectives is the preservation, enhancement and sharing of the cultural heritage of Canadians.

TEN DAYS for Global Justice, a Canadian inter-church coalition and network of community-based ecumenical groups, challenges dehumanizing and destructive forces, and promotes alternative models of society that put people and creation first. Each year there is a 10-day education and action campaign (usually in February) aimed at mobilizing Canadians to effect change on particular global justice issues. As well, many local groups, churches and other organizations carry out **TEN DAYS** education and actions year round. The Anglican, Lutheran, Presbyterian, Roman Catholic and United churches are among the groups involved.

The healthy-communities movement in Canada is an important source of ideas for bringing people together in new ways. One organization with links to communities across Canada and in the U.S. is the **Ontario Healthy Communities Coalition**. For fascinating ideas about urban neighbourhoods, check out the **Jane Jacobs, Ideas that Matter** web page. As well, the *New Internationalist* is well worth reading for its excellent coverage of development, social and community issues.

For those with a particular interest in the natural environment and conservation, there is the **Canadian Nature Federation**, which has affiliates in every province and links with dozens of local groups across the country. At the international level, through the **Earthwatch Institute**, many thousands of volunteers have taken part in active conservation projects all over the world, to improve the prospects for everything from black bears to turtles. **Earthwatch** has now set up a *Global Citizenship* program to link all of its volunteers and help them put their values into practice on a daily basis.

4.3 Not in My Back Yard

Is it wrong to fight for the places we love?

Ordinary people are increasingly demonstrating that they are prepared to protect the places where they live, protesting noisily—and often effectively—against those trying to impose new developments in their "back yards." Although this can make it a nightmare to get things done—even things that are very necessary—it should also be seen as a positive trend. Indeed, if people cannot protect the places that mean the most to them, what can they protect?

There goes the neighbourhood

The stronger our sense of community, the more likely we are to fight development proposals that may damage the character of our surroundings. But the very term "NIMBY"—short for "Not In My Back Yard"—is generally used in a critical context, with protesters accused of selfishly looking after their own neighbourhoods without thinking of the "needs" of the wider community.

The assumption is that the NIMBY form of environmentalism is somehow less altruistic, less pure, than campaigns for distant whales or rainforests. At one level this is true, but the catchphrase of environmentalism has long been "Think Globally, Act Locally." These down-to-earth campaigns can have a real impact on local—and sometimes national—policies, and encourage people to work together to improve their situation.

We have seen a boom in single-issue politics, which have proved very effective at achieving their goals—campaigns against new airports or airport expansions, for example. The real challenge, however, is not simply to kill off new projects but also to suggest how society can meet its needs more intelligently and with fewer unnecessary impacts. The best way to shoot down a proposed development is to come up with a better solution to the problem that it is meant to answer.

Problem neighbours

Airports, grocery stores and factories are just some of the commercial activities that can make unwelcome neighbours. Not only do they cause concerns about noise, pollution or explosion risks, but they also help to generate the huge volumes of traffic that account for such a high proportion of complaints.

But our problems may well be caused by ordinary individuals. Indeed, most people would not find it hard to come up with a local candidate for the "world's worst neighbour." Some neighbourhood disputes can become extremely bitter, evolving into long-running feuds. One effect is to erode community spirit and seriously undermine the quality of life and even the health of those involved or affected.

Noise is one of the most common sources of complaints against neighbours. This is not simply a problem of shouting or dogs barking, but of an ever-increasing range of noisy machines, among them radios, sound systems, mowers and power tools. Other controversial local issues can include litter, smells, graffiti, dog fouling (particularly in parks), pets invading neighbour's gardens, and—depending on whether people like trees or not—the planting, pruning or felling of trees. Property boundaries and parking cars on neighbourhood streets can also be sources of conflict.

Waste matters

One of the trickiest issues for local governments is getting rid of waste. We all produce it, but for most of us it is a case of "out of sight, out of mind" once we have replaced the garbage can lid. However, when we find that there is a proposal for some sort of waste facility, whether it's an incinerator or even a recycling plant, we can wake up with a vengeance—and a cause. In the end, there is no single ideal and practical way of dealing with all the waste we produce. We need a system that uses a combination of reuse, recycling and disposal options. To help focus on the real priorities, let's look at some of the most commonly used options—and some of the issues associated with them.

There is no single ideal and practical way of dealing with all the waste we produce.

Landfill: Most waste in most countries still goes into holes in the ground. But the number of available and appropriate sites is shrinking all the time, while growing numbers of people are prepared to fight to prevent new "dumps" in their area. Although landfill is becoming more expensive, it is unlikely to disappear. But the conditions imposed on this industry will become steadily tougher. Apart from dealing with the problem of leaching into waterways, smell and litter problems, landfill sites will need to capture the methane gas (page 28) produced as the waste rots, particularly since it is a powerful greenhouse gas.

Burning: Most people hate the idea of any sort of incinerator being located nearby. Although most incinerators now meet tough environmental standards, many of us worry about toxic emissions, such as dioxins (page 32), being released into the air and affecting our health, most particularly that of children. Some plants reclaim the heat and convert it into useful energy, but many do not. Incinerators produce a fair amount of greenhouse emissions, but—surprisingly—less than landfill sites.

Composting: A favourite with most environmentalists, composting is now beginning to be applied on an industrial scale. The idea is to break down organic waste—such as vegetable and garden waste—so that it can be used to fertilize gardens and fields. Of course, this method can only be used for waste that will rot, so metals, glass and plastics must be separated out. Also, heavy metals like cadmium can sometimes be found in the final compost, making it unsafe to use for growing food. Despite these problems, composting will be a growth industry of the future. It also contributes to fighting global warming by reducing methane.

Recycling: The basic idea with recycling is to recapture materials that would otherwise go to waste, returning them to some productive use. There has been huge progress in this area, but important barriers remain (see next section, "Recycling Questions"). This is another major growth sector for the future.

Reuse: We often assume that if something is recycled it is fine, but the first step—before discarding a product or material—should be to see if it can be repaired or reused. Ontario, for example, has laws requiring stores to provide returnable pop bottles; however, these laws are ignored in favour of recycling—a second-best choice. The more complex a product, the greater the savings to be made by reusing it rather than breaking it up for its components and materials. Unfortunately, however, many modern products are designed for disposability, particularly electronic goods. Often the simplest and cheapest option is to junk a product and buy another one. Designers—and their clients—need to ensure that we increasingly design both systems and products for easy reuse.

Recycling Questions

- ***What we do with our waste is crucial.* That said, recycling is rarely the easy option. Governments must create the right infrastructure, waste collectors need to have put systems in place, the public has to participate and industry must be able to use the waste materials produced in a profitable way. Given the fact that all these links in the chain must work together, it is hardly surprising that recycling has sometimes struggled to get going. The successes of greener countries like Denmark and Switzerland show what can be done. But for most countries perhaps the biggest hurdle is the debate over whether recycling actually makes sense in the first place. Myths abound. Below, we look at some of the most commonly asked questions, and try to set the record straight:**
- ***Is it economic?* For most urban communities where space is under pressure, recycling makes a great deal of sense. The real issue is not whether to recycle, but which materials, where and how. Recycling will clearly be more cost-competitive if landfill and incineration are expensive–and if it can benefit by operating on a large scale. Also important are the price of the raw materials that the waste might replace and the size of the markets for the products made from the recovered materials.**
- ***Does it save energy?* Recycling most resources does save energy, particularly if you take into account the whole process of mining (or growing) the raw material, processing it and distributing**

the final product. But we should never forget to do the energy analysis. Some forms of recycling are much more energy-efficient and profitable than others. Recycling aluminum cans, for example, saves a huge amount of energy because the raw material is energy-intensive to produce. But some other materials (like products made of mixed plastics and many low grades of paper) are simply not worth the effort.

- ***Does it save trees?*** **Recycling paper can save trees. The real issue is, what sort of trees? The paper industry argues that it plants more trees than it cuts down to make paper, so why bother saving them? First, this claim is often untrue–and even with planting, seedlings may not survive in large clearcuts. Moreover, plantations traditionally use a lot of pesticides. Also, these new plantations are generally very different than the old-growth forests–which may contain ancient trees and a great variety of wildlife–that they often replace. In general, the more virgin paper we use, the greater the risk that plantations will replace old-growth forests.**

The more virgin paper we use, the greater the risk of destroying old-growth forests.

- ***Do you use more energy getting to the recycling centre?*** **If you drive a large car a considerable distance solely for the purpose of depositing one bottle in a bottle bank, you would obviously not be saving resources. But most recycling centres are situated close to shopping centres and the extra weight of the waste being transported for recycling will use a negligible amount of extra gas.**
- ***Is it possible to recycle plastics?*** **Plastic manufacturers often promote the idea of burning plastics and reclaiming the energy, while playing up the difficulties of recycling. There certainly are real problems with separating plastics, particularly when there are different types of plastic in the same product, but new technology will help. Manufacturers must be encouraged to design products for easy recycling.**
- ***Are useful products made from recycled materials?*** **Without question. Think of the industries that are best at recycling, such as the gold industry: every speck of gold recovered (or at least 99.9999 per cent) is reused. Another valuable metal is aluminum, where the energy savings from recycling can be dramatic. Stylish furniture is now being made from recycled Tetrapak cartons. With paper, there is a wide and growing range of applications for recycled materials, from fine papers through to cardboard boxes. But much more needs to be done to make sure that useful applications and markets are developed for recycled materials.**

Signs of change

There are many reasons why people get involved in protesting, but one of the most important is the feeling that things are getting "out of control." Below we take a look at three areas where change has been particularly marked and where many protests have been focused.

The built environment

We take the buildings we pass every day for granted—until someone changes them or threatens to knock them down. It's a bit like losing a tooth: you really only notice when it is gone. But, whether it's the people next door putting up a new wall or adding on an attic, or some unknown company buying up buildings on the local main street and planning to put up offices or a new grocery store, changes in our built environment can be deeply unsettling.

At the same time, the pressures to develop are often considerable and intensifying. Expanding populations, increased rates of divorce (page 90), more people living on their own and more cars: these are some of the factors behind our requirement for new building and development. Here are some of the friction points where the strains can build—and where, as a result, protests often erupt.

Infrastructure projects: The scale and impacts of some megaprojects, such as new airports, sewage works or highways, make them both noticeable and unpopular. We may protest about the impacts, but at the same time our lifestyles—and many of our life choices—are helping to drive the change process.

Urban sprawl: Anyone who has known a particular part of the countryside for many years cannot fail to notice how fast things have changed. Few people would argue that all those changes have been for the better. The root causes are the same: more people wanting more space, more cars, more facilities.

Greenfield sites: Most of us can see that it makes more sense to build on land that has already had some development on it ("brownfield" sites), rather than dig up the countryside. But for developers it is far easier, and often cheaper, to start afresh—and there is always demand for houses in scenic locations. So the pressure on "greenfield" sites continues to grow.

Vicious cycles: As the climate becomes warmer, people use more air-conditioning, which uses energy, which helps drive global warming. Increasingly, we must break out of such cycles. One idea is to paint roofs with reflective coating and plant more trees and other forms of vegetation to cool the local environment. Studies of Los Angeles suggest that the result could be a 20 per cent cut in the need for air-conditioning, a better than 10 per cent cut in local smog, and massive cost savings.

Street lighting: Street lighting gives us a real sense of security. But the result is that it is increasingly difficult to get a clear view of the night sky. The stars are often obscured by "light pollution," a sickly orange haze. New forms of lighting are available that reduce the problem, while matching the energy efficiency of the offending sodium lamps—but they have yet to win widespread acceptance.

Our home and threatened land*

Most Canadians live in cities and towns, but we like to think of all of our vast land as our back yard. Our breathtaking natural landscapes have been a source of spiritual sustenance and recreational opportunities for generations, yet they are under intense and growing pressure. Canada is losing one square kilometre of wilderness every hour to logging, mining, agriculture, and urban and tourism developments. At this point, less than six percent of Canada is legally protected from industrial development. Over one-third of these protected wilderness lands are found within the nation's 38 national parks and national park reserves. Conservation groups are urging governments to expand the system of national parks and protected areas to ensure that a representative sample of each of our

**Statistics and facts on Canadian wildlife sourced from the Canadian Nature Federation and World Wildlife Fund Canada.*

country's natural regions is preserved for future generations. The spiritual and aesthetic values of wilderness are readily recognized by most people. In the long term, however, even our physical survival and that of our children depends on a healthy natural world, which includes intact wild places. In addition to protecting designated areas, we need to use the lands and waters outside the protected areas in a sustainable way.

Canada is losing wilderness at the rate of one square kilometre every hour.

An integral part of the richness and beauty of the wild landscapes of the earth are the animals and birds these lands support. But human population growth and industrialization keep encroaching on these lands. In what looks like a war for space on the planet, the wild animals are losing out to the people. In Canada, for example, loss and degradation of habitat is estimated to be responsible for more than 75 percent of the danger to species. Much of this book is about reversing the loss of animal habitats, so that there will be a healthy future for all species—including us humans.

Canada's farmlands are also under siege. This is worrisome, given that 94 per cent of our land is not suitable for farming. Some of our best agricultural land continues to be lost at an alarming rate to erosion, salinization and urban sprawl.

Ninety-four per cent of Canada's land cannot be farmed, while our best agricultural land continues to be lost.

In some residential areas, mines and quarries are seen as blots on the landscape. Canadians may recognize the economic contribution of the mining industry, but they also want companies to clean up after themselves. In British Columbia, for example, there has been public outrage for decades over an abandoned copper mine mill that scars the face of Mount Sheer, an otherwise spectacularly beautiful setting on Howe Sound, located 45 kilometres north of Vancouver.[17] In Ontario, meanwhile, regional municipal councillors say Caledon's gravel pits are a blight on the landscape and the mining companies should be forced to rehabilitate the sites after they have been shut down.[18]

That said, urban sprawl remains one of the most serious threats to the landscape. The pace of new home construction seems set to grow as people live longer and populations around urban centres continue to increase. More homes mean more water, more energy, more hospitals, more schools and more cars. And—unless the laws of physics are repealed or heavy eco-taxes introduced—more cars mean more roads.

As people want to make ever-greater use of the land, so the need for more facilities—including holiday resorts, marinas and golf courses—inevitably grows. Even where there are no roads, the impacts can grow as more people walk through—or, dramatically worse, take to the countryside in off-road vehicles.

In fact, we don't even need to visit the countryside to have an impact on it. If you use a cellular phone, for example, you are part of the pressure that is driving the construction of new communication towers (page 178). (And, by the way, the jury is still out on whether cellular phones are safe. A recent *Lancet* article recommended they be sold with a health warning.)

Interestingly, however, one unexpected effect of modern communication technologies may be the end of the era of skyscrapers. With teleworking (page 188) and virtual offices, the pressures to build skywards should decline. Powerful people may still be tempted by the sheer visibility of skyscrapers[19], but in future companies may put more effort into improving their websites than into building massive towers.

Culture and traditions

Buildings and landscapes may be difficult to conserve, but our culture and traditions are often even harder to protect—partly because they need to be a living part of our lives if they are not to die.

Few of us want to drown in history, but a sense of continuity is important. Families often develop their own traditions, around Christmas, for example. These can be key in developing our sense of who we are. Outside the home, buildings and landscapes—and not just the highly valued cultural ones—are important in providing a physical framework for our lives, which is why we are so shocked when they are destroyed.

Wherever we live, it is important to honour and renew our contacts with the less obvious parts of our past. This is not simply a question of placing flowers on war memorials or beautification projects, but also of the active exploration of local history and architecture—and the conservation, celebration and revival of old crafts. Celebrations and festivals can all help build our sense of community—and ensure that our feelings for the places where we live, and for those we share them with, are given positive expression.

Yet, around the world, the evidence suggests that local diversity—be it biological, cultural or economic—is under enormous pressure. Tourism, for example, is usually hailed as a blessing when it first arrives in a new area, because of the money it promises. But such is its nature, and its scale in popular areas, that it suffers from a modern (and reverse) version of the Midas Touch. It often seems that everything mass tourism touches is commercialized and, as a result, cheapened.

Happily, there are some signs that those who were fans of yesterday's developments can become today's NIMBYs—and may even become tomorrow's fully fledged greens.

The recent completion of a fixed link between the mainland and Prince Edward Island came only after 10 years of struggle between pro- and antilink Islanders. The antilink fishers, environmentalists and academics argue that if the new bridge brings the increased tourism touted by its promoters, it will end up spoiling the serenity that attracted many of those tourists in the first place.[20] Well, the pro-link business, tourism and labour groups won the day, but the impact on PEI's environment and way of life remains to be seen. The link promoters may one day find themselves joining the NIMBYs and the greens in trying to limit the impacts of tourism.

On the other side of the country, the federal government has placed a moratorium on further development in Banff National Park, in an attempt to restore the threatened ecology of this world-renowned natural treasure. But two Banff-based conservation groups have sued the government for not going far enough and, in particular, for exempting from the moratorium a convention centre that Canadian Pacific Hotels wants to build at Lake Louise.

Not In My Back Yard

✔Citizen 2000 Checklist

1. Stand Up for Your Local Community and Its Environment

The **Canadian Environmental Network** can put you in touch with local groups dealing with issues directly affecting your community. The **Canadian Environmental Law Association (CELA)** will act at hearings and in courts in Ontario on behalf of citizens or citizens' groups unable to afford legal assistance. The **Canadian Nature Federation (CNF)** lists over 100 affiliated local naturalists' clubs, which offer opportunities to learn about, protect and enhance the environment around your home, school, community and region. Each provincial affiliate of **CNF** also lists local clubs. **EcoAction 2000** (formerly the **Action 21 Community Funding Program**) is an **Environment Canada** initiative to encourage Canadians to take the actions needed to create and sustain healthy environments in their communities. The **Canada Trust–Friends of the Environment Community Fund** supports local environmental initiatives. **Sierra Club** has chapters across the country and offers activist training workshops as well as expert help on local issues.

PITCH-IN CANADA involves millions of volunteers in various action programs, from initiating recycling and composting programs to cleaning up and beautifying local communities, streams and wilderness areas. Most of these programs are funded and implemented locally, with **PITCH-IN CANADA** providing information and other resources. **PITCH-IN CANADA** is a founding member of the **Environmentally Sound Packaging Coalition of Canada (ESP)**.

Healthy communities networks offer opportunities to get involved, and their websites have many useful links to other relevant organizations across the country. Among these are the **B.C. Healthy Communities Network**, the **Manitoba Healthy Communities Network**, the **Ontario Healthy Communities Coalition** and the **Sustainable Communities Info Service Databank** (based in Nova Scotia).

With its primary office in Canada, the **International Council for Local Environmental Initiatives** serves as an international clearinghouse on environmental initiatives and techniques being implemented at the local level.

For stimulating and inspiring ideas about the role of neighbourhoods in maintaining the quality of urban life, read Jane Jacobs' 1961 classic, *The Death and Life of Great American Cities*. Since the 1960s, Jacobs has lived in Toronto, where her books and community involvement were celebrated in the 1997 **Jane Jacobs: Ideas That Matter** conference. A report on the fascinating discussions that took place is still available (see the "Jane Jacobs" entry in the Directory at the back of this book). *The Neighborhood Works: Building Alternative Visions for the City*, the magazine of the Chicago-based **Center for Neighborhood Technology**, tells the stories of organizers who fight incinerators, plant community gardens, battle for jobs, build housing and make themselves heard. **Citizens for Local Democracy** was originally formed to oppose the amalgamation of five municipalities into the "megacity" of Toronto, but the group is now linked with a number of other urban and rural groups opposed to the closing of neighbourhood schools and other amalgamation schemes. They also have links with groups involved in neighbourhood and urban issues in other provinces and in the U.S.

Such groups as **The Preservation of Agricultural Lands Society (PALS)**, **Preservation of Agriculture and Living Space of Sundre**, **Préservation Environnement Pierrefonds** and the **Coalition on the Niagara Escarpment** work to protect agricultural lands and green spaces.

2. Stand Up for Spaces and Species

Habitat protection and saving endangered species of birds, fish and animals from extinction go hand in hand. **World Wildlife Fund Canada (WWF)**, the **Canadian Nature Federation** and other conservation groups are calling for protection of natural areas representing all of our natural regions, both lands and waters. Each year, **WWF** grades the provincial, territorial and federal governments on their progress towards completing this goal. A crucial part of reaching the goal will be protection and expansion of our national parks. But it will take strong public support and pressure to compel our politicians to take action to preserve our nation's dwindling wilderness. The **CNF** has produced *A Citizen Action Guide to Completing the National Park System* to help Canadians learn about and participate in the campaign to protect representative ecosystems across the country. The **CNF** is also working with the **Canadian Wildlife Federation**, the **Sierra Club of Canada**, and the mining, pulp and paper, and agriculture industries to advocate a strong federal Endangered Species Act. On the West Coast, **Greenpeace Canada** has been a very effective force in protecting B.C.'s temperate rainforests.

The **Nature Conservancy of Canada**, along with the provincial land trusts, plays an extremely important role in preserving natural habitats across the country. The **Conservancy** accepts land donations or funds for land purchases and then manages the properties in perpetuity to preserve the natural plant and animal life. It will also strike agreements with landowners setting out legally binding restrictions on development and land use. Since its founding in 1962, the organization has secured over 700 properties, through donations of land or money from private citizens, businesses, communities and governments. The **Conservancy** also works with provincial land trusts across the country. The organization now protects more than 546 000 hectares (almost the size of Prince Edward Island) of forest, coastal habitats, wetlands and grasslands across all provinces.

3. Reduce, Reuse, Recycle and Buy Recycled Products

The recycling council in your province is listed under "Recycling" in the Directory. These organizations produce practical guides on practising the 3Rs (Reduce, Reuse, Recycle) in the home, school and workplace. Many municipalities throughout Canada also distribute excellent 3R tips, along with handy information pieces on how to make the best use of Blue Box and other curbside recycling programs. Many also distribute backyard composters. The **Green Communities Association** helps homes, businesses, institutions and governments to save energy and water, reduce waste, prevent pollution, and protect and enhance green space, habitat and ecosystems.

If your community or shopping area doesn't have recycling facilities, ask your local council if they will install them–grocery stores are also worth asking, as they frequently have potential sites in their parking lots. Remember to drive the market for 100% recycled products. Insist on 100% post-consumer paper at your school or workplace.

4. Celebrate Your Home Patch

Heritage and historical societies work to preserve and protect the built, natural and cultural heritage of communities. Heritage foundations are sponsored by provincial governments across Canada, either as distinct not-for-profit agencies or as programs within such departments as tourism, culture and recreation, environment or natural resources. Contact your provincial government for details. Historical societies play a similar role at the local and county level. You can help such organizations in your community by volunteering your time, making a donation or touring a heritage site.

A wide range of campaigning groups promotes local or seasonal produce. Among these are **FarmFolk/CityFolk**, (based in Vancouver), **Earth to Table** (Calgary) and **Knives & Forks** (Southern Ontario). Organic retailers across the country tend to emphasize local and seasonal produce.

5. Help Others to Protect Their Own Home Patch

Ecotourism has been described as travel to natural areas that fosters environmental understanding, appreciation and conservation and that sustains the culture and well-being of local people. Some ecotour operators servicing regions in Canada: **Adventures on the Grand** (Ontario's Grand

River), **Alberta North**, **Green Planet Tour Company** (Niagara Region) and, in British Columbia, **Tzoonie Outdoor Adventures**, **Kokanee Ecotours Ltd.**, and **Pedals & Paddles**. The **Aboriginal Tourism Authority Inc.** is a not-for-profit organization dedicated to promoting, preserving, protecting and celebrating the integrity of aboriginal tourism in Western Canada.

For international tourism, **Eco Travel Services (ETS)**, a California company, links clients with "green" tour operators through a computer database. **ETS** also publishes a free newsletter, *Eco Travel News*, which carries reports and discussions about the environmental and ethical aspects of tourism.

Wherever you travel, make sure the operator you choose is environmentally and socially responsible.

4.4 Greening the Home

How can we pull out all the stops?

If we are going to take effective green action, the best place to start is at home. Whether we live in a caravan or a castle, a mobile home or a mansion, our daily life results in a range of environmental impacts. But, more positively, we have direct personal control over the resources we use and can enormously reduce our impact through the product and lifestyle choices we make.

Given the complexity of many of these issues, we need better information to make the right choices. But as we make these choices, we can all help send powerful signals to government agencies and big business about the sort of world we want to live in.

The hole in the ozone layer is an issue that has illustrated the tremendous power of the consumer in pushing for environmental change. Scientists, governments and campaigners all played key roles, but ordinary people signalled their concern by supporting "ozone-friendly" products and boycotting problem products. Our consumer choices can have a big impact. Unfortunately, however, market surveys show that people—both consumers and producers—often want to do the right thing, but they are more likely to say they are doing it than to be actually doing it.

So in this section, we look at some of the barriers that prevent people from being "greener" or more socially responsible, and at what can be done to remove them.

The barriers

So what are the really important barriers? Let's focus on the following 10:

Need: Most of us would admit that we sometimes buy products that we don't really need. If, for example, we buy a product that we have not really used or appreciated, then every environmental or social impact of its production, use or disposal is a price being paid with little or no return. Coming up with a universal definition of what is "necessary" or "unnecessary" is impossible, but it is a bit easier if we focus on our own needs. Don't buy what you don't need.

Demand: Every time we buy products we encourage retailers and manufacturers to believe that there is a demand that must be satisfied. Although responsible companies invest heavily in reducing the impact of the products they sell, this is not true of all—and even well-designed products have some impacts.

Information: Tracking down the "green" credentials of most products is still an uphill struggle. And often even the so-called experts are in dispute over what the issues are—and about what the best choice might be. Next, there is the issue of whether to trust the manufacturer's claims, since companies obviously want to present their products in the most appealing way. Although advertising is controlled in many countries, there is also the problem of exaggerated, misleading or false claims.

Labelling: Even where there is agreement, and the product labels are up-to-date, truthful and helpful, we may not have the time or energy needed to understand the issues and weigh up the options. There is a growing number of independent labelling schemes, but they do not yet cover a very wide range of products (page 127).

Trust: We tend to assume that if there was a real problem with a product, it would have been removed from the shelves—or that responsible companies would withdraw problem products or that law-makers would stop them from being sold. But, unfortunately, this is not always the case, perhaps because there is not yet agreement on the seriousness of a problem or because alternatives are seen to be equally damaging. Often, too, it is because there are strong vested interests in keeping a product on the market. Companies may have invested millions of dollars and want to protect their assets.

Availability and cost: We take for granted the fact that green products are available, but often they are hard to find. Green products are also considered to be more expensive, although this is not necessarily the case. Some companies do try to exploit our green intentions by overcharging, but one certain way to be greener is to buy less—and this costs less, too. Energy and water efficiency usually saves money, although some measures—such as installing double-glazed windows or fitting energy-efficient lightbulbs—require an initial investment before there is a payback. For other products such as greener detergents or recycled toilet paper, cost should not be a barrier. But there are some greener or more ethical products that are more expensive. Organic and fair trade products, for example, require more labour and inevitably cost more.

Competition: Companies may not wish to "green" their products for fear that they would lose out competitively. But if you buy greener products you will be making green improvements worthwhile—and ensuring that products will be available and cheaper, too.

Convenience: With more of us working and increasingly time-pressured, few of us are prepared to go far out of our way for the sake of ethical concerns. The demand for convenience has driven the huge growth in demand for such products as microwave ovens and convenience food. This issue also erupts when it comes to such areas as sorting and recycling waste (page 105). We will look at diapers and clothes dryers later in this section.

Mind-sets: One of the biggest barriers that we face in making progress towards a greener world is our throwaway mind-set. The whole thrust of modern consumer culture is toward disposability as we create ever-larger waste mountains. We make little effective use of waste materials, adopt new materials that do not break down in nature, forget about the possibility of repairing products, and fail to invest enough in the systems needed to recover and recycle waste. Later in this section, we look at the effects of this throwaway culture in the world of clothes and shoes (pages 122–127). The throwaway mind-set has been *learned*. For example, the green garbage bag is a Canadian invention. Initially, consumers rejected a product that they could only use once and throw out. As a result, garbage collectors used to dump the garbage and leave the bag on the curb!

One of the biggest barriers we face in making progress toward a greener world is our throw-away mind-set.

Image: For some people, the whole business of asking for organic produce—or taking waste to the recycling centre—is just a bit too, well, *conspicuously* green. There is also the concern that "green" products offer poorer performance overall than their competitors. Really, who wants to go downmarket—and possibly pay for the privilege? The fact is that some greener products do cost more to produce and to buy, but often they offer qualities that people are prepared to pay for.

So, having looked at some of the barriers stopping us from living greener lifestyles, let's now look at what can be done in relation to some specific product areas and consumer choices. The following sections are designed to help prioritize the actions that we should all have on our "to do" lists.

Beneath the froth

Two French companies have started to make clothes that need to be washed less often, because the materials are impregnated with chemicals that kill bacteria generated by sweat and odour. They have started with socks, underwear and sportswear. Good luck to them. Although they predict a rapidly expanding market for "bioactive" garments, for most people, freshly laundered clothes sound more appealing!

Laundry blues

Looking back, it is clear that the introduction of washing machines reduced the amount of work involved in washing a load of clothes. But, by making it more convenient to achieve cleanliness and hygiene, it also boosted the number of times clothes were washed. So it's quite possible to spend as much time at the chore today as earlier generations did.

This is an interesting example of the way the choices we make every day determine how much impact we create. The decision to choose ever-greater levels of cleanliness by washing more often results in more environmental impacts because more energy, water and detergent are used. If we had better information, perhaps we would make some of these choices more carefully.

In Canada, the EnerGuide labelling system, which rates the energy efficiency of appliances, has been one of the factors persuading washing-machine manufacturers to carry out some improvements in the energy and water efficiency of machines. But washing machines still account for 16 per cent of energy consumed by new electrical appliances (including lighting) in a typical Canadian household. The clothes dryer accounts for another 12 per cent. Taken together, the washing and drying functions consume about as much energy as lighting.

The most significant factor in cutting the amount of electricity used in washing clothes is the temperature of the water. Washing-powder and washing-machine manufacturers have been working together to reduce wash temperatures, with some success. Whereas 30 years ago most washing was done at boiling temperature (100°C), now it is done at between 30°C and 50°C. This downward trend is likely to continue, although at some point it will mean washing machines will have to be radically redesigned. Once this happens, it will still take between 10 and 15 years for the full benefits to come through, as people slowly replace their existing machines.

Those who know this area well note that the Japanese already wash their clothes in cold water. So why don't we? The answer is that, although they also have different types of washing machines and detergents to enable them to do this, they also have a different approach to laundry. In most Japanese homes, space is a major problem. So they don't let the laundry pile up—they wash every day. Because the dirt has less time to work its way in, the clothes are easier to clean without hot water. The Japanese also tend to soak clothes more, scrub particularly grimy parts and use extra bleach. Put all of these factors together and the overall savings in energy and water may be much less than we might imagine.

Another area of debate focuses on which ingredients have what impact—and on the question whether concentrated detergents offer any real benefits. If you use the correct dosage of a concentrated product, it may not cost you any less, but it will certainly mean that you need less packaging and less energy to transport the detergent. You need less space in your home to store the products and, because you use less chemicals, you also cause less water pollution.

Let's take a look at some of the issues associated with the sorts of ingredients you will see listed on the labels of detergent products. If you want to cut the impact of your laundry, don't wash clothes too frequently, wash a full load when you use the machine, and use a super-compact detergent—which will contain enzymes, enabling you to cut down on both energy and packaging.

Hung out to dry

When the washing is done, many people still hang it out to dry in the wind and—hopefully—sun. Even with this free service, the number of people with dryers is growing all the time, to the point where, in North America at least, you might be considered deprived without one. To be fair, dryers do soften clothes as well as dry them. And there are real advantages for people who lack the space to dry their washing. On the other hand, most people should not find it too great an inconvenience to manage without one—or to use these machines only when weather conditions prevent drying. The energy savings would be considerable.

Taken to the dry cleaners

Given the powerful chemical smell you encounter in most dry-cleaning shops, it should come as little surprise that some of the chemicals used by this industry are potentially hazardous. One of the more ozone-unfriendly dry-cleaning agents, CFC-113, has been phased out in the richer regions, although it can still be used in countries such as Russia.

Perchloroethylene (or "perc") is by far the most widely used dry-cleaning chemical. It has the advantage of not attacking the ozone layer, but has contaminated underground water in some areas, may be carcinogenic, and there has been concern about possible links with miscarriage in cleaning-industry workers. It is also quite volatile and accumulates in fatty substances. An ice-cream shop located next to a dry cleaner's could well be selling perc-contaminated ice cream.

We should support the efforts of those who are trying to develop "environment-friendly" cleaning schemes and opting for less harmful chemicals. One new technology—"wet cleaning"—may emerge as a greener alternative. This uses controlled agitation and finely measured quantities of water, detergents and additives to achieve the same effect as dry cleaning, but manages to do all of this without the shrinkage we would normally expect when water is used. So far, however, it is not as efficient as solvent systems in cleaning oily or

Table 4.1: WHAT'S IN THE WASH?

Ingredient	***Function***	***Issues***
Surfactants	Make water more efficient as a cleaning agent.	Have caused foaming in rivers in the past, but this problem was largely solved some time ago. Nowadays, they biodegrade rapidly—before they get through the sewage system. Tend to be made from petrochemicals, but can also be made from plants such as coconut, palm, linseed, soya and oilseed Trape.
Builders (e.g., phosphates)	Make the water softer and more alkaline, to enable the surfactants to work better.	Phosphates in waste water cause eutrophication, which allows algae to bloom, depriving the water of oxygen and killing fish. Phosphates in water come in equal measure from detergents, agriculture and sewage. So an effective solution is to ensure sewage works have "phosphate strippers." Although zeolite, the key phosphate alternative, does not cause eutrophication, it still has an environmental impact because it adds bulk to sewage sludge. NTA, also used as an alternative in some countries, has been banned in some jurisdictions because of concerns that it might cause cancer.
Enzymes (the biocomponent in "biological" products)	Digest stains caused by protein (e.g., blood or chocolate), starch (e.g., potato or flour) or fat (e.g., oils or lipstick).	Enzymes, contrary to long-standing concerns, do not cause allergies. In rare circumstances, they may aggravate some existing skin conditions. Overall, however, they bring major environmental benefits—because they help detergents to remove stains at lower temperatures, saving energy. Once in the environment, they break down very fast.
Bleaches	Remove stains and prevent yellowing in laundry.	Residues of the bleaches added to mainstream washing powders go down the drain. Contrary to the assumptions of some people, these are not part of the chlorine cycle.
Optical whiteners	Make the clothes look whiter and colours brighter.	Not major pollutants. The often-repeated claim that they can lead to skin sensitization has no basis in fact.
Preservatives	Need to be used in some liquid laundry products.	Preservatives are not normally used in most detergents because their formulations do not encourage bacterial growth.

greasy stains, and may crack the materials (particularly acetate and viscose) used in some "structured" garments. Some dry cleaners in Canada have expensive perc-recycling within their dry-cleaning system.

For the moment, the best option is still—wherever possible—to avoid clothes that have to be dry-cleaned. Longer term, fashion designers must learn to use materials that look attractive but which do not require expensive special care. Whereas today's smart dressers have to shop around for clothes that do not need dry cleaning, tomorrow we must hope that it will be the textile designers who will be smart—helping to develop and popularize materials that can be thrown into the washing machine and come out looking like new.

Watt guzzlers

Our homes now contain a wide range of energy-guzzling equipment—and plans are afoot to persuade us to have many more such items. If you believe the futurologists, we will soon have houses that follow the weather and adjust the windows, control everything from the baths to the stereo, and turn on the rice cooker when we are on our way home from work. More, the toilets will analyse our blood pressure and urine, and wash our bottoms to boot. Let's focus, however, on some of the conveniences that already exist in our homes.

Fridge world

They hum inconspicuously in the corners of our kitchens, yet few domestic appliances have so transformed our lives as fridges and freezers. Indeed, most of us now take them pretty much for granted—until they break down. Behind the scenes, however, fridge and freezer manufacturers have been under intense pressure to make their products more energy-efficient. Huge advances have been made, but there is still a long way to go. In the U.S., the government has legislated for a 30 per cent increase in energy efficiency. Once achieved, this should save 25 billion kilowatt hours of electricity every year, equal to the power generated by eight large power stations.

But there have also been new issues to worry about. Ozone-eating CFCs (chlorofluorocarbons) were widely used by the industry in insulation materials and cooling systems. Each molecule of CFC can destroy over 100 000 molecules of the earth's protective ozone layer, leading to increased risks of sunburn, eye cataracts and cancer. Worse still, CFCs are major contributors to the greenhouse effect (page 28).

To begin with, the industry argued that CFCs were not a problem. Then they accepted that they might be, but argued that there was no alternative. Next, as the pressures on the industry continued to mount, they began to switch to HCFCs and HFCs. These are less ozone-depleting, but are significant greenhouse gases, and are also being targeted for elimination by campaigning organizations.

Greenpeace then forced a growing number of manufacturers to produce completely ozone-friendly models (with reduced greenhouse effect, too) by launching a campaign highlighting an alternative technology, based on hydrocarbons. This is an excellent example of a successful campaign focusing on solutions, not just problems. But CFCs will still be used in fridges in some parts of the world; in China, for example, their use will be allowed until 2010. And HFCs are likely to take even longer to phase out.

Let there be light

The incandescent filament bulb is 70 times brighter than a candle and lasts 100 times longer. But modern lighting still consumes a great deal of electricity: around 30 per cent of household electricity use in Canada. So the industry has developed compact fluorescent bulbs, which are five times more energy-efficient and last ten times longer.

How many lightbulbs does it take to change a planet? One. A 13-watt compact fluorescent bulb gives the same amount of light as a 60-watt incandescent bulb and lasts 10 times longer.

Strangely, however, most households do not have a single fluorescent light bulb. Fully 15 years after their introduction, these amazing bulbs only account for a few per cent of bulb sales. Why is this? There are two main reasons: availability and cost. For those aware of the benefits of compact fluorescents, they must go to hardware or ecology stores, and generally can't find them on grocery-store shelves with other bulbs. Second, even though they work out cheaper than ordinary lightbulbs over the long term, in the short term they are much more expensive to buy. This "first-cost barrier" also works against purchases of more energy-efficient appliances like fridges. But these purchases *do* pay their own way.

Other concerns have focused on the colour of the light they produce and their ability to marry up with existing fittings. Those who saw early long-life bulbs still remember the stark white light that they produced, but now there are much warmer options. The fittings problem has also been addressed, so long-life bulbs can be inserted into ordinary sockets and work with many different types of shade.

On the environmental front, a key concern was over the mercury content of fluorescent lightbulbs. Interestingly, however, the amount of mercury in compact fluorescent bulbs is more than offset by the mercury that would otherwise be released into the environment by power stations if a normal bulb had been used.[21] So the overall conclusion is that these bulbs are well worth the investment.

Battery power

Until recent years, household batteries were not a happy story, environmentally speaking. Not only did they contain toxic materials, but they were neither rechargeable nor recycled. As a result, some analysts concluded that batteries were not only polluting, but produced 50 per cent less energy than it took to make them!

In Canada at least, the story has moved much closer to a happy ending. As of 1997, the household battery industry had eliminated mercury from alkaline batteries and discontinued the sale of button-sized mercuric oxide batteries. As a result, mercury entering the solid waste stream in Canada from the sale of household batteries has been reduced to zero from 75 tonnes in 1968. As well, the industry has set up the Canada-wide *Charge Up to Recycle!* program, enabling consumers to recycle used rechargeable nickel-cadmium (Ni-Cd) batteries. To the industry's credit, all of these actions have been voluntary.

Home improvements

Look in the right places and you will find evidence that near-miracles are possible in terms of greening homes. High in the Rocky Mountains, for example, environmentalist Amory Lovins has built a house that is so well insulated that he can grow avocados, bananas, mangoes, papaya and other exotic fruit even when the snow is lying thick outside, without a heating system.

Thanks to the building's super-insulation, 99 per cent of its energy comes from the sun. Among the most important features of the building are its "super-windows," which contain a heavy gas, like argon or krypton. This means that they can insulate as well as six, nine or even twelve sheets of glass. As far as the ordinary home is concerned, properly installed double-glazing can also help save a good deal of energy and greatly reduce outside noise. But the payback can take a long time—and in poorly insulated homes significant energy savings can often be made simply by draught-proofing around windows and doors.

Remember that heating is responsible for over two-thirds of the energy consumption in the typical home. Key actions here are to ensure regular servicing of furnaces and boilers, the insulation of walls (particularly cavity walls), and the installation—or topping up—of attic insulation.

Between 15 per cent and 50 per cent of heat loss from a house is through draughts.

Out of the woods

Tropical hardwoods, including mahogany and teak, are attractive and extremely long-lasting—but the felling and extraction of these trees has resulted in widespread destruction of the world's rainforests (page 38). This issue has been hugely controversial—and deservedly so. But, sadly, even though many people know there is a real problem, it has not been easy to get action. The reasons for this are many and various.

So, for example, the causes of deforestation are complex (whether you look at the tropical regions or places like Siberia); the market for tropical hardwoods is well established, but not structured in ways that help deliver greener products; in the past, the trail from forest to superstore was particularly difficult to track; the demand for tropical hardwoods is growing rapidly in parts of the world where environmental issues are seen as less urgent; and the greener alternatives have been hard to find and trust.

More positively, new labelling schemes are evolving—and more wood is available that has been certified as coming from well-managed forests. Indeed, it is now possible to buy certified teak that has been grown in plantations. We should also do everything we can to encourage the locally grown hardwoods, if sustainably logged, and to boost the success of good labelling and certification initiatives (page 127).

As far as alternatives are concerned, one way to replace hardwoods is to use board made out of wood (including thinnings and scrap), bound together with glues or "binders." MDF (or medium-density fibreboard) has been one of the "wonder products" of recent years and is used to make everything from furniture to wardrobes. It is also been a favourite with do-it-yourself enthusiasts. More recently, however, alarm bells started ringing.[22]

The problems flowed from the fact that MDF is made by mixing together wood dust and scrap with a resin, formaldehyde. As with some other woods, the clouds of fine dust released when sawing MDF are hazardous to health. There is evidence that people working with the material over a long period have a higher-than-usual incidence of nose, throat and lung cancer. There are also concerns that the formaldehyde smell in MDF may contribute to "sick building syndrome."

The MDF industry points out that formaldehyde occurs naturally—and often in higher concentrations—in produce like tomatoes and kippers. It also says that the evidence on cancers is open to different interpretation. But if you are planning to saw up MDF, or any other timber likely to create a dusty atmosphere, use a face mask. And, if you really want to play safe, ask for low- or zero-formaldehyde MDF boards.

The boom in MDP and oriented strand board (OSB) has also led to increased logging of Canada's forests.

Behind the gloss

Paints hardly seem to be a major threat to the natural world—and are certainly much safer than they used to be. But their manufacture, use and disposal do raise a number of important environmental and health issues.

Lead: Lead pigments are no longer permitted in paint, but were commonly used prior to 1960. Ingesting even small quantities of lead paint can be a serious health hazard, particularly for children and pregnant women. Exposure can be caused by chipped paint getting into household dust or, more likely, by the sanding or damaging of paintwork during renovation. If you face this problem, the paint industry has now produced detailed guidelines on what to do (see Citizen 2000 Checklist, page 128).

Solvents: Most paint is based on hydrocarbon solvents, which are designed to evaporate. As a general rule, the glossier the paint the greater the quantities of solvent involved. These solvents cause smog and, it turns out, can also harm the central nervous system, causing headaches, loss of coordination and tremors. Sufficient exposure, significantly beyond the levels most domestic users would be exposed to, can even cause brain damage. In Denmark, "painter dementia" is a recognized industrial disease. Happily, water-based paint products now offer a much safer alternative for both our health and the environment.

Pigments: The most commonly used pigment in paints is titanium dioxide. This is used primarily as a whitener and to make the paints more opaque, so that less paint is then needed to cover any given area. The production of titanium dioxide can be environmentally damaging—although there are considerable differences between the standards of different manufacturers. As the biggest customer for titanium dioxide, the paint industry has a great deal of influence on their suppliers and can stipulate higher standards. This is another area where consumer pressure and eco-labelling can help.

Disposal: The best way of disposing of paint is to use it for its intended purpose. However, it is unusual to finish a paint job with no waste paint left. Pouring paint down the drain can contaminate the groundwater, mess up the sewage system and even help to contaminate drinking water supplies. So if you are using large quantities, check with your municipal waste department regarding proper disposal. Some communities have occasional household hazardous waste collection days and/or depots where you can drop off such materials. If you have paint left over, see if neighbours or community groups can use it. Remember: in some regions there are organizations that collect and use waste paint for community purposes.

Water works

Literally on tap wherever we turn in the rich world, water—particularly clean water—is a resource that is increasingly in short supply (page 23). And there is a great deal more we could do to improve water efficiency in our homes. Effective water-saving measures include the following:

Fixing leaks: Check taps, tanks and hoses. Even a slow drip or leak can waste more than 450 litres (100 gallons) of water a week.[23]

Metering: Free resources are most likely to be wasted. Where water is metered, and people pay for what they use, water consumption usually falls significantly.

Water-efficient appliances: If your water is

metered, replacing showerheads or taps with water-efficient models will often pay back within a year. Other types of equipment that are worth checking for water-efficiency include washing machines and dishwashers. Remember, when you waste hot water, you are wasting both water and energy.

Grey water: Waste water is often referred to as "grey water." Using this water for purposes where "clean" water is not needed can be a great saver.

Washing: Taking a shower typically uses less than half the amount of water used when having a bath, although—not surprisingly—high-pressure showers use rather more water. Keep showers short!

Toilets: About one-third of the average household water consumption is flushed down the toilet. Given that most of us are flushing away good clean drinking water, this is very wasteful. Low-flush toilets can be two to three times more efficient. In New York, where they have been installed on a fairly large scale, it is estimated that the city has saved 227 million litres (50 million gallons) of water a day—which helped it get through one of the worst droughts on record.[24]

Gardens: Average sprinklers and hose-pipes get through about 10 litres (2.2 gallons) of water a minute. Talk to most gardeners and their vision of water conservation is a mixture of brown lawns and drooping or dying plants. But this really need not be the case.

Measures that can be taken include the following: using water-barrels to capture rainwater; installing drip irrigation systems or soaker hoses; and—most effectively—designing your garden to minimize the need for water, for example by using native and drought-tolerant plants.

In the nursery

Safety issues in relation to toys are usually well regulated, but new issues do surface. For example, PVC (polyvinyl chloride) plastic has been under pressure from environmentalists for years because of dioxins produced when it is burned. But recent concerns, raised by a Danish study, focused on the presence of phthalates, used in PVC (page 30), in products such as teething rings and other children's toys. In November 1998, Health Canada issued an advisory to parents and caregivers of very young children regarding soft vinyl toys designed to be mouthed (chewed or sucked). The department's risk assessment concluded that a health risk stemmed from the phthalate plasticizer used to make the vinyl soft.

PVC toys are also under attack because of the levels of lead and cadmium they contain. In some cases, according to Greenpeace, the amount that could be ingested exceeds legal limits.

Changing diapers

Few people are as pressed for time as those with babies to look after. As a result, convenience is usually at a premium. Once disposable diapers were introduced, they effectively took over the market, leaving the nondisposables as niche products.

The disposables vs. nondisposables controversy has been one of the most charged in recent environmental history. So in Table 4.2 we review some of the issues raised by both types of diaper. The overall conclusion seems to be that neither option is a clear leader in environmental terms. On balance, nondisposables win out in terms of less raw material impacts (forestry for paper pulp), less solid waste, and cost, while disposables win out on convenience, less environmental impacts from washing, and energy savings. But disposables are supposed to be rinsed in the toilet before disposal to remove any feces. However, very few people do this even though feces do not belong in landfills. Disposables also help to reduce diaper rash, although chemicals used to produce them may irritate sensitive skins.

So which issues are most important to you? In Holland, for what it's worth, they reckon that the best environmental option is to use "green" cotton diapers, washing them on your washing machine's energy-saving program and hanging them out to dry in the sun.

Fashion footprints

There are those who argue that the fashion industry is relatively harmless—indeed, a delightful part of being human. Others conclude that fashion, by its very nature, can have a powerful negative impact both socially and environmentally.

A dramatic illustration of the potential harmful impacts of fashion can be found in the public response to the megahit film, 101 Dalmatians. Backyard dog breeders produced large numbers of dogs in the expectation that thousands would see the film, decide they wanted one or more Dalmatians, and rush out to their nearest pet-store or kennels. The dogs certainly look loveable on the screen, but many new owners found them uncomfortably big and boisterous. Soon, hundreds were being dumped on the streets or at humane societies, where they were put down if they had not been re-adopted within a few days.[25]

Nor is it simply a question of dogs being dumped—western fashion trends generally mean that most people have far more clothes, shoes and other accessories than they need. As we will see, it is becoming increasingly clear that the industries producing these products have some serious social and environmental issues to address.

Material world

Typically, advice on the greening of fashion recommends "natural" materials rather than synthetic ones. Natural materials are seen as biodegradable and not linked to the problems of the chemical industry. But this last assumption does not bear close inspection. Choosing the "greenest" material is not as easy as might be imagined. And it's important to remember that how you wash and dry your clothes (page 114) is at least as important as which material you choose. Below we look at some key issues associated with different textiles.

Cotton: Cotton growing can cause widespread soil erosion, uses vast quantities of water and also requires heavy applications of insecticides—because the plants are vulnerable to a range of insect pests, such as borers and weevils. Worldwide, more than 25 per cent of insecticides are sprayed on cotton. Like other textiles, cotton also needs to be bleached, dyed and treated; each stage of the process is linked to significant environmental impacts. Buy organic cotton clothes. Patagonia is one company that is committed to using only organic cotton in its designs.

Growing the cotton for a single T-shirt requires 450 litres (100 gallons) of water.

Hemp: For the moment, hemp is the number-one "green" choice. It can be grown in cooler climates; it grows rapidly, without the need for pesticides, fertilizers, defoliants or herbicides; it is a good crop for "cleaning up" heavy metals in the soil; and it can be harvested so that the nutrients are returned to the soil. Because of its associations with cannabis, however, growing hemp is banned in some countries—and requires a special licence in others. But it is perhaps worth noting that you would apparently have to smoke 0.8 hectares (two acres) of the low-narcotic variety to get high! The processing stage for hemp is similar to cotton and the final material is both strong and durable. There is a budding hemp industry in Canada, which some predict has a glowing future in North America. Hemp was grown on about 400 Canadian farms in 1998, the first year that federal regulations allowed the crop. It was expected that about 600 farms would grow hemp in 1999.[26] It is an ideal replacement for tobacco crops.

Nylon: Until recently, the amount of ozone-depleting nitrous oxides released during nylon manufacture was a significant problem. In 1994, in Canada, over 31 per cent of nitrous oxide emissions came from the manufacture of nylon. However, DuPont has recently created and implemented technology to eliminate nitrous oxide emissions from the adipic acid manufacturing process (used in making nylon) at all of the company's sites. DuPont is sharing the technology with other companies. Manufacturers also point out that nylon entails reduced environmental impacts in dyeing—less dye is needed for such synthetics—and in washing. Less energy is also used because nylon can be washed at lower temperatures.

Polyester: Made from oil, this fibre is energy-intensive to produce and involves emissions of ozone-depleting methyl bromide (page 43). As with nylon, the chemical industry argues that the environmental problems during processing are offset by less impacts during use, but some people think that tighter clean-air legislation could well force this material to be phased out.

Viscose and Lyocell: Viscose is normally made from wood pulp—and the conversion process, to get it ready for spinning, can be highly polluting. So some viscose producers are turning their attention to producing Lyocell—brand-named Tencel. This fibre has the feel of natural fibres and the durability of synthetics. And most of the chemicals used in manufacture are recycled, which means there are very limited emissions to air or water. The main disadvantage of Lyocell is that chemical treatment is required to stop pilling (or balling of the fibre).

Wool: Not as "green" as its image might suggest. Although the use of organophosphates (page 41) in sheep dips is being phased out, the replacement chemical turns out to be 1000 times more toxic to aquatic life. The process of cleaning the fleece also uses detergents and large volumes of heated water. The result can be significant quantities of greasy effluent, often contaminated with toxins from the dipping process. For every kilogram of scoured wool, 1.5 kilograms of waste impurities and effluent are produced. And it is worth remembering that shrink resistance and moth proofing can also involve the use of toxic chemicals.

Although hemp comes out a winner, clearly the fibre debate is not a simple one. Nor is the issue any simpler with dyes. Natural dyes can only be used on natural fibres and they are considered unsuitable for industrial use, because of the large variations in colour tone—and their tendency both to fade over time and to run in the wash. To help fibres absorb the dye, fabrics must be treated with highly polluting heavy metals. And the concentrations of natural dye found in nature are often extremely low. Black walnut shells, for example, have a dye content of 0.2 per cent. So if walnut shells were to be used to supply mainstream dyeing needs, the

Table 4.2: DISPOSABLE vs. NONDISPOSABLE DIAPERS

Issues	***Disposables***	***Nondisposables***
Convenience	One of the main benefits of disposables is their convenience.	Washing diapers can be time-consuming. But diaper laundering services, which pick up soiled diapers from your home and deliver them back clean and ready for use, have helped—as have Velcro-fastened terry-towel diapers, which are easier to fasten than safety pins, boosting local small businesses.
Cost	Disposable diapers are expensive.	Many people believe that a major benefit of nondisposables is that, over the diaper-wearing life of a baby, they work out much cheaper than disposables. Use a diaper laundering service, however, and disposables are still cheaper. For home washing, too, the "hidden" costs of detergent, electricity and wear and tear of the washing machine make the gap between disposables and nondisposables smaller than we might imagine.
Bleaching	Chlorine bleaching of diapers was found to cause dioxin pollution— and there were also concerns over possible health problems for babies. These concerns were not supported by scientific research, but no diaper manufacturers now use chlorine bleaching.	Chlorine bleaching is not generally used for cotton nondisposable diapers.
Energy	Energy is required to produce the diapers, but none is required for washing.	The main environmental negative is the amount of energy used in washing diapers.
Health	The absorbent gels used in diapers are very effective at keeping the baby dry, thereby reducing its vulnerability to diaper rash. Babies and children with sensitive skin may, however, react to the gel.	Contact with urine and feces aggravates diaper rash, so nondisposables may need to be changed more frequently.

Table 4.2: DISPOSABLE vs. NONDISPOSABLE DIAPERS *continued*

Issues	***Disposables***	***Nondisposables***
Pollution	There has been some unease over human excrement going into landfill sites, although there is no evidence of adverse effects among waste-disposal workers.	The biggest issue here is the extra pollution caused by washing diapers.
Raw material	Trees are made into pulp, which is then used to make diapers. So disposable diapers are linked to all the issues of clearcutting and plantation forestry.	Cotton is the main material used to make nondisposables. Chemical pesticides are used to produce cotton, often causing health and safety problems for workers.
Resources	Use more material resources, because of their disposability. It may be, however, that parents change them less often because of their absorbency.	Far fewer material resources used to make diapers overall, but we also need to account for the detergents and soaking agents used in washing diapers.
Waste	A high proportion of household waste is made up from diapers, potentially increasing problems of disposal.	One of the key benefits of nondisposables is that they generate much less waste; indeed, old diapers can be used as rags.

demand—and the waste—would be huge.

Synthetic dyes, too, have a problem of wastage. Between 20 and 50 per cent of reactive dyes, the most commonly used dyes, are flushed away. And, after dyeing, several washes are required, using considerable volumes of water. Typically, 100 grams (4 ounces) of salt are used for every litre of water. Much of this dyeing work is done in poorer countries, where pollution controls are weak or nonexistent.

Another related problem is that cotton textiles partly processed elsewhere and then shipped to the richer countries can cause water pollution problems, because toxic chemicals (some of them banned in the richer countries) have been used to prevent moth damage and mildew during transit.

Leather goods

Leather is another natural product and is found in a wide range of fashion applications, particularly shoes. Again, leather raises some tricky issues:

Waste product: You could say that leather is environmentally friendly because it is a by-product of the meat industry. Cows and pigs, for example, are rarely reared solely for their skins. An effective, high-value use of a material that might otherwise go to waste, you might conclude. Unless, of course, you don't eat meat.

Vegetarians: Those boycotting leather mainly do so because of vegetarian or vegan principles, largely driven by concern for animal welfare or personal health. It is interesting to note, however, that many vegetarians do not follow through when it comes to shoes, partly because no really suitable alternative to leather has yet become available. Wearing canvas shoes or "jellies" with a suit is not always considered to be appropriate!

Tanning: De-hairing, softening and treating leather can be highly polluting processes. Leather tanning is often carried out by small-scale operators, many of whom are unwilling or unable to abide by strict environmental standards. Heavy metals (such as chromium, arsenic and cadmium) and other toxic substances (including formaldehyde and pentachlorophenol) are all used to treat and preserve leather.

Endangered species: On occasion, the demand for expensive leathers from rare species has threatened wildlife. In some parts of the world, crocodiles or alligators are caught in the wild, the inevitable result being a depletion of their population numbers. Crocodile farms can produce a ready supply of this material, although the availability of farmed materials can make it more difficult to successfully identify and stop poaching and the illegal trade.

Nearly new

Whatever clothes or shoes are made of, it obviously makes sense to sell them rather than throw them away. Indeed, second-hand clothes shops are a greatly underrated resource—and should be celebrated as key contributors to the environmental cause. Those clothes that are not bought and reused are often recycled into, among other things, clothes, furniture stuffing, sound insulation or wiping cloths. Other clothes may be sent off in response to emergency requests for aid. In some cases, too, they are shipped off to Third World countries to be reworn. Inevitably, perhaps, concerns have been raised about the danger of undermining local industries with western imports, which suggests that any export schemes should be handled sensitively.

When it comes to shoes, a large proportion are thrown away each year, instead of being repaired. Sadly, the traditional shoe repair shop has all but disappeared. However, shoe repair franchises are popping up in some shopping malls. As well, a small number of firms are beginning to recycle shoes and sell them to the Third World or Eastern Europe at affordable prices.

Price tags

These days, most textile processing and production is carried out in Third World countries, where labour is cheap and safety and environmental regulations are less stringent. The fashion industry has not yet addressed these issues effectively, with relatively few companies specifying the standards they want met by suppliers and contractors.

This is clearly undesirable, but hardly surprising given the nature of these markets. There is fierce competition between retailers, desperate to keep the price of clothing down. This has resulted in intense pressure being put on manufacturers, particularly in the Third World, to cut wages, increase working hours and—even if this is not always the original intention—ignore health and safety guidelines.[27]

Investigators have found workers exposed to toxic fumes while working around open glue pots, which has resulted in breathing difficulties, brain damage and, in the young, stunted growth. Shifts in these factories can go on for as long as thirteen hours, seven days a week, and beatings for offences such as talking at work are commonplace.[28]

As a result, there has been growing pressure

on shoe companies and textile manufacturers to ensure that their employees—and the employees of their suppliers—are better treated. Some suppliers have been publicly accused of ruthless exploitation of their employees.

Among the issues that have surfaced have been forced overtime, pitiful wages, the banning of unions and—perhaps most controversial of all—child labour (page 92). As a result, as the 21st century gets into its stride, it seems very likely that we will all be encouraged to take a much closer look at what lies behind our wardrobe.

Greening the Home

✔Citizen 2000 Checklist

1. Work Out an Action Plan

This is the vital first step. **Environment Canada**, in addition to providing many excellent printed materials, has compiled a wide-ranging databank of green tips about things you can do for the environment in and around your home. Go to the **Green Lane/EcoAction 2000** on the Internet. The nonprofit **Green Communities Association** runs a *"Green Home Visit"* program, which helps people to reduce their energy, waste and water and take other measures to minimize their environmental impact. The **Association** is currently operating in communities across Ontario, and helping to build green communities across Canada.

The **Green Building Information Council (GBIC)** disseminates information about energy and environmental issues in the building sector. This small nonprofit Canadian organization has extensive international links.

2. Look for Labels

The **Environmental Choice Program (ECP)**, which licenses the use of the **EcoLogo**™ symbol (see this page), is Canada's only national eco-labelling program. It was established by **Environment Canada** and is now run through an independent agency, **TerraChoice Environmental Services Inc**. The **EcoLogo**™ appears on nearly 2000 household, commercial and industrial products and services, including appliances, building materials, paint, cleaning products, automotive products and office products such as paper and printing services, plastic products and so on. Other labelling schemes are included in other sections. Compliment retailers where the labelling is well done. And, it hardly needs saying, buy products that have an improved performance.

You may also want to consider joining the nonprofit, nongovernment **Green Canada Club**. Members save money on products and services and, at the same time, protect and enhance their community's environment.

3. Save Energy and Water

By law, every new appliance in Canada must carry an **EnerGuide** label to show you how much energy it consumes. It tells you at a glance how the appliance you're considering compares with other makes and models in its category. The lower the kilowatt hours (kWh) per year, the higher the energy efficiency. Provincial and municipal electric utilities provide excellent guides on what to look for when buying major appliances, on energy-efficient lighting and alternatives, and on how to save money–and make a positive contribution to the environment–by using energy efficiently in the home. All the major lightbulb manufacturers now produce compact fluorescent lightbulbs. The major natural gas utilities also provide guidance on energy efficiency with reference to high-efficiency furnaces, low-flow faucet aerators, energy-efficient windows and other products. **Natural Resources Canada** is developing the *EnerGuide for Houses* evaluation system in cooperation with **Canada Mortgage and Housing Corporation** and other partners. The evaluation focuses on how the home's energy performance can be improved while maintaining or enhancing the indoor environment. Some gas utilities also offer an assessment service that looks at the heating efficiency of your house.

Environment Canada has information on how to reduce water consumption in the home by 40 per cent or more, through such measures as retrofitting toilets and low-flow showerheads with shut-off buttons.

The use of alternative forms of energy is still in its infancy in Canada. **The Solar Energy Society of Canada Inc. (SESCI)** is gathering information for the second edition of the *Canadian Renewable Energy Guide.*

4. Reduce Your Building Material's Impact

The **Canadian Wood Council**, an industry group, promotes wood as the building material of choice for environmentally conscious Canadians. Not only is it a renewable resource, they say, but a study by the **Canadian Research Alliance** demonstrates that the manufacture of wood products is cleaner, less wasteful, and consumes less energy than other building materials. The **Forest Stewardship Council** focuses on the sustainable use of forests as its main criterion for labelling products as environmentally preferable. **Greenpeace Canada** says selective logging can be environmentally sustainable, but that clearcut logging is devastating to the rainforest ecosystems on the West Coast. The group is calling on all B.C. logging companies to follow **MacMillan Bloedel**'s lead in phasing out clearcutting in old-growth forests. According to the **Sierra Club of Canada**'s authoritative book, *At the Cutting Edge: The Crisis in Canada's Forest* (Key Porter Books, 1998), 90 per cent of all logging in Canada is clearcutting.

The **Canada Mortgage and Housing Corporation (CMHC)** provides a range of excellent publications on green housing design and indoor air quality. On the Internet, **CMHC** provides a "Virtual Sample Room" of green building materials, complete with pictures, product data and full search capabilities. The program allows you to compare the environmental benefits and drawbacks of all kinds of building products–floors and floor coverings, walls, ceilings, paints and coatings, and much more.

If your house was built before 1980, the interior or exterior paint may contain lead. Removing old paint is potentially very hazardous. Before doing so, contact your local **CMHC** office to obtain its safety rules for removing and disposing of lead-based paints.

5. Green Your Wardrobe

The foremost source of information on industrial hemp in this country is **Hemp Canada**, dedicated to the promotion of the commercial hemp industry in Canada and around the world.

Nike is redesigning its "Air" shoes to remove a gas, sulphur hexafluoride or SF_6, which is highly damaging to the environment, staying in the air for more than 3000 years and acting as a powerful greenhouse gas. The gas is used to fill the cushioned heels and soles, giving them buoyancy. The company plans a total phase-out by 2001, switching to nitrogen, given the nonessential nature of the use.

Clean used clothing can be donated to **Goodwill Industries**, **Salvation Army**, the **St. Vincent de Paul Society** and other charitable organizations.

6. Remember Fair Trade Issues

The **RUGMARK Foundation** has set up a scheme to help children escape from the notorious South Asian hand-knotted carpet industry. Its program involves a combination of independent certification of suppliers and the rehabilitation and education of child workers in India. **Fair Trade** campaigns have also focused on many other industries where child labour has been used or human rights have been violated: tea, coffee, footwear, soccer balls, agriculture products, and the work of artisans, to name a few. These campaigns aim not only to ensure that workers' rights are protected, but also to provide them with a living wage. Look for a **Fair Trade** label when shopping for items where you suspect child labour may have been used. If you can't find one, ask why. **Fair TradeMark Canada**, which involves church groups, social justice organizations and the **Canadian Labour Congress (CLC)**, has started a campaign that asks workplaces that use a coffee service to convert to fairly traded coffee.

No Sweat, published by Verso and edited by Andrew Ross, is a book exposing some of the workers' rights abuses perpetrated in the name of fashion.

7. Be Prepared to Spend Time Finding Out More

Some issues are not as clear-cut as we might hope. The issue of disposable diapers vs. reusable cloth diapers is one such issue (pages 124–125). The **Diaper Club**, a subsidiary of **Knowaste Canada**, has taken the unique route of recycling disposable diapers. It is a residential delivery service that both distributes disposable diapers and picks up soiled ones for recycling.

A different approach is promoted by U.S. company **ETECH**, which has developed a reusable miniature wetness detector, "WeeTrain." It is slipped into the waistband of a diaper and–in conjunction with normal potty training–is intended to help get babies out of diapers sooner, thereby saving 30 per cent of diaper costs. At the time of writing, this product was not available in Canada.

Alternatives to CFCs are being developed all the time, because there is a deadline for replacing them. **Greenpeace** has led the way in pushing the refrigeration industry toward ozone-friendly options with their "*Greenfreeze*" fridge. They are also campaigning for alternatives to HFCs. If you need a new fridge, check out these issues as well as its energy efficiency.

Greenpeace's anti-PVC campaign tackles another controversial issue. One of the particular concerns is about the use of potentially hormone-disrupting phthalates in toys and many building products, such as cabling, flooring and blinds (page 33). The **Vinyl Council of Canada**, on the other hand, says **Greenpeace** has "needlessly incited a tremendous amount of fear." Clearly, we need to know more.

On the battery front, use rechargeable nickel-cadmium (Ni-Cd) batteries. Spent batteries can be recycled for free at **Canadian Tire**, **RadioShack**, **Zellers**, **Blacks Photography**, **Astral Photo Images** and **Battery Plus**. Further information is available from the **Rechargeable Battery Recycling Corporation (RBRC)**. That said, use of wall outlets whenever possible is usually more energy-efficient. As an intriguing alternative, try **Baygen**'s clockwork radio and other products, as they appear. Where practicable, such mechanical devices would be the ultimate in net energy savings.

5 Transport & travel

ACCIDENTS • AIR TRAVEL • BIOFUELS • BULLET TRAINS • CAR CULT • CAR SHARING • CATALYTIC CONVERTERS • COMPANY CARS • CYCLING •DRIVING • ELECTRIC CARS • EXHAUSTS • FUELS • GLOBAL WARMING • GRIDLOCK • HYPERCARS • INTEGRATED TRANSPORT • RAIL • ROAD RAGE •HYDROGEN CARS • PEDESTRIANIZATION • PUBLIC TRANSPORT • ROAD PRICING • SCRAPPING CARS • SMART HIGHWAYS • SMOG • SUPERSONIC AIRCRAFT • TRAFFIC CALMING • TRUCKS • TIRES • ZERO-EMISSION VEHICLES

It is hard to imagine a future without the internal combustion engine—and more specifically, the private automobile. But the world's increasingly urgent transport problems guarantee that the 21st century will see radical changes in the ways in which we get around. The environmental costs of our love affair with the car are huge—smog, climate change, health problems, as well as damage caused by additives. Lead in gasoline is now banned in Canada. But its replacement, MMT, is still controversial.

Our love affair with vehicles in general, and with the car, has deep roots. But it was only in the early years of the 20th century, when men like Henry Ford brought the automobile within the reach of the masses, that the "car cult" really got under way. As ever-faster cars have colonized our roads, like a new form of predatory beast, some people may wish that the clock could be wound back—but this is simply not possible.

Whatever the costs in terms of traffic jams, accidents and environmental damage, the car is highly unlikely to become extinct. And as much of our world has been designed around cars—rather than people—the pressures have grown to travel ever-farther afield to get to the shopping centre, to school or to work. This, in turn, has fuelled the demand for even more road travel.

This growth trend cannot go on forever. But it will be extremely difficult to put into reverse. We increasingly live in a world on the move. And it is not just a question of cars or road travel. Even air travellers now face congestion in the sky, with pressure mounting continuously for more planes, more flights and more airports.

So how can we ensure access to the things people value without having to cater for ever-growing mobility and traffic? In this chapter we look at what we need to do to create integrated transport systems that are affordable, user-friendly and environmentally efficient, as well as at the impacts of the different transport options, including cars.

In summary, we ask three simple questions:

- *How can we design transports of greater delight?*
- *How can we transport the masses?*
- *Where will our love for roads take us?*

5.1 Smart Moves

How can we design transports of greater delight?

Our transport future will not be a matter of either this mode of transport or that one. Instead, it will be both/and. So in this section, before turning to look at some specific issues associated with mass transit and the use of the private car, we will look at ways in which future integrated transport systems may be developed—and at possible ways in which we might be encouraged to use our cars less.

Changing direction

The 21st century will see a new balance between the use of the car and other forms of transport. But we should not underestimate the challenge of getting people out of their cars and onto other forms of transport.

Squeezing the car

We love our cars, often with good reason. In many situations they are the cheapest, most flexible and most comfortable mode of transport. We can leave when we want, stop off more or less where we like—and listen to our own music while we travel. Crucially, we also feel safer.

The number of cars in use in Canada has tripled since 1950 (there are now 445 for every 1000 of us) and sales of minivans and sport utility vehicles (SUVs) have soared in the last decade. Sales of SUVs and light trucks are now more than half of the new-car market in Canada. This moves us *backward* from the strides made toward energy-efficient vehicles in the early 1970s. Only one percent of Canadians cycle to work and just 10 percent use public transit to get there. (In Toronto, this number increases to 22 percent, which is the highest for Canadian cities, followed by Montreal at 20 percent and Ottawa at 17 percent.)

Only one percent of Canadians cycle to work.

Even when the price of gasoline is raised fairly dramatically, motorists usually refuse to give up their cars. But reducing road space does make a difference in the long term. People review their need for a second car, move closer to where they work or decide to stay at home. Perhaps they might even start teleworking (page 188).

In the German city of Bremen, the authorities planned a 1500-home car-free community, offering houses connected by narrow footpaths, with children playing freely on the green spaces, and not a car in sight.[1] The idea was that old-style forms of community would blossom again. But having to promise not to own a car apparently put people off. Now the developers plan to be less strict. Car-owners are allowed, but they must park on the outskirts of the community.

Carrots and sticks

So what carrots and sticks will need to be offered to drivers to encourage transport patterns that work better for everyone? Clearly, changing people's habits will not be easy. Often the changes will be unpopular, partly because costs tend to surface faster than benefits, and partly because the benefits do not always go to those who have to pay the costs. So we need brave politicians to guide the transformation.

Another problem with many of the measures used is that opponents always manage to argue that they disadvantage the poor more than the rich. But restrictions, however they are imposed, will always hit some sections of the population harder than others. Clearly, it will be important to target those people who actually use their cars most, rather than penalizing people simply for owning a car.

And it should be stressed that improvements in air quality and a reduction in the number of accidents are a benefit to rich and poor alike. Indeed, given that many poorer people live closer to roads and other mobile sources of air pollution and noise, the poor might benefit even more. Further, if tax revenues are spent on public transport and improving walking and cycling facilities, the poor could again benefit more—because they will be more likely to use them.

Let's look at some of the car-calming measures that have been tried, at their effectiveness and at some of the problems they may bring.

Taxes: Taxes are already levied on cars and on fuel. The price of gas has actually, in real costs, dropped in recent years—gas is cheaper in Canada than bottled water! Taxing fuel has the advantage of being directly linked not only to vehicle use, but also to vehicle efficiency. Although increases in car fuel tax would not seem to have had much effect in discouraging drivers, it is thought that the ridiculously cheap fuel prices in the United States are a key factor in promoting the car-based society. Another option promoted by environmental groups in Canada is amending the property tax assessment system to encourage smaller buildings and more intensive use of land. This would help to limit urban sprawl, a major factor in increasing automobile use.

Enforcement: Fines for parking offences, speeding, noise and excess emissions need to be both imposed and enforced. And dangerous driving, road rage and other driving-related violence should be discouraged with rigorous policing and heavy court sentences.

Priority lanes: Some cities have introduced priority lanes for buses, cyclists or drivers with more than one occupant in the car, to encourage people to share transport. These schemes often work well, although they are open to abuse. In the U.S., some lone drivers were filmed with blow-up dolls of the President strapped into their passenger seats. Others have taken the less humorous, but more effective, approach of hiring kids from adjacent poor districts to sit in the passenger seat![2]

Traffic calming: Slowing traffic down, particularly through urban areas, has proved very effective in reducing accidents and making roads quieter for residents. Speed cameras, whether or not they contain film, have also dramatically reduced motorists' speeds. Other measures include "pinch-points," (an island or curb extension mid-block), corner bulges, "rumble strips" (noise-inducing strips), roundabouts (traffic circles at intersections) and speed bumps. Given that driving slower is more fuel-efficient, though, it is ironic that new research shows that speed bumps increase car exhaust pollution by at least 50 percent, and worsen gasoline consumption, because of the braking and accelerating they encourage.[3]

Scrap old clunkers: Even a well-maintained old car can produce almost four times as much air pollution as a new car. Some countries have now introduced schemes to buy up old cars to encourage people to switch to newer ones. In the U.S., this approach has brought major benefits, but in Italy this led to the local recycling industry being swamped, so that large numbers of cars were shipped to North Africa and simply dumped. A more effective approach, which is being introduced in Germany, is a higher road tax for gas-guzzling, highly polluting cars. The Government of Ontario's *Clean Air* program, begun in 1999, is testing emissions levels in all cars over three years old.

Car rental: Rather than buying a car, the idea here is that you buy the right to use a vehicle from a large pool of available models. You can choose from a range of vehicles, which are available at any time—and can be delivered direct to your door. This is a great idea, particularly for city dwellers who mainly want the use of a car on weekends. The approach could be much cheaper than owning a car "full-time."

Car pooling: This involves sharing a car—perhaps your own—with other people who may want to travel where you are going. It is most commonly used for commuters, although the fact that people often arrive and depart from work at different times, and many are not keen to socialize first thing in the morning, has meant that this idea can be difficult to put into practice.

Squeeze company parking, reward transit use: The provision of company cars as a perk is, thankfully, on the decline in Canada, but free company parking remains an inducement for many employees to drive to work rather than use public transit. Free parking is supposed to be a taxable employee benefit, but in many cases the tax is not collected, in part because of difficulties in assigning a value to parking spots. Ironically, transit passes given to employees are always taxed! Pollution Probe and other groups have been lobbying Revenue Canada for 10 years to waive this tax. The amount involved would be a drop in the tax revenue bucket, the public relations benefits to the government would be enormous and use of public transit would be encouraged. Yet successive finance ministers have shown no interest in changing the rule. Another way for employers to encourage use of public transit would be giving the cash value of a parking space to employees who do not use it.

Road pricing: Highway tolls have been in existence for a long time, but are not universally welcomed by environmentalists. One effect can be to encourage people to find other, free routes—increasing total kilometres driven and simply transferring congestion. Also, the money raised is often used to fund yet more roads. Charging people to drive in city centres, on the other hand, can be effective in pushing people toward public transport options.

Increasingly, schemes like this will become more "intelligent," with different types of users charged at different rates. The prices might be set higher, for example, for those with bigger cars, for vehicles with just one occupant, or on days when the air pollution is likely to be particularly bad.

Car-free

We have looked at some of the measures that could be taken to relieve pressures in an auto-dependent world. But, if we are to make a real difference in the quality of our lives, we must look at alternatives to cars—and at how to make them more attractive. We should also consider systems that cut the need to travel.

Public transport

The future for buses looks bright. Once on the move, they take up less road space than two cars, yet can carry many times more passengers. As our roads become more crowded, we will see radically new forms of bus systems on offer. New technologies are already being introduced that will make life easier for bus users. For example, smart traffic lights can give priority to buses and other preferred vehicles. We are also seeing bus stops that tell you where the next bus is, at what speed it is travelling and when to expect it to arrive.

Another big step toward convenience on all forms of public transport will be the use of "smart cards" in place of tickets. These can open station turnstiles without even being taken out of your pocket. Such cards can be "charged" with a stored value, allowing access to public transport systems for a set time or set number of journeys. The result is to allow seamless transfers between different forms of public transport, reduce ticket prices and help cut down on fare-dodgers.

Complicated ticket pricing, plus difficulty in getting through-tickets to many destinations, can add to our problems. Then, on arrival at a station, you may find no transport services to take you on to your final destination—or only expensive taxis. None of these challenges should be beyond the capabilities of public transport operators. If they are, then we need new operators.

The kind of creative thinking needed to lure people away from their cars can been seen in Rimouski, Quebec, site of the first public taxi service in North America. For a monthly pass costing $70.55, Taxibus clients use the service to go where they want when they want. City planners say this kind of on-demand transit could be the wave of the future for low-density parts of large cities and for smaller centres that find it hard to justify a regular service.[4]

Meanwhile, creating quiet spaces for people to live and for pedestrians to walk is a critical need for the future. Sizeable areas of major cities such as Rome, Naples and Milan are now closed to cars, or open only to residents and delivery vehicles. Plans are afoot to develop more in London. And Paris is working on a patchwork of "quiet quarters," where car entry is restricted, strict speed limits imposed or the areas are sealed off altogether.

Mobility or access?

Our modern lifestyles depend on cheap, convenient modes of transport. No one denies that we need the mobility and access that transport gives us, but that does not mean that we have to—or can—keep going with things as they are.

The car, which is at the heart of the modern transport system, was certainly an extraordinary invention, and will undoubtedly be a part of most future transport systems. But there is a growing recognition that systems that work for some cities or even some countries cannot be applied to the planet as a whole.

Happily, there are a number of ways to make our transport systems work better—and our communities more livable. This will require considerable investment, but we can take comfort in the fact that it will pay real dividends, both in terms of improved quality of life for citizens and, hopefully, in export earnings from sales of our technologies and expertise. And it will often be far cheaper than road building.

In the real world, well-travelled roads develop deep ruts—and in the same way, we all get stuck in the old, comfortable ways of thinking. We need to think afresh. Instead of simply focusing on cars, we need to think about transport systems as wholes. Instead of transport, we should think about getting about. And instead of getting about, we should think about how people can get to the things they really need and want.

So, for example, we may decide to invest in telecommunication systems and the Internet (page 165). The use of teleshopping, teleworking and teleconferencing (page 188) will reduce the demand for certain types of transport.

Nortel, part of a burgeoning trend among Canadian companies adopting teleworking, has calculated that the five percent of its worldwide workforce who telework (about 4000 people) reduce automobile air pollutants by 7 million kilograms per year and save $8 million a year in real estate costs. Most of the approximately 5000 federal government teleworkers save one hour's driving time every day they work at home, making their telework days environmentally friendly by any standards. The Canadian Telework Association (CTA) notes that, as one of the world's least densely populated countries, Canada is a prime candidate for telework as an alternative to driving long distances. In addition to the well-documented productivity improvements and increased employee satisfaction, the potential environmental benefits of teleworking on some or all work days are enormous.

The more we can move around electronically, rather than physically, the more we will help to free up space on our increasingly crowded roads. Many services, like banking, will increasingly be handled electronically, although many—like hairdressing—will not.

However successful these new technologies become, though, most people will not move in short order and *en masse* from real-world highways to the new, virtual "information superhighways." We will still want to meet face-to-face. And given that most people on this planet do not yet own a car and have never travelled by plane, there is still a vast untapped demand for travel. For the moment, at least, the travel industry's future seems assured.

Smart Moves

✔Citizen 2000 Checklist

1. Organize Your Life to Travel less

In the future, this may be easier than it sounds. Teleworking is fast growing in Canada, involving major telecommunications companies, major banks, all three levels of government and hundreds of smaller businesses. **The Canadian Telework Association** provides statistical information and case studies documenting the personal, productivity, cost and environmental benefits of telework.

Canadian cable television networks are carrying home-shopping channels and beginning to offer TV-Internet access. An increasing variety of goods and services can be purchased via the Internet, though you need to be careful concerning the security of confidential information, such as credit card numbers, that you transmit. Canadians currently benefit from some of the world's cheapest Internet access, and it is predicted that 28 per cent of homes will be linked to the Net by the year 2000.

Pollution Probe holds a one-week *Clean Air Commute* every June, in which approximately 100 companies in the Greater Toronto Area encourage their employees to use more environmentally friendly means of transport: public transit, car pools, telecommuting, teleconferencing and so on. Similar commuter challenges are run by environmental groups in Calgary, Edmonton, London and Vancouver, and by the B.C. Environment Air Resources Branch in Victoria (specific groups are listed under "Commuter Challenge" in this book's Directory). **Probe** also runs an education program encouraging proper car maintenance to reduce emissions. **Natural Resources Canada's** *Auto$mart Program* and the **Canadian Automobile Association (CAA)** both give tips on buying, driving and maintaining vehicles in ways that reduce fuel consumption and spare the environment.

2. Use—and Support—Public Transport

If you are renting or buying a new home, it is well worth considering its proximity to a subway or bus stop or other means of public transport. If public transport becomes more efficient and attractive over time, the value of your home could well increase as a result. Plus, homebuyers could afford larger payments for more desirable downtown homes and near mass transit with the savings from not owning one (or two) cars. As far as background information is concerned, try contacting your local public transport operators and local authorities. **Transport 2000** has also produced an interesting publication entitled *Blueprint for Quality Public Transport*.

3. See If You Can Manage Without Owning a Car

This can be a chicken-and-egg problem. Until better public transport exists, we prefer to use our car–and yet, until enough people are willing to use public transport services, such services cannot be significantly improved. But there are ways of breaking out of this trap. For example, countries such as Canada, Holland and the U.S. are experimenting with a range of car-sharing and "car pool" initiatives. In Canada, members of **Vancouver's Co-operative Auto Network (CAN-VAN)**, **Victoria Car Share Co-op**, **CommunAuto** in Montreal and **Auto-Com** in Quebec City share the use of cars owned by their co-ops. These are grassroots initiatives to decrease the number of cars polluting the atmosphere. In Toronto, **LIFT (Low Income Families Together)**, and **LETS (Local Employment and Trading System)** are starting up **AutoShare**. They are targeting people with second cars as well as those with modest incomes in hopes of persuading them to get their old clunkers off the road. **Taxibus** in Rimouski, Quebec, is the first on-demand public transit service in North America. For a monthly pass costing $70.55, riders use the service to go where they want when they want. To promote public transit and car-sharing in downtown Toronto, certain lanes are reserved during rush hours for buses, bicycles, taxis and cars with three or more riders.

5.2 Trains & Boats & Planes

How can we transport the masses?

How do we travel when we are not in our cars? There are many alternative transport modes, of course, and most of them suffer from intense competition with the car. But several of them are doing better than most people imagine.

Off the roads

The energy efficiency of walking is pretty amazing—and the health benefits hardly need emphasizing. For thousands of years, our towns and cities were mainly designed for people on foot, along with a growing number of beasts of burden, which helped to ensure that they were built (and operated) on a human scale. But current conditions for pedestrians and cyclists leave a great deal to be desired in most cities and towns.

Shall we walk or cycle?

Almost all of us walk every day. Indeed, it is estimated that if all human footsteps from a single day were placed in line, they would reach 88 times to the Sun and back.[5] But—particularly in the developed world—travelling by foot is on the decline.

Think for a moment of how things have changed for schoolchildren. Only a decade ago, Canadian school children walked many more kilometres each year than they do now—and cycled more, too. In the Greater Vancouver Regional District, for example, planners were alarmed by the increase over the past 10 years in the numbers of children being driven to school—from one in three to one in two.[6] We are in real danger of producing generations of children who take much less exercise and, as a result, are less fit and healthy. The Heart and Stroke Foundation estimates that two-thirds of Canadian children and youths are at risk of premature death and disability because of inactivity.[7] To counteract this trend, Active Living Canada runs an annual Walk a Child to School Day. In Toronto, some neighbourhoods have embraced the "Walking School

Bus," where children and adults walk, hand in hand, to school—improving their physical condition and the environment.

Cycling is even more energy-efficient than walking. When other traffic is at a crawl, it can also be the quickest and most reliable form of transport available. In fact, some urban police forces are forming "cops-on-bikes" units to reach crime scenes faster.

Among other advantages, cycling is cheap, door-to-door, can be great fun in the right conditions and wastes much less time in hunting for a parking space. It also has major health benefits. A short cycle journey of just six kilometres (four miles) a day will halve your risk of heart disease. On average, those who cycle regularly enjoy a fitness level equivalent to non-cyclists 10 years younger.

Just six kilometres (four miles) of cycling a day will halve your risk of heart disease.

Unfortunately, both walking and cycling are actively discouraged by the traffic conditions in most major cities and towns. For schoolchildren, too, there is the fear of being attacked, although this may be exaggerated in that no more children are killed by strangers today than 50 years ago. Meanwhile, removing children from any contact with the outside world may well leave them with little idea of how to deal with public dangers. So support pedestrianization or traffic-calming schemes wherever possible.

Waterways

Huge quantities of cargo still move by inland waterways, and much greater volumes by sea, but we are significantly less dependent on water transport than we once were. This is unfortunate because ships and boats take advantage of the fact that water is an almost ideal medium for low-friction transport.

One encouraging development is that more food can now be shipped because new air-tight containers for storing fresh produce have been developed. The rotting agent ethylene (page 61) is sucked out and fresh produce lasts longer.

Most commercial freight is shipped in vast container vessels and super-tankers. So large are these—and so great is the momentum that they build up—that they can take several kilometres to slow down once the captain has put the engines into reverse. Generally, however, these ships steer clear of the headlines. The exceptions are those carrying oil or particularly hazardous cargoes that manage to run aground—or break apart on the high seas.

Much of the damage caused by such ships is inflicted out of sight of land, so is also often "out of mind" for those of us ashore. But the scale of the damage can be considerable. Although many captains are very responsible, a significant number still clean out their tanks at sea.

Dumping garbage out at sea is another highly polluting habit, aggravated by the fact that many ports do not have sufficient facilities to deal with waste, or charge for the service. Over time, we will need much stricter laws and will have to monitor shipping movements much more closely, either from the air or, more likely, from satellites orbiting in space.

On the right tracks

Trainspotters are not the only people with a passion for railways. In certain areas, like the long-haul transport of heavy freight, railways are unbeatable. In Canada, for example, independent research has shown that freight trains are three times more fuel-efficient than trucks. It also turns out that they emit 35 to 54 per cent less nitrogen oxides, 79 to 85 per cent less particulates and 65 to 75 per cent less carbon dioxide (page 28).

So why did we fall out of love with trains? A key part of the answer is that, for some time, trains have been losing their long-distance passengers to airlines and their short-distance passengers to cars. A great deal of freight, meanwhile, has been switching from rail to road. And new types of industries have been set up to be serviced exclusively by trucks.

Via Rail has been disadvantaged by serious cuts in its government funding, leading to reduced service. There is no longer any passenger rail in Newfoundland; Nova Scotia's service no longer reaches Cape Breton; and much of the Prairies and British Columbia no longer have access to Via. Worse, CN Rail owns the tracks and Via passengers are often inconvenienced so that freight can roll through.

Inside cities, planners are turning back to streetcars, or their modern equivalent, light rail systems. Subways may be the ideal solution, but they are usually too expensive and disruptive to build. Streetcars are easier, but many cities tore up their streetcar tracks decades ago. Toronto has bucked this trend, maintaining its streetcars as an important part of its transit system and continuing to extend its subway.

Between cities, trains usually travel at much higher speeds. In the early 1960s, for example, the Japanese introduced "bullet trains." France opened Europe's first high-speed rail line in 1981, effectively halving the time needed to travel between Paris and Lyon. France has subsequently opened a number of other lines for its *train à grande vitesse* (TGV)—and other European countries, among them Germany, Italy and Spain have followed suit, running trains at speeds of around 250 km-h (156 mph).

These trains are proving highly popular, carrying an eighth of railway traffic in western Europe. And there are further plans for expansion. Belgium has opened a high-speed link and some 20 000 kilometres (12 000 miles) of new lines are planned for across Europe. The result will be to create a high-speed web, with France very much at its centre.

High-speed rail in Canada?

A rail train tested in Japan in 1997 travels so fast that a trip from Winnipeg to Vancouver would take just under five hours. An attractive prospect, but don't look for high-speed rail travel in Canada any time soon. Bombardier Inc., which holds the Canadian licence to the French TGV train, has formed a consortium with several other companies to propose a high-speed rail link from Quebec City to Toronto. It would be a huge project, in the order of $11 billion, involving the building of new track and overpasses over hundreds of kilometres. The project would require partial funding from the federal government as well as from Quebec and Ontario. The federal government is taking a very slow and cautious approach before committing itself to any funding. Even if the project does get government funding, the high-speed link would still be at least a decade away. Meanwhile, there are plans to revitalize Via Rail for faster and more frequent service. Clearly, the Canadian government has not yet recognized the benefits of improved rail service. Transport Minister David Collenette told the House of Commons Committee that the greenhouse effect was not yet figured into transportation planning. "We have a 20-year window to implement Kyoto," said the minister in the fall of 1998, baffling most observers.

In the long run, however, high-speed rail may be the way to go. Of course, if you happen to live near a proposed high-speed train track, you will be acutely aware of the disruption the trains cause and the scars their new lines can leave on the countryside. But, high-speed trains generally score well on the environmental front. Some studies show that a plane can use four times more energy than a TGV per passenger kilometre, and a car two and a half times.[8] The airlines, however, say that their fuel-efficiency figures show that planes are close to—and in some cases overlap with—the TGV figures. It all depends on how the trains and planes are used.

Next in line, we are told, is the "maglev" train. Instead of running on wheels, this will "fly" on a magnetic field or "cushion." Indeed, given that these trains will effectively fly a few millimetres above the line, they could almost be viewed as planes without wings. The German government has given approval for one of these 400-km-h (250-mph) maglev lines between Berlin and Hamburg. More will almost certainly follow, helping to make inter-city rail travel increasingly competitive.

Into the sky

It is extraordinary to recall that the Wright brothers pretty much gave birth to the aviation industry in 1903 by taking to the air for just 12 seconds. The pace of development since then has been breathtaking, although it has not gone quite in the direction that early enthusiasts expected.

Winging it

In America, at least, the original goal was an aircraft in every home's garage. Indeed, by the 1940s, surveys showed that over 40 per cent of U.S. householders expected to own a plane. That dream failed, mainly because early air travel proved to be both dangerous and expensive.

Then the airlines stepped in, offering travellers more comfortable and safer conditions, at ever-cheaper prices. Fifty years ago, for example, it took 15 hours to fly from Montreal to Vancouver, weather permitting.[9] It took four days to fly from Sydney, Australia, to London, England—rather than under 24 hours today—and it cost 12 times more.[10] The result: great human migrations. Every day, there are some 45 000 scheduled flights carrying more than 3.5 million passengers—and at any one moment probably over 250 000 people are up in the skies.[11]

The equivalent of the entire population of the U.S.A. flies around the world twice a year.[12]

Worryingly, the growth in air travel could well put pressure on the industry's safety record, as the airlines try to keep pace. Already, the number of "near-hit" incidents, in which two or more planes nearly collide, has grown significantly at some of the busiest airports.

One U.S. Federal Aviation Authority official even predicted that, with the rapid growth of discount airlines, safety standards could become so poor that "we can expect a major crash every week or so after the turn of the century."[13] This is a real issue, even though this official hopefully was exaggerating for effect.

Despite these problems, however, the airlines in most parts of the world have achieved remarkable levels of safety. Indeed, it is worth pointing out that in 1996, while just 1934 people were killed globally in commercial air accidents, 885 000 people were killed on the roads.

But so great is the fear of flying that the industry will continue to push for ever-safer skies. At the same time, it will have to make concerted efforts in reducing its environmental impacts at every point in the chain. We look at some of these impacts below.

Making planes

It is predicted that the world commercial airplane fleet will double to 23 000 between 1996 and 2016. To meet the demand for new planes and to replace obsolescent ones being retired, the industry estimates that it will have to make more than 16 000 new jets over the next 20 years.

With growing concern about the ozone layer (page 21) and about global warming (page 27), the aircraft manufacturers are beginning to be pushed into the spotlight. They defend themselves by arguing that enormous progress has already been made with aircraft design and manufacture. Over the past 30 years, they note, emission levels have been halved—and the noise from the best modern aircraft is only half that of older ones. Still, travelling by air produces nearly three times as much nitrogen dioxide as cars, and eight times more than trains.

Although noise and emissions are the most important issues for aircraft designers, there are other important areas for improvement. For example, aircraft are repainted roughly every six years. Painting aircraft releases considerable volumes of VOCs (volatile organic compounds, page 150), while stripping off the old paint is usually done with highly toxic chemicals. Now some aircraft manufacturers and airlines are using water-based paints and electrostatic paint spraying to cut the solvent emissions, and high-pressure water hoses to strip paint without using the toxic chemicals.

Running airports

Interestingly, many airports rank right up there alongside traditional smokestack industries in the pollution stakes. Los Angeles International Airport (LAX), for example, is one of the biggest sources of smog in the L.A. region. Indeed, it is calculated that every day aircraft, shuttle buses and other ground vehicles at LAX emit 28 tonnes of hydrocarbons and nitrogen oxides (page 150).

A single wide-bodied jet can emit 45 kilograms (almost 100 pounds) of pollutants every time it takes off or lands. But some aircraft manufacturers are failing to guarantee that their planes are fitted with the best cleaner technologies. With the increase in the number of airplanes flying, we can only hope that more airports follow the lead of Zurich's, which was the first airport in the world to introduce emission charges for incoming craft. Planes meeting their limits receive a five percent discount on landing charges—while those failing to meet the limits are charged 5 to 40 percent more.

A single wide-bodied jet can emit 45 kilograms (almost 100 pounds) of pollutants every time it takes off or lands.

Another factor in the emissions debate, albeit a relatively small factor overall, has been the sale and shipment of duty-free goods. There would be fairly substantial fuel savings if people stopped transporting duty-free goods around the globe simply to avoid tax. Indeed, it has been estimated that 70 000 tonnes of duty-free alcohol is flown annually across the Atlantic each year, wasting more than 27 million litres (6 million gallons) of fuel.

The airlines also handle the catering for airplanes. This is another area of enormous waste. Many airlines, for example, serve meals on disposable trays with disposable plates, napkins, plastic glasses and cutlery. Often customers barely take a mouthful. Those services that use real glass are no better, because of the extra weight this involves. But reusable trays and cutlery—known as rotables—can be used, saving considerable resources.

Interestingly, one airline tried saving on food by allowing passengers to choose what they wanted before flying. They found that 60 percent of people chose nothing—or at most a piece of fruit. This experiment showed clearly that the all-or-nothing approach to airline catering may save time for flight attendants but is extremely wasteful.

The airlines believe that they must make a clear distinction between the services offered to customers who travel in different classes. Catering is one of the main ways they can do this. So business and first-class passengers are routinely fed smoked salmon (page 72), shrimp (page 74), caviar (page 71) and other exotic foods, as well as fine-quality wines and champagne. Little regard is paid to the seasons (page 82), or to the environmental impacts of producing or transporting these foods.

Travelling by air uses four times as much primary energy per passenger kilometre as travelling by car and nearly twelve times more than travelling by train.

Footprints in the sky

The amount of pollution produced by the world aircraft fleet has soared. For any of us carefully driving our cars in an environmentally efficient way, it is sobering to think that just one long-distance flight can wipe out all the energy we would save by not driving for an entire year. One way to reduce your personal impact of flying is to avoid short-haul flights. Most fuel is burned on take-off and landing, so taking a 30-minute flight from Montreal to Ottawa is extremely wasteful compared to two hours on a bus or train.

Despite the greening of aircraft technology in the intervening period, it is expected that by 2015 aircraft emissions will have doubled their contribution toward global warming. And by then civil aircraft could also be responsible for around half of the total annual destruction of the ozone layer.

As it turns out, there is a tension between an airline's response to ozone depletion and its response to global warming. In recent years, for example, cost-conscious airlines have been sending their aircraft even higher, to take advantage of the decreased drag of the thinner air. Ironically, the savings in fuel—with a subsequent decrease in their contribution to global warming—may well be offset by the fact that the airlines are believed to be increasing their contribution to the destruction of the stratospheric ozone layer.

So, for example, around half the fuel burned on long-distance flights is actually burned while flying in the ozone layer. And NASA estimates that up to 60 per cent of ozone-destroying nitrogen oxides now come from aircraft. This could become a major 21st-century problem.

Supersonic flights, such as those made by Concorde, are particularly damaging. But with air traffic doubling every 12 years or so, subsonic flights—which do not break the sound barrier—are also emerging as a major source of air pollution. There is no doubt that both aircraft manufacturers and the airlines will be under increasing pressure to put even greater efforts into cleaning up their emissions.

Destinations

So, how many travellers ask about the environmental performance of travel companies when booking a ticket? Very few, we suspect. Yet when a leading tour operator surveyed its customers, fully 87 percent said that they would prefer to travel to a destination with a good environmental record.[14] The survey also found that most tourists thought waste, pollution and the quality of the local environment were important issues when on holiday. A huge proportion of those surveyed claimed they would take these issues into account when choosing an airline or tour operator.

It would seem that there is room for a bit of competitive pressure here. And there are social issues to be considered, too. Those questioned, for example, were concerned when they realized that local people in developing countries had been evicted to make way for tourism development. Nearly all of those surveyed said that these issues should be brought to public attention—and they felt that tour operators, in particular, have a responsibility to lobby against such abuses.

Trains & Boats & Planes

✓Citizen 2000 Checklist

1. Walk or Cycle Wherever Possible

It makes sense to campaign for better walking and cycling conditions in your local community. Contact your local authority and complain about current conditions. Better still, suggest what they might do.

The Maritime provinces are leading the country in supporting turning unused railway lines into parks and multiuse recreational trails. Contact **Canadian Rails to Greenways Network** or **The Trans Canada Trail Foundation** for more information. The **Foundation** is developing a 15 000-kilometre shared-use recreation trail from coast to coast, partly along the railway rights of way. For a $40 donation, you can build a metre in any province or territory.

Organizations supporting walking include local hiking clubs, **Hike Ontario**, **International Youth Hostels** and **National Parks and Recreation**.

Cycling organizations include the **Canadian Cycling Association** and various provincial and city/municipality associations. On the Internet, check out **Yahoo Canada's** cycling page, the **B.C. Cycling** and **Hike Ontario** websites, and the **Atlantic Canada Cycling bulletin board** for local clubs. Many cities have annual *Bike to Work* weeks, often sponsored by municipal and environmental groups. Toronto even has a bicycling choir! Serious cyclists would be interested in such magazines as *Cycle Canada*, *Canadian Cyclist* and *Pedal*.

Cyclists take note! If you're travelling on **VIA Rail**, you can take your bicycle with you anywhere in Canada for just $15 (boxed or unboxed)! Via Rail even provides a free box if transfers between trains are needed.

2. Support Good Rail and Boat Travel

We should not only use our railways and related services, but should also campaign vigorously for better services. **Transport 2000 Canada** promotes rail travel. It represents the interests of users of public transport services in Canada and is a federation of seven regional associations. It researches, educates and represents consumer interests before federal, provincial and municipal public hearings and regulatory bodies, helps direct consumer complaints to public carriers and maintains an extensive library of transportation-related publications and documents.

3. Ask Your Favourite Airlines to Cut Their Impacts

Given the growth of air travel, this is a crucial area. Show a lively interest in what the airlines are doing to cut their environmental impact. Ask for a copy of their latest environmental report. Read it–and then write to the airline with your comments on it. And fill in their feedback forms asking them what else they plan to do on the environmental front.

Among the things that airlines can do are to buy and operate cleaner, quieter and more fuel-efficient aircraft. Both **Airbus** and **Boeing** have been putting a great deal of effort into this area. Indeed, the best thing that could happen would be for all of yesterday's aircraft to be replaced by today's latest models: the environmental results would be extraordinary. A number of airlines, among them **British Airways (BA)**, **SAS** and **Swissair**, report that they have made great efforts to buy aircraft with engines that emit less nitrogen oxides, without compromising fuel efficiency. **Air Canada** is gradually phasing out its Boeing 747s and replacing them with Airbus 330s and 340s, which are much more fuel-efficient. As well, the airline's use of small regional jet fleets provides daily regional service without the need to fly larger jets, which would have to run half-empty on such short-haul flights. Manufactured by Bombardier, the 50-seater jets are very fuel-efficient and excellent for flights of less than two hours. It is also worth asking the airlines you use what they do to reuse or recycle materials used for in-flight catering. Where destination points have appropriate recycling facilities, **Air Canada** separates for recycling all plastics, cans, bottles and newspapers used in its in-flight service.

If you enjoy taking organized tours abroad, ask your tour operator what they have been doing to cut the environmental and social impacts of tourism.

5.3 Driven Mad

Where will our love for roads take us?

And now for the biggest near-term transport challenge: taming the car. The personal automobile remains one of the greatest inventions of all time, and its future seems guaranteed. But it already causes so many problems that it will have to evolve radically in order to survive in the third millennium.

Wheel worlds

Once, the best way to experience a real sense of power was to sit on a throne, an experience usually only open to emperors, kings and queens. Not an option open to many. Today, however, millions of people can experience something of the same when settling into the driving seat of a car. Indeed, the phrase "to be in the driver's seat" is now used as shorthand for real power. We live in a period of history when the car cult is more developed—and more widely supported—than any other cult in history.

Our car cult

Let's take a quick look at some of the cult's main features:

Only one god: Most cults—indeed most religions—only allow for one god, and the car cult is no different. Cars compete mercilessly with other forms of transport, both for road space and for public affection. As more cars are used, they drive other types of transport off the road.

Growth: The cult is growing rapidly in just about every country on earth. It has been calculated that the number of cars already on the planet would form a six-lane highway to the moon.[15]

Power: For most people, speed is exhilarating. The power and acceleration of a modern engine would have been mind-boggling to anyone used to a horse-drawn world. And some high priests of this global auto cult have still greater powers. In 1997, for example, a 10-tonne, jet-powered car was driven through the sound barrier, with two giant engines delivering the power equivalent of no less than 141 Formula 1 cars. With its parachute released, it still took 11 kilometres (7 miles) to slow down.

Offerings: The power of a cult is often indicated by the value of the gifts provided by devotees. In the U.S., the auto industry spends an estimated US$20 billion each year to ensure that cars are seen as sexy, sporty and the only real option for those on the move. Meanwhile, North Americans devote one-quarter of their waking lives to the purchase, use and upkeep of their cars.[16]

Size: Like muscles, penises or breasts, the size of their car matters to most people. Big off-road, four-wheel-drive vehicles increasingly line city streets. Some of the biggest found in Europe, however, are dwarfed by vehicles now appearing on U.S. and Canadian roads. Light trucks, passenger vans and sport utility vehicles now account for more than half of all sales of private automobiles in Canada. These gas-guzzling giants are used for transporting children to school, commuting in heavy traffic and everyday shopping. "I just love the fact that I'm higher than everybody," said one U.S. woman who drives a vehicle fitted with no less than four TVs, "and that if me or my kids get hit, I'm going to survive and so are they."

Accessories: Once, not so long ago, American cars sprouted wings and other protuberances worthy of sci-fi spaceships. You don't see many UFO-like vehicles on the roads these days, but colour and accessories remain crucial for many motorists. One of today's great thrills is to fit "bull bars," which are almost tailor-made to kill children, because of the way they concentrate impact in vehicle-on-pedestrian collisions. The car cult requires child sacrifices, usually other people's children.

Blood sacrifice: The car cult demands a regular, horrifying input of victims (page 145). In the U.S., some 40 000 people are killed on the roads each year. Taking total population into account, Canada's annual highway death toll of around 3800 a year makes our record as bad as the Americans'. It is also estimated that air pollution from traffic kills as many people each year as road accidents. Nor is it simply a question of human sacrifices. The loss of wildlife hit by vehicles is very high. The death toll even includes such large mammals as white-tail deer and moose. Birds in pursuit of prey—great grey owls, great horned owls and snowy owls—are caught unawares by oncoming vehicles.

Gridlock

Much of the time, however, our vehicles are not speeding along. Most people would agree that congestion problems are worsening. In Canada, every large city has its rush hour, though Vancouver's rush hour is said to last all day. The Greater Vancouver Regional District (GVRD) is Canada's fastest-growing region and, due in part to inadequate public transit, its roads must accommodate a net increase of about 60 cars a day.[17] Highway 401 outside Toronto currently holds the title of North America's most congested stretch of highway. For the country as a whole, the Canadian Urban Transit Association estimates time lost in traffic jams costs the economy $4.125 billion per year. So far, however, we have not matched the traffic snarls of France, which was the scene of the world's worst traffic jam. One day in 1980, traffic on the road from Paris to Lyons was at a standstill for a staggering 176 kilometres (109 miles).[18]

The roads of the Greater Vancouver Regional District must accommodate a net increase of about 60 cars a day.

So why is there so much congestion? The obvious answer is that more people want to drive more cars, more often—and further. But there are other factors at work, too. Many European and older American cities, for example, were not designed for cars. Whether you are driving through Bergen, Brussels, Bologna or Budapest, the highways and autoroutes end in the suburbs, leaving traffic to crawl slowly into the city centres. But the major cause of congestion in cities such as Los Angeles and Vancouver is suburban sprawl, which creates far-flung, low-density developments where public transit is not feasible without huge subsidies. Nor is the congestion problem found only in the richer countries. Bangkok, for example, probably has the worst traffic problems in the world.

And even countries that have previously had bicycle jams, such as Vietnam and China, are joining the race toward car dependency. But it is difficult to argue that these countries should learn from our mistakes. As the European Transport Minister put it: "A car, a pair of jeans and a burger are evidence of liberty, fraternity and equality."

By 2025, North Americans will be wasting almost 8000 centuries of their time, annually, sitting in stopped traffic.

Although technology will play a central role in civilizing the auto industry and its products (page 155), the underlying problem is indicated by the sheer growth in numbers. In 1950, worldwide, there was one car for every 46 people. Because of rapid population growth, this leaped to one car for every 18 people in 1970—and to one for every 12 by the early 1990s.[19] For the moment, this trend seems unstoppable.

Trucking hell

Our modern lifestyles are totally dependent on the movement of freight. We rely on trucks and other heavy goods vehicles for transporting products and produce both within and between countries. Given their size, it is hardly surprising that these vehicles generate more pollution than the typical car—and cause considerably more road damage and disturbance to the communities they pass through.

Central buying systems, overseas imports and chain superstores are all fuelling the trend. The Canadian government, with one policy reversal, moved huge amounts of grain from rail to road when it killed the "Crow Route," hurting farmers and the environment. In most cases, for a number of reasons, trains are not viewed as a viable alternative. As a result, the volume of trucks on our roads is expected to grow for the foreseeable future.

But there is a smattering of good news. Some trucking companies, for example, are working hard to lessen the environmental burden by teaching drivers to slow down, using intelligent systems to improve on their efficiency, and cutting the distance they need to travel. Some companies, too, are trying to make sure that their vehicles are full whenever possible—by delivering their cargo and, at the same time, collecting waste materials for recycling.

Travel sick

A key factor in many of our most pressing transport-related problems is that we consistently overvalue the ability to move around, while undervaluing the true costs—particularly where those costs are borne by others.

Accidental deaths

Every year, there are at least half a million deaths on the world's roads and 15 million injuries. Indeed, for men aged 15 to 44, road crashes are the biggest cause of sickness and premature death.

A child pedestrian is 151 more times likely to be killed or injured than an adult is to catch AIDS.

Fortunately, there is no universal law that says that the number of accidents exactly tracks the number of cars and motorists. Through a combination of producing safer cars, wearing seatbelts and implementing tough controls on drinking and driving, Canada has managed to buck the worldwide trend toward higher and higher numbers of people killed on the roads. By 1996, the death toll had declined somewhat—to 3802 as compared to about 4000 in 1980.

Conversely, studies have found that extra safety features in cars can make people—either consciously or subconsciously—drive more dangerously. Surprisingly, they found that there were fewer accidents in rain and stormy weather because people drove more carefully. One driving instructor jokingly suggested that putting a spike in the steering wheel, which stabbed the driver in the chest if they crashed, might be the most effective way of reducing accidents!

Cutting speed, particularly in built-up areas, is a key factor in reducing the chances of fatal accidents. It is an unfortunate fact that old age also takes its toll in this area—more than half the drivers aged over 65 killed in accidents turn out to be suffering from Alzheimer's disease. Loss of judgement and memory, poor coordination and confusion are all symptoms of this illness. As the population ages, regular driving tests for people over a certain age will probably become a standard requirement in more countries.

Your choice of car also has a big influence on your chances of surviving an accident. Indeed, European research suggests that deaths in car crashes could be halved if buyers avoided cars with poor safety records. When a Swedish insurance company looked at the records over the last 27 years, it found that the risk of being killed in the least safe cars was 20 times higher than in the safest models.[20]

Road rage

It's an extraordinary fact, but American drivers are now as likely to be carrying spare bullets in their vehicles as spare tires.[21] Over a five-year period, aggressive driving incidents in the U.S. rose by 51 per cent, resulting in 218 Americans being killed and 12 610 injured.

And levels of violence seem to be getting worse. What used to be a situation involving two people screaming at each other is now often a case of one person losing their temper and pulling the trigger. In the cases studied in the U.S., 37 per cent of the offenders used firearms against other drivers, 35 per cent used their cars as battering rams (an 800-kg car is a particularly lethal weapon in the wrong hands), and 28 per cent used an assortment of other weapons—including knives, car jacks and even tins of food pulled from shopping bags.[22]

While there are no statistics on Canadian incidents of road rage, a great deal of anecdotal evidence suggests that it is increasing on this side of the border as well. Reported incidents range from verbal threats to fist fights to the bizarre. A 60-year-old man whacked a 19-year-old woman with a billy club because he didn't like her boyfriend's driving.[23] An incensed driver shot at another man's penis then sped away, leaving the bloodied victim lying on a downtown Calgary road.[24]

None of us is immune from the symptoms of road rage, but some people are more likely than others to succumb. They tend to be tired and overstressed, resulting in them not paying attention to road conditions—and being more easily surprised by other motorists' behaviour. They are also more likely to have an aggressive, competitive approach to driving, getting worked up when they are overtaking or being overtaken.

Psychiatrists advise that you should simply take a deep breath when someone upsets you on the roads. And let the problem go. Rather than going on the offensive, take the other vehicle's number and report the driver. Remember, too, that we often assume that we can be rude to others because we are anonymous. But one poor driver woke up to his road-rage problem when he yelled an obscenity at the woman in the next car—and she turned out to be his boss's wife.[25]

Breathing difficulties

Not so long ago, photochemical smog problems were associated with only a few cities around the globe, such as Los Angeles and Tokyo. Now they are everywhere. Toronto has "smog alert" days every summer (13 smog alert days in 1998), while the Lower Fraser Valley in British

Columbia and southern New Brunswick have the highest smog concentrations in the country. Travel around Europe and you find similar problems in a growing number of cities. In 1996, for example, the centre of Rome was closed to all but emergency traffic when air-quality levels reached the danger zone. Paris often has higher levels of low-level ozone—caused by traffic emissions—than Los Angeles. In the United Kingdom, a brown film of air pollution often blankets cities on windless days.

One cause of the summer smog problem in Canada is U.S. industry emissions carried across the border by air currents. But cars account for three-quarters of smog-creating pollutants and so are implicated in increasing the number of asthma cases, or at least exacerbating them. In Ontario alone, the Ontario Medical Association estimates that air pollution from all sources is responsible for 1800 deaths in the province each year.

And the problem is now even found in countries like Norway. In Oslo, the nation's capital and yet a city that has a population of only half a million people, the air quality can be bad enough for there to be regular winter-time warnings that children should not play outdoors.

Paving the planet

There is a simple law of modern cities: cars create urban areas that can only be serviced by cars. Put another way, urban sprawl and out-of-town developments mean that cars are needed to make more journeys.

Take the inhabitants of the oil-rich city of Houston, Texas. The average Houston motorist consumes about 50 per cent more gasoline than the average New Yorker, about twice as much as people living in Melbourne, Australia, and around seven times more than city dwellers in Europe. This is not simply a matter of wealth. The main reason for the differences is the structure of the cities themselves.[26] Compared to European cities, and fuelled by cheap gas, Houston sprawls over a much wider area and public transport options are few and far between.

A number of Canadian cities are in danger of becoming "Houston north." In Toronto, for example, planners and transit officials say that unless transit systems outside the city improve, highways in the Toronto region will resemble the clogged freeways of Los Angeles and Houston, complete with attendant urban sprawl and increased air pollution.[27]

Cities that spread out with low-density housing often result in an increase in social isolation and a loss of neighbourliness (page 98).[28] As they spread, the effect is to pave over much of the countryside—which disappears under roads, cloverleafs, parking lots and other space dedicated to cars. The scale of all of this activity is indicated by the fact that there are 900 000 kilometres (560 000 miles) of road in Canada alone—and their construction is estimated to have required over 300 billion tonnes of aggregates.

Taking into account highways, bridges, gas stations, parking lots and garages, close to one-third of all land in cities goes to accommodate the car.[29]

In the U.S. alone, it is estimated that road surfaces now cover some 96 000 square kilometres (60 000 square miles) of land, enough land to produce food for 200 million people a year. What happens when the car cult arrives in countries where food supplies are less adequate? Losses of cropland on such a scale could have major implications for countries such as China and India, both of which are in the early stages of car booms.

For example, if China adopted the private

automobile on the same level as the Germans, the result would be 500 million cars on China's roads—considerably more than the 330 million in the global car fleet today. Quite apart from the pressures on land for growing food, the implications for air pollution and global warming would be awesome. The planet's life-support systems would shut down.

Auto lives

Slowly but surely, we are beginning to wake up to the social and environmental impact of cars throughout their lifecycle. Indeed, if the auto industry wants to avoid becoming the pariah industry of the 2020s or 2030s, it faces a period of wrenching change. This will transform the ways in which vehicles are designed, built, used and dealt with at the end of their useful lives.

Making cars

Cars are enormously complex machines, containing thousands of parts made of such materials as steel, aluminum, copper, zinc, plastic, rubber and glass. Making an average car produces well over 50 tonnes of waste. Worse, because some of the raw materials used are often found deep below the planet's surface and in very small traces in the relevant ores, their production almost always causes a great deal of environmental damage—including rainforest destruction. Producing just one tonne of copper, for example, can involve the removal and processing of 140 tonnes of rock.

Nowadays, much more plastic is used to make cars. Indeed, 50 per cent of the world's plastics are used in car-related products. This has the advantage of making them lighter and therefore more fuel-efficient, but the disadvantage is that disposal is more complicated (page 154). Clearly, the production of plastics requires oil and a vast array of other chemical substances designed to achieve, for example, flexibility, flame resistance, colour, cushioning or strength.

Spray-painting cars results in the release of huge volumes of solvents, which contribute to smog. The bigger companies usually have to obey the relevant laws, but smaller garages often manage to avoid such controls. Fortunately, however, new types of paints, such as water-based or powder paints, coupled with high-efficiency sprayers, mean that companies obeying the rules are no longer at such a disadvantage.[30] One issue here, however, is that water-based paints take longer to dry, which can mean that infrared flash ovens are used, resulting in higher energy use.

Walking round to the back of the car, the most obvious problem is the exhaust (page 150). The vehicle catalysts (page 152) used to reduce harmful emissions consume over 40 percent of the world's platinum, almost a fifth of its palladium and nearly all of its rhodium. Worryingly, the countries where these materials are mined and processed end up paying a heavy environmental price. Indeed, a German study noted that almost all the world's production of the platinum group of metals is concentrated in Russia, Canada and South Africa.

In the worst case, a single Russian platinum processing plant was found to be emitting two to three times more sulphur dioxide than the entire German economy. The result was that an area as big as Switzerland was being damaged by acid rain.[31] There can be no overall environmental benefits in making catalysts with platinum from plants operating so inefficiently. Obviously, such plants should be closed or cleaned up, and the catalysts we do use should be recovered and reused when cars reach the end of their useful lives.

One Russian platinum processing plant was emitting two to three times more sulphur dioxide than the entire German economy.

The real price of oil

The oil industry depends for its future on transport in general and on the car in particular. Nowhere is this clearer than in the U.S. With less than 5 per cent of the world population, the country uses 25 per cent of the world's oil and produces 25 per cent of the world's greenhouse gas emissions—and over 60 per cent of that is used for transport.

Think about it. In Canada, a bottle of bottled water often costs more than a litre of gasoline. So what is the real price of oil? Well, however you add it up, one thing is clear: the pump price reflects only a small fraction of what we should be paying.

You don't have to be a geologist to know that oil takes millions of years to form from the remains of organisms buried deep underneath the earth. In a very real sense, then, it is irreplaceable. But, although there has been much concern over whether—and when—we might run out, more oil has always been discovered. Today, in fact, there is a widely held belief that by the time the resource does run out we will have found ways of replacing it.

The problem is that much of the new oil and gas is being found in areas that have not yet been developed or industrialized. These include pristine wildernesses such as the rainforests, polar regions or deep under the oceans. Usually, at least on land, roads must be built to provide access into these areas—and, too often, trees are cut down, local communities disrupted and rivers polluted.

One company spent 20 years pumping a billion barrels of oil from wells in Ecuador's rainforest. During this time, the company was estimated to have destroyed 2600 hectares (6400 acres) of rainforest, spilled some 19 million litres (4 million gallons) of crude oil into the rivers and soil of the upper Amazon, and discharged more than 21 billion litres (4.5 million gallons) of waste waters, often contaminated with hydrocarbons, heavy metals and salts. It also left behind hundreds of unlined toxic waste sites.

But scores of giant oil companies, among them Shell, Exxon, Elf and BP, are scouring the world in search of new oil fields to keep the industrial planet turning on its axle.

Inevitably and increasingly, the social impacts of their activities are coming under the spotlight. Imagine, for example, the impact upon indigenous tribes that happen to live in an oil-rich area targeted for exploitation. Either the tribes are moved from the area, or they may be employed to work in the new, westernized businesses. A few may get rich. The young people may be provided with schools to learn our western ways. But then, just as inevitably, the oil runs out. What is left for them? The result is often alcoholism, discontent and the obliteration of a culture.

One seminomadic tribe of 5000 in Colombia threatened mass suicide when a petrochemical oil company announced its intention to drill for oil in their territory. They said, "Our soil is our blood and it is not for sale or negotiation."

People are prepared to fight for oil, too. Wars like that in the Persian Gulf are fought to protect sources of oil to feed our insatiable energy appetite. The resulting wealth is often distributed very unevenly. Consequently, as we have seen in Nigeria, the oil-supply industry can find itself drawn into local—and sometimes quite vicious—politics. The oil companies often say that it is not their business to police human rights in such countries, but increasingly they will have little option but to use their influence on dictatorial governments.

Once the oil and gas have been extracted, they must be shipped around the globe. The result, often, has been catastrophic. Remember the headlines on such massive oil spills as those caused by the *Torrey Canyon*, the *Amoco Cadiz*, the *Exxon Valdez* and the *Braer*? Some of these have been ecological and social tragedies on a huge scale. Others have been less damaging than was at first feared, but all can affect such coastal industries as fishing and tourism, quite apart from the wildlife oiled and suffocated in the process.

When the *Exxon Valdez* ran aground, piloted by an intoxicated captain, Greenpeace ran a poster campaign summing up the situation: IT WASN'T HIS DRIVING THAT CAUSED THE ALASKAN OIL SPILL. IT WAS YOURS. Whether or not we agree with this analysis, it is clear that at least some of the big oil companies are beginning to recognize that they should be spending more on developing other fuel sources. Indeed, the fact that some of them are now investing significant sums in solar and other renewable sources of energy suggests that they can see the writing on the gas-station wall.

Exhausted

For the moment, and perhaps also for some time to come, most of our cars will continue to be fuelled by oil-based products. In the process, they pump out huge quantities of a wide range of air pollutants.

An individual car may not be a pollution source on anything like the scale of a power station, but add up all the thousands of cars on our roads and they soon emerge as one of the biggest pollution sources on the planet. In fact, the toxicity of some of these pollutants is underscored by the fact that many people have successfully killed themselves by inhaling exhaust fumes.

Below, we look at the main emissions that come from cars—and at some of the health and environmental problems they cause.

Benzene: There is three times more benzene in gasoline than in diesel. Ironically, it is a particular problem in super-unleaded gas, although benzene levels are significantly reduced by the use of catalytic converters and carbon canisters designed to decrease hydrocarbon emissions, also known as VOCs (volatile organic compounds), see opposite. Our main exposure, however, is likely to come from fumes while filling up the car—particularly if you are in the back seat, with the window open—rather than through exhaust emissions. Benzene can be absorbed by the skin and is very carcinogenic, and so the maximum level in gasoline is being reduced.

Carbon dioxide (CO_2): On average, a car will produce one tonne of CO_2 a year. Emitted whenever and wherever fossil fuels are burned, it is the main contributor to the greenhouse effect (page 28).

Carbon monoxide (CO): Lethal both at high and low doses, CO is what kills people when they reroute the exhaust into their car to commit suicide. It can also cause headaches, fatigue and stress—by reducing the oxygen-carrying capacity of blood. As a result, it can impair concentration, helping to cause accidents. It is a risk to those with heart disease, and can also aggravate asthma.

Hydrocarbons: VOC emissions from motor vehicles represent 40 percent of human-made emissions in western Europe. Although the biggest source is the exhaust system, they also escape at many other points along the fuelling chain. So, for example, if you see a haze around the gas pump when you are filling your tank, you are watching VOCs evaporating into the sky. They are also released from the fuel tank as the temperature changes, with vapour evaporating as the fuel gets hotter. VOCs help create photochemical smogs, which include low-level ozone, and can cause breathing distress, asthma attacks and even trigger heart failure.

Lead: A major issue in recent years, lead is obviously found in leaded fuels and not in unleaded. Canada has banned most leaded fuels (farm machinery is still allowed to use leaded gas). Less obviously, it is not found in diesel. Originally put in gasoline to increase its octane level and to boost energy efficiency, lead can build up in our blood and bones, damaging the brain and central nervous system. Children are particularly vulnerable, because their nervous systems are still developing. Lead in gasoline is being phased out, although many older cars will continue to need leaded fuel.

MMT: This is a manganese-based gasoline additive used in Canada, but not in Europe, nor most of the United States. Car manufacturers argue MMT increases air pollution by impairing emission controls. Health and environmental groups are concerned that manganese, which is a neuro-toxin (brain poison) poses health risks. Canada banned MMT in 1997, but lifted the ban in 1998 when the manufacturers sued the Canadian government for $350 million under provisions of NAFTA. Ethyl Corp., which also continues to manufacture lead additives for gas for use in developing countries, claimed compensation for lost profits and damage to its reputation! Canada removed the ban and gave Ethyl $13 million in compensation in an out-of-court settlement. The government also issued a statement of apology and stated that the government had no evidence that MMT was a threat to health or the environment.

Nitrogen oxides (NO): Nitrogen dioxide (NO_2), the most significant component of NO, is a major part of vehicle emissions. It can increase our susceptibility to viral infections by disrupting the body's immune system, irritating our eyes and nose, causing tightening of the chest and also exacerbating asthma, bronchitis and pneumonia. It is also implicated in photochemical smog and acid rain problems.

PAHs (PolyAromatic Hydrocarbons): These pollutants are produced by reactions in the exhausts of diesel vehicles. In laboratory tests, they have turned out to be among the most powerful cancer-causing chemicals yet discovered. Although they are only present in very small quantities in diesel exhausts, it is thought that they make a significant contribution to disease and death rates in traffic-congested areas.

Particulates: Particulate pollution is at its worst at the curbside—and the main source is usually the burning of diesel. Estimates of the number of people whose deaths are accelerated by particulates range from between 2000 and 10 000 in the U.K. alone[32], and run closer to 60 000 in the United States. In recent years there has also been growing concern about tiny particulates known as PM10s (less than one-hundredth of a millimetre in diameter) and even PM2.5s (a quarter of the size of PM10s), which can penetrate deep into the lungs. A single breath taken in a heavily polluted environment can contain several million PM10s—and there is no known safe limit for such particles, which can have a particularly harmful effect on those already suffering from heart and lung problems.

Sulphur dioxide (SO_2): Emitted from diesel exhausts, and to a much lower extent from leaded and unleaded gasoline, SO_2 can irritate the eyes and nose—and may also exacerbate asthma, bronchitis and pneumonia. SO_2 is also a major precursor of acid rain. Traffic, however, is not the biggest SO_2 culprit—industrial sources are a greater problem.

Which fuel?

Looking at car emissions, it is difficult to decide which fuel is best. Even the energy industry itself is divided on this issue—and its opinions change with time. One key problem is that we have to measure costs and benefits on very different scales. So, for example, some critics now say that the introduction of unleaded fuel was a disaster—because it is dependent upon fuels that are rich in benzene.

What they forget, however, is that unleaded gasoline wasn't simply a way of getting rid of lead, but of ensuring that more cars could use "catalytic converters"—pollution control devices, which don't work with leaded gas.

So, before comparing specific fuels, we need to look at a couple of the technologies that have been developed to reduce harmful emissions.

First, then, catalytic converters—often shortened to CATs. These can significantly clean up emissions before they leave the exhaust pipe. A typical CAT consists of a very thin coating of rare metals, particularly platinum (page 148), laid on a honeycomb structure of ultrastrong ceramic. As the hot exhaust gases pass from the engine through the exhaust, the CAT converts the carbon monoxide, hydrocarbons and NO_2 into carbon dioxide, water and nitrogen—all of which are naturally present in the air we breathe.

The efficiency of a car's CAT, and they have been fitted to all new gas-engined cars sold in North America since 1978, can be as high as 90 per cent. But they do not work well until they have been warmed up, making them much less effective in controlling pollution caused by short journeys. Given that the average car in Canada makes 2000 trips per year of five kilometres or less (about three miles)[33], this is a significant disadvantage, although, encouragingly, new pre-heated catalysts are being developed, which might alleviate this problem. It is also worth remembering that poorly maintained catalysts can be much less effective. In Canada, the gas additive MMT impairs the functioning of CATs.

Second, there is the carbon canister, a device that can be fitted to vehicles to soak up VOCs that would otherwise be vented to the atmosphere. VOC emissions can also be reduced at gas pumps by fitting a bellows-like device—something that is already done in some high-pollution areas.

So how do some of the main fuels compare?

Leaded gasoline: The worst of all worlds. Not only does it produce lead emissions, but also most of the pollutants vented by cars running on other fuels. Cars running on leaded fuel cannot be fitted with catalytic converters (CATs), which are "poisoned" by the lead. So, increasingly, leaded fuel is being squeezed out. Indeed, it will effectively be banned in most western countries from 2000.

Unleaded gasoline: The big advantages here are that the lead emissions are removed as a problem and cars can use CATs. But some unleaded fuels have the big potential disadvantage that they can produce higher levels of benzene.

Super unleaded gasoline: Not so "super" from an environmental point of view. It packs more punch than ordinary unleaded gas, but does so because it has a high benzene and aromatic content. It also produces more benzene emissions. Super unleaded gas is increasingly being phased out in western countries and will eventually be banned.

Low-sulphur, low-benzene gasoline: Similar to

reformulated fuels found in Japan, parts of the U.S. and Scandinavia, and likely to become standard throughout Europe over the next 10 years.

Diesel: Diesel engines normally emit much less carbon monoxide and hydrocarbons than gasoline engines and they are lead-free. But they produce more particulate pollution, smoke and smell, twice as much nitrogen oxides and six times more sulphur dioxides. Diesel is more energy-efficient than gasoline engines, particularly for urban driving. Catalysts reduce the carbon monoxide and hydrocarbons but not nitrogen oxide emissions.

Ultra-low-sulphur diesel: This has less than 50 parts per million of sulphur, compared to at least 300 parts per million in ordinary diesel, and can be used by all diesel vehicles without modification, at a small extra cost. Another advantage is that clean-up catalysts work more efficiently with it.

Ethanol: Grain fuels offer a much cleaner option. In Canada, Mohawk Fuels was recently purchased by Sunoco. Renewable fuels and cars with two tanks to allow fuel switching will become increasingly common.

Overall, the cleanest option among current cars is probably an unleaded gasoline vehicle fitted with a catalyst and a carbon canister, or use of ethanol-based or blended gas. In some countries, people are also beginning to switch to natural gas, which provides a much cleaner ride. And, as we see later in this chapter, the future holds the promise of some very much cleaner vehicles altogether (page 155).

Air-conditioning

More and more cars are now being fitted with air-conditioning systems, even in cooler climates. About one-quarter of the 12 million new cars sold in western Europe in 1995 had air-conditioning systems, but by 2000 this proportion is expected to rise to nearly half of all new cars sold.[34]

The problem has been that the coolants in air-conditioning systems were ozone-depleting CFCs. And during the lifetime of air-conditioning systems, 10 to 30 per cent of these gases escape. Although CFCs have now been replaced with less ozone-depleting HFCs (hydrofluorocarbons), these replacement gases are themselves even more significant contributors to the greenhouse effect than CFCs. A serious problem, given that before the switch the greenhouse emissions from air-conditioning systems of western European cars already had the global warming impact of five modern power stations.

Butane or propane hydrocarbon gases are viable alternatives to CFCs and HFCs, although they are highly flammable. But these have not yet been taken up by the industry.[35]

Behind the wheel

Once cars are built, the most important factor determining how polluting they are is the way we use them. Let's look briefly at speed, the distance we travel and the issue of car maintenance.

Speed: The car industry seems completely irrational. At exactly the same moment that environmentalists are persuading the public that the car must be reined in, leading car manufacturers are launching cars able to scorch down the highway at 280 km-h (175 mph).[36] From the point of view of fuel efficiency and emissions, 65–90 km-h (40–55 mph) is the optimum speed.[37] And driving at slower speeds also means you are both less likely to have an accident and less likely to kill someone if you do.

At 110 km-h (70 mph), you are probably using 30 per cent more fuel than at 80 km-h (50 mph).

Distance: Emissions are highest when a car's engine is cold. Indeed, in hot weather a gasoline car may have to be driven for eight to nine kilometres before the engine is fully warmed and operating efficiently. In cold weather, it will need to be driven even farther. This makes short journeys, such as for shopping and school runs, particularly dangerous in respect of emissions.

Maintenance: Well-maintained cars are more energy-efficient—and run cleaner than those that are not. So it is important to have your vehicle serviced regularly, checking the tuning, tire pressures and emission controls. Remember: radial tires are more energy-efficient, and correctly inflated tires can save up to five per cent of your gas bill.

Scrapping cars

Our vehicles need to be disposed of when they come to the end of their useful lives. Just as ship-breaking yards evolved to break up and recycle obsolete vessels, so an entire industry has developed to break up cars and reuse at least some of the materials. In Canada, for example, over 4300 tonnes of cars are scrapped each day, though at least a third of this tonnage is recycled.[38]

For much of its history, however, the recycling industry has been poorly financed and, often, a pretty bad neighbour in terms of noise and pollution. Recently, too, its task has been made much harder by the introduction of more plastics and rubber in cars, complicating the challenge of separating materials—and of reclaiming nonmetal materials in forms that industry is prepared to buy to make into new products. New cars will need to be designed with ready recyclability in mind.

Some countries, meanwhile, have introduced pioneering schemes to encourage car manufacturers and importers to take back and recycle cars at the end of their useful lives. In Sweden, this scheme is mandatory. The Swedish auto industry has been told that by 2002 it must aim to recover 85 per cent of the materials in cars through reuse, recycling or burning with energy recovery, and 95 per cent by 2015.

One possible problem is that if we succeed in encouraging the car industry to recycle more materials, they may decide to use more metals in cars. This is a problem for fuel efficiency, given that metals are heavier than plastics. But with industry's vast resources, this should not be an insurmountable challenge.

A linked challenge is to make good use of the materials reclaimed from cars. To maximize the environmental and cost benefits, much more needs to be done to ensure that the recycled materials are produced in quantities—and qualities—that make them attractive for other uses.

In parallel, there are plans to produce cars out of other forms of waste material. The Chrysler Concept Vehicle, or CCV, has a body made from 2132 plastic bottles—which once contained pop and mineral water. To make the new material for the car, the manufacturers ground up the bottles, then mixed the resulting material with a bucketful of finely chopped, hair-thin strands of glass fibre.

The CCV, apparently, would be almost 100 per cent recyclable. And it would be simple to repair: you would simply cut out the damaged part and melt in replacement plastic patches. Although the car is something of an ugly duckling, Chrysler has had high hopes that such a cheap-to-build, easy-to-operate car would offer real advantages, particularly in the Third World.

A Canadian company, Husky Injection

Moldings, is working with Chrysler to develop a lightweight plastic car body. Since most of the gas burned in a car is used to move the weight of the car body, significant fuel-economy improvements occur with lighter vehicles.

Tire mountains

Most motorists junk their tires much more frequently than they junk their cars, but few think of what happens next. The real problem here, apart from the fact that such vast quantities of tires are junked, is that no one has found a good way of dealing with them.

Every year an estimated 19.5 million tires are discarded in Canada alone (13 million of them from passenger vehicles).[39]

About half of the disposed tires end up in landfills (page 104), illegally tipped or stockpiled. One of the problems with stockpiling is that if the piles of tires catch fire, which has happened a number of times, the fire can take years to put out—and the resulting pollution costs a great deal of money. The infamous 1990 tire fire in Hagersville, Ontario, located south of Hamilton, burned out of control for 17 days, forcing 2000 people from their homes and poisoning local water supplies. In other parts of the world, junked tires provide ideal breeding grounds for disease-carrying mosquitoes.

Another route for tires is to burn them in custom-designed incinerators and use the heat to generate electricity. This approach is not yet supported by environmentalists because of concern over toxic emissions. Other ideas include grinding up the tires and using them for rubberized tarmac, making shoes in the Third World, and chaining them all together and dumping them onto the seafloor to make new coral reefs. Although more tires could be used for these purposes, none of these solutions will use up all the tires available. This is a problem for which no ideal solution has yet been found.

Future cars

Apart from using cars less or more efficiently, and switching fuels, a number of "technical fixes" can help cut emissions and boost a car's overall environmental performance.

Cleaner cars

As a general rule, the smaller the car, the smaller its environmental footprint. Cutting the weight of a car by 10 per cent reduces its fuel consumption by around 7 per cent—and every time you reduce the weight of the vehicle, you can also cut the size of its engine a bit.

Interestingly, too, lightness is a characteristic of the information age, whereas heaviness was an attribute of the machine age, which we are increasingly leaving behind. As a result, we are even seeing major car makers linking up with watch makers to design new, ultralight cars. They should soon be able to achieve around 33 kilometres per litre (100 miles per gallon).

Meanwhile, however, each year brings a dazzling new crop of car designs, most of which—despite appearances—remain dinosaurs under their skins. In evolutionary terms, they are grotesquely inefficient and, it now seems certain, doomed to extinction.

Worried about their futures, car companies are beginning to look at how to completely redesign engines to run on new or adapted fuels—in the process producing much lower (or even zero) emissions. However serious the challenge, they know that their products will need to be fun to use, a key characteristic of successful vehicles in tomorrow's world.

Tomorrow's fuels

A range of other fuels are competing for attention. Below, we look at some of the options:

Natural gas: Increasingly popular, because it is readily available and burns cleaner, natural gas still emits about three-quarters of the carbon dioxide produced by gasoline. Even so, it is winning important niche markets, powering taxis or company car fleets, where maintenance engineers can be trained to cope with the problems of the novel fuel technology. Cars using compressed natural gas lose space when the tank is installed. Very few gas stations currently offer the fuel, although it has been suggested that motorists could buy their own equipment and draw on domestic gas supplies.

Methane: A major component of natural gas, methane is also a "biofuel," produced by fermenting sewage and by rotting waste in landfill sites. Some vehicles already run on fuels produced from such sources. One major benefit is that cars burning methane would help control global warming. They would still produce CO_2 in their emissions, but they would be burning a greenhouse gas (methane) 25 times more powerful than CO_2.

Liquefied petroleum gas: LPG is usually based on propane or butane and normally has a high octane rating, which makes it ideal for use with existing engines. It also offers reduced emissions when compared with conventional fuels.

Ethanol: This is the simplest form of alcohol and can be produced either from wood or natural gas. The most popular biofuel, ethanol is usually made by fermenting sugars produced from crop plants such as sugar cane and root crops. Brazil was an early pioneer of this fuel, but the government's support was undermined by an unexpected rise in sugar prices. Although ethanol burns fairly efficiently, it may not become a key fuel source for a number of reasons. First, you need more of any alcohol fuel to power a car over a given distance. Second, there is not enough farmland to grow enough plants to fuel the world's cars. And, third, the huge volumes of fertilizer required for growing the crops, coupled with the large amounts of energy required to turn the plants into fuel, undermine at least some of the environmental benefits. One way of getting around these problems would be the use of ligno-cellulose ethanol, produced from wood waste from Canadian pulp mills. Overall, the ligno-cellulose option involves less energy than turning crops into fuel, and less greenhouse gas emissions. In fact, the use of ethanol may not be far off (see page 153).

Methanol: This is also a biofuel, but it can produce formaldehyde (page 119) when burned, which is a suspected carcinogen.

"Biodiesel": Confusingly, this term is used either to describe diesel-like fuel produced from plants or a blend of normal diesel with a biofuel (such as ethanol). In the second case, a blend of 80 per cent regular diesel with 20 per cent soybean oil can cut emissions because it contains a higher proportion of oxygen. In New Jersey, the town of Medford has been using this fuel for some of the town's school buses. The main complaint has been from the children, who say it smells like French fries and popcorn—making them feel hungry. However, although there is a reduction in hydrocarbon emissions, there can be an increase in NO_2 emissions.

Hydrogen: The hydrogen car is the great hope for the future, possibly using water as a source for fuel and emitting water vapour or steam. The idea is to remove the hydrogen from water—the H from H_2O—and use this as a fuel. Unfortunately, the process of separating the hydrogen from the other elements in water is energy-intensive—and whichever form of energy is used (even covering vast areas of desert with photovoltaic panels to get solar energy), there will be negative impacts.

Furthermore, hydrogen is extremely volatile and likely to explode, so it must be stored at freezing temperatures. Together with the chilling equipment, this clearly adds a good deal of weight to a car and takes up space. As a result, larger vehicles —such as buses—may be better early bets for this sort of technology.

Cars would need to use fuel cells to make the hydrogen burn efficiently. Developed for use in space missions, fuel cells are not only highly efficient but their only emission is water vapour. The real problem with hydrogen is that it has only one three-thousandth of the energy density of gasoline. One way to increase its energy density is to freeze it, with the problems outlined above. A promising approach to dealing with this problem is to fill the vehicle's tank with fuels such as methanol or gasoline—which would then be converted by a fuel cell into hydrogen before being burned. One of the central challenges with the hydrogen car will be to drive down the price of fuel cells.

A world leader in this emerging technology is Ballard Power Systems Inc. of Vancouver, which has developed a fuel cell that uses methanol as the fuel source and converts it into hydrogen. In 1997, this fuel-cell system was used to power a Mercedes-Benz prototype vehicle. Dispensing with the hydrogen tanks not only reduced vehicle weight, but also improved practicality, because gas stations can handle methanol as easily as gasoline or diesel fuel. The methanol fuel tank fits neatly under the rear seat. In January 1999, Ford launched its prototype P2000 sedan, also powered by a Ballard fuel cell. Both Ford and DaimlerChrysler have invested heavily in Ballard Power Systems. By the middle of the next decade, most auto companies will be introducing fuel-cell-powered cars. So will bus companies, with both Vancouver and Chicago testing Ballard fuel-cell-powered buses.[40]

The car moves on

One obvious place to look for clues of what future cars might look like is California, where the environmental rules are among the strictest in the world. The legislators have specified that 10 per cent of vehicles offered for sale in the state by 2003 should be "zero-emission vehicles" (ZEVs).

As a result, auto companies have been racing to develop electric vehicles (EVs). These are great, at least in theory: they are smooth, silent and nonpolluting when you use them. But they still need electricity, produced in power stations, so the pollution problem is often simply transferred from the exhaust pipe to the power-plant smokestack. Where nuclear power is used, the problems are also transferred, but are traded for low-level radiation and other hazards.

Electric cars depend on batteries, which are still hopelessly heavy. Even the best batteries cannot match the performance of gasoline; indeed, it would take three tonnes of sodium sulphur battery, currently viewed as one of the best hopes, to drive a car over the same range as its gasoline equivalent.

The range for electric cars is currently limited to around 100 kilometres (60 miles) before they need recharging. And it takes a long time, typically six hours, to recharge—rather different than zipping in for a refill at a gas station (although futurists see the day where you could zip into a "battery station," dropping off a low battery for a recharged one). So the main use for these vehicles will probably be as urban runabouts. Given that 80 per cent of car journeys in North America are under 15 km (9 miles), this may not be such a problem.

Meanwhile, the technology will certainly evolve. One company is already promising a form of fast-charge, which would mean that EV drivers could park and charge within 15 minutes, perhaps while doing the grocery shopping.

An alternative approach, which some companies are also exploring, is the hybrid car, using battery power topped up by a traditional gasoline or diesel engine. Fitted with the right computers, a hybrid vehicle—whether it is a car or a bus—can "decide" whether it should be running on gasoline (or diesel) or on its battery when accelerating, cruising, braking or idling.

Even this solution is not quite the complete answer, however. These hybrid cars combine at least some of the disadvantages of electric and the gasoline and diesel alternatives. Again, buses will be more likely to use the technology, because they can carry the additional weight—and operate mainly in urban areas.

Liquid nitrogen cars, it is claimed, might help reverse global warming. The idea is that refrigeration plants would be used to cool the nitrogen—it boils at minus 196°C—and would freeze CO_2 at the same time, thereby removing it from the atmosphere. The air flowing over the "reverse radiator" would provide all the heat needed to vaporize the nitrogen and this would generate power. The exhaust would pump out pure nitrogen gas, which already comprises 78 per cent of the Earth's atmosphere. But even though producing the nitrogen would take no more energy than electric vehicles, this fuel is no easy option. Cars would have a very limited range, using a vast amount of fuel and enormous freezing equipment. Crashes might even result in frostbite!

Further along, the hypercar would be superlight and ultraefficient. A hypercar built from advanced composite plastics would weigh a quarter to a third less than today's autos. Small electric motors would power the wheels, with the energy for the motors produced on-board by a small gas-burning power plant.

Thanks to such design features, and their "ultraslippery" carbon fibre construction, hypercars could nearly halve the weight of current cars and therefore achieve 150 miles per gallon (50 kilometres per litre), with an extraordinary theoretical maximum limit of over 600 miles per gallon (200 kilometres per litre).

In simple terms, the promise is that such vehicles will boost fuel efficiency by 4 to 10 times, while cutting pollution from the vehicle itself by up to 1000-fold. No wonder some of the major car and component manufacturers have already invested more than US$1 billion in this area.

Solar cars today are mainly used for publicity stunts. They tend to have tear-drop shapes, to minimize wind resistance, and sport blue-black arrays of solar cells all over their upper surfaces. They are often pictured in races across desert areas—where the heat of the sun is intense. The solar cells capture sunlight and turn it into electricity, which is either used to run an engine direct or is stored in a battery.

Mass-produced cars that run exclusively on solar energy don't look very likely, but solar energy could be captured from cars while they were parked (96 per cent of the time) and fed into batteries, or the regional or national grid.

Smart movers

Whatever fuel cars use, the 21st century will see growing pressure to ensure that they use the available road space as efficiently as possible. One idea is to automate highways, to ensure that cars can travel much closer together, but with a much lower risk of accidents. Eventually, it is claimed, cars, buses and trucks will be able to travel safely at up to 160 km-h (100 mph), in almost any weather condition. The technology could squeeze a lot more cars onto highways, reducing the need for new lanes or more roads.

Although the cost of equipping a highway with the necessary magnets and radar technology would be substantial, this could be far cheaper than building new highways. But it would probably take a long time to implement, because every car on the road would have to be automated with compatible systems.

More importantly, critics point out, the effect of the new system would simply be to remove traffic jams from one place to another. The cars would be streaming off the highways into a stand-still as they transfer onto "normal" roads taking them into city centres.

Meanwhile, cars are getting smarter. Some, for example, are being designed to ensure safe driving and prevent accidents. If you get too close to the car in front, these experimental vehicles automatically slow your speed and increase the gap.

On-board chips and computers help both to manage engine performance and, increasingly, to navigate. A car phone being manufactured in Lethbridge, Alberta, for example, uses satellite technology to locate a vehicle and automatically calls for help after an accident. In addition to this important safety feature, lost drivers could use the phones to dial up a service that give directions; travellers with engine trouble could immediately access the nearest garage; and hungry tourists could even learn the whereabouts of the nearest restaurant.[41] There could be significant benefits here, given the significant number of drivers that are lost at any one time and thus adding to traffic jams and pollution. Given the number of arguments between couples and friends as they get lost, and one or the other tries to read the map, the new navigational aids promise to be a godsend.

A significant number of drivers are lost at any one time, adding to traffic jams and pollution.

A growing number of new "intelligent" devices are also designed to prevent car crime. Future motorists will be offered lower insurance premiums to ensure that they are used. Among other things, the car of the future may fill with a nontoxic fog after a break-in, lock the would-be criminals in while it calls the police, and even insult the car thieves while they wait. If they do manage to get the car going, the engine could also be programmed to cut out after a short distance and electronic homing devices could help the owners, and police, locate both the stolen vehicle and the thieves.

But will our cars ever be smart enough to tell us when to leave them at home—and to insist if we try to override their objections?

Driven Mad

✔Citizen 2000 Checklist

1. Don't Buy a Car

As mentioned in earlier chapters, huge savings can be achieved by avoiding car ownership costs. Renting a vehicle now and then provides a good option if daily commutes can be managed on public transit.

2. Buy the Right Car

Apart from buying a home, the purchase of a car is probably the biggest single financial outlay that most of us make. This is also the moment when we have greatest influence on the lifecycle of the car. Ask retailers–and manufacturers–about safety, fuel efficiency, CFCs, air-conditioning, the use of recycled materials and environmentally significant emissions. Write to the various manufacturers on your list and ask for comparative information on the environmental performance of different models.

Because they want to make the sale, these businesses will work hard to meet our information needs–and they will also get the message that there is real interest in their overall environmental performance. Manufacturers that have done a good deal to improve their environmental performance include **Volvo** and **Volkswagen**. You might also ask whether the manufacturer supplies customers with a handbook on greener driving.

In 1997, **Toyota** launched the first mass-produced hybrid car (page 158), which cuts exhaust gases by 90 per cent and does 28 kilometres per litre (66 miles per gallon). A range of car companies also say they will introduce new direct-injection engines, to cut emissions and improve fuel efficiency. Among them, **Mitsubishi** and **PSA Peugeot Citröen** are introducing new direct-injection diesel engines, which they claim will significantly cut gas consumption and polluting emissions.

Remember, though, the smaller the car you buy, the better its environmental performance is likely to be. From the **Mercedes** *A Class* through to **Ford**'s *Ka* and *Puma*, and **Volkswagen**'s *Pico*, the international car industry is scrambling to produce a range of small cars. By contrast, both **BMW** and **Porsche** have recently launched high-speed cars, raising concerns on the environmental front and about the possibility of encouraging fast driving (page 145).

Most of the big car manufacturers have "concept cars" at various stages of completion. **General Motors'** *EVI* electric vehicle and the **Volkswagen** *Golf Ecomatic* are already on the market. Others include **Citröen**'s *Citela*, **DaimlerChrysler**'s *NECAR II*, **Fiat**'s *ZEV* vehicle, **Ford**'s *EcoStar*, **Toyota**'s solar challenge vehicle and **Volvo**'s concept truck. For more information on electric vehicles, contact the **Electric Vehicles Association** or **Alternative Vehicle Technology**.

It may be a while before it is mass-marketed, but **Honda** has developed a promising ultra-low-emission vehicle that uses gasoline. The ZLEV (stands for zero-level emission vehicle) relies on a catalytic converter that solves the problem of existing converters that do not begin to work until they warm up, which usually takes about one minute of engine running time. The ZLEV converter has a large surface area that hydrocarbon particles stick to until the surface warms up, at which point the particles are released and broken down into harmless substances before being released to the atmosphere.

A crucial area for further work is recycling. **The ReinCARnate Program** in Ontario will tow away your old vehicle, issue a tax-deductible charitable receipt and ensure the vehicle is dismantled and recycled for parts, fluids and materials. B.C.'s **"Scrap It"** program provides trade-in or transit pass incentives to remove from the roads older models with noxious emissions.

3. Support and Use Cleaner Fuel Options

Probably the cleanest option among current cars is an unleaded gasoline vehicle fitted with a catalyst and a carbon canister. This is a complicated area, but there is now plenty of reliable information to be had. Regarding alternative fuels, **Natural Resources Canada's Office of Energy Efficiency (OEE)** has publications and information on transportation fuels, including propane, methanol, and a list of natural gas refuelling stations in Canada. **The Canadian Renewable Fuels Association** promotes expanded use of liquid fuels made from renewable biomass as sources of fuel. **Sunoco** (see also **Suncor** below) has 270 retail outlets for its ethanol-enhanced fuel, which is designed to decrease environmental impact.

The **Canadian Automobile Association (CAA)** and **BCAA** are both asking their members and other motorists to join them in lobbying the government for stricter emissions laws. A federal bill passed in 1981 but not proclaimed (brought into force) would allow the government to set fuel consumption standards that could force manufacturers to decrease polluting emissions. The **David Suzuki Foundation**, which seeks science-based solutions to environmental challenges, is supporting BCAA's campaign.

When it comes to individual models, we are seeing a number of the features of yesterday's concept vehicles coming through into today's vehicles. **Volvo**'s *850 Estate* can run on both unleaded fuel, for highway running, and on cleaner, compressed natural gas (for use in towns).

Meanwhile, **Ford** and **DaimlerChrysler** have formed a new car development company called **Eco**, alongside Canada's **Ballard Power Systems**, the world's leading fuel-cell company. They predict that hydrogen-powered cars could be on the market as soon as 2004. **Mercedes** has already produced hydrogen concept cars, including the *Necar 3*, based on the company's A-class car–and **BMW** is trying out hydrogen cars, too. The Necar 3 and Ford's prototype P2000 sedan, launched in January 1999, both use Ballard fuel cells that create hydrogen from methanol.

Less positively, we have seen many of the major car companies lobbying hard against new emissions limits. **Ford**, for example, lobbied against the U.N. climate change agreement in Kyoto and opposed tougher air-quality standards in the U.S. In Canada, it is **Imperial Oil** that has worked hardest to block Kyoto, while more progressive energy companies are ready to move forward.

In general, however, circumstances in the U.S. have worked to push the Canadian car industry toward stricter engine-emission standards. It all begins in California, a huge part of the North American auto market and the state with the strictest emission standards on the continent (never mind that their hand has been forced by the enormous smog problems caused by their over-dependence on the automobile). It makes more sense for the Big Three U.S. auto makers (**Chrysler**, **Ford** and **General Motors**) to build all their engines to California standards, rather than to build to various standards. **Environment Canada** has seized the opportunity to also call for stricter emissions standards. But providing the required level of refinement in gasoline to meet the requirements of these low-emission engines means huge costs for Canada's giant oil companies. So there have been bruising battles between the oil companies and the **Canadian Vehicle Manufacturers Association (CVMA)**, which represents the Big Three in Canada. Now the oil companies are fighting the **CVMA** over lowering sulphur levels in gasoline. Sulphur is one of the culprits in the creation of smog. If you side with the auto makers on this issue, you may want to let both the **CVMA** and the **Canadian Petroleum Products Institute (CPPI)** know. If Canadian refineries were modernized, they would not be producing such high-sulphur gas.

4. Use Your Car Wisely

Natural Resources Canada's *Auto$mart Program*, the **Canadian Automobile Association (CAA)** and **Pollution Probe** all give tips on buying, driving and maintaining vehicles in ways that reduce fuel consumption and spare the environment. They can help you calculate fuel consumption and how much pollution your car journeys produce.

Once you have a car, maintenance is critical. Poorly maintained cars cause problems not only in relation to safety but also fuel efficiency and emissions. Make sure that yours is serviced regularly, and check the tire pressures at least once a month. Properly inflated tires are not only safer but also save fuel. When the vehicle is tested, make sure that the garage checks the emissions, as they are now required to. Show a real interest in the results.

As the environmental pressure on the car and oil industries grows, we will likely see some interesting new initiatives. Leading energy companies, for example, are undertaking initiatives in which releases of carbon dioxide emissions in one part of the world are offset by the preservation or creation of carbon sinks in another part. **Suncor**, for example, is the first Canadian company to join with the **U.S. Nature Conservancy** in acquiring and preserving 7600 hectares of an endangered forest in Belize. Because forests absorb carbon dioxide, this action will prevent at least 400 000 tonnes of the greenhouse gas from being released into the atmosphere. A fascinating initiative in the U.K. personalizes carbon offsetting. We are aware of no such initiative in Canada, so we refer interested readers to the Oxford-based **Carbon Storage Trust**, which is hoping to involve car makers, airlines and utilities.[42] The idea, for example, is that someone seeking to offset their global-warming emissions might pay an extra $10 on an airline ticket, with the money being used to plant carbon-absorbing trees. A monthly surcharge of $6.25 on domestic energy bills would cover the cost of carbon emissions. And a typical car would need a $750 surcharge over its life to cover carbon dioxide emissions. According to the Trust, someone living to 65 would need to invest $7500 in tree-planting schemes to live a "carbon-neutral life." There is an opportunity here for a Canadian group to take up this concept.

Finally, remember that the more courteous you are in your driving, the more likely you are to be a safer and more environment-friendly driver. Remember to give space to pedestrians and cyclists, who are doing their part by avoiding driving. Don't strand pedestrians in the crosswalk in order to turn right on a red light. Cut your speed and try to keep calm, even when other people are driving badly. Leave room between your car and the one ahead. Government agencies and groups such as **Against Drunk Driving** and **Mothers Against Drunk Driving (MADD)** actively campaign to prevent road accidents.

6 Communication & computers

ADVERTISING • CENSORSHIP • COMPUTER GAMES • CYBERWORLD • CYBER-FRAUD • DIGITAL UNTOUCHABLES • E-CASH • ERGONOMICS • HACKERS • HOME SHOPPING • INFORMATION OVERLOAD • INTERACTIVE TV • INTERNET • INTRANETS • JUNK MAIL • MICROCHIPS • MILLENNIUM BUG • MOBILE TELEPHONES • PESTER POWER • PRIVACY THIEVES • SATELLITES • SMART CARDS • SPACE JUNK • TELEWORKING • UPGRADEABILITY • VIDEO-CONFERENCING • VIRUSES • VIRTUAL REALITY

Communications technology has gone through explosive changes over the last century. From radio to interactive television, from typewriters to laptop computers and the Internet, these new technologies have helped to transform our lives.

The speed of this change is now accelerating further as a huge range of new technologies comes on-stream—mobile telephones, video-conferencing, virtual reality and many more. As a result, it is almost impossible to imagine the end-points of this revolution as it races into the third millennium. It would be like trying to forecast all the ways in which the horseless carriage would affect our lives as the first Model T rolled off the Ford production line nearly a hundred years ago.

Inevitably, the increasingly powerful communication and computer technologies now appearing in our workplaces and homes raise a host of new issues, some of which we explore in this chapter. For example: What can computers really offer us? How are they likely to evolve? And how will they affect our lives in the future?

As information technology (IT) spreads around the planet and infiltrates every aspect of our lives, we probe some of the environmental and social impacts that computers bring in their wake. We focus on some of the ways in which IT is being greened. And we investigate the implications of having our privacy invaded. How are people getting what information about us—and how is it being used?

In summary, this chapter asks three main questions—and then looks at some of the practical issues arising from them:

- *Will computers end up running the world?*
- *What are the upsides and downsides of IT?*
- *Can we green IT?*

6.1 Cyber Citizens

Will computers end up running the world?

The panic that hit many companies when they first heard about the "Millennium Bug," which threatens to send the world's older computers crazy as the new millennium dawns, shows just how dependent on chips and computers we have become. They are everywhere: in our cars, elevators, watches, even toys.

Welcome to the "cyberworld"

This is where we and our descendants will spend the 21st century and the third millennium. It is a strange world, bringing us many extraordinary gifts—and introducing new threats. Some people—particularly children—are taking to it like ducks to water. Some of us are drowning in information. And some people don't even know it's happening.

How did it happen?

The cyberworld has been evolving for a long time. You can track its roots back to early calculators, like the beads-on-a-wire technology of the abacus, or the cogs-and-gears computer of the last century. But the real take-off came in the 20th century—and the resulting revolution has rocketed forward in recent years.

In some ways, the computer was a latecomer. In the 1830s, it might take eight months for a letter to travel from India to England. By 1870, a telegram might take just five hours. The telegraph involved sending electrical signals, which could be converted to words at a distance. Hence *tele* for "far" and *graph* for "written." Then came the telephone—the word *phone* being used for "sound," also at a distance. Unlike the telegraph and the telephone, the next big invention, radio, didn't need wires to carry the messages. That's why people called it the "wireless."

Each of these three teletechnologies helped to link distant places, with the speed and usefulness of the message increasing each time. But, even after such stunning progress, the next step forward was revolutionary in a new way. Television, from *tele* and *vision*, enabled us to see at a distance. In simple terms, it brought the planet into our living rooms—and the world would never be the same again.

By the 1960s, the first ("baby boom") generation had been reared on TV, a fact that transformed the way they viewed the world and the way in which they behaved. TV revolutionized many things, even war. The Vietnam War was fought as much on TV as on the battlefields, and the world's most powerful nation, the United States, lost.

Behind the scenes, however, something was happening that was to lay the foundations of an even greater leap into the future. The first radios used large, bulb-like "valves" to amplify the messages. From the late 1940s, however, valves began to be replaced by "transistors." These are tiny electrical switches—much smaller, more robust and less energy-intensive, which also means that the equipment does not heat up as much.

More than anything else, transistors were the building block for the Digital Age. Other major milestones included the invention of the integrated circuit—or "chip"—in 1958, and the launch of the Apple "personal computer" in 1984.

There is more computing power in a musical greeting card than there was in the whole world in 1950.

Apple's founders aimed to provide "wheels for the brain," and they succeeded spectacularly. But the pace of progress has been so staggering that even fleet-footed Apple couldn't keep up.

The power and speed of the computer chips has been doubling every 18 months—and the cost halving. Most people in the industry forecast that this trend will continue for years to come, suggesting that each year computers will become more powerful, faster, smaller and cheaper.

Indeed, probably the most startling indication of the scale of this revolution is that every month the global IT industry now makes no less than four *quadrillion* transistors. That's over 500 000 for every man, woman and child on the planet.[1]

The pace of progress is unlikely to stop—or even slow down—any time soon. Scientists are now working on superwhizzy computers of the future that will be based on transistors made from single molecules. This will involve unimaginably sophisticated technology, with engineers increasingly working at the atomic level. But if we can be sure of anything, we can be sure it will happen. It is simply a question of when.[2]

Net and Web

Given the near-miraculous powers of these new machines, it is not surprising that most of us still focus on the hardware and software, which we will discuss at the end of this chapter. But computers have now been linked in new ways—via the Internet and World Wide Web. The effect has been to open up a new universe, or cyberworld. It is a world that many parents fear has swallowed their children.

The Internet (or "Net") is a vast international computer network. It evolved from an urgent question raised over 30 years ago: how would the U.S. authorities communicate after a nuclear war? The answer was to begin the process of linking millions of individual computers so that the network would survive even if large parts were obliterated. Today, any individual with a computer can use the Net and get information from anywhere in the world down the telephone line.

Plugging in is like having millions of experts at your disposal—or a vast, constantly updated encyclopedia at your fingertips. You can use the Internet for zillions of things, including sending messages, finding a job, listening to music, discovering new recipes, playing games, linking up with like-minded people around the world, doing research or simply looking around—known as "surfing."

So let's quickly explore some of the main building blocks of the cyberworld:

World Wide Web: For many people, the "Web" is the Internet. It is a universe of linked pages that you access over the Net. Reading a page off the Web is like reading a magazine, except that it is interactive: you can click on particular words or phrases and "jump" onto other pages or other websites. Each jump can take you, just as swiftly, to another document by the same organization—or to a new organization in another part of the world.

Home pages: Many companies now have a "website" address, where you can find out more about them—and in many cases buy their products. As long as you have a computer and an Internet connection, you can also have a "home page" on the Web, which anyone can access. These websites can be used for something as simple as a family scrapbook, or for broader interests such as fan clubs, religious cults (page 98) or hobbies. And they can be furnished with anything that can be digitized—from your ideas, voice and causes, through to pictures of your ancestors, pets or scars.

Search engines: These are the Internet's equivalent of the librarian who looks up your book request in a card index at a public library. The difference is that search engines, also known as "web browsers," can operate at lightning speed, covering millions of records in a matter of seconds. Although constantly updated, they are never comprehensive—and there is always the risk, if you are not very specific, of being buried under an avalanche of useless information. Welcome to "information overload" (page 176).

E-mail: Electronic mail is a tremendous way of keeping in touch with people, many of whom you may never meet in the flesh. You can send e-mail to anyone connected to the Internet, from the prime minister to your next-door neighbour. You can also attach large documents, spreadsheets, computer programs or pictures for the recipient to put onto their computer and use or alter as required.

Chatting: Chatting over the Internet with people on the other side of the planet still only costs the price of a local call. There are thousands of sites with a "chat" or discussion area, often set up as "forums" for people with shared interests. You can find forums on gardening, Scrabble, Dr. Seuss children's stories or the Grateful Dead, and meet like-minded people. One problem is that such sites still operate by typing in what you want to say, but it shouldn't be long before we will be able to hear—and then see—our e-friends as video-conferencing facilities become more common.

Games: You can also play games on the Internet, taking part either on a one-to-one basis or in games with multiple players. There is everything from war games to live versions of bridge, chess, Scrabble and so on. You enter a site, register that you want to play and are then able to join other people at their "table."

Intranets: The Internet is open to all who have a computer, but an "intranet" is more exclusive. Usually, it is developed within an organization, so that employees can use it, but outsiders can't. Well-developed intranet systems become the shared memories of such organizations, also helping to deal with the problem of losing knowledge when key people leave the organization.

Cable TV: For better or worse, cable TV will eventually mean that there are thousands—if not millions—of channels. Although you need a computer to access the Net and Web, millions of people will soon be doing so via interactive TVs. You will be able to surf the Net, or do your shopping from your own TV screen. This is likely to be important to the TV companies and broadcast media, which are beginning to worry that they will lose viewers to the increasingly seductive Net. Their main hope must be that the different media will converge and merge.[3]

Virtual worlds

"Virtual reality" describes a computer-generated environment that is almost lifelike—in which the user, or users, can become immersed. Most of us think of virtual reality in terms of people wearing strange helmets and electronic gloves, so they can see 3-D worlds, as well as feel and even (eventually) smell what is going on. They can play games, fight virtual battles, carry out surgical operations or walk through buildings that have not yet been built.

There are many potentially useful applications for virtual reality. Medical students, for example, can now train by dissecting a "virtual corpse." Aircraft pilots can learn their trade on the ground. And emergency evacuation procedures can be tested in "virtually real" situations; indeed, so frighteningly real are some of these simulations that great care has to be taken not to frighten people out of their wits. But given that sex is the most widely searched-for topic on the Web, virtual sex with anyone of your choosing seems set to be a sure-fire winner!

Just as TV transformed the world, so will "virtuality." Many of us will be members of multiple communities, physical ones and virtual ones. Some of our virtual neighbours will live next door, but many—who share interests such as medicine, art, plumbing, the environment or homosexuality—will link via the Internet. Already some schools no longer have physical classrooms, instead operating virtually, potentially meaning that you could be educated through the U.S. system, for example, while living in Vietnam or Venezuela.

Companies, too, are learning to operate virtually, with different parts of a project team keeping in touch electronically from different parts of the world. As a result, we will hear much more about—and many of us will increasingly find ourselves working for—"virtual corporations," operating from "virtual desks" and attending "virtual meetings."

Who controls IT?

Early in the 20th century, people like George Orwell feared that the future would be controlled by dictators, like "Big Brother." When the first giant computers came along, some as big as houses, there were real concerns that these machines would compete with us for control of the planet. The technology has evolved dramatically, but still people fear that a few ultrapowerful individuals will establish a stranglehold on the cyberworld.

Digital gold rush

Many fear that the extraordinary success of Bill Gates, founder and chairman of software giant Microsoft, means that he and his company could stage a new form of world domination.

Gates sees today's IT industry and cybermarket as just the beginning. "The global information market will be huge," he says. "It will combine all the various ways human goods, services and ideas are exchanged. On a practical level, this will give you broader choices about most things, including how you earn and invest, what you buy and how much you pay for it, who your friends are and how you spend your time with them, and where and how securely your family live."[4]

This is not just hype from someone who wants to sell us more computer equipment. Whether we like it or not, IT will change just about everything we do—even our sense of who we are. We will soon be calling for new rights, assuming new responsibilities and supporting new laws to tackle new problems (page 185).

As the Digital Age gets into its stride, the gold-rush phase continues. Indeed, many people worry that wealth is being concentrated in too few hands, as it was in the early years of the Oil Age—when families like the Gettys and Rockefellers made their fortunes.

Interestingly, whatever you may imagine, surveys show that people who regularly use computers are likely to be closer to the ideal model of an intelligent, informed, outspoken, participatory and patriotic citizen, with real faith in the future.[5] This is a stark contrast to the usual image of computer "nerds," locked into their own world—and possibly addicted to violent games and pornography.

More worryingly, however, computers are now beginning to challenge us intellectually. IBM's *Deep Blue* and *Deeper Blue* computers were eventually able to evaluate 200 million chess moves per second. Even Gary Kasparov, arguably the greatest chess player of all time, was struggling. The sheer pace of progress suggests that computers will soon have the edge.

Should we be worried? Some people think so. In the film *2001*, the supercomputer HAL takes over a space station and tries to kill the humans who want to reprogram it. The idea that machines might one day become so powerful that they take over the world has often popped up in science fiction. And it may not be totally fanciful. But, although a computerized Big Brother might just help to curb the worst excesses of humanity's strong will to violence and destruction, a world controlled by a single computer would also be extremely vulnerable to malfunctions, natural disasters or terrorism.

Global operators

Nowadays, all sorts of business—from grocery stores to banks—operate over the Net. Many are expanding overseas, operating in a fast-expanding but largely invisible market. They are selling everything from books to high-tech weaponry. Soon, many slower-moving companies will find they have lost their customers, often without even being aware of how it happened. So far, America and Japan have led the computer revolution, but new leaders are emerging. India, for example, has taken a lead in developing software. One Indian business leader pointed out that this industry is particularly suited to his country, since it is people-intensive rather than capital-intensive. It demands highly skilled young people, has few undesirable environmental side-effects and is growing rapidly. Indeed, it is no accident that about 10 per cent of Microsoft's total workforce is Indian.

Whatever business you work in, computers are helping to accelerate globalization, breaking down traditional notions of office hours as we move toward a 24-hour-a-day world. In America, where the consumer rules, many shops now never close. In Canada, we have seen all-night gas stations, followed by 24-hour on-line banking and round-the-clock grocery shopping in some major cities.[6]

As these trends build, we will see the evolution of an increasingly seamless digital workplace. Projects increasingly move around the world on a 24-hour cycle, from person to person or from group to group, one working as the other sleeps. In this new economy, an ever-growing wave of projects will follow the sun as it travels around the globe.

Computer dependency

Clearly, we are becoming increasingly dependent upon a cyberworld that spans the globe—and is now beyond the capacity of any single individual to understand. This is a world that operates to its own rules, making it difficult to predict what will happen next.

So tightly interconnected is this new world, some argue, that we must now develop a series of measures for evaluating and communicating the scale of "Net crashes," as when 40 million Americans lost their telephone connections for 19 hours. Just as the Richter scale is used for earthquakes in the physical world, this new system would measure the economic impact of a "Netquake" in the cyberworld.

In the 1970s, a megabyte of memory cost $2.5 million, compared to perhaps $12.50 today.

Squashing the Y2K Bug

The scale of our IT dependency was brought home to people when news started to filter out about the "Millennium Bug," also known as the Year 2000 or Y2K problem. The problem results from the fact that in the 1950s and 1960s, computer engineers tried to save memory, which was incredibly expensive. In the 1970s, for example, a megabyte of memory cost $2.5 million, compared to perhaps $12.50 today. To save money and memory, they programmed dates using two digits, instead of the normal four: for example 99 instead of 1999. Unfortunately, when (19)99 becomes (20)00, computers may think they are back in the year 1900 and wipe out any data that come after that date.

Even if many of the problems forecast never materialize, the Y2K Bug—in simple cost terms—will probably have been the greatest industrial disaster ever. The estimates of global losses range from an incredible US$300 billion to an unthinkable US$3.6 trillion. Not surprisingly, one leading economist has concluded that there is a 40 per cent chance that a breakdown in communications caused by the Y2K bug could be enough to cause a worldwide recession.

Banks, we are told, could mistakenly withdraw their loans. Airplanes might fall out of the sky. Elevators could freeze in their shafts—and cash machines spew out wads of money onto the street. Hospitals could grind to a halt, losing their records and the lives of many unfortunate patients.

The potential problem is made much worse by the fact that such dates are embedded in almost every microchip in a system. Breakdowns could be caused by a chip that no one affected was even aware existed. So how else do the experts think the Y2K bug could affect us?

Banks and credit cards: Now that the money world has gone electronic (page 203), anyone spending, saving or investing could be hit. For example, a customer's accounts could be deleted—or a century's worth of interest added.

Offices: Intelligent buildings may suddenly act dumb, refusing to let people in. If they get in, computer systems may not work and heating, ventilation and security systems may fail.

Health-care services: In the Canadian health-care system alone, it looks as if addressing the Y2K problem could run into the billions of dollars. Even in a small province like Nova Scotia, it is estimated that ensuring the Y2K bug doesn't cripple vital medical equipment could cost the provincial government $60–$70 million. Ontario, meanwhile, has committed $278.5 million to enable hospitals to make their computer systems Y2K compliant. This is money that could otherwise have helped to cure illnesses and save lives.

Local services and shops: Some retailers have already had problems in handling credit cards or expiry dates in the year "00"—so some fear that many services will fail as 2000 approaches.

Transport: Getting to work might be a headache. Traffic lights, street lighting and ticketing systems all depend on date-dependent software.

Air travel: Airlines and airports have been working on this problem for some years. It is unlikely that airplanes will fall out of the sky, but very likely that many flights will be cancelled as undetected bugs show their effect. Some airlines may refuse to fly to certain countries, where they fear the Y2K Bug might cripple air-traffic control systems.

Satellites: In space, some of the older satellites have clocks that cannot make the century change. Replacing their chips is impossible. End of story?

Defence: Hunting down the Y2K Bug in today's highly computerized military systems has been a nightmare. So if you are planning to declare war, don't do it late on December 31, 1999.

Home: Inconvenience is likely to be the most serious problem for householders as video recorders cannot be set for the year 2000, and some sophisticated heating and security systems disobey orders.

Personal computers: Older machines used two-digit dates. Many machines bought as recently as 1997 failed at least some millennium-compliance tests. Even if the hardware passes, the software may not.

Telephones: It may be advisable to make your calls on December 31, 1999, rather than on January 1, 2000, since there is still a possibility that the lines could fail.

Although the Millennium Bug can be relatively simple to sort out, the changeover requires advance planning—and there is a shortage of skilled technicians for the job. Furthermore, the rogue dates are often embedded in systems and need to be changed systematically.

Worse, in some chips it may simply be impossible to change the date. So how many of these are there—and where are they? Nobody really knows, although a train, for example, has hundreds, in power-control systems, doors and brakes.

Who knows what will happen? The millennium may dawn with no problems at all, or the cyberworld may suffer withdrawal symptoms quite as traumatic as a heroin addict's "cold turkey." But one thing will have been made clear to most people: we all have a heavy—and growing—computer dependency.

Haves and have-nots

One problem with this computer dependency is that our world is increasingly divided into a new form of "haves" and "have-nots." Some people are speeding along the "information superhighway," while others are left behind in their dust-cloud.

People who are highly informed and skilled in the ways of this digital world even have their own name: the *digerati*. Citizens of cyberspace, on the other hand, have been dubbed *netizens*. But there are a number of reasons why not every one wants to—or is able to—join their ranks.

Age: Many older people are deeply uneasy with new technology—and particularly fearful of computers. Young people, by contrast, are exposed to computers from the beginning—and soon accept them as an integral part of their lives. Children come from a world of "crash and burn," happily experimenting with little or no reference to the instructions. They consult, confer and learn very fast, delighting in helping others, regardless of age. For them the computer is natural, not something to be feared.[7]

Sex: Although computers are generally believed to be more of a male interest, in a survey testing levels of competency in navigating the Internet, females led by a nose.

Wealth: Once wealth meant money, but in the cyberworld it also means access to technology and information. It is an extraordinary fact that fully 80 per cent of the world's people still lack even basic telecommunications. Although the range and power of computing technology is soaring, and the cost tumbling, there is a huge—and often growing chasm—between those who are "wired" and those who are not. "Teledensity," or the number of phones per 100 people, is now seen both as a spur to wealth and as a means of measuring it.

Three-quarters of the world's telephones are installed in just eight countries.

Language: English—particularly American English—has emerged as the language of the Net. The French are among those worrying about their language being squeezed to extinction in cyberspace. In 1997, only 4 per cent of Internet sites were created in French, mostly by French Canadians. Part of the problem is that English speakers are winning hands-down in coining new terms. "Hacker," for example, is unlikely to be replaced by the French "*un pirate informatique*." Longer term, however, powerful new translation software may make it easier for non-English speakers to feel at home on the Net.

Jargon: A real problem with the cyberworld is that we are creating a landscape littered with acronyms. Exciting for those in the know, perhaps, but worrying for people who see them as so much gibberish. Some are pronounced as a series of letters (e.g., CPU, ISDN), while others (e.g., ASCII, DOS) are pronounced as words. Yet others have evolved on the Net as shorthand; for example, FWIW (*for what it is worth*) and IMHO (*in my humble opinion*). Expect more.

Getting started, keeping going: Getting started can be a big stumbling block. You may have got all the equipment, the manuals and the enthusiasm. But then you cannot understand the instructions, or you set something up and it won't work. Then the system crashes. Or you may be unclear exactly what you are trying to do. Don't worry: everyone goes through this stage. And the technology is getting better all the time. Computer crashes are becoming something of a rarity.

Technophobes: However user-friendly these machines may become, you still have to want to use them. Those who can't or won't risk being left behind. Perhaps technophobia in general—and cyberphobia in particular—will even come to be seen as treatable diseases?

IT impact zones

The so-called bits of information that computers process are not edible, so they can't directly stop hunger. Nor are computers moral, so they can't resolve complex issues like the rights to life and death. But computers, chips and bits are now shaping every aspect of our world and future. Like a force of nature, the Digital Age is now pretty much unstoppable, so learning how to "be digital" will be almost as important as learning how to read or write.[8]

Let's look at just a few areas of our lives that will be transformed.

Intelligent buildings

We started out in trees and caves—and now seem to be creating homes and workplaces that will be almost as complex as entire ecosystems. Think of Microsoft's Bill Gates, who spent years building a new US$53 million cyberhome in Seattle. Everything had to be automated, from the garage doors through to the art collection shown on wall-mounted screens. Ironically, the whole system broke down soon after it was installed.

But this is a trend that will gather force in the 21st century. Our homes and other buildings will become increasingly "intelligent," eventually knowing more about our lives or companies than we do. Indeed, what will it be like to move into a home that remembers the previous occupants, their habits and tastes? Will we have to retrain it—and perhaps even have its memory banks wiped, so that it doesn't keep telling us how the previous people did things?

Walk around many kitchens at night and you see little red lights: on the fridge, on the range, on the mobile phone. These are early twinklings of intelligence in homes that are still largely "dumb." Even today, however, we have programmable heating systems and ovens, lights that can be set to go on and off to deter burglars, and alarm systems that will soon recognize us by looking deep into our eyes.

Early on, many of these systems will gobble energy, but eventually they may help our buildings become much more energy-efficient. Just as our homes were invaded by videos and CD players, it won't be long before these machines are joined by—and often hooked up to—others. These might include "virtual chefs," to cook the meals, and "intelligent garbage pails," which recognize and separate recyclable materials.

Some enthusiasts even picture a future where our "smart" shoes send a signal to an "intelligent doorknob" as we walk up the front path—and the building itself takes our bags and asks us what sort of day we have had. Maybe, but the Gates family's hiccups suggest this scenario is still very much in the future.

Home shopping

Many people who hate going to the grocery store love the idea of teleshopping. Indeed, already you can buy almost anything over the Internet, from books and coffee through to cars, holidays and homes. And the relative convenience of teleshopping will grow hugely as the services get better—and the pressure on our roads gets worse.

Just as the supermarkets are trying to reproduce the traditional main street all under the one roof, with specialist counters offering everything from meat to dry cleaning, so we are seeing the early stages in the evolution of what the Japanese dub "roboshops." The idea is that you will get all the service you want, being guided by willing and knowledgeable assistants, and yet never meet another human being.[9]

So what will it actually be like? Well, we are told, we will be able to sail down virtual grocery-store aisles with the aid of a mouse (the computer kind, of course), clicking on items we want to check, know more about or buy.

We will soon be able to choose a virtual shop assistant who knows exactly what we want and where to find it. We may even be able to have our own virtual butler or maid who follows us everywhere in cyberspace, knowing our needs and tastes almost as well as we do.

Imagine being able to ask for a romantic vegetarian dinner for two, perhaps to a specified budget, or ordering a suitable present for a 12-year-old granddaughter interested in bypass surgery and flower arrangement.

No wonder people are keen to see progress in this area, particularly those who are "cash rich but time poor." Although the grocery stores have been bombarded with requests to expand their pilot schemes to other regions, there are still lots of glitches in the system—from the wrong foods being delivered through to the order arriving at the wrong address.

Expect rapid progress, though. Already there are trials under way with on-screen personalities available to help us shop. These "personalities" actually understand not only what we say, but also gestures, such as nodding or shaking our heads.

In Japan, there is "Takishi," a helpful computer-generated shop assistant with slicked-back hair, bow tie and braces. He already recognizes several hundred words in Japanese, such as "What is that?" and "Show me." In the U.S., meanwhile, "NetHead Red" not only greets customers and answers questions, but she can even distinguish between people who are genuinely interested and those who are simply passing by.

Finding Mr. or Miss Right

It can be hard to express emotion when sending e-mails. Inevitably, however, computers are getting more emotional, even more romantic. Users have come up with a range of "emoticons," or "smileys," which mimic facial expressions and body language. And computers are now being used not simply as dating agencies, storing details of the romantic interests of their clients, but also for studying what mating strategies are most effective in the modern world. Indeed, one leading feminist has even suggested that women might start to share what they know about particular men through the Internet, to unmask and avoid the "cads."[10]

At one German institute, scientists are trying to work out how many people we would need to date to find the right partner. Although statistics and economics suggest that you would need to check out 37 per cent of the world's population (of 6 billion), the scientists—reassuringly—conclude that it should be enough to try just 12 serious candidates when looking for a partner.[11] It sounds a bit optimistic, but they argue that this sample would give a good idea of the general standard of possible mates available, dramatically increasing the chances of identifying Mr. or Miss Right.

In Japan, meanwhile, men are at last able to find the woman of their dreams—a tall, slim school pupil with doe-like eyes. This computer-simulated character, known as "Horose Nozomi," offers herself for dates and comes in various guises, from sporty to scatter-brained. The problem may be that these sweet, shy and submissive idols may make it even harder for men to relate to real women, who are growing more assertive.

Computer-simulated submissive female models may make it harder for men to relate to real women.

Remote voters

Imagine voting without having to go to the polling station. Maybe today's radio and TV stations give a foretaste of the future with their "phone-in" lines to register your opinion on different issues. Some would argue that those who phone in are not representative, but perhaps the polling booth system is no better.

Clearly the job of a politician is to take time to understand the nuances of complicated issues. Politics involves compromise, which is nearly impossible without a relatively small number of representatives making informed decisions on behalf of the people who elected them. But the new technologies will haul all politicians into the spotlight. Instead of getting away with glib sound bites, voters will be able to get a much more direct sense of what their representatives are doing—and how they are voting.

The day when a member of Congress, MP or MPP gets 100 000 e-mails on a single topic, or is able to have his or her beeper announce the results of a real-time opinion poll from his or her constituents, will be the day a new era in politics really begins.

Who goes there?

Most of us now have wallets—or purses—full of plastic cards: credit cards, bank cards, airline cards, retail cards and so on. But in the future we may carry a single smart card encoded with all the necessary details of our identity, medical records, insurance policies, financial status, bank accounts and the like.

On the other hand, maybe we won't need cards at all. Already there are technologies that can identify you without anything being inserted into them. Machines that take a photograph of your eyeball, for example, have proved very effective, since every individual eye is unique. Once correctly identified, you will be able to carry on with your transaction without delay. An even more radical approach, which we are unlikely to see for some time, would be to implant a chip under our skin that contains all the information about us anyone will ever need to know. Having worked out how to identify a person when he or she is on the spot, scientists are now turning their attention to identifying a criminal suspect, for example, from biological samples left at the scene of a crime. They are using traces of blood, sperm or hair to build up a picture of what the suspect looks like. The DNA in the samples could reveal the suspect's race, eye and hair colour, and even the shape of his or her head.

Getting smaller

Do you ever get the sense that things around you are shrinking? Already many of us wear digital watches and carry pagers and ever-smaller mobile telephones. Forecasters predict that we will soon be wearing our computers rather than lugging them around. So, just as people today listen to the latest musical hits while jogging, soon they will be able to call up websites and send e-mails as they exercise.

Computer wearers will listen to music broadcasts over the Net, call up travel timetables, check their diary arrangements or look up a word in the encyclopedia almost as easily as we look at our watches. And, as voice recognition technology improves, we will also soon be talking to our wearable computers. Noise nuisance, already a problem with mobile-telephone users, will intensify as ordinary citizens walk through the streets, stations and airports apparently chatting to their wrists —or using chin microphones.

Take heart, though. The world may yet become quieter. Some experts say that the time is coming when biocomputers can invade our brains and take instructions direct from our thought waves.

Use less

Ever since the computer first appeared on the scene, enthusiasts have been telling us that one result would be to reduce the amount of paper we use. For years, this forecast has provoked hollow laughs as people struggle with the ever-increasing mountains of paper generated by computers, faxes, photocopiers and other electronic equipment. But behind the scenes some important changes have been under way, which are beginning to deliver on that original promise.

Looking back, one of the big mistakes we made was simply to take the paper-based office and transfer it onto our computing systems. Because the whole idea was to produce paper—something the new technologies were spectacularly good at—the inevitable result was a massive growth in paper use.

Now, however, some people are beginning to use computers differently. Today's executives often do their own typing and e-mail messages, which zip through cyberspace at speeds that would have been inconceivable when typewriters and typing pools were state-of-the-art.

It has to be said, however, that the speed and efficiency of the new technology have dramatically increased the total amount of communication, so the reductions may be relative rather than absolute. So, for example, if people travel less because they are working from home (page 188), this will only mean less traffic on the road if they do not increase their travel at other times or for other purposes. Likewise, e-mail will only save on printing and paper if most e-mails are not printed off and photocopied.

Teleconference facilities, where executives "meet" on-screen from their offices in different parts of the world, can mean a real reduction in overseas travel or long-distance travel, as well as substantial savings in hotel bills and executive time. Major savings can also be had when it is possible to buy a single machine that can serve as a phone, fax, answering machine, scanner and printer.

Another area where savings can be made through computer use is in safety testing. Whether it's for simulated car crashes or for trying out new tactics and weapons for the armed services, cyberspace can be an effective alternative to expensively crushed vehicles and holes blown in the countryside.

If we stand back and look at the big picture, it is clear that computers are shifting us to a new economy, in which we increasingly move bits of information rather than atoms of material. This trend could hardly be more timely, given that our movements of materials and energy are increasingly producing worrying impacts upon the global environment. So let's look at how environmentalists feel about IT.

Global brains

As a group, environmentalists did not fall head over heels in love with computers the way scientists and Nintendo-loving teenagers did. Indeed, computers seemed to be helping the enemy. As *Time* put it: "The big mainframes in the old days—IBM's generous contributions to environmental causes notwithstanding—all seemed to be working for giant corporations bent on cutting forests, paving wetlands or filling up the sky with hydrocarbons."[12]

The early PCs, even if they did have fruity names like "Apple" and "Apricot," came wreathed in packaging and, once switched on, were seen to be sources of dangerous electromagnetic fields. But the arrival of the Web changed all that. *Time* again: "With nodes wherever a local environmental group could afford a PC and phone line, and a structure suited for mobilizing far-flung activists in a common cause, the Internet was ideal for thinking locally and acting globally to save the earth."

When the magazine tried a quick keyword search, it was stunned to find just how many green sites popped up. In 1997, it reported that it had found "an astonishing number of matches for such hot-button environmental issues as ozone depletion (41 110 Web pages), global warming (75 160) and pollution (354 580)."

Much of the stuff you find on the greener parts of the Web[13] are repetitive and, in some cases, not very accurate. But all of this activity points to the possibility that the Web could develop, over several decades, the makings of an amazingly powerful, global "green conscience."

There is even the suggestion that we wire up the entire global ecosystem to the Web. The idea is that we would seed millions of tiny video cameras and powerful sensors around the world to monitor everything from smokestacks to wetlands. Environmental groups—and the public—could then start to track everything from CFCs going up into the ozone layer to shipments of toxic waste on their way to Brazil or Malaysia.

"We haven't a clue what happens if we begin to network the ecosphere and make the results accessible to anyone who wants them," one expert commented. But one thing we can be sure of: plugging ordinary citizens into the planet is likely to make us all much more environment-conscious. So a technology that began as a means of coping with nuclear bombs could help us from winning our undeclared war against our own planet.

Cyber Citizens

✔Citizen 2000 Checklist

1. Get Computer Literate

All of us have something to learn about computers, but now that they are an integral part of our lives, we need to keep up-to-date. The best way to get started is to find a friend or colleague who is prepared to talk you through the basics–children are often a good bet! Then go to the computer section in your local bookshop and see what's available. If you decide to enrol in a local course, perhaps through a community college, choose a course teaching you how to use computers rather than program them.

If there is a cybercafé in your area, this will be a good place to get a feel of how the Internet works. Your local library might also be able to offer you time on the Internet. Bestselling books on the Internet include *The Canadian Internet Handbook* and *The*

Internet Directory and Research Guide, published by Prentice Hall, *The Rough Guide to the Internet*, published by HarperCollins, and Trevor Owen's *The Learning Highway*, published by Key Porter Books. Other books to look for include the *Dummy Guides*, including *Word for Windows for Dummies*.

2. USE IT EFFECTIVELY

Let IT cut down the amount of paper you use, and the amount you travel. Investigate the options, and let them work for you. Many environmental groups now have websites. Expand your awareness of current issues while learning to "surf the Net."

3. TAKE THE MILLENNIUM BUG SERIOUSLY

Many sources of information are available on the Y2K bug. Read the newspapers. Scan computer magazines for articles on the theme. A number of Canadian and U.S. websites are also well worth perusing from time to time. **Canadian Y2K** counsels preparedness but not panic. It provides excellent background information, discusses the potential effects of the Y2K bug on health-care, banking, transportation and so on, and collects news items. **Y2K Watch** on *GLOBEtechnology.com* provides free access to *The Globe and Mail*'s archives for articles related to the Millennium Bug. Both **Canadian Y2K** and **Y2K Watch** provide links to other useful Y2K sites.

Utne Reader, a periodical that excerpts articles and summarizes ideas from "the best of the alternative media," has produced a *Y2K Citizen's Action Guide*. The guide takes a communitarian approach and suggests ways to prepare yourself, your family and your neighbourhood for the year 2000 problem. The guide is available on newsstands or by mail order, or it can be downloaded from the Web.

6.2 Chips with Everything

What are the upsides and downsides of IT?

The promise is seductive. Soon we will have huge calculating power and all the world's information at our fingertips. Students, for example, can now take powerful calculators into exams to do calculations that once would have taken mathematical geniuses hours or days to perform. Certainly, we will be much better informed, but will we be able to sort the wheat from the chaff? Will we be more knowledgeable? And wiser?

Good for us?

Communications technologies can bring major benefits—otherwise people wouldn't spend so much on them. Some of the early suppliers and users overpromised, but now we are seeing some of the real benefits. However, as these new uses evolve they will inevitably bring new problems. Let's look at some of the bigger ones.

Overload

More and more of us are being overwhelmed by avalanches of data. It is as if words have suddenly found the ability to breed like rabbits. For example, the Lord's prayer is just 73 words long, whereas documentation on the pricing of cabbages in the European Union now takes nearly 7000 words.

In the past generation, more words have been churned out than in all the rest of recorded time.

Every day more than 1000 books are published and nearly 20 million words of technical data are recorded. Thanks to computers, e-mail, faxes, mobile phones, voice mail and answering machines, many of us are exposed to ever-growing torrents of information.

As one information worker joked, half-seriously: "Check your e-mail, voice mail, fax, database—and it's time to go home." A recent U.S. survey found that the average corporate worker sends and receives 177 messages a day![14] Many workers, apparently, are so desperate to get the recipient's attention that they send the same message in different ways and at different times. Most of us already experience volumes of junk mail through the mail (page 191), but with more ways of getting in touch, the direct-mailing opportunities are expanding all the time. Junk e-mails have followed junk faxes. Indeed, bombarding people with unsolicited information in this way even has its own name: *spamming*. This practice, used to sell everything from adult videos to diet pills, has become so widespread that at times it has disabled parts of the Internet.

The result can be growing stress among those using these technologies—doctors call it "information overload syndrome." First detected among British and American intelligence decoders during the Second World War, it is becoming an increasingly common feature of modern life. Initial symptoms include forgetfulness, headaches, bad temper, loss of concentration, sleep disturbance, anxiety and "computer rage"—literally beating up the computer.

As the number of messages grows, the real challenge is to work out what is significant—and what is not. Internet service providers are now offering filtering services to reduce spamming, while management consulting companies charge clients to weed out useless information. One hopeful idea is that the phone should offer services on phones, faxes, e-mail, voice mail and so on, that have a much higher degree of built-in intelligence, so we can teach them who we do—and do not—want to receive messages from.[15]

Cellular phones

The growth in the use of cellular phones in recent years has been dramatic. They offer huge advantages to people on the move, represent a key ingredient in any successful "virtual business" (pages 166 and 186) and will inevitably continue to proliferate. But even such tiny devices can cast a long shadow.

One of the main concerns has been that the use of cellular phones may be causing health problems. The concern is that electromagnetic radiation generated from cellular phones is absorbed directly into the head—and particularly the brain—of the user. Some scientists argue that even a few minutes' exposure to this type of radiation can transform a five per cent active cancer into a 95 per cent active cancer. One Australian study found a near-doubling of tumours in animals exposed to this form of radiation. A recent *Lancet* article recommended that cellular phones contain health warnings.

That said, and although U.S. authorities advise cellular telephone users to limit their calls and make them as brief as possible, most scientists agree that there is not yet firm evidence that these phones are causing cancer. And research continues. That can always change, of course, and there is still concern that low-level radiation might cause short-term memory loss.[16] Research on rats showed that it affected their ability to learn simple tasks. But those with the latest digital phones will no doubt be relieved to hear that they emit less radiation than the older analogue phones.

Then, again, there are the social problems. It often seems that cellular-phone users have joined smokers, drunks, nose-pickers, hawkers and pan-handlers as social outcasts. Some people feel it is bad manners to use cellular phones in public places, their trills disrupting civilized life. Worse, users tend to adopt a loud voice that is not easily ignored. As a result, these phones are now banned from many restaurants, theatres, gas stations and airplanes. And at least one train company has announced that it will be coating the windows of some of its cars with metallic film, which is impenetrable to radio signals.[17]

Then there is all the infrastructure needed to support cellular phones. Cell-phone towers are sprouting up around our cities, and sometimes in the oddest places—in the midst of a Calgary cemetery and concealed in a church cross in Vancouver. On a per-capita basis, Alberta has the highest cell-phone use in Canada and is believed to have the highest percentage of cell-phone users in North America.[18] Not surprisingly, it has also seen a number of successful protests against towers that were installed without community consultation.

We need to see greater cooperation between competing companies, so that they can share towers or even use structures that already exist—but not crosses! New phone systems will require hundreds of new satellites in low-Earth orbit, more than doubling the risk of collisions with other satellites.

Alberta is believed to have the highest percentage of cell-phone users in North America.

One of the systems planned would involve no less than 840 satellites to ensure worldwide coverage. An effect of so many satellite launches into space will be a 30 per cent increase in space debris bigger than one centimetre. The destruction of a French satellite in 1996 by a fragment from an Ariane rocket launched 10 years earlier has concentrated space scientists' minds on this issue.

Are you sitting comfortably?

Constant high-pressure typing, particularly when the keyboard is placed at the wrong height, can lead to serious wrist problems. In severe cases of what is called "repetitive strain injury" (RSI), the ability to type may be lost forever. Although manufacturers have produced keyboards that minimize the risk, the consensus is that this is not the major problem. Instead, it may originate from different parts of the workstation—or from the environment in which the computer user works. After a number of court cases, where victims have claimed compensation not simply for pain and suffering but also for the loss of their livelihoods, many companies are taking the issue more seriously. They are improving the seating, displays, keyboards, work surfaces, office lighting and even software design in an attempt to minimize the risk.

It has been estimated that an average of 37 working days are lost per episode of chronic back pain.[19]

Choosing the right type of chair and adopting a good sitting position can substantially reduce the strains on your back. Helpful advice on how to minimize damage includes the following: choose a five-wheeled chair, so that you are more likely to wear out its bearings than the ones in your back; sit with your elbows at a 90-degree angle to your desk and with your knees at 90 degrees to the floor; keep your legs uncrossed and place your feet flat on the floor, slightly apart; and finally, move around a lot, so that you are not stuck in the same position for hours on end.

Lighting can also be a problem. Recommendations for improving conditions include the following: if necessary, cut lighting glare by tilting the screen; don't use screen filters, because they reduce legibility; and beware of positioning yourself between the window and your workstation, with light coming from behind.

Computer games

Parents and schools tend to hate them, but many young people love computer games with a passion. Each new game launched triggers anxiety about violence, sex, addiction or the diversion from homework and "real life." So are we right to worry?

Certainly many of the games are far from politically correct. Some researchers warn that a large number of young people are losing themselves in a world of evil foreigners, big-chested women and the need to prove themselves through violence.[20] The worry is that playing a game can become a child's true reality, and that they may become addicted to sex, sexism or violence. As one expert put it: "Movie violence is like eating salt. The more you eat, the more you need to eat to taste it at all."[21]

A few years ago there was Nintendo, whose addictive power was shown by the fact that some people found it impossible to stop. More recently, *Tamagotchi*—small computerized pets—have sold in the millions. Even adults have not proved immune to their charms; indeed, the beeps of their neglected "cybertots" have been heard in offices around the globe. Many schools have banned them, because classes were being interrupted and children distracted when their "pets" demanded "food," "cleaning" or "a walk."

The idea of nurturing a pet and catering for its needs may not seem to be very harmful, but what does it teach our children about life and death when they can push a "restart" button to bring a neglected pet back to life? And what of the Hong Kong manufacturer that offers a *Tamagotchi*-like toy that enables you to raise a "cyberpunk"? He won't thank you for milk and biscuits, preferring alcohol and cigarettes. And forget the idea of a game of catch with his friends: this knife-wielding thug prefers a street scuffle any day.

Despite such problems, many of these technologies and toys are pointing to the very real need to develop new ways of enabling young people to make sense of the huge range of information now on offer—and to make learning fun. As parents, how do we encourage moderation and get the balance right between learning and obsession?

Couch potatoes

Parents were worried about the seductive appeal of those glowing screens long before PCs came along. And it's easy to see why. Children today spend more than five times as long watching television as they do playing outdoors.[22] The result, typically, is a lifestyle with much less physical activity and less family interaction. Children eating in front of the TV, for example, have no time to talk to their siblings or parents, losing the opportunity to learn in more traditional ways.

Perhaps it was an urban myth, but the intoxicating power of TV was indicated by what is said to have happened in the peak period of the Lebanese civil war. The shooting would suddenly die away as the gunmen went indoors to watch the latest episode of the TV soap *Dallas*. True or not, such programs have carried images of rich, glamorous and high-consumption lifestyles around the globe. In the process, they have infected people with the desire for cars, consumer goods and wealth, American-style.

And there are other real concerns. One has been about the "dumbing-down" effect of TV. Once, we believed that TV would "abolish ignorance" and promote "universal literacy," yet now the TV is often described as an "idiot box."[23] Could the Internet, for all its current promise, turn into the "idiot net" of the 21st century?

In many homes, TV has become a babysitter. As a result, many children are exposed to sex, violence and foul language aimed at an adult audience. It is hard to imagine this diet of the seedier side of life having no impact on the receptive minds of the young.

By the time they start school, Canadian children will have seen an average of 9000 murders and 100 000 other acts of violence on television.[24]

Nor is it simply a question of films showing images of fictional horror. News programs, too, throw the spotlight on a world apparently running out of control. If a Chernobyl explodes, children know about it—often before their parents. If hundreds of thousands of people are hacked to death in Rwanda, children are among the first to see the gory results. If torture chambers are found where pedophiles have murdered young people, what do young minds think as the nightmare images flicker across their screens?

The level of violence in many modern TV films and videos must be seen to be believed. In one recent survey of the top 10 rental videos, the police found that the average video had 295 images of firearms, 13 deaths by firearms and 6 deaths by other means. One film had an image of a firearm every 7.9 seconds—and a firearm killing every 2.7 minutes.[25] There has been much debate about whether video violence translates into aggressive behaviour and even murder. The jury is still out, but the circumstantial evidence seems increasingly strong.

Parents also worry that their children have become "couch potatoes," "passive, sloppy, bombarded by images, spoilt by choice, drifting towards an adolescence of druggy stupor, towards an unready, unreflective adulthood."[26] But all is not lost. Paradoxically, it may be that the more TV output there is, the less children watch. In the U.S., for example, young people's watching time has fallen by a dramatic 18 per cent from a dozen years ago. Because we have to choose actively what to watch, we tend to watch less—and what we do watch we tend to watch more attentively. In Canada, young people's viewing habits have not changed much in recent years.

Meanwhile, the unsuspected health effects of TV watching were indicated by an incident in Japan, when hundreds of children watching a cartoon program developed epilepsy-like symptoms. Their fits began when a scene showing an explosion was followed by five seconds of flashing red lights from the eyes of one of the characters. Ironically, others came down with the same symptoms when the TV news replayed the offending scene as part of an item warning that such sequences should be avoided.

More than half of 10- to 15-year-olds in North America have a TV in their bedroom.

The depth of many children's addiction to TV is worrying. One couple, for example, decided to ban TV on school nights. Predictably their children cried, but what surprised them was that the children continued to cry for four solid months. Once the withdrawal period was over, however, family activity resumed—and the children's imaginations became more active. Finally, the parents allowed a single program per week, with the result that the children became extremely discriminating about what they watched.

For today's parents, rationing television and even videos may seem less of a problem than the challenges raised by computers and, increasingly, the Internet (page 185). On the positive side, this new technology opens up a cornucopia world of information and communication. Young people will be able to tailor their education to their own needs and pace. But the ready accessibility of the Internet, coupled with our inability to censor material effectively, does raise concerns.

As the technology becomes increasingly sophisticated and interactive, we will also worry more about whether it matters if children have "electronic friends" rather than real friends. Will they help them learn how to relate to humans—or hinder their development?[27]

Billboard planet

More than half of teenagers dream of working in advertising and the media. Many adults dismiss these dreams, having seen too many stupefyingly idiotic ads, but maybe the youngsters have a point. In a world bombarded with information, where every message must fight to be heard over the background roar, the role of the advertising industry can only become more important.

In a recent survey of Swedish company bosses, a whopping 58 per cent saw marketing as their problem.[28] Increasingly, the strength of brands will be what separates the winners and losers, and this is entirely dependent on a company's ability to communicate.

Once we worried about the power of subliminal messages in TV advertising, the so-called hidden persuaders. Today, however, there are other concerns. These include the use of "pester power." Many companies have specifically targeted children, trying to get them to pressure their parents to buy particular products.

One of the great victories of the advertising industry has been to persuade us that life's problems can be solved by buying things.[29] Many ads work by making us discontented with our lives and what we already have. In the process, they help both to drive materialism and to build people's underlying dissatisfaction with themselves and their lifestyles. So, civilizing the world of advertising remains one of the great challenges of the 21st century. But even if the original Marlboro Man has now died of cancer, and the company behind the brand is facing restrictions (at least in the U.S.) on using images that make smoking look so seductive, we still have a long, long way to go.

Already, there are some signs that advertisers recognize that they are going to have to communicate differently in the future. The world's largest ad agency has even set up a separate company specifically to communicate with women.[30]

Now that some 80 per cent of all purchasing decisions are made—or heavily influenced—by women, growing numbers of companies want to understand how women relate to brands. One likely change will be to replace flawless beauties and use more humour instead.

Some people, of course, will see this more sophisticated approach as deeply worrying—and one more symptom of the appetite of the commercial culture for our attention and money. As a result, we are seeing the development of new groups—like Canada's highly effective Adbusters—dedicated to countering the torrent of advertising messages in which we are all increasingly immersed.

Computers go to school

Most schools have to continually fight for more resources to pay for teachers, educational materials and the upkeep of buildings. They are not always helped in this struggle by the growing pressures to install computers—or by the ongoing needs to upgrade them.

Schools certainly do need computers for their pupils to use. These are extraordinarily powerful tools for learning. But do we need one in each classroom? On each desk? And if they are on each desk, with the Net waiting to be accessed, how can teachers keep track of what the students are doing?

These questions inevitably lead to others. For example, at what age should children be exposed to computers at school? And how much time should they spend on them? There are at least two different schools of thought. One argues that children should be exposed as early as possible and be given every opportunity to use computers, so that their use becomes second nature. Alternatively, there are those who argue that there is no great hurry. Sure, children will need to learn about computers, but first let them enjoy their early childhood before they are allowed to wander out onto the "superhighway."

On balance, many children find these new machines exciting and useful. If they can't get access to computers at school or at home, many will use them in friends' homes. Apart from the sex and violence issues (page 185), one of the charges levelled at both TV and computers is that they encourage a short attention span. With images flickering across the screen in seconds, and important news stories communicated in short sound bites, critics wonder what the impact will be on our ability to concentrate and to focus on complex issues for more than a few seconds.

Either we—and our youngsters—learn to make sense of it all or the shock waves will knock us senseless. Just as previous generations had to teach their children to cope with a world of horses or cars, so we must now help ours to avoid the perils along the superhighway and to become effective, engaged cyber-citizens. Ironically, however, it will often be a case of them teaching us.

Major hazards ahead

Technology being what it is, and people being what they are, it is hardly surprising that the early days of the cyber-revolution have already seen some spectacular disasters. The future will see many more, but it helps to have a sense of the sorts of problems we should be keeping an eye out for.

Hackers, crackers, viruses, worms

Just as highwaymen sprang up to prey on the early coach services, so "hackers" have emerged to waylay computers, no matter who owns them and what they are used for. For today's hackers, the more complicated the computer system—and the tougher the security protection is to crack—the more attractive the challenge. Matters are made worse by the fact that the latest hacking and code-breaking software is often released over the Net.

So why do they do it? Most hackers say that all information is "yearning to be free." But most just do it for the hell of it, for the thrill of outwitting people who are usually much more highly trained and better paid. That said, most would agree that it is bad form to damage the system they break into. "Crackers," on the other hand, break into computer systems and websites with mischievous or even malicious intent, altering or destroying files.

More of us will be exposed to "viruses" than hackers or crackers. Like the "germ" that causes the common cold, computer viruses can spread rapidly, multiplying as they go. Often introduced by malicious pranksters, there are now a large and growing number of different types of virus. Some operate whenever you turn on your computer, while others continually mutate to avoid detection.

For example, a "computer infection" may be designed to spread when something is copied off the Internet. The unlucky recipient may then find that this virus will search out all the files on his or her computer and delete them—or it may come up with a threatening message every time the computer is switched on. Some warn people that all their data will be deleted in 10 minutes, but say there is nothing they can do about it—simply sit back and watch it happen.

The term *virus* is used for anything that causes unexpected behaviour or leads to damage, but technically there are significantly different types. A virus must be attached to other programs to work. A *worm*, on the other hand, is a program designed to spread on its own across systems. *Trojan horses* are programs that appear to be useful, but then spring an unpleasant surprise, for example crashing your machine. And logic bombs lie dormant until something triggers them off—for example, you fail to pay a licence fee within 30 days.[31]

In 1988, a worm nearly triggered the collapse of the Internet.

The impact of computer viruses can be severe, as when hospitals lose their medical records and "forget" which patients need treating when, or who is allergic to what drugs. As a result, there are a number of businesses whose product is protecting computer users from this sort of damage. Antivirus software is available and, like the viruses themselves, can often be found on the Internet.

Flying pickets on the superhighway

Another problem that will increasingly come to haunt cyberspace is the cyber-strike. At a time when many executives may feel that strikers are almost an endangered species, the new technologies are putting enormous power into the hands of ordinary workers to disrupt the operations of the organizations they work for—or other organizations against which they hold a grudge.

One U.K. company was subjected to a 24-hour "electronic picket" during which time sister organizations jammed the company's communications lines by flooding them with faxes and e-mails, stopping potential customers from getting through.[32] This form of retribution by workers or others may become increasingly common.

The time lost by companies because of strikes has fallen sharply in recent years. In the "Winter of Discontent," in 1979, the U.K. lost nearly 30 million working days, whereas by 1997 the annual figure was down to around 250 000 days. There are many reasons for this dramatic change, including new government controls on certain types of industrial action, but a crucial problem was that traditional forms of industrial action—such as walkouts, overtime bans and flying pickets—were simply not working. That may change when the potential power of cyber-strikes is recognized.

flashpoint: Going Too Far? Electronic ID Cards

- **Canadians, like many other people in countries where they are not already required, are nervous about the prospect of national or provincial identity cards. Our federal and provincial governments have been looking at a "common client identifier." In October 1998, it was reported that the Ontario government hoped to have a fingerprint ID card within five years to replace drivers' licences and health cards. More worryingly, the province floated the idea of electronically storing peoples' medical history on their health cards. The chances are, however, that governments will introduce such identity cards through the back door. In the U.K., for example, the government plans to introduce a computerized card designed to give people faster service from the tax and social security agencies. But civil rights groups view this as the thin end of a disturbing wedge.[33]**
- **The U.K. government, which aims to computerize a growing proportion of the services it offers, argues that such cards will help reduce bureaucracy. For example, a single card could carry our**

driving licence, our social security details and enable us to vote. In France, such simpler identity cards are already commonplace; indeed, 12 out of 15 EU countries have some form of identity card.

- **On current plans, the U.K. cards will not carry photographs, but they will contain a code embedded in a microchip. They could also carry "biometric" data, such as a finger, thumb or eye print, enabling you to be uniquely identified by electronic scanners. Public opinion polls show that around two-thirds of Britons would support the introduction of compulsory identity cards, but most presumably would also be nervous about the cards being introduced by stealth.**

Cyber-criminals, cyber-cops

Crime has flourished throughout human history, and will continue to flourish as long as there are people. Now the computing skills of many young people mean that they can sometimes run rings around the law. Ireland's first charged Internet criminal, for example, was a teenage boy with a sweet tooth. He ordered US$2000 worth of chocolate using a made-up credit account number, which turned out to belong to an Argentinean. When discovered, the boy was said to be "remorseful and sick of the sight of chocolate."[34]

Most cyber-criminals, however, are adults—and the range of their activities is growing all the time. Let's browse through a few examples.

Stealing: A new breed of criminal robs banks without even having to visit the scene of the crime. Hackers broke into a Citibank system, for example, in an attempt to steal millions of dollars through wire transfers to other countries. In another case, one pair of cyber-criminals offered so-called prime securities (which don't even exist), promising to double investors' money within four months. The scheme was shut down by the authorities, but not before millions of dollars had been sent in and stolen.

Credit card fraud: Cyber-fraudsters can hover around the "electronic doorways" to databanks, hoping to steal credit card numbers as they streak through.[35]

Tax avoidance: Few people are likely to pity tax collectors, but they are finding that increased electronic trading overseas, the use of private intranet systems and difficulties tracing the routes of transactions are making their job much more difficult.

Corporate espionage: Trade theft costs U.S. companies US$100 billion a year in lost revenues. Stealing codes from computer programs and passing them on to competitors can be a profitable exercise and significantly impact the advantage of the company targeted. With the end of the Cold War, some intelligence agencies have turned their hands to corporate espionage—on the grounds that it is in the national interest.[36]

Cons: Common scams include chain letters, pyramid selling schemes, work-at-home plans, the sale of bogus medicines, phony investments and fake off-shore banks, all requesting that money should be sent "up-front."

Hoax sites: Also known as "phantom websites," these involve taking over or mimicking an existing organization's "home page." Once a site is cracked, the intruders can steal any income generated or slander the host organization. This might involve considerable hacking skill, but in some cases it can be as simple as changing the telephone number—so that orders go to a rival company. Affected businesses may be hit in two ways. They can lose sales and their reputation can be seriously dented.

Rumours: Rumours—and outright lies—can spread like wildfire with no way of stopping them. Remember the rumour that the "distinguishing mark" on President Clinton's penis, which featured in an ongoing sex scandal, was a tattoo of a bald eagle. It shot around the Net, but how are we to know who—or what—to believe?

Copyright/libel/slander: It is horribly complex to establish property rights to material on the Net, and to sue for any defamation in the cyberworld. The difficulty generally lies in identifying who is responsible—and under which country's laws they might be charged. For example, actress Pamela Anderson of *Baywatch* fame found herself displayed nude on the Net without having given her consent.

Hate mail/threats: Worse still, actress Jodie Foster was the subject of rape threats over the Net—and many other well-known people have been the victims of hate mail.

Unfortunately, the legal system is usually light-years behind the criminals in terms of their understanding of the new technology and of its potential for good and evil. Lawyers, too, are being slowed down by the fact that there is little in the way of legal precedent to draw upon.

Given human gullibility and greed, cybercrime seems to have a guaranteed future, but there are things we can all do to protect ourselves. These range from regularly changing passwords to installing security systems that help to keep would-be hackers at bay and software that hunts for and kills viruses. But, like the arms race, this will continue to be an area of intense competition between those trying to defend IT systems and those trying to break into them.

Sex and violence

Like it or not, it is now possible to discuss sex, arrange dates with like-minded sexual partners and see live sex acts on the Internet. Pornography, including child pornography, is one of the biggest growth areas. It is hardly surprising, therefore, that there is now great concern about the ability of pedophiles and pornographers to operate in a "Wild West" environment, with no effective policing.

Sex is the most searched-for topic on the Web.

Given that young people can easily access these sites, what can parents—or other adults—do to tackle the problem? Apart from unplugging every computer in the home, it is possible to pull down censorship packages from the Internet. They come with names like "Net Nanny," "Surf Watch" or "CYBERsitter." What they do is limit access to sites with high levels of sex or violence.

At the moment, however, most of these programs are fairly unsophisticated. By measuring how much naked skin and foul language appears, they may well switch off programs that are light entertainment, such as *Baywatch*, or which are providing useful information, for example, on sexually transmitted diseases such as AIDS.

Meanwhile, at work, some employers have woken up to the fact that much of the Internet access they are paying for is for sex-related sites. Many of them now keep track of what sites have been visited by their employees, with the result that there are red faces when workers are confronted with the evidence.

Whether they use TV or computer screens, there will inevitably be more controversy about the impact of on-screen violence and sex on young people—and on people who later commit related crimes. Our tolerance is constantly being tested. The film *Crash*, for example, explored the sexual gratification derived from seeing bodies mutilated in car crashes. And a computer game showed very real images of people being mown down: the whole idea was to kill people by running them over.

Where do we draw the line? The research doesn't always help. So, while there have been cases of criminals copying things they have seen on screen, it is still far from clear that most watchers change their behaviour. But do they become desensitized to suffering?

The whole issue of censorship on the Net has been much discussed and is highly controversial. Some argue that the Net should be wide open, with a totally liberal approach to content, while others argue that censorship is absolutely necessary. Is it right, for example, that people can put the recipes for making the sort of bombs that caused the Oklahoma City devastation, let alone anthrax bombs, on the Net? Should we just ignore the people who fixed it so that anyone searching for "Princess Diana," after her death, would get linked to their pornography site? We will have to draw the line somewhere—and then enforce it, which is never going to be easy in cyberspace.

Virtual jobs

Every revolution attracts counteractions, and the digital revolution is no exception. Early in the last century, for example, Ned Ludd and other workers opposed the increasing mechanization of textile factories, which was costing them their jobs. They destroyed machinery and burned mills in protest. Today's protestors against the cyber-economy are known as "neo-Luddites," and they too are concerned at job losses, but this time, as a result of digitalization.

Jobs on the endangered list

Many people wonder whether machines will take over the world. The reality is that in some areas they already have, as anyone hoping for a lifetime's employment as a machine minder or a clerk just a few years back will have discovered.

In some cases, the computerized world will have made people unemployable as, for example, when a steelworker loses his job—because of foreign competition—at the age of 50. Unlike his 25-year-old-daughter, the laid off steelworker has no computer skills to help him into another job. For others, the issue is simpler still: their jobs have been taken over by machines.

So which jobs are most vulnerable? Below, we look at how some jobs or sectors will be affected by computerization:

Machine minders: Computers and robots have been taking over jobs from people for some time. Despite cheap labour, including child labour in other parts of the world (page 92), this trend will continue to destroy traditional work opportunities.

"Middle-men": Because electronic commerce dramatically reduces the number of links in the chain between manufacturer and consumer, we will see huge pressures on the people in between, such as wholesalers, distributors and retailers. Although new roles will be created, as in operating electronic payment systems, these are likely to be less labour-intensive.[37]

Bank clerks: As more of our financial transactions are done on-line, the need for all the people who work in banks, keeping track of paper recording details of our financial lives, has begun to disappear. Credit cards, electronic cash cards and the like are only the thin end of a wedge that will rapidly squeeze "cash" as we know it out of our lives (page 203).

Grocery clerks: Scanners replace the need to enter the price of items into a cash register. Grocery-store checkout staff will be replaced as shoppers do their own scanning and bagging of groceries and pay electronically.

Financial experts: When a financial centre like the Toronto Stock Exchange switches from physical trading floors, where people gather to deal in stocks and shares, to electronic dealing rooms, the result is a dramatic surge in job losses. As computers become more powerful and better able to recognize and respond to underlying trends in financial markets, they will continue to make thousands of brokers and other financial experts redundant.

Musicians: Computerized synthesizers are replacing freelance musicians for much well-paid session work, including recording music for commercials and advertising jingles.[38] Longer term, it is even possible to imagine computers nibbling into the work of composers.

Book, music and video shops: These are some of the retail outlets most likely to be at risk of being replaced by teleshopping (page 172). You will be able to download the music and films direct into your PC or digital TV, while virtual bookstores will offer a wider choice of books, together with as many reviews as you want to browse through.

Publishers: Publishers will find their markets are being cut into by people buying cheaper books over the Internet. For Canadian publishers and booksellers, for example, it is likely to be particularly difficult to undercut the prices being offered by U.S.-based companies.

Mail carriers: The Swedish postal service has provided every Swedish citizen over the age of six with an e-mail address as part of the first national service of its kind.[39] The idea is that electronic mail will replace the old "snail mail," although the need for mail carriers will not disappear completely. Messages for people who do not use computers, for whatever reason, or packages that cannot be transferred by e-mail, will still be delivered.

Software sales: Instead of being sold in shrink-wrapped boxes, more and more software is being directly downloaded from the Net. Now that customers can try before they buy and, if satisfied, use the product immediately, what sort of long-term future can there be for the boxed versions? Even software designers may be threatened. Ironically, some of them are working on software that takes responsibility for its own evolution, using the digital equivalent of genes and natural selection to develop in ways—and at speeds—way beyond the capacities of human programmers.

Travel agents: If we can book holidays over the Web, often more conveniently and more cheaply than through travel agents, what is left for them to do? The answer is that they will need to offer a deluxe service, tailor-made to each customer. They will also have to come up with new holiday ideas that we may not have thought of ourselves, as well as supplying an efficient service to sort out any problems we may encounter along the way. But they will need computers to do all of this.

Clearly, the number of jobs under threat can only continue to grow. As more and more business is done over the Internet, many more companies—and even entire industries—will find themselves coming under similar pressure.

It costs more than eight times as much to process a traditional airline ticket as it does an e-ticket.[40]

Opportunities

Now for some good—and some less good—news. Inevitably, such technologies also bring opportunities and new jobs. The biggest short-term opportunities are probably for those skilled in computer support services, but the range of cyber-jobs (from cyber-cops to cyber-lawyers) seems set to explode.

Another near-term need: the number of people employed by hotlines for Internet service providers is booming as customers clamour for help in setting up websites and overcoming glitches. Computer retailers, too, are recognizing the opportunities in providing customers with technical support, not just selling them equipment.

Perhaps surprisingly, public interest campaigners have been pioneers in exploiting the digital revolution. But then they aim to get information out to as many people as possible. Check out the Internet websites of environmental and other campaigning organizations and you will be struck by their sophistication and appeal.

Less happily, think about the spread of telephone "call centres," where workers answer inquiries 24 hours a day. More people now work in call centres than in the coal, steel and car-making industries combined. But many of the operators are under heavy pressure. In most centres they have no control over whether to answer a call, and as soon as one is finished, another is put through. Worse, every aspect of their performance can be monitored, from how friendly they sound to how much time they spend persuading customers to part with their cash.

Like so many battery hens, however, the operators get used to the conditions. They get good rates of pay, particularly in areas where there is little other work to be had, and they even get used to being spied on. But what sort of model is this for the workplace of the future?

Home working

In the cyberworld, too, work can be done in new ways, in new places, at different times. As advanced computers, e-mail and telephone systems boost the power of home IT systems, home working will become increasingly common. The transition is already well under way. It is estimated, for example, that there are 1 million people teleworking in Canada, and this figure is predicted to be 1.5 million by 2001.

So what is it like to work from home? You will find many people who miss the company and other pleasures of the office. Working from home can be too peaceful. But growing numbers of people genuinely appreciate the saved time, flexibility, lower stress and reduced need to commute—with all the associated strains and emissions (page 194). They also often say they have more time for their families and local communities.

Nortel has calculated that the five per cent of its worldwide workforce who telework (about 4000 people) reduce automobile air pollutants by seven million kilograms per year.

On the environmental front, telecommuting is often advanced as an answer to urban transport problems (page 150), but it, too, has its downsides. Enabling people to work in the more rural areas adds to the pressures to build as people move out of the cities in search of a country life. On top of that, the need for home offices has fuelled the trend toward people requiring bigger living spaces.

Some of the negative impacts of telecommuting can be counteracted by working from a "telecentre" or (in rural areas) "telecottage," if one exists nearby. Here, resources such as computers and office equipment are shared among a number of people, giving people access to the latest technology as well as, in some cases, helping with services such as bookkeeping or translation.

Companies that have introduced teleworking for their employees have usually found that it brings financial savings and increases productivity. The employees often appreciate the greater flexibility in terms of when and how they work—and less central office space is needed, cutting costs.

Privacy thieves

But this will be a very different world. All of us, in different ways, will find that the Digital Age opens up new threats to our reputation and privacy. At the extreme end of the spectrum, for example, one American actress was murdered by a deranged fan who found her address through California's motor-vehicle records.

Then there was the U.S. banker who was also a member of a state health commission. He pulled up a list of cancer patients, crosschecked it against his bank's customers—and revoked the loans of those who were both clients and cancer patients. And, as they say, we ain't seen nothing yet.

Who is watching us?

Companies and other IT users are finding that their employees are sending huge streams of e-mail that their employers have no way of monitoring. "Theoretically, you could enforce a policy of reading every electronic message your employees send out over their corporate PCs," advises one of the world's leading IT experts. "It is perfectly legitimate to do so, provided you disclose the practice to your employees. But how could you hope to attract and retain talented people with such policies? And besides, who would you trust to read all those messages?"[41]

Even on your home computer, it is now possible to uncover other people's ex-directory telephone numbers, street and e-mail addresses, social security numbers, credit ratings, employment records, job applications, travel arrangements and details of their romantic liaisons. Moreover, most of the movements you make on the Internet can be tracked. People can find out which sites you have visited, intercept your e-mail or uncover your financial details if you pay by credit card.

Nor are we simply vulnerable via the Internet. New technologies are continuously keeping track of where we are—and what we are doing. Your activities and location will have been noted every time you: withdraw cash from a bank machine; use your credit card; shop at a grocery store where you have registered for a loyalty card; go to work where they have employee ID scanners; or make a telephone call on a cellular phone.

If you want a sense of how the system works, feed in a slightly misspelled name on some of these forms. And see how rapidly you begin to take on a new identity with a range of businesses that want you as a customer—and buy lists of possible customers from other businesses. And there are other trends at work. When a young child is abducted from a shopping mall or a princess dies in a car crash, some people still wonder how it is that parts of their final, fateful journeys are captured by video cameras? The answer, of course, is that security problems—including burglaries, store thefts and terrorism—have encouraged the rapid spread of these electronic eyes throughout our cities and towns.

Many of these new systems are sharp-eyed indeed. A camera mounted on top of a building can sometimes identify car licence-plate numbers more than a kilometre away. Satellites have more powerful cameras still. Their bird's-eye view from space can even spot you taking a skinny dip with a close companion!

Big brother, little brothers

If such surveillance cuts crime rates, most people will welcome it. Some will also often accept that personal ID cards with our fingerprints—or other forms of identification—on them could be immensely useful in crime prevention, helping police identify criminals and reducing bogus social security claims, for example.

Speed cameras, too, have proved effective at cutting speeding on the roads. And sifting through computer data can assist the authorities in cases of racial discrimination, malpractice and fraud. Companies that think they are colour-blind or sex-blind can find that computers identify strong patterns of discrimination in appointments or promotions.

Most of us may have little to fear from having our movements traced and information known about our finances. But what if our records got into the wrong hands or our government was less benign—run by someone like Hitler or Saddam Hussein? We might worry a bit more. In reality, however, Big Brother may turn out to be less of a threat than a whole raft of Little Brothers—mischief-makers intent on upsetting the rest of the world.

So, for example, you may find that your electronic identity has been sabotaged or destroyed. Your credit card ratings could be tampered with, your telephone conversations eavesdropped upon, your e-mail siphoned off, your mortgage called in, your health insurance discontinued or your social insurance number obliterated.[42] In short, you could become a "digital untouchable," unable to work, shop or operate in a world that no longer recognizes your existence.

Many of these problems reflect a world that has got out of kilter. In the traditional village or small town, everyone knew everyone else's secrets—and people learned to live with this. These days, by contrast, we no longer know who lives next to us, who is watching us—and what they know.

Bionic brains

We might well be even more vulnerable to snooping if some of the way-out ideas of computer scientists come true. For example, some scientists have been working to integrate living nerve cells with microchips. The experiments show that it would be possible to bridge between human nerves and powerful computers, raising the prospect of artificial sight, bionic brains and hugely expanded human memories.[43]

The idea of extending human intelligence has often been discussed in science fiction, with fictional cyborg robots like *Robocop* and *The Terminator* also showing what might happen if we were able to build bionic beings. Most people would not want to go this far, but given the number of people happy to accept breast implants, we should assume that many people would also be happy to accept brain implants that boost their intelligence.

If they did, one possible danger is they might find that people using scanners could track what they were thinking—or, by sifting through their stored memories—discover what they had (or had not) done.

In the really long term, even more extraordinary developments might become possible. In his book *3001: The Final Odyssey*, the science-fiction writer Arthur C. Clarke even suggested that in the future the thoughts and memories of a lifetime could be downloaded into a "soul catcher" chip, for insertion into another person's brain.[44] But don't count on it any time soon.

Chips with Everything

✔Citizen 2000 Checklist

1. Don't Let TV and Computers Harm Your Health

Don't become a "couch potato": take exercise. And if you are using a computer, check that your desk and chair are at the right heights. You can very easily damage your back, or develop repetitive strain injury (RSI) problems in your wrists or arms if you work in the wrong way. Consult a massage therapist, chiropractor, doctor or other health professional quickly to prevent such problems from becoming chronic and difficult to treat. Be sure they give you a basic grasp of workplace ergonomics and self-care tips. Other resources include **The Back Association of Canada** and the **Institute for Work and Health**. Check out *The Ultimate Back Book* by Judylaine Fine and the latest edition of Dr. Hamilton Hall's series of books on back pain/care.

At the same time, make sure that you have fresh air–and that you are not sitting near equipment such as photocopiers or printers that give off emissions such as ozone. Plants can help to keep the air pure. Read Gerry Mander's *10 Arguments for the Elimination of Television* for a serious look at the damage done by this pervasive medium

2. Fight Back Against Junk Information

If you like sorting through endless direct mail–and its fax and e-mail equivalents–that's fine. But for those who are struggling to cope with information overload, a number of things can be done.

Remember, if you sign up for a grocery-store loyalty card, you may soon be bombarded with junk mail. If you are receiving unwanted direct mail, contact **The Canadian Direct Marketing Association (CDMA)** and ask for your name to be removed from junk-mail lists. They represent 80 per cent of the Canadian direct marketing industry, and their privacy code prohibits members from trading or renting customer information to third parties without permission. For unwanted phone advertising, write **Tele-Direct (Publications) Inc**. and get your name deleted from the lists it sells to organizations (see front of the "Yellow Pages," which TeleDirect publishes, for contact information). Or get an unlisted number from your phone company.

If you are worried about "spamming" (junk e-mail) or scams, log onto **Scambusters**. This website advises on how to avoid letting "spammers" get your address–and sends you details of pyramid selling schemes (page 211), and other get-rich-quick ideas and wonder products that probably don't work. The site also warns people about the latest frauds. So, for example, one fraud involved an organization sending fake bills–and requesting people to call a number to get more details. If they did call, they were charged for the call at up to $25 a minute! Of course, they didn't find out until later. Alternatively, you can log onto the **University of Alberta's Computing and Network Services** website for information and links on "Spam, Velveeta and Third-party Mail Relay."

3. Take a Stand Against Excessive Sex and Violence

Of course, censorship can be dangerous. All too often, censorship is taken to its ultimate limit, which is murder. In countries such as China, Guatemala, Iraq, Myanmar (Burma) and Sri Lanka, people are killed simply for expressing their views. Among the groups campaigning to protect the right to self-expression are **Amnesty International**, **Article 19: the International Centre Against Censorship**, and **PEN Canada**.

On the other hand, there are occasions when

some forms of censorship can make sense. Canadians' long-term concern about media education and literacy has grown along with the increase of media sex, violence and bad language, and easy access to Internet pornography and hate literature. **The Media Awareness Network** provides information, ideas and resources for media education and media issues affecting children. It provides a toll-free public inquiries number, brochures and posters, on-line discussion groups and information on regulation and codes and procedures for consumer feedback. **MediaWatch** offers kits for parents, teachers and administrators to use with children to counter sexism and violence in broadcast TV, videos and video games. The kits are used to help children learn about media manipulation, privacy, netiquette, cyber-hate and how to search for quality information on the Internet. Filtering programs for the Internet and V-chips for television are becoming increasingly available to concerned parents.

There are also groups working for media literacy across Canada, looking at issues of values and consumerism.

Other organizations active in preventing sexual exploitation or abuse of children include the **Child Welfare League of Canada**, **the Manitoba Child Care Association**, various provincial and municipal Child Care or Children's Aid Societies and **Childnet International**, who campaign for the interests of children in relation to communications issues.

4. Think Before You Jump Into Teleworking

Growing numbers of people will telecommute in the future, teleworking and attending teleconferences. Given that there are downsides to this style of working, as well as upsides, you would be well advised to contact some of the key organizations in this area to find out how to make the best decision. Organizations that support people working from home include **The Canadian Association for Home-based Businesses**, **The SOHO (Small Office Home Office) Business Group**, **The Canadian Organization of Small Business Inc.**, and **The Women Business Owners of Canada (WBOC)**. "Telecommuting: The New Workplace" is an interesting short article summarizing advantages and disadvantages, written by an Edmonton lawyer (see in *Law Now*, June-July 1997). If you've made your decision, **The Canadian Telework Association**, and **The Canadian Advanced Technology Association (CATA)** have set up a free on-line telework job database.

6.3 Computer Footprints

Can we green IT?

Most people think of the computer industry as a clean industry—and it is, at least compared with traditional heavy industries such as steel making. But computers have also thrown up an extraordinary range of environmental, safety and health issues at different stages in their lifecycles.

Silicon Valley is the heart of the global IT business—and its problems underscore the shadow-side of the industry. Hundreds of chemicals are used in electronics and computer manufacturing. For example, more than 700 compounds are used to make a single computer work station. As a result, this part of California has one of the highest concentrations of toxic waste sites in the world. And the semiconductor manufacturing industry uses more toxic gases than any other industry.

As public concern mounts, growing numbers of IT companies are talking about "green computers," but their products continue to have a significant environmental impact throughout their working lives. Let's take a look at some of the issues that surface when making, installing, using, upgrading and disposing of IT equipment.

Getting started

Although some companies have tried to introduce "green PCs," their success to date has been limited. The reasons for this range from poor customer understanding of the issues through to the higher prices often charged. But the speed at which computers become out-of-date, together with the exploding amount of memory space needed by new software programs, is now provoking a reaction from many computer users. And computer manufacturers seem likely to come under growing pressure on the environmental impacts of their industry and its products.

Chips and circuit boards

Oddly, given that the end-products are so small, huge volumes of natural resources are used to make computer chips. The process of making a chip is very complicated, with each stage involving a range of safety, health and environmental risks.

So, for example, the production of a typical 15-centimetre (6-inch) silicon wafer used as the basis of a chip may use 960 cubic metres (3200 cubic feet) of bulk gases, including 6.6 cubic metres (22 cubic feet) of hazardous gases; over 9000 litres (2000 gallons) of water; 9 kilos (20 pounds) of chemicals; and 285 kilowatt hours of electricity. Furthermore, the waste from the production of each chip will be around 11.5 kilos (25 pounds) of sodium hydroxide, over 1245 kilos (2800 pounds) of wastewater and 3 kilos (7 pounds) of hazardous wastes.

Printed circuit boards are the physical structures on which a range of electronic components, including chips, are mounted. To make them, the industry prepares the boards, applies coatings, solders, fabricates and assembles. Among the problems generated in these stages are acid and ammonia fumes, organic vapours and wastes from the plating baths.

In recent years, the media spotlight has shone on the industry's enormous consumption of ozone-depleting CFCs to clean chips and circuit boards. Under intense pressure, the industry soon recognized that there were viable alternatives, including water, with the result that the use of CFCs has now largely been eliminated.

Screens and casings

The manufacture of a computer monitor, the part that looks like a TV, results in such pollutants as solvents, caustics, acids and surfactants. Around a quarter of a typical computer workstation is made out of plastic, often PVC (polyvinyl chloride), polyethylene and polystyrene. Although these materials are recyclable, they are not often recycled (page 106)—and PVC, in particular, raises a number of environmental issues. One issue that has caused controversy is the use of particular flame-retardants in monitors and a range of other computer and electronic systems. The concern is that these polybrominated flame-retardants might produce dioxins when burned—and these are highly toxic. Some companies have stopped using them, while others continue to defend their use.

Another chemical used for this purpose is tetrabromobisophenol-A (TBBA), found in the materials used for personal computer housing. One by-product of TBBA is methyl bromide, which is both toxic and ozone-depleting (page 21).

Cabling

To work effectively, computers need a great deal of cabling. Fibre-optic cables, made from abundant materials like sand, are replacing the more traditional cables made from copper (a much scarcer material). They are much more powerful and energy-efficient. Much cabling, however, tends to be sheathed in PVC (page 33), a plastic that has had a troubled history in terms of health and environmental issues.

For telephones, televisions and computers alike, huge quantities of new cabling are being laid. The idea is that you will be able to receive multiple TV channels, as many telephone lines as you wish and much faster computer connections. But laying the cables can damage or kill trees, if done badly. Those digging the trenches, working to deadlines, often cut roots, damage bark and compact the soil (slowing the flow of oxygen and water to the roots). Some cable companies are now aware of the problem—and give guidelines to cable layers on how to minimize damage.

Packaging

Anyone who has ever unpacked a computer or printer knows that it comes with huge amounts of packaging material. This is not easily recyclable, nor easily disposed of. In response, some companies are using waste materials as packaging, such as corrugated paper packaging and cushioning foams. Some are even using edible popcorn! But this issue will need to be tackled more effectively.

Most equipment comes with huge paper manuals, often in a number of languages. But some companies are now making the obvious next move to electronic manuals, preinstalled on their PCs. In some cases, this has already made substantial savings in the amount of paper used. Given that many manuals are written so badly, perhaps they should abandon them altogether!

In use

Compared to a steel factory or an intensive pig farm, a computerized office is scarcely a major environmental problem. But as more and more computers are used, the scale of their safety, health and environmental impacts are attracting growing attention.

Energy supply

Computers consume a fair amount of energy in use. But a large proportion of this is because computer users never turn their machines off, partly because they do not want the inconvenience of rebooting the machine and reopening applications. This can be solved by buying a machine that "suspends" applications when switched off, so they don't need to be reopened each time.

In general, most computer users turn their machines off overnight. TV watchers, on the other hand, leave their machines in standby mode when not in use. This still uses 25 percent of the energy that would be used when the TV is switched fully on.

Leaving TVs on standby still uses 25 per cent of the energy that would be used when the TV is switched fully on.

Meanwhile, the rapidly expanding market for portable computers, laptops and subnotebooks, as well as mobile telephones and video cameras, has led to huge demand for rechargeable batteries. Early laptops used lead-acid batteries, smaller versions of those found in cars—but growing demand for longer-lasting, more powerful and lighter-weight batteries has meant that manufacturers have switched to NiCad batteries, made from nickel and cadmium.

In one respect, at least, these new batteries are worse than the old lead-acid ones. The battery deteriorates if it is recharged before it has been completely discharged. So the best approach is to carry two, working each one "to death" before recharging it. The average life of these batteries is around two years, but given that they contain toxic, heavy metals it is hardly impressive that few, if any, computer makers have set up recycling—or even safe-disposal—schemes for such batteries.

Finally, for areas where grid or battery power present problems, new solutions are emerging. For example, the inventor of the clockwork radio has now come up with a clockwork computer. It runs for over half an hour after just a 30-second twist, with no need for batteries, utility or solar power. Clearly, there is exciting potential for using this innovation in every Third World village—or in other places where power supplies are unreliable. To date, however, it still costs more than the electric utility supply alternative.

Radiation, static and ghosts

As with mobile telephones (page 177), computers emit small amounts of electromagnetic radiation from their monitors. This radiation is a result of the electrical current flowing through the system, although the present view is that it is not a significant risk to health. More of a problem, it appears, are the so-called visual display units (VDUs), which can cause headaches through a combination of stress, poor vision and poor posture (page 178).

Static can also be a problem with computers. A light static field will give you a mild tingling feeling in your fingers when the charged object is touched. A heavier field will give an electric shock. Positive ions, which occur in dry and dusty weather, in the typically dry air of well-sealed offices and in smoke-filled rooms, can also be increased through higher static conditions. These ions are suspected of causing tiredness, irritability and ill health, as well as skin complaints, sore throats and itchy eyes. Printers and copiers can also be a source of indoor pollution in offices. They emit ozone and should be operated in well-ventilated spaces.

There are a number of ways of tackling all these problems in an office environment, including the following: opening windows; regularly spraying office plants with water; minimizing the amount of artificial fabrics used or worn; and using antistatic screens, mats and rugs.

For those who leave their machines on for long periods of time, however, particularly if they tend to use the same software package, there is a danger that they may begin to find "ghost" images permanently etched on their screens. Most people operating computers will have come across good "screen savers." In fact, if you have an up-to-date computer and use the energy-saving or "sleeping" mode, a screen saver is not even necessary.

Even computers die

And so your computer has finally bitten the dust. What do you do with it? Dump it in the garbage—or try to get it recycled?

Reusing, recycling and upgrading

When it comes to disposing of a personal computer (PC) or larger computer, your original choice of machine will prove to have been crucial. Some manufacturers have gone to some trouble to ensure that their PCs do not contain heavy metals, such as cadmium, lead or mercury, either in the plastics or in the batteries. Others have not.

Some manufacturers, too, are designing their computers for easy disassembly. In simple terms, this means that the machines can be taken to pieces when their useful life is over—and it simplifies the task of separating components for reuse and materials for recycling. A number of countries have introduced new laws to make manufacturers responsible for recycling or reusing the computers and packaging they make and use. More will do so in the future.

By 1999, there will be 100 million obsolete PCs around the world.

As such pressures on the industry grow, it is likely that many computer companies will begin to assume responsibility for their computer systems from "cradle to grave"—or, if recycling does happen and the materials are reused, from "cradle to cradle." This may mean that they will start leasing computer systems rather than selling them outright. Hopefully, this would give them a stronger incentive to upgrade equipment rather than junking it.

The pace of progress in computing often means that your computer is obsolete even before you get it out of the store. As newer models of PC come on the market, the temptation is to junk the old—or less new—machine. Talk to other people using computers and there is always something more they can do on their machine than you can on yours.

We find we need more memory, a faster processor or another software package, which then turns out to need a new machine to run on. But some manufacturers are now trying to design their machines for easy upgradeability. The idea is that users can easily replace or upgrade the memory, the storage and even the central processing unit (the machine's "brain"), without having to replace the entire PC. This trend should be encouraged.

Computer Footprints

✔Citizen 2000 Checklist

1. Make Sure Your PC Is Clean and Green

This is the critical first step. Ask retailers and manufacturers about the energy efficiency and environmental performance of the products you are considering. Such requests for information can have a significant impact on companies that are dedicated to keeping their customers happy.

Dell Computers, which mainly supplies systems to corporate customers, have launched a range of computers designed to be easily serviceable, upgradeable and recyclable. Other companies offering "greener" computer models include **Digital** and **IBM**. But companies such as **Apple**, **Compaq** or **Toshiba** may be doing something and making less noise about it. Check them out.

When buying computers or other communications equipment, check for **Environment Canada's** *Ecologos* on fax and photocopy machines or the U.S. **Environmental Protection Agency (EPA)** *Energy Star* logos on computer equipment, faxes, photocopiers, scanners and VCRs. These products "power down," "sleep" or shut themselves off when not in use. A **Natural Resources Canada** brochure (or their website) will let you calculate your office's likely savings–often up to 50 per cent of operating costs–using *Energy Star* equipment. The **EPA** website lists products in the program. Other things to look out for include an energy-save mode; upgradeability; use of recycled materials and recyclability; copiers that print double-sided; whether retailers will take back packaging and recycle it; and the environmental policies of the companies involved.

2. Use It Intelligently

Once you have the machine, remember to switch it off when it is not in use–and cut down on the amount of print-outs you make. Where you print out for your own use, always use the back of paper already used once. This is very convenient (as long as you remember to remove the staples!) and can save a tremendous amount of virgin paper.

3. Upgrade, Reuse and Recycle

Don't junk your PC too soon. If you want it to operate faster, or to have more memory, upgrade it. If it really has reached the end of its useful life as far as you are concerned, remember that–although there is not much of a second-hand market in these systems–there may be others who can use it.

Schools, nonprofit organizations and community groups are often interested in acquiring cast-off computers. In Nova Scotia, governments, teachers' associations and businesses have been operating programs to recycle computers into classrooms and libraries. Other initiatives involving repairing, reselling or recycling computers and donating some to low-income families and nonprofit organizations include **Human HiTec Assist** in Vancouver and **TLC** in Toronto. **Syrotech Industries** in Winnipeg will pick up your computer (for a fee) and ensure it is recycled and that none of it goes to landfills. **Progeni Computers** in Toronto recycles computers, and **Reboot Canada** is a registered charity distributing used recent-model computers to charitable and nonprofit groups nationwide.

The **Canadian Foundation for World Development**, famous for distributing used eyeglasses to less-advantaged countries, accepts used computer donations and sends them abroad.

The **GreenDisk** company takes higher-quality used computer diskettes and turns them into good-as-new products, often selling them for less than new, lower-quality disks. Check their website for vendors near you or contact your local Grand &Toy or Today's Office/Lyreco Office Products head offices.

Digital, **IBM** and **Xerox** have set up recovery centres to recondition machines for re-use, recycling or–failing that–safe disposal. A number of companies, including **Hewlett-Packard** and **Xerox**, take back toner cartridges.

4. Research Before You Buy

One of the most frustrating and wasteful aspects of IT is that we often buy products or systems that do not, in the end, turn out to do what we want them to do. The result can be that we have to buy more equipment than we really need and that it goes out of date quicker. Software companies are often part of this problem, as they bring out new programs that take up more computer memory–potentially making your machine redundant overnight. Before you buy any equipment, it is worth checking out what companies such as **Microsoft** have in the pipeline and what the hardware requirements will be.

Part of the problem has been that different parts of our IT systems have been made by different manufacturers, which may not be totally compatible. Increasingly, however, it is possible to buy integrated systems that provide a number of functions in one piece of equipment, for example, printing, photocopying, scanning and faxing.

7 Money & investment

Affinity cards • Arms • Banking • Black economy • Charities • Downshifting • E-cash • Eco-taxes • Ethical investment • Gambling • Genetic screening • Globalization • Fat cats • Free trade • Happiness • Haves and have-nots • Human rights • Insurance • LETS • Lotteries • Medical records • New economics • Pensions • Plastic money • Poverty trap • Third World debt • Trade, not Aid • Unemployment • Wealth • Workfare

Remember the old adage that "money makes the world go round"? Well, money is now zipping around the world at such unimaginable speeds that even the most switched-on politicians and business leaders can find the pace of events dizzying. And as more money travels as electronic signals rather than in more solid forms, like gold bars, the speed of change can only accelerate.

In the following pages, we look at some of the powerful trends that are reshaping the global economy. We hear a good deal about "globalization," but what does it really mean? Who—or what—is driving it? How many of us are really prepared for it? What are the implications for our jobs? And what will be the impact on the world's richer and poorer countries?

And just as the world's economies are being transformed, so is the world of economics itself. Some people even talk of a "new economics." What do they mean? What form might new economics take? Can we really begin to put a price on such things as clean air and water, biodiversity, the world's rainforests or unspoiled wilderness? And is it possible to measure and take account of how happy people are, rather than just how much money—and how many things—they have?

We also look at the meaning of work. Why do we work? Other than money, what are the rewards? And how should we use the money we have earned? Money is certainly a powerful force for change—and, if used in the right way, change for the better. Giving money to charity is one way of making sure that we support organizations that are in tune with our wider values. But is this enough? Should we also be involved in ethical investment? Would this simply be a way of salving our conscience, or is there real money to be made?

In this chapter, we address three main questions:

- *Is money developing a mind of its own?*
- *How do we know when we are well off?*
- *How can we make a healthier profit?*

7.1 Global Economies

Is money developing a mind of its own?

Anyone wanting to understand what may happen to their job or investments needs to understand how economies work. And this challenge is much tougher when—as is the case today—the economy is starting to behave in new ways.

In 1997, the world was sharply reminded just how far globalization had already gone. The extraordinary economic crisis in the East Asian region showed that the globalization of markets can bring major headaches.[1] Countries such as Indonesia and South Korea, which for years had shown explosive growth and had served as the engines of global growth, suddenly crunched into a lower gear—throwing just about everyone off balance.

As the shock waves spread, two lessons were clear. First, economies will always move in cycles, oscillating from boom times to crashes. And, second, the health of our own economies is now intimately linked to the health of economies that would once have seemed a world away. Let's look at some of the reasons why.

Boom and bust

For most of us, the work of economists seems remote from our daily lives, but it is anything but. The human species is unique in its use of complex and ever-changing patterns of production, distribution and exchange. This is essentially the realm of economics. And understanding how economies work is crucially important if we are going to be able to use the market as a tool for creating a better world.

What is an economy?

At its simplest, an economy is a system that brings together those who want something, be it a new hat or a second-hand car, with those who can provide it. It is about setting the price for goods based on how much we want and how much is available. Making things a little more confusing, there is not just a single economy but several. The "black" or underground economy, for example, is made up of illegal, untaxed trading, whereas the "green" economy aims to meet our needs for environmental goods and services.

The ups and downs of the economy make headline news. But many of us don't really understand the significance of what is being reported, nor how it is likely to affect us. Below we summarize and explain some of the key economic issues.

Growth and recession: Economists and politicians alike love growth, because it suggests that all is right with the world. Recessions, when people lose their jobs and government tax revenues fall, suggest the opposite. But both growth and recessions are closely tied to human nature. In the financial world, "bull" markets (when investors stampede to put their money into perceived growth opportunities) will always be followed by "bear" markets (when investors realize the market is overvalued, lose confidence and try desperately to pull their money out). Many people wonder why markets can't behave sensibly, expanding steadily year after year. But human nature means that economic cycles are inevitable.

GDP and GNP: Most of us have heard people using these terms. GDP (Gross Domestic Product) is the total value of goods produced and services provided in a country in one year, whereas GNP (Gross National Product) also includes net income from abroad. Both are measurements of economic activity, used to compare the relative wealth of countries. The major concern with this approach is that measuring the economic activity of a country does not necessarily reflect its well-being or the quality of life of its people. Road crashes and oil disasters, for example, contribute to the GDP and GNP of a country because they boost the use of transport, fuel, and a range of products and services.

Black markets: The worldwide black economy has shown dramatic growth. Based largely on invisible transactions designed to avoid tax or controls (as with fishers avoiding restricted quotas), it has grown three times as fast as the official economies.[2] Indeed, in 1998 it was estimated that the black economy accounted for some 15 per cent of economic activity in the developed world. But in relatively lawless Russia it is now worth more than the official economy! This matters, not only because governments lose tax revenues, but also because it is almost impossible to apply reasonable social, health, safety or environmental standards to "black" transactions.

Demand and supply: Although our basic needs for things such as air, water and food do not change very much, demand for goods can change dramatically. So, for example, the demand for pantyhose was completely transformed by the invention of nylon, while the demand for bicycles generally plummeted as car ownership spread. This is important because governments manage economies through mechanisms designed to accommodate or restrict either demand or supply. For example, they may decide that the demand for road travel means they have to go on building more and more roads. On the other hand, they may decide to limit the number of new roads as a means of encouraging people to use alternative modes of transport.

Jobs and employment: Economies are composed of virtuous and vicious cycles. To take an example of the latter, if people find that they don't have enough money to buy goods, then business finds it cannot sell its products and is able to employ fewer people. With fewer people employed, the money supply shrinks again and the cycle is repeated. If this starts to happen, the governments may decide to increase demand by making it cheaper to borrow—or by reducing taxes. This often means that people start buying again and companies can begin to create more jobs.

Inflation: But what happens if people have too much money? Then there are not enough goods or services to go round and prices go up. This is inflation, and if it is left uncontrolled, it can go into overdrive. Sometimes normal currency becomes almost valueless and prices soar, on a daily basis. When this happens, governments cannot keep pace by printing higher-denomination notes and (in cases of hyperinflation) people end up pushing wads of cash around in wheelbarrows just to buy everyday necessities. In such conditions, people start hoarding or bartering rather than using money, and black markets boom.

Deflation: Just as economies can have inflationary cycles, so they can have deflationary cycles. With much of the postwar period having been an inflationary era, many of us have forgotten—if we ever knew—what deflation is like. Instead of prices rising steadily over time, they fall. That may sound great, but people find that the value of many assets—including property—can fall dramatically. In Japan, for example, the value of commercial property has fallen by over 75 per cent in just a few years. The economic and social impacts of such changes are obviously profound.

Although we cannot remove the cycles from the economy, most of us know instinctively that a reasonably stable economy is good for most people. It means that government can invest in longer-term projects in such areas as education, health care, research and infrastructure. It means that companies can confidently plan for the future and invest in new plants, training, employees, businesses and new products. And it means than individuals can be reasonably assured of employment, income and a secure future.

If, for whatever reason, the economy becomes unstable, the implications may not only be financial but also social and political. If people find themselves facing hardship and unemployment, they will often look for scapegoats.

Sometimes they may vent their anger on politicians, but sometimes it may be directed toward different ethnic groups who, they feel, have taken their jobs or exploited them financially. Think of the Chinese in Indonesia. Although they account for about 3 per cent of the population, they may control as much as 70 per cent of the country's wealth. This tends to make them highly vulnerable to racial hatred in times of financial hardship.

Small world

Globalization is a key factor in all of this. So much trade is going on between different countries that their financial security is interdependent. If even a relatively small country borrows large sums from other countries, and then collapses, the domino effects can be considerable.

Another result of globalization is that it forces companies to make themselves more competitive in a global marketplace. As they try to slash costs and make themselves more profitable, huge numbers of companies are "downsizing" or changing their structure. The result has been wave after wave of job losses.

So why is all this happening? And why is it happening now? In simple terms, globalization is driven by two things. The first is freer trade, less restrictions on trading with other countries, and less protection of home markets. And the second is the ease with which money can now be moved around the globe. Computerization (page 168) has helped on both these fronts. Computers make it easier to keep track of suppliers right down a complex chain, and to trade on 24-hour financial markets.

Let's look at the arguments for and against globalization. First, the arguments for:

Efficiency: The bigger a company's markets, the more it can benefit from economies of scale, driving down costs. And the more efficient a company's operations, the more it can elbow other competitors, including local producers, out of the market.

Profits: Many international companies are salivating at the potential money-making opportunities. They can imagine the profits, for example, of selling just one extra cup of coffee, one more packet of cigarettes or one more hamburger a week to two billion Chinese or Indian consumers.

Equal opportunities: Why should the richer countries deny the rest of the world the potential benefits of an economic model they have discovered and have shown to work?

Voting with their wallets: Whether consciously or not, people are voting for globalization with their hard-earned money. Companies like Coca-Cola and Pepsi, for example, use massive advertising budgets to get ahead of the local competition. Presented with giant billboards overshadowing the main shopping areas, and with Coke and Pepsi vending machines lining their back streets, many Chinese are showing they are prepared to pay more for international brands of carbonated sweetened water—which are seen as symbols of the western lifestyle.

Now, some of the arguments against:

Unemployment: As companies become more efficient, they generally use fewer people. This trend will accelerate as companies try to move more of their production activities to cheap labour areas.

Footloose companies: As global competition builds, so many companies are becoming less loyal to the places and communities where they have operated in the past. Although the social impacts for the countries they move to may be extremely positive, the communities they leave behind can sometimes be devastated.

Weaker controls: Laws to encourage "free trade" can mean that it is difficult to impose restrictions on imported products that do not meet certain environmental or social standards. For example, when campaigners launched a boycott on tuna caught in nets that also trapped dolphins (page 70), the producing countries claimed it to be a "barrier to trade." In essence, they wanted to deny consumers the choice between "dolphin-safe" or "unsafe" tuna. Trade rules can affect a country's export decisions. In late 1998, a California company that wanted to import Canadian water sued the B.C. government under the North American Free Trade Agreement (NAFTA) over the province's ban on water exports.[3] This has disturbing implications for Canada's sovereignty over its natural resources. Also, a NAFTA challenge led Canada to lift its ban on a toxic gasoline additive.

Unfair trade: Some small-scale enterprises are being driven out of business by the giants. The Caribbean banana growers (page 79) point out that it is simply not possible for them to reach the efficiency levels of the giant plantations in Latin America. But the European Union, which had long favoured the Caribbean producers, was pressured to stop giving them preferential deals—because it meant they were blocking trade in bananas from other countries, such as Costa Rica. The Caribbean banana growers have warned that they may go bust as a result, and will certainly face tremendous hardship.

Small farms lose out: In one sector of the economy after another, globalization has tended to strengthen the strong and further weaken the weak. For example, small family farms find it much harder than large farming units to take on board the new legislation imposed within the major trading blocs. So vast monoculture plantations win out over small-scale, more environment-friendly enterprises.

Out of control: Normally, if a country's economy got out of control, it knew roughly what it had to do—and could do it. Today, however, the problems tend to come up faster, tend to be linked to other countries' problems to a greater extent, and the options open to national governments tend to be constrained by international agreements, particularly those designed to promote free trade.

Equity: Globalization is accelerating the truism "the rich get richer and the poor get poorer." According to the United Nations, the wealthiest three people in the world have more wealth than 43 developing countries.

So where are we headed? Without question, and whether we like it or not, we are headed down the path toward greater globalization. But with such a weight of issues on the downside, this trend will inevitably continue to be controversial—and there will be vigorous protests about the social and environmental implications. We also seem to be moving toward a world where many political leaders have less power and many business leaders have more.

Cash flows

Globally, US$1.5 trillion whizzes around the world every day in currency transactions. These are mostly speculative—a large casino, with destabilizing impacts, as was seen in the Mexican peso crisis and the Asian flu. Most of us know what money is—and many of us handle it on a daily basis. Increasingly, however, we are becoming dependent upon electronic forms of money—credit and debit cards, for example—which allow our money to move between bank accounts without it ever having touched our hands. And money moves between countries and back again, affecting the economies of nations of all sizes and levels of affluence. But does "easy" money have a hidden cost? Increasingly, like it or not, our world spins on a financial axis. What happens in the world of money can have profound implications for our employment prospects, our savings and our pensions.

Virtual wallets

To begin with, money was fairly basic. A certain weight of this sort of metal bought you a certain quantity of this product or that service. But then it became more symbolic. We were asked to trust the state to pay "money" to the stated value of a token or note. And now money is going through another stage in its evolution.

The increasing use of electronic money, in the form of credit cards and computer transactions, shows that the real value of money is not so much in its physical form as in what it does.[4] "E-cash"—which so far is largely experimental—is a system whereby you have a "virtual wallet" in which you keep a certain amount of credit. The plan is that you will be able to use such cards for everything from parking meters and telephone booths to buying newspapers and food. The current problem is that people don't see any point in carrying e-cash until it is widely accepted, while retailers are unwilling to accept it until it is widely carried. But digital currency or e-cash is increasingly accepted on the Internet, where it can be used even for purchases that would be too small for credit cards. And it has the added benefit of being less vulnerable to fraud because the system does not need to store your personal details. Although the ordinary credit card is still the currency of choice, despite its security problems, it won't be long before the use of e-cash explodes, encouraging a totally new way of trading.

Debt crises

Whatever forms money comes in, however, there will always be ways of getting into debt. Borrowing against tomorrow in order to spend today can be a good idea if the money is used wisely, perhaps for research, technology, infrastructure or education. But if the money is simply funding more current consumption, the long-term result can be impoverishment, even bankruptcy. This general rule holds true for individuals, companies and governments alike. Many poorer countries have run into particularly severe debt problems through ill-advised borrowing. They may have wanted to fund imports from richer countries or to build major developments, such as hydroelectric dams, roads or housing. Unfortunately, many have then found that not only are they unable to pay back the capital, but that even the interest payments are crippling.

Many people in the richer countries imagine that we are kindly supporting the poorer countries, for example, by pouring in aid during times of disaster. Well, only up to a point. It turns out that poorer countries pay three times more interest to the richer countries than they get back in the form of aid. The debts incurred by many of these countries have helped to create—rather than end—poverty within their borders. By the late 1990s, the world's developing countries owed over US$2 trillion to international money organizations. And they were paying considerably more interest on these loans than they received in aid.

By the late 1990s, the world's developing countries owed over US$2 trillion to international money organizations.

Not surprisingly, campaigning groups have called on governments to cancel—or massively reduce—the debts, as a celebration of the millennium.[5] The Jubilee 2000 campaign has spread from the United Kingdom to Canada, and indeed all of the industrialized world. But in the end, the decision will not be totally in the hands of governments. Inevitably the money would come from all of us, either through higher taxes, or more directly through reductions in the value of our investments, such as pensions. Some people may think it odd that pension funds invest in poorer and riskier economies, but during the periodic booms in such regions the temptation to get involved can be intense. So some of our pension funds will have been invested in this way. How many of us would be prepared to write off the resulting debts, if we knew that we would be helping pay for it so directly?

Taxing issues

There are only two things in life that are certain, we are told: death (pages 275–280) and taxes. Taxes may not be popular, but they are certainly necessary—and for a number of reasons. Among other things, governments raise taxes to fund their own activities, to fund other people's activities and to encourage or discourage certain activities.

Eco-taxes

The idea behind eco-taxation is to encourage people to do things that have less impact on the environment, such as using public transport, or to discourage people from doing things that are bad for the environment, such as creating pollution or using lots of energy.

Taxes are one of the most powerful ways of provoking change. Companies, for example, tend to view their profits as more important than their environmental and social impacts. But if pollution is going to cost more than cleaning up, it's a pretty good incentive to stop polluting. Eco-taxes can also mean that governments have a better chance of meeting their tax revenue targets, increasing employment and helping to clean up the environment at the same time. For instance, revenues from eco-taxes can allow governments to reduce payroll taxes and the GST, thus stimulating employment and economic activity.

So much for the theory. Among the eco-tax proposals currently on the drawing board are industrial energy taxes (to cut the amount of energy industry uses); higher gas and diesel taxes (to encourage the development and use of more efficient vehicles); road pricing (to reduce the number of cars using particular roads); higher waste disposal taxes (to encourage people to generate less waste); a quarrying tax (to encourage greater efficiency with resources); and an end to company car tax perks (to reduce the number of vehicles on the road).

One of the most discussed eco-taxes has been the proposed "carbon tax." Governments are faced with the challenge of reducing the total amount of carbon dioxide (CO_2) produced, because of its contribution to the greenhouse effect (page 28). Burning fossil fuels—which contain carbon and include oil and coal—releases CO_2. Carbon taxes are designed to cut the amounts of these fuels that are burned. All the Scandinavian countries and the Netherlands have introduced carbon taxes.

The problem with any tax scheme, however, is that there will always be winners and losers. And the losers usually tend to shout the loudest. Industry, for example, is concerned that high energy taxes will make it less competitive against companies operating in countries where the tax is not applied. Taxing car fuel inevitably triggers concern about people living in rural areas or worries about penalizing the "poor." And a tax on household fuels, which would help boost energy efficiency, is unpopular also because of concerns among the poor—particularly the elderly.

It should be noted, however, that if there are serious problems caused by raising tax through any route there are always ways that the disadvantaged can be compensated. A tax on household fuel, for example, would generate more than enough money to compensate those in need. This is just a question of recognizing the problem and designing the legislation accordingly.

Although political battles will inevitably slow down progress in this area, a range of eco-taxes looks set to be a key feature of the 21st-century financial landscape. One linked idea is that governments should begin to shift taxation from jobs to consumption. The result would be that people would be rewarded by lower taxes when they create jobs—and penalized by higher taxes when they buy things. Clearly much more can be done through taxes to promote things that we want, like employment, and discourage things that we don't want, like using up resources.

One significant proposal for a tax is the so-called "Tobin tax," named for Nobel Laureate James Tobin. It would be a very small tax, less than one per cent, applied to currency transaction, applied and collected globally. In Tobin's words, it would "cool down the hot money." Funds raised through a tax on currency speculations could fund programs to eliminate poverty globally, run the United Nations and clean the environment.

Global Economies

✔Citizen 2000 Checklist

1. UNDERSTANDING MONEY

If we fail to keep track of what is going on in the money world, we are much more likely to experience unpleasant surprises.

As we are asked to take responsibility for our pensions and other aspects of our lives that would have once been handled by government, we need to equip both ourselves and our children with a good grasp of financial management. Indeed, we should see financial literacy training as at least as important as computer training and it should be included in the school curriculum.

Most of the major newspapers across Canada carry columns and articles on personal finance–*The Globe and Mail* is particularly good. The "Financial Post" section of *The National Post* also carries useful information and advice. Television and radio are also good sources of consumer-friendly financial advice, including **CBC Television**'s *Marketplace*. There is a wide range of magazines related to money issues on the news stands, at least one of which, *I.E. Money*, is devoted solely to personal finance. For the novice who wants an introduction to the basics of personal finance, there is David Chilton's *The Wealthy Barber* (Prima Publishing, updated third edition, 1998). If you are looking for specific advice on managing your own finances, it is worth contacting the **Canadian Association of Financial Planners**, who will put you in touch with a certified financial planner (CFP). The CFP designation is recognized internationally. On the Internet, *i/money* functions as a secure, unbiased gateway connecting financial product providers directly with consumers in order to facilitate on-line transactions.

2. Support Sensible Eco-Taxes

There are strong arguments in favour of cutting the taxes on employment (thus helping to create new jobs, which we want) and making up the difference by putting taxes on waste and pollution (which we don't want).

As long as eco-taxes are introduced in a way that takes account of the interests of the poorer members of societies, they should provide a very efficient way of helping markets to deliver a safer, saner world. But eco-taxes will need strong public support if politicians are to take the bull by the horns and put them into practice. Find out more about this area and write to your MP and MPP/MLA asking what their position is on the issue. The **Pembina Institute for Appropriate Development**, **Sierra Club of Canada** and **Canadian Centre for Policy Alternatives** have done some work in this area, including the publication of an annual "Alternative Budget" for Canada. For those wanting to know more, the U.K.-based organization **Forum for the Future** publishes an excellent magazine, *Green Futures*. Interestingly, the concept of eco-taxes fits well with the philosophy of the **Canadian Research Committee on Taxation**, which, since 1964, has maintained that current forms of taxation infringe on individual liberty and effort, negate the productive capacity of our economy and often subsidize environmentally detrimental practices. The International Institute for Sustainable Development (IISD), based in Winnipeg, also has a number of excellent publications on perverse subsidies and tax policies.

3. Help the Underprivileged Help Themselves

The financial climate is going to get even tougher on some poorer nations. A few may be able to "leapfrog" western technology, but most will find it very hard. This trend makes the work of those who try to help the underprivileged to help themselves even more important.

The **Canadian Ecumenical Jubilee Initiative** (see Ten Days for Global Justice) is part of a worldwide movement calling for the cancellation of the unpayable debt of 50 of the world's poorest countries. The Anglican, Roman Catholic, United and other churches are involved. **CUSO** supports alliances for global social justice and sustainability. The **Canadian Foodgrains Bank** is a Christian-based food aid and development organization that collects donations of grain, cash and other agricultural commodities for distribution to the world's hungry. They work with international partners to ensure the food gets to where it is intended to go. **Halifax Initiative** is a Canadian coalition of environment, development and church groups, with excellent public education materials.

If you want to find out more about these issues, and to do so on a regular basis, two excellent sources of information are *The Ecologist* and *New Internationalist*.

7.2 Real Wealth

How do we know when we are well off?

Most people feel quite happy about the idea of wealth and wealth creation. The real issue has generally focused on who really benefits—and who they then share their new gains with.

New economics

The 21st-century challenge is likely to be very different. A series of new questions are now building up to add to the old. Some of these are the focus of what is often called "new economics."

Doing the math differently

If traditional economists help ensure that markets work reasonably efficiently in financial terms, what do "new economists" do? The biggest difference is that they also want to ensure that markets work well in terms of environmental, social and ethical measures of progress. Easy to say, of course, but often the measures they need to do this do not yet exist—or, if they do, are not yet widely known and accepted.

Indeed, sparks can fly when old and new economists start talking. One critic from the new economics camp has even complained that most of what passes for modern-day "economics" is actually a form of "brain damage." She was exaggerating, of course, but it is certainly true that mainstream economists have often proved to be strikingly shortsighted when it comes to the social and environmental effects of economic activity.

Part of the problem is the language economists use. Much of the jargon is almost impossible to understand if you are not a member of the profession. So, for example, economists may refer to "externalities," when what they are really talking about is some new development forcing native people off their land, destroying rainforests, poisoning rivers or increasing the risk of children suffering from asthma. So the terms are sometimes used to make real-world problems seem more remote.

Economists have enormous vocabularies, too, for describing how and why prices go up or down, or for explaining the changing value of shares. But they are often surprisingly mute on some of the ethical, social and environmental issues that are being forced onto their agenda. Now, economists want to know the answers to new questions about how people value the world around them. Some are trying to put a price on such things as the sense of community, silence or even remote wilderness areas where no one goes. But it is almost impossible to come up with a value that people can make sense of. The U.S. government, for example, is reported to have valued a grizzly bear at US$18.50.

Of course, it really does matter how much we are prepared to pay for the conservation of a colony of Monk seals or a coral reef, to protect the ozone layer or to slow down global warming. If the answer is nothing, then most of these resources will disappear. But for many people, the attempt to put price tags on nature is worrying. They argue that it should be thought of as priceless, and should be conserved whatever the cost.

This is understandable, but not very helpful in making decisions. The truth is that we already put price tags on things that are not directly bought and sold. If you buy a house with superb views in unspoiled countryside, for example, you expect it to cost more than an equivalent house situated next to a busy road, airport or industrial park. What environmental economists are trying to do is make us think a little harder and recognize some of the trade-offs we are already making.

The so-called new economists aim to offer new perspectives on a range of economic, environmental and social issues. So little importance has been attached to community, they argue, that there are no generally accepted ways of measuring community well-being. Therefore, new economists are trying to develop the necessary measures. One survey included questions on topics such as loneliness, neighbourhood safety, racial harassment, neighbourly help proffered or expected, and the frequency with which people move.[6]

Measuring happiness

If one area marks new economists out from the rest, it is their focus on happiness and well-being. Normal economists assume that economic growth and a higher standard of living automatically bring greater happiness and an improved quality of life. But new economists suggest that sometimes—paradoxically—the reverse may be true.

Normal economists suggest that growth and a higher standard of living automatically bring greater happiness and an improved quality of life.

Currently, a nation's well-being is measured by "Gross National Product" (GNP)—how much we produce (page 199). GNP improves in times of disaster, which means that car crashes, oil spills and earthquakes can all actually improve the GNP, because they boost the economic activities that are measured. Spending time with the family and charitable or voluntary work do not.

Clearly, GNP is not a good measure of our general well-being and happiness. Most research confirms that money is a key factor in happiness—at least until people have reached a certain level of affluence. Beyond that point, its importance may fall away, at different rates for different people. But there is also research that shows a more worrying trend. In many countries,it seems that since the 1970s increased wealth has led to a decline in the public's sense of overall well-being and happiness.

Nova Scotia is experimenting with the Development of Real Progress Indicators in an innovative effort that may set the course for more meaningful measurements.

There are many reasons for this trend, but part of the problem is that our growing dependence on consumption brings with it some major social problems—not just more waste and pollution. We put time and energy into buying and consuming, which we might otherwise put into our families, neighbourhoods and communities.[7] This is not just the time spent shopping, but also the time and money needed to look after our possessions, insure them, make sure that no one steals them and so on.

So, can science tell us anything about why we may be wealthier but less happy? Possibly. One Dutch professor has developed what he calls the "World Database of Happiness" and a "Happiness Index." He believes that happiness is far from random, that it can be measured and that over time his approach to measuring it will become as familiar to us as such measures as GDP and GNP. Key factors of happiness (page 96) are linked to areas of our lives as diverse as our sense of community and our faith in our government. Personal factors fall somewhere in between.

Local trading

One key idea promoted by the new economics movement is local trading, often based on an updated form of barter. The idea of LETS (Local Employment Trading Scheme), for example, is to establish a new form of currency that allows people to trade, including those who may be outside the mainstream economy, such as young mothers, teenagers or retired persons.[8] Under a LETS scheme, you might build up a stock of credits by mowing people's lawns, babysitting or providing out-of-class tutoring. You can then spend your credits with other people in the system by buying services, such as painting, mending or car washing.

Such schemes have been springing up in a number of countries, although in France they have run foul of the tax system—because the tax inspectors suspect that they might be a ruse to avoid tax! Even so, they seem likely to spread. Apart from enabling people to work who might otherwise find it impossible, this approach has proved to be very positive in regenerating community spirit.

The meaning of work

Most of us know people who are unhappy being unemployed, but we also know people working who are not happy either with what they do or what they earn. Then again, we may be able to think of people who are surprisingly happy despite either having no job—or having to work very hard for what seem like relatively low rewards. What is going on?

Why work?

Work occupies a larger part of our lives than any other single activity, except sleeping. For many people, however, work is a question of drudgery endured to earn enough money to buy things. But work can also provide us with a number of other things that we value, such as:

Social life: Work gives us welcome opportunities to meet new people and make friends. We may even meet our future husband, wife or life partner at or through work. Indeed, for many people the community they are part of at work is more important to them than the community in which they happen to live.

Challenge: Great work can be about finding a worthwhile challenge and facing up to it. So it can be a liberation, allowing us to escape from ourselves. Indeed, part of the problem with unemployment is that it does not provide the outside stimulus that so many of us need. TV, most people find, is no substitute for the real world. Worse, it can make us even unhappier with our lot.

Self-esteem: The importance of work for our sense of identity and self-esteem varies from person to person. For most men, in particular, being able to support the family is still crucial for their sense of worth—even though there are now more women in the workplace (page 87).

Direction: Equally important, the very rhythm of work can provide a structured environment and a real sense of belonging and direction, which many people need. Instead of watching TV, going for walks or sitting on the beach—or, in some cases, turning to crime—going to work can help give meaning to life. Or at least until we begin to approach retirement age.

Skills and training: Most of us are keen to acquire new skills. Now, with all the new technologies coming on stream, work can be a useful way of getting up-to-date training and experience, pretty much for free.

Given that our working life gives us so much more than just an income, it is not surprising that many people who have reached retirement feel as if they have been thrown out on the garbage dump. No longer are other people asking their opinions or looking up to them—and often their children have left home. Filling this void with travel, study, campaigning, community or other charitable work can be an effective way of solving the problem.

Increasingly, too, many retirees—particularly those taking early retirement or who have been made redundant—are setting up their own businesses. In some cases, they consult in the field in which they once worked, often for the same organizations. But sometimes, too, they set up completely new businesses, developing totally new skills in the process. This seems likely to be a key trend for the early 21st century as the baby-boom generation ages.

Rewarding effort

There have always been—and will always be—disputes about how much people are or should be paid. Some of the really spectacular controversies in this area have tended to focus on the pay and rewards of so-called fat-cat CEOs. But while professions such as nursing and early childhood education are often paid appallingly, young stock market whiz kids frequently earn even more than the CEOs of many companies. Even more striking is that they may be earning these amounts at an age when most of those CEOs were at a fairly low level in the company.

The odd thing is that most people don't take nearly as much offence at the huge amounts of money earned by rock bands, actors or sports heroes. In one case, however, the disparity of earnings was so great that it did raise public protest. Sports-goods company Nike paid leading sports hero Michael Jordan a staggering US$20 million in one year for endorsing its products. At the same time, Nike's Indonesian suppliers were paying workers just US$2.23 a day to do Nike work. Whatever we think about the scale of rewards to "stars" in any sector, it seems likely that this trend will continue. The number of U.S. billionaires, for example, leapt from just 13 in 1982 to 149 by 1996. Indeed, the 450 members of the "Global Billionaires Club" are now richer than the group of low-income countries accounting for 56 per cent of the world's population.[9]

The 450 members of the "Global Billionaires Club" have a greater combined wealth than 56 per cent of the world's population from low-income countries.

Wealth clearly makes people powerful, and, as the "CNN world" increasingly enables us to see what these powerful people are doing and consuming, the disparity of incomes between rich and poor is likely to cause tensions. But revolution may not be the automatic result. Indeed, the outcome may be to make many people even more interested in ways of earning large amounts of money with little effort.

Easy money

However much money we have, the prospect of "easy money," or "something for nothing," is appealing. In the modern world, easy money comes in many forms, but usually there are hidden catches. Let's look at just a few of the options.

Inherited wealth: This is the hardest type of easy money to arrange, given that we cannot choose our families. Although inheritance and wealth taxes have made it more difficult for parents to pass on their assets to their children and grandchildren, the urge to do so is so strong that nothing will completely stop it from happening in some form or other. For those inheriting large sums of money, the downside is that evidence shows that getting too much, too early, too easily can be enormously destructive. Apart from anything else, you lose any sense of what money is really worth.

Plastic money: Credit cards are sometimes seen—misleadingly—as a form of easy money. Indeed, they can encourage us to imagine that the normal laws of finance have been suspended. Some people even seem to assume that a "cashless society" means that everything will somehow be for free. In the United States, where there are 700 million credit cards in use, many young people actually include the unused credit on these cards when asked to draw up a statement of their financial "assets." Clearly, the credit card companies are partly to blame. Along with store accounts, mail-order and bargain offers for anything from sofas to cars, we are offered vast sums of "free" credit—which, of course, is anything but.

Get-rich-quick schemes: Most people get caught in some sort of "get-rich-quick" scam at some point in their lives. "Pyramid selling" is a common technique and can be done responsibly, although it is often abused. You may be appointed to recruit others to sell products, and each of your new recruits must pay you a percentage of what they receive. This has led to some pretty hard-sell tactics, with little regard to the quality of the products sold.

Unstable pyramids: Even worse are the "ring of gold" schemes, which promise enormous returns for recruiting just 10 people, say, each of whom then pays a small sum of money to the person at the top of the pyramid. Each of those 10 then has to recruit 10 more, and so on. Obviously, this can be a money machine for those who start the scheme, but very shortly there are not enough people to recruit—and the scheme crashes, with a lot of losers. In Albania, schemes of this sort helped cause the whole economy to crash, with many people losing their jobs and their homes. The results included armed violence and a dramatic increase in economic refugees to other countries such as Italy.

Lotteries: These are probably the biggest source of easy money. Lotteries currently represent a US$120 billion-a-year global business, with the U.K. lottery in the lead in terms of overall value, followed by the Spanish, Japanese and French systems.[10] Social activists worry that poor people end up spending a greater proportion of their income than the better off, arguing that lotteries are a "tax on the ignorant." In a recent CIBC survey, for example, 11 per cent of respondents listed buying lottery tickets as part of their financial planning.[11] But even with almost no chance of winning, many people feel that there is no harm in dreaming about what might happen if they did. They are buying hope.

Welfare: And then there is the welfare system. For many people, welfare is a last resort and in no sense easy money, but for some these systems are wide open to abuse. Recent years have also seen a spreading recognition that welfare dependency can itself be socially destructive, undermining the desire to work and trapping large numbers of people in a culture of dependency. It can also drain the resources of the state to the point where other important things, like education, are poorly funded.

This debate will run and run, but one thing is clear: money forms the foundation of almost everything we do, including how we live, how we plan our futures, and how we view the world around us. Both the "haves" and "have-nots" are caught in the same trap—whatever our level of income, we all think we need more. But the divide between these sectors of society is ever increasing, and if it is allowed to grow unchecked, it may well be the most corrosive agent our society has ever witnessed.

Life at work

Most of us want to do more than simply rely on the remote chance of coming into easy money. So what job prospects are there in today's world?

It is not always easy to see what may happen to the industries we are working in. Resource industries like fishing and mining on Canada's East Coast and forestry on the West Coast provided lifelong jobs for many generations. Today, the mining industry in Cape Breton has collapsed and the Atlantic cod fishery faces an uncertain future. In British Columbia, 12 lumber mills closed permanently in 1998 and

13 more were expected to close by the end of 1999, resulting in a loss of 15 000 direct and indirect jobs.[12] The forest industry still has a viable future, but it will require a shift from shipping raw lumber to manufacturing and shipping finished products. It will also require learning to work with environmentalists, who have mounted very effective boycotts against B.C. forest products in Europe and the United States. Other industries will certainly be changed or wiped out, while new industries will emerge. One way to check out the industry you might be working for would be to see whether ethical investors think it is a good bet (pages 216–218), although there will always be exceptions to the rule: lotteries and other forms of gambling will probably always survive.

Whatever we do, our working lives will be very different than those of our parents. The idea of jobs-for-life is being replaced by far more flexible working patterns. In the future, there will almost certainly be more opportunities for part-timers, contract workers, temporary workers and the self-employed.[13] The real winners in this game will include so-called portfolio workers who have—or are able to develop—a range of skills, and can therefore work for a number of employers in quick succession, or even at the same time. The spectrum of work available will be for everything from odd-job people, through to consultants paid thousands of dollars a day. Among the core skills needed for many of these types of jobs will be people skills and the ability to use new information technologies (pages 188–189).

In the process, too, more of us will have to negotiate our own pay and conditions. To do so effectively, we will need to have a good idea of what both we and our skills are worth. Negotiating pay used to be left to the unions, but now many of us must do it for ourselves. Interestingly, most women often find this process of self-valuation and negotiation harder than most men. This seems to be part of our early programming, with boys using bargaining tactics to get what they want, while many girls resort to sulking and pleading. We will all need to be trained to negotiate fairly and effectively.

Meanwhile, in a spectacular reversal of the old order, many women are taking over household finance tasks from men.[14] A recent survey found that more than half of women now wear the "financial pants" at home, making major financial decisions, checking statements and paying bills. Indeed, this may prove to be one of the longer-term driving factors of the growth in ethical investment, since women are twice as likely to say that they are willing to sacrifice profit for principle.

Real Wealth

✔Citizen 2000 Checklist

1. Stand on Your Own Feet

Increasingly, we will have to manage our own finances. To do so properly, we need to begin by putting our financial affairs in order. Accredited members of provincial associations of credit counselling services provide consumer credit education, confidential budget and debt counselling, and debt repayment programs to families and individuals. You can call 1-800-267-2272 to find an accredited service near you. We also need to think about what balance between money and other rewards is likely to maximize our quality of life. It also makes a great deal of sense to review, at least once a year, the state of the organization you are working for, or planning to work for–and the sort of trends likely to affect its future prospects.

2. Remember, Money Is Not the Measure of Everything

One alternative to the traditional GNP measure (page 199) are social indicators which aim to give a more accurate picture of where wealth is being created–and where it is being destroyed. You can find out more from the **Canadian Council on Social Development** and **The Social Indicators Site** on the Internet. For anyone just starting with this subject, one very helpful book is *Wealth Beyond Measure: An Atlas of New Economics,* by Paul Ekins.[15] Two other thought provoking books in this area are *For the Common Good, Redirecting the Economy Toward Community, the Environment and a Sustainable Future* by Herman E. Daly and John B. Cobb and *The Case Against the Global Economy: And a Turn Toward the Local* edited by Jerry Mander and Edward Goldsmith. As more people experiment with downshifting, there is a growing number of useful books in this area. These include *Is It Too Late to Run Away and Join the Circus* by Mark Smye, *Downscaling: Simplify and Enrich Your Life,* by Richard Carlson and *Living the Simple Life: A Guide to Scaling Down and Enjoying More* by Elaine St. James.

The key anticonsumerism group in Canada is **The Media Foundation**, which publishes the famous *Adbusters* magazine and runs the **Powershift Advocacy Agency**. They also organize "Buy Nothing Day" (held every year in late November just as the Christmas shopping season heats up), an event that has spread to the United States, England, Ireland, The Netherlands, New Zealand and Australia. **Sierra Youth Coalition** also hold Buy Nothing Day events and has youth-friendly materials available on consumerism and its environmental and social impacts.

And if you want to find out how to set up and operate a successful **LETS** (Local Employment Trading Scheme) (page 208), contact the **LETS Toronto** who have information about LETS activites in Canada and around the world.

3. Work Out How the New Economies Might Enrich Your Life

A wide range of interesting new initiatives is advancing this agenda. In terms of sustainable lifestyles, one key U.S. organization is the **Center for a New American Dream**, dedicated to reducing North American consumption while fostering opportunities for people to lead more secure and fulfilling lives. You may also want to check out the **Shorter Work Time Network of Canada** and the website of **The Simple Living Network**.

7.3 Conscience Money

How can we make a healthier profit?

Can money ever have a conscience? In most cases, it seems, the answer is no. It pursues the highest return and the greatest profit. It is usually assumed that if people or the environment are damaged in the process, this is simply "the way the world works." But now there is a growing range of options for those of us who want to ensure that our money helps drive positive changes, not negative ones.

Doing good

The simplest way to use our money for good is to give to charity. Let's look at charity first, then turn to foreign aid and ethical investment.

Good Samaritans

Nowadays, the whole business of helping the helpless has become much more organized. Even so, as anyone who walks the city streets of even the world's richest countries will know, many people are still hungry or homeless.

To address such problems, charities in most richer countries have expanded rapidly in recent decades. Indeed, they have taken over many initiatives that were once the responsibility of governments. Whether or not we are aware of it, they have had a remarkable influence on the way most of us see the world, how we prioritize the big social issues and how we put our beliefs into practice.

Most charities today operate like businesses and are run by highly professional people. They need to be, because the challenges they encounter are often just as great as those faced by companies. A central task is to strike a balance between employing enough people to run effective, high-profile campaigns while keeping overheads down, so that most of the money raised can be spent on the causes that supporters espouse.

One way of stretching limited resources is to use volunteers or get "help in kind," such as free building materials, or use of vehicles or sites for fundraising events. Company giving is also a very significant source of income for many charities. Indeed, there is intense competition between various charity sectors to tap this source effectively.

The emphasis of business charitable giving has been changing, however, with fewer companies giving hard cash and more involved in "cause-related marketing" schemes. The idea here is that a given company can get actively involved, sell more products, improve its profile and, along the way, help charities raise money.[16] For individuals, one effective way of linking consumer spending with charitable donations has been through the use of so-called affinity cards. The idea is that you swap your normal credit card for one that supports the charity, or charities, of your choice. This is done by skimming off a small percentage of every transaction you make. The bank involved will also generally pay a small lump sum to a specific charity for each new customer signed up. To get an affinity card, either respond to advertisements or check with your favourite charity to determine whether they provide this service.

Trade, not aid

As the richer nations have become ever-wealthier, while the poorer parts of the world struggle to feed their growing numbers, foreign-aid donations have become a necessary growth industry. Sometimes the money or food gets through to those in need, sometimes not. But often the unintentional result has been to create new forms of dependency, with poorer nations—often run by highly corrupt elites—becoming almost addicted to foreign aid and loans (page 203).

Clearly, whether or not corruption gets in the way, there will always be a need for well-focused aid. Some of this money will go to help people after disasters, or during emergencies, while some—hopefully a growing proportion—will be invested in longer-term needs such as clean water, public health care and education.

Many people feel that more countries should be giving a greater proportion of their money to support the world's poor. But instead of putting money into begging bowls, or giving poorer countries "tied aid" to buy western goods and services, an alternative approach is being tried. Implementing "trade, not aid" schemes can help poorer countries stand on their own feet in the future. Up to now, much of the aid money that has flowed into the poorer regions of the world has gone in huge dollops—and often been invested in somewhat questionable mega-projects. Yet there are much more effective ways of using the money to help people.

In Bangladesh, one of the world's poorest countries, the Grameen Bank has attracted an international reputation by providing very small loans to the poor. The average loan is less than US$20, with most of those taking the loans being women. The astounding thing is that the repayment rate—at 98 per cent—has been higher than for many mainstream banks. The moral is that it really does make sense to help people help themselves.

Moral money

How can we put our money to good work—and at the same time earn a reasonable return?

Choosing investment options is never easy: in Canada alone, there are hundreds of financial products to choose from. But one way of narrowing the choice is to invest ethically.

What is ethical investment?

These days, directly or indirectly, most of us are involved in the stock market. While some people own shares directly, others have invested in mutual funds, pension funds and even insurance policies that involve investments in stocks and shares. Others of us may work for companies listed on the stock exchange, or live in communities that depend on such companies.

In recent years, a growing number of major companies have found themselves in the media spotlight because of issues such as human rights, sexual harassment or the use of child labour (page 92). Some have seen their reputations and brands severely tarnished as a result. For this reason, many companies now find that they have no option but to pay serious attention to some of the "softer" values, such as integrity and respect for employees, customers and the environment, in addition to "harder" values such as profitability.

In parallel, a growing number of financial institutions are responding to the demand for "ethical investment" products and services. The central idea is that each of us should have the option of investing according to our conscience.

Even today, however, many people have never heard of ethical investing. And some of those who have may assume that you can only invest using your conscience if you are prepared to lose your money. In fact, when the first U.K. ethical fund was set up, it was nicknamed the "Brazil" fund, because surely only a "nut" would want to put money into it. But, over the years, ethical funds—including those in Canada—have shown their real colours, with very competitive returns and, in some cases, outstanding performances.

Ethical investing goes back a long way. In 1920, for example, the Methodist Church of America, which had previously considered investing as a form of gambling, decided to put money into the stock market. They were particularly concerned, however, to ensure that they did not invest in companies involved in alcohol or gambling. The Quakers—who had long invested in ethical business ventures of their own—soon followed suit, although they were more concerned with avoiding weapons manufacturers.[17]

According to the Social Investment Forum, some nine per cent of funds under management in the U.S. are held in socially and environmentally responsible funds, with an estimated value of around US$1.2 trillion. In Canada, the growth of assets held by ethical funds has been dramatic. Vancouver-based Ethical Funds, Inc., for example, has grown from $100 million in assets to more than $2 billion over the last decade.[18]

It is possible to choose from a growing number of ethical financial products, including pensions, mortgages, saving schemes and even insurance (see below). This is a sector of the economy that will grow. Norway, for example, is trying to ethically invest over US$15 billion of the funds earned from its gushing oil wells. This fund on its own is forecast to grow to some US$60 billion by 2001.[19]

Some of the existing ethical funds—and particularly those with strong research units—are beginning to exert real influence on the boards of some major companies. And as the number of these managed funds grows, the influence of those who represent the interests of ethical investors will also expand. Nor is it simply a matter of controversies erupting at a company's annual general meeting of shareholders. Often a well-timed letter or phone call from one of these ethical trusts can send a powerful signal to a company's board or management that a change of tack is overdue.

Most people who do know of ethical investment will know that—as a minimum—it usually involves avoiding companies or businesses involved in the production of such things as alcohol, tobacco or weapons. But, increasingly, there is much more to it than that. Some funds may still simply screen out problem investments, although growing numbers are also set up to challenge the management of the companies in whose stocks and shares they have invested—to encourage them to improve their performance against a range of ethical criteria.

More important even than the sums of money involved is the high public profile that many of these ethical funds have developed. They ensure that companies understand why an investment is being made and, if a decision is made to disinvest, why this has proved to be necessary. Some company boards may view such funds as little more than a nuisance, but they also know that sometimes a well-publicized disinvestment, even by a relatively small stockholder, can have a disproportionate impact on a company's reputation.

Clearly, it should make sense to invest in companies with a good ethical record—and to avoid problem companies. The tobacco industry, for example, is almost certainly storing up problems for itself in the future, while companies active in cleaning up or that have a strong ethical stance should have a better sense of where things are going. Some investors, however, have grouped together to invest in all the "rogue" industries, partly as a reaction against ethical investment, and have also done well. Longer term, though, they face major reverses.

For those who do travel the ethical route, there are plenty of issues to wrestle with. One of the most controversial areas focuses on just how much involvement any company can have in a problem activity or sector before it is removed from the list of acceptable investments.

Many funds do accept that at least some of the companies they invest in will have up to a one per cent, five per cent or even ten per cent involvement in a particular problem area. For many, it is a matter of just how close the company is to the problem, whether it is weapons manufacture or gambling. To help them decide where to draw the line, the main ethical funds use panels of independent experts to vet their investment choices. If you are selecting an ethical fund, check whether it has such an advisory group, who sits on it, how often they meet and how much influence they have on investment decisions. Do they have the power of veto?

What are the key issues?

Run down the list of "no-go areas" for most existing ethical funds and you find a surprising range of issues on the hit list. Check which of the following areas they cover, and how, before investing. In terms of the "how," ethical funds must decide whether to screen certain problems out of their portfolios—or to buy some shares in problem industries and companies as a way of achieving a bigger say in what goes on. The second option is obviously much more powerful, but if you are choosing a fund that pursues this strategy, make sure that they have the research capabilities to do it justice.

Alcohol and tobacco manufacturers generally top most "negative" lists, but let's also look at some of the others:

Addictive products: Alcohol, tobacco and gambling are potentially addictive or corrupting products or activities, and are all screened out by most ethical investors. The introduction of lotteries has intensified the debate over gambling, because of concerns that money can be diverted from low-income families, often at the expense of children. Tobacco companies, too, have been in the spotlight as they would seem to have concluded that the best way of boosting sales is by targeting the poorer, rapidly industrializing regions of the world (page 256).

Alcohol, tobacco and gambling are all screened out by most ethical investors.

Animal testing: Interestingly, concern about the testing of products on animals cuts across age groups, social backgrounds and political persuasions. But it tends to be strongest among women and the young—and is much stronger in some countries, for example the U.S. and Canada, than it is in others, such as France or Japan. Typically, companies are not only assessed on whether they have directly carried out such tests but also on whether their key suppliers have.

Arms: Some investors and funds rule out any company dealing in arms or related equipment. For others, their concern may be triggered by companies selling equipment such as warplanes, tanks or landmines to murderous or oppressive regimes. Among the most sensitive countries have been Burma, China, Indonesia, Iraq and Libya. Not surprisingly, these protests intensify when the items exported relate to the development of nuclear bombs or germ warfare weapons.

Environmental issues: There are scores of environmental reasons to avoid particular companies, and these issues can emerge at any stage in a product's life, from "cradle to grave." This makes it particularly hard to set up agreed criteria that can be universally applied. Every company will be responsible for some negative environmental impacts—it is often simply a matter of degree.

Health and safety problems: These days most of us accept that employees should be able to work in safe, healthy conditions. Some companies may make an occasional mistake, linked to human error, and we may accept this. Others, however, have a long-term bad health and safety record, or knowingly use suppliers whose standards are poor. These should be avoided—or actively encouraged to clean up their act.

Intensive farming: Our societies have become increasingly dependent on factory farming and intensive agriculture. But the range of linked problems, from pesticide residues and antibiotic resistance to mad cow disease and other forms of food contamination, means that there is growing interest in finding better alternatives (page 49).

Human rights: During periods when slavery was rampant, there were boycotts of products like sugar on ethical grounds. But the big breakthrough came during antiapartheid campaigning in relation to South Africa. The idea of human rights campaigning took root and spread, with a growing range of right-wing, left-wing and over-the-edge regimes targeted.

Nuclear power: The Three Mile Island and Chernobyl disasters helped push this industry further up the list of must-avoids for ethical investors. Apart from the link to nuclear weapon proliferation, there remains massive concern that the nuclear power industry has failed to solve the problem of radioactive waste disposal.

Pornography: Many investors would probably not choose to invest in firms dedicated to producing pornography, but it can be highly profitable—and some large mainstream publishing or distribution companies may have tentacles extending into such areas. Critics of pornography worry that it can deprave and corrupt. They believe it can be degrading, promoting the idea of men, women and children as sex objects. Pornography is also linked with sex discrimination and sexual violence, including rape. Recently, there has been particular concern about child pornography, which is illegal, as well as about the ease with which children can access pornography via the Internet (page 185).

Rainforests: The destruction of the tropical rainforests—often described as the planet's green-belt or lungs—has been one of the most dramatic and alarming trends of the past few decades. Although the spotlight has tended to focus on logging companies, many other types of business are involved, directly or indirectly. These include the banks and other financial institutions, mining and oil companies, agricultural companies, suppliers of chainsaws and other earth-moving equipment, and the developers of dams and other major construction projects.

Canada's ancient forests: Companies clearcutting Canada's forests are also targets for eco-investors.

Roads: The real concern here is that some companies are pushing products or technologies that are not only damaging the environment but also potentially undermining the prospect of developing an integrated transport system (page 136).

Third World concerns: Some investors are concerned that companies put profit ahead of principles at the best of times. But they are even more likely to do so in the poorer regions—where the pressures for development are more intense and the media less critical. There have been major controversies, for example, about the selling of overpriced or ineffective drugs, the promotion of formula baby milk instead of breastfeeding (page 239), the involvement of western banks in extending Third World debt (page 203) and a growing range of "fair trade" issues (page 79).

Obviously, any company or industry trying to find solutions to some of the problems identified above might be a good bet. But this is far from automatic, because a company may well be working on a solution, such as renewable energy, while at the same time being involved in a problem activity, such as oil exploration in rainforest areas. The globalization trend (page 201) makes these conflicts all the more likely as companies grow into vast entities owning businesses involved in thousands of different activities.

Some activities that would obviously qualify for ethical investment include the provision of public transportation; the manufacture and sale of products such as bicycles or alarm systems for elderly people; environmental technology and waste-recycling companies; suppliers of renewable energy; health care and the production of health-care equipment; and most forms of education and training.

Other things to look for in companies are their level of community involvement (page 101), their approach to equal opportunities and their openness about their track record and targets for improvement. You cannot invest ethically if you cannot get the information you need to make the relevant choices. For more information on companies and on ethical funds, turn to the Citizen 2000 Checklist (pages 222–223).

Banking on change

If you have invested in an ethical fund—or plan

to do so—then the logical next step is to apply the same principles to other areas of your financial affairs. So, for example, most of us walk into the bank, do what we came to do, and then walk out. How many of us, as we cash cheques or withdraw money from automatic teller machines, wonder what the money in our hand did before we got it—and what it will do once we have spent it?

The answer is that few people do—but their numbers are growing, and the banks, which know they have no option but to please their customers, are beginning to take note. Yet banks are as likely as other companies to have problems in such areas as sex discrimination or the environment. In addition, there are also the obvious risks of fraud and mistakes in calculating people's mortgages. But the biggest impact that banks have is through the investments they make in, for example, the Third World. Many ethical finance advisers have considerable reservations about the major banks because of the way they lend money to companies almost regardless of their ethical performance.

In Canada, credit unions are generally a better bet. Part of the cooperative movement, which has a long and honourable history in this country, they are democratic institutions run by their members, so that decision-making power is kept in the hands of savers.

Health insurance and pensions

As the populations of the richer countries age, the pressure on their pension systems will grow. Four workers used to support every pensioner. By 2040, it will be down to two workers.[20] As a result, some national pension schemes may buckle under the strain. Whatever happens, governments are likely to devote more effort to persuading us all to invest much more in personal health insurance and pension policies and to work for longer in our lives.

Four workers used to support every pensioner. By 2040 it will be just two.

As more people work freelance, or have a number of professions (page 212), they will need flexible health insurance and pension policies—which they can take with them as they move from job to job. Income replacement insurance pays you an income if you are too ill to work, while critical illness insurance pays out a lump sum if you are diagnosed with one of a number of specified diseases. In both cases, there are now ethical options available.

Whatever the financial product, however, there are concerns that the ethical options are not well enough known. One key problem is that only people with personal (rather than company or state) pension plans can choose such options, and they, too, are dependent on their financial advisers to tell them that the ethical options exist. Yet nothing makes more sense than taking into account such issues as climate change when investing for the long term. Say you are 25 and planning to put money into a Registered Retirement Savings Plan. Surely you want to know that someone is paying attention to some of the social and environmental problems that might surface over the 40 years that your RRSP would take to mature?

The risk business

The idea behind insurance is relatively simple. Life is a risky business. Accidents happen, fires break out, companies collapse and storms sink ships. Obviously, the insurance industry bets on two things: first, that a large number of people will pay them money for protection and, second, that only a small number will ever make claims. Usually, this proves to be the case, but every so often there is a run of bad luck or new issues arise that can wipe out insurers.

Rising costs

From time to time, the insurance industry spots a worrying pattern in the claims it is paying. In the last couple of decades, for example, it has noticed more claims caused by environmental factors. One likely result is that insurance premiums will rise for some time. Another is that insurers will ask more penetrating questions about the possibility of environmental problems.

When insurance companies covered environmental risks linked to asbestos, toxic and nuclear wastes, and contaminated land in the U.S., they thought they knew what they were doing. But then the law changed and the costs of cleaning up pollution or compensating injured parties soared. Some 20 per cent of the losses that almost brought the Lloyd's insurance market to its knees were linked to these types of claims. Indeed, it is estimated that the world insurance industry lost at least US$30 billion on asbestos-related claims—and another US$60 billion on claims related to toxic waste.[21]

Twenty per cent of the losses that almost brought the Lloyd's insurance market to its knees were environment-related.

Now there is another threat looming. In just five years during the 1990s, insurers found themselves having to pay out over three times more compensation for weather-related damage than they had for the entire decade of the 1980s.[22] One leading insurer even voiced the fear that "climate change could bankrupt the industry." The risk is not simply of distant tropical islands drowning and coastal areas flooding, but also of massive short-term increases in less dramatic problems such as building subsidence—which can be enormously expensive to make good. Drier climates force nearby trees to drive their roots deeper, sometimes causing severe structural damage to foundations. Paradoxically, however, if the trees are removed the problem may not be cured: because their roots are no longer drawing up water, the underlying clays can expand and distort foundations. Houses affected in this way can become unsaleable.

Whether or not our homes are hit by subsidence, storm damage or other weather-related problems, the insurance industry survives by spreading the pain. As the claims go up, some insurers may go bankrupt—but most simply raise their premiums. So if climate change does prove to be a real threat, we are all going to end up paying. On another front, some insurance companies are refusing to cover companies that they think are too risky because of their environmental policies—or lack of them. They say that even if the companies paid higher premiums, the loss from accidents, spills and so on would not be tolerable.

Nor is this simply a matter of avoiding business. One American insurer was so appalled at its losses through land contamination problems that it set up a business to provide the best clean-up technologies to clients. The idea was to prevent pollution from happening—and all parties have found they benefit. The insurance company cuts its liabilities and gets an excellent insight into new start-up companies it might want to invest in. The insured companies are helped to clean up and end up paying a lower premium. And the companies making the clean-up technologies get more business.

Medical snoops

To put it mildly, the insurance industry and the insured do not always totally trust each other. But ordinary policy-holders are now even more worried that life and health insurance companies might start charging higher premiums based on the results of new genetic tests. Why is this important? The answer is that genes (page 245) influence and direct the development and functioning of all the organs in our bodies. Without the right genetic blueprint, our hearts would not beat, our lungs would not breathe, nor could our body fight off infection and disease. None of us, however, has a perfect genetic make-up. Many of these genetic defects are not particularly serious, although some may be. For obvious reasons, insurers would like to know which problem genes each of us has inherited.

Screening for genetic disorders began as a preventive health measure in the 1960s, with the development of tests for such conditions as phenylketonuria (page 47) in the newborn, a disease that can result in permanent disability if left untreated.

Over time, a growing number of new genetic tests have been developed, with the U.S. Human Genome Project promising (or threatening, depending on your viewpoint) to uncover the genetic component of most major diseases (page 249). The information produced will raise taxing ethical issues in the family, in the surgery and, inevitably, in the insurance industry. Insurers would be able to find out who among us has genes that will make us more likely to suffer from cancer, diabetes or heart disease, for example. They could then begin to weed out the highest-risk individuals from their customer base.

Clearly, this would make a great deal of sense commercially. But this new approach would leave many people either crippled by the premiums—or without insurance coverage altogether. Surely, critics argue, the whole purpose of insurance is to cover risks, so why should insurers be able to stack the odds totally in their favour?

Another concern is that these companies may well start to use "genetic detectives" to track down high-risk individuals or families. Their task will become ever easier. Already a single drop of blood or strand of hair contains enough DNA for hundreds of genetic tests. And these tests can reveal highly sensitive information, not only on potential health risks but also about paternity and other personal issues. Beware of your hair stylist!

No one disputes the fact that such tests can play a crucial role in tracking down criminals, like rapists and serial killers. But what will happen to all the data collected during these searches? Who will have access? Those involved say they will protect the information on their databanks from misuse. But can we really be sure?

Consider the following example. The Medical Information Bureau in Massachusetts contains the medical records of millions of Americans. The databank was originally developed to prevent insurance fraud, but is now routinely used by U.S. insurance companies to set the premiums on new health and life insurance policies. Indeed, they are legally allowed to deny applicants insurance coverage on the basis of the genetic information in the databank.

So will we see the emergence of a "genetic underclass," uninsured and, indeed, uninsurable? If so, the trend could have wider implications. For one thing, people might begin to avoid genetic tests, for fear of higher insurance premiums, potentially slowing medical research and endangering their own health.

No one disputes that having more information in such areas can be a real boon, but our ethical and professional standards sometimes struggle to keep up with the sheer pace of development. This is an area for governments to regulate, with citizen action likely to be most effective if it focuses on energizing politicians.

Conscience Money

✔Citizen 2000 Checklist

1. Put Your Money Where Your Mouth Is

Money has huge power. Use your financial muscle to support the causes you believe in. Look for ethical banks, insurance companies and investment funds. When planning to put your money into such organizations, write to them to ask for information on how they operate–and why their services are better than those offered by their competitors.

In the U.S., the **One Percent Club** has been set up for all companies giving at least this amount of their profits to charity. There is also a **Five Percent Club**, with plenty of members–and, then one with many fewer members, the **Ten Percent Club**. In this country, the **Canadian Centre for Philanthropy** has set up the **Imagine** Caring Companies concept. To date, over 400 companies have made a commitment to Imagine's corporate giving standards–donating a minimum of one per cent of their pretax profits to community organizations and encouraging employee volunteering.

Another way to put money into causes you support is to use an "affinity card" (see page 214). These are now offered by many charities.

Companies, too, are now major sources of charitable funds. **The Body Shop**, for example, gives 2.37 per cent of its profits to charity. As another source of funding, **The Body Shop** has also been very active in promoting "trade, not aid"–they source some of their ingredients from places where they can make sure their business is helping the local people to help themselves.

2. Check Your Bank or Credit Union

Banks have huge power and influence. Usually, we expect to be pressured by our bank manager–but the relationship can work the other way. Try asking your bank manager what his or her bank is doing to tackle the issues associated with both its office operations and its lending and other financial services.

An alternative to the major chartered banks are community and employee credit unions, which have a long history in Canada. They are owned and democratically directed by their members. Credit unions make a point of offering ethical investment funds. While credit unions are traditionally community based, one credit union has "gone national." The federally chartered **Citizens Bank** was formed by the Vancouver **City Savings Credit Union (Van City)** to provide a "branchless" national bank. The two companies operate cooperatively but as two separate institutions. **Democracy Watch** is the leading Canadian advocate for banking reform.

3. Invest Ethically

Key things to remember when looking for ethical investment funds are as follows: (1) check whether the funds have their own research units of well-qualified researchers; (2) ensure that the funds publish the reasoning behind each company holding in their managers' reports; (3) only invest in funds that provide regular newsletters or briefings on their investments, indicating a strong underlying research process; and (4) decide whether you want to invest in a pure ethical fund or in a fund that aims to support the transition toward more socially progressive and sustainable forms of business.

The 1998 Canadian Ethical Money Guide by Eugene Ellmen (Lorimer) provides up-to-date social and environmental ratings of Canada's 14 ethical mutual funds as well as a comprehensive listing of labour-sponsored venture capital funds. A new chapter entitled "Getting Started" details all the things necessary for investors to determine their ethical priorities along with their financial strategies. **The Social Investment Organization (SIO)** is Canada's largest social investment information clearinghouse, with a membership of over 450 investment professionals, social justice and environmental groups, corporations and socially concerned individuals. **EthicScan Canada** and **Michael Jantzi Research Associates** provide detailed social and environmental profiles of Canadian companies operating at home and abroad. **EthicScan** also publishes the bimonthly magazine, *Corporate Ethic Monitor*.

Shareholder actions by, for example, religious bodies and pension funds are coordinated by the New York-based **Interfaith Center on Corporate Responsibility (ICCR)**. The **Taskforce on Churches and Corporate Responsibility (TCCR)** focuses on Canadian corporations, especially banks, military organizations and resource industries (mining, forestry, etc.).

The U.K.-based **Ethical Investment Research Service (EIRiS)** researches the policies and practices of around 1500 transnational companies, based in U.K./Europe and North America.

There is now a growing number of ethical and green funds in Canada that are designed to provide good returns while being socially and environmentally responsible. **Ethical Funds Inc.** will not invest in companies involved in the production of military weapons, tobacco or nuclear power. They also screen out those with unfair employment practices or poor environmental performance or who support repressive regimes. **Clean Environment Mutual Funds** and **Fiducie Desjardins** invest in environmentally responsible companies. **The Investor's Group** offers the **Summa Fund,** which adds connections with gambling and pornography as factors that would disqualify companies from their investment list.

4. Support Responsible Insurance Practice

Genetic testing by insurance companies is already widespread in the U.K. and the U.S. As the science of genetic testing expands to cover more disease areas, the ethical and privacy issues will intensify. To learn more about this issue, contact the **Canadian Cancer Society**. Also interested in this area are the **Huntington Society of Canada**, the **Multiple Sclerosis Society** and other organizations concerned about genetic diseases. The **University of Toronto Joint Centre for Bioethics** addresses ethical issues related to genetics.

8 Life & death

ABORTION • ADDICTIONS • ADOPTION • ALTERNATIVE MEDICINE • ANIMAL TESTING • ANTIBIOTICS • BIOLOGICAL WEAPONS • BIOPROSPECTING • BIRTH • BREASTFEEDING • CLONING • CONTRACEPTION • DRUGS • DYING • EATING DISORDERS • EMBRYOS • EUGENICS • EUTHANASIA • FEMALE CIRCUMCISION • GENETIC SCREENING • GENE WARFARE • GREEN DEATH • HRT • INFERTILITY • IVF • ORGAN TRANSPLANTS • PAIN RELIEF • PATENTING LIFE • PREGNANCY • SEX SELECTION • TEST-TUBE BABIES • VACCINATIONS

This is an area where questions and dilemmas multiply faster than rabbits. So, for example, should we feel the same pressure to have children as previous generations did?

For those who do want children, but cannot get pregnant, will new technologies like in-vitro fertilization (IVF) offer solutions or more problems? How much do we really want to know about the possible defects of children before conception, via genetic screening, and about the health of the fetus, via prenatal screening? And, if something is wrong with the unborn baby, is abortion the answer—or might gene therapy increasingly be a possibility?

Nor do the questions stop coming once the child is born. Next come such issues as: Should he or she be vaccinated? What can be done through diet and exercise to avoid later health problems? Why do we become addicted to things that are bad for us—and how will this affect our family and friends?

Later in life, when women experience menopause, is hormone replacement therapy (HRT) worth the risk? When financial or medical resources are limited, how should we decide whom to treat? Then, as we move toward the final curtain, are there better ways to cope with death and dying?

These are just some of the issues we will now explore, highlighting some emerging solutions.

Of all the areas covered in *Manual 2000*, this chapter probably throws up the most challenging issues. From cradle to grave, from womb to tomb, life keeps getting more complicated. We—or those responsible for us—face a growing number of taxing life choices. Sometimes these choices are made consciously, sometimes not.

But the evidence suggests that in the future we will be asked to make more of these choices for ourselves.

In this chapter, we ask five simple questions:

- *What are the issues before, during and after birth?*
- *How far are we prepared to go to preserve human life?*
- *Why have addictions exploded in the 20th century?*
- *What keeps the medical profession awake at night?*
- *Are there better ways of dying?*

8.1 In the Beginning

What are the issues before, during and after birth?

The human race is genetically programmed to reproduce. Some scientists insist that it is our only real purpose in life. But at a time when the world population is exploding and the future seems uncertain, it is no surprise that at least some people are wondering whether to have children at all, while others are deciding to have fewer than they might have done in the past.

To be or not to be?

The world must come to grips with the population issue (page 20). As our numbers build, population pressures help to trigger wars and destruction—as in Rwanda. But programs aimed at reducing population growth by limiting the number of babies have, in most cases, been less successful than programs aimed at educating women and giving them access to effective birth control.

Sixty per cent of people in industrialized countries use contraceptives, compared with less than 20 per cent in Africa.

In some countries, too, there are religious constraints on the use of contraceptives. The Vatican has consistently opposed the use of contraceptives for Catholics—and, therefore, surely must take some responsibility for the continuing population explosion.

On the other hand, population control brings its own dilemmas. Think of the Chinese limit of one child per couple. Parents tend to choose male babies over female ones, and healthy babies over sick ones. Some unfortunate misfits, by virtue of sex or illness, are smothered or abandoned to die. And who knows what sort of future the Chinese can expect when these trends produce far more men than women (page 230).

Birth control

Children born into the industrialized world have a much greater environmental impact through their lifetimes than children born into the less developed world. For some, this is reason enough not to have children at all. For others, it means having fewer children than they would like. But for most people it is simply not an issue they want to worry about. Of more concern, to many, is the question of whether they can afford children at all—and whether the time is right.

The choice of which contraceptive device to use has been complicated by growing concern over side-effects and by fears of sexually transmitted diseases, particularly AIDS. The best method for each of us depends on our age and circumstances. Apart from condoms, each new contraceptive technology tends to bring new health issues, as with the pill and intrauterine device (IUD). But it is fair to say that the risks of side-effects for tried and tested contraceptive methods are now minuscule when compared with the risks of pregnancy, childbirth and the impacts of having an unwanted child.

Interestingly, it can be difficult to assess possible side-effects because pill users, for example, may behave differently from non-users. One study found that pill users were "on average taller, more physically active, more likely to smoke or drink in moderation (though not more likely to be heavy smokers or drinkers), to sunbathe more frequently, to have initiated sex earlier, and to have had more partners, than non-users." This could mean that their lifestyles have had more to do with particular health problems than the pill.[1]

Table 8.1 reviews the extraordinary range of ways in which people around the world try to

Table 8.1: SOME WAYS TO DEPRESS HUMAN FERTILITY

Contraceptive	***Description***	***Issues***
Castration	Severance of the testicles.	Extreme option. Oddly, if physical castration happens after puberty, the sexual appetite—and linked performance—does not necessarily disappear. "Chemical castration" is sometimes suggested as a way of dealing with persistent sex offenders.
Abstinence	Forego sex, like monks and nuns—or even like the wives of some Crusaders, in their "chastity belts."	Less exciting, perhaps, but almost a zero risk of sexually transmitted disease. Worth considering, but not a mass option.
Sterilization of women	Women's fallopian tubes are cut or clamped to stop eggs from reaching womb.	Pretty well guaranteed to stop pregnancy, but almost impossible to reverse.
Vasectomies	Men's sperm tubes are cut or clamped.	Said to be reversible, but this is not guaranteed.
Female circumcision	Removal of the clitoris or outer labia; sometimes including sewing up of the vagina. Not a contraceptive device, but designed to curb female sexuality.	Barbaric, but still carried out as part of tribal traditions in some parts of the world—and also, privately, in hospitals of developed countries. The first two methods can make sex painful, and certainly make it less pleasurable; the third is meant to make it impossible, until the stitches are removed.
Natural family planning	This includes the "rhythm method" favoured by the Vatican. Women calculate when they are ovulating and abstain from sex at that time.	Requires time and attention on the part of women in tracking their menstrual cycle, but if couples are taught by experienced teachers, it can be as effective as barrier methods. Women's interest in sex may rise when they are at their most fertile, so be careful.
Ovulation prediction kits	Kits that enable women to know when they are fertile. Also Vatican-approved.	Expensive to use. Not appropriate immediately after childbirth; same problems as with natural family planning.

to their opponents: in 1994 alone, there were four murders and eight attempted murders of doctors carrying out abortions in the U.S. In 1998, a doctor who performed abortions was killed when an assailant shot a bullet through his window. In Canada, three doctors were wounded between 1994 and 1998, in Vancouver, Winnipeg and Hamilton. The anti-abortion lobby favours solutions such as family parenting and adoption.

Worldwide, there are 50 million abortions every year.

The "pro-choice" lobby argues that any woman has the right to terminate a pregnancy before the fetus is viable—and even later if there is a risk to the mother's life. Among the factors held to justify abortion are rape, incest, fetal abnormalities, medical complications, teenage pregnancy and even lack of money. "Pro-choice" campaigners argue that keeping abortion legal means that operations can be carried out professionally and safely. The alternative, they say, would be to drive the practice underground.

As far as risks to women are concerned, professionally conducted abortions in the early stages of pregnancy are statistically safer than carrying the fetus to term. But some 20 million abortions are performed annually in countries where such operations are not legal, with the result that many of them are unsafe. Over 10 per cent of all pregnancy-related deaths are caused by such abortions. And, wherever they are done, it is clear that the complications and death rates rise rapidly with the age of the fetus.

Over 10 per cent of pregnancy-related deaths are caused by illegal abortions.

Where abortion is used as a standard form of birth control, as in Russia, there is widespread concern. But where it is used as a method of last resort, there tends to be wider support. In some groups, indeed, it can offer a means of avoiding giving birth to children afflicted with terrible diseases.

Playing God?

Once, disease was more or less accepted as God's will. Today, by contrast, we increasingly assume that good health is a basic human right. New genetic techniques make it even more likely that at least some people will expect their parents to have done everything in their power to make them as perfect as possible. It is predicted that before long a child will sue its parents for being born. It will claim that its parents were negligent not to have found out about—or to have disregarded evidence of—genetic defects that have since made its life a misery.

Choosing genes

One way of avoiding the need for abortions is genetic screening. It is already possible to test the probability of a couple producing a child with a particular disease. One in 25 of the Canadian population, for example, has cystic fibrosis in their genetic make-up—perhaps unknowingly. If both parents are "carriers," there is a one in four chance of each child having the disease.[2]

Cystic fibrosis is a disease of the lungs and digestive system. It is the most common, serious genetically inherited disease in "white" populations and those who have it have a life expectancy of no more than 25 years. Couples who are aware of the risk may choose not to have children.

It is difficult to argue against genetic screening for such diseases. But screening fertilized eggs, already done during IVF (page 232), is likely to be more controversial when it is used for less serious conditions, perhaps even for personality traits, such as homosexuality. Is this another step along the road to a human race dedicated to designing out defects? If so, what will the consequences be?

Choosing sexes

One thing that parents-to-be have long wanted to decide is the sex of their children. For better or worse, new techniques are surfacing that could make the task of selecting the sex of your child simplicity itself. Will the future be a world of boys?

Several doctors in Canada have offered sex-selection services, and at least one entrepreneur is offering a "natural" method of sex selection. The Selnes (Selection Naturelle du Sexe) Method, sold by Toronto-based Right Baby Inc., caused an uproar in Europe in 1996. The method is based on the claim that each mother has a biological clock, which alternates within a predictable cycle, accepting or rejecting the Y (boy) or X (girl) sperm. Health Canada has declared a voluntary moratorium on sex-selection techniques, asking doctors not to recommend them. But the Selnes method is exempt because it isn't considered a medical procedure.[3] When a "gender clinic" opened in Holland, it provoked a nationwide debate. The resulting report by the Dutch Health Council distinguished among three different forms of sex selection: by abortion, by embryo transfer and by insemination.[4] Let's look briefly at each of these.

Sex-selective abortion: Given that some diseases are linked to our sex, parents may have medical reasons for aborting particular fetuses.

Sex-selective embryo transfer: Techniques have been developed that can test the sex of embryos before inserting them back in the womb during IVF (see page 232). This technique is still in its early stages, however, and may damage the embryo.[5]

Sex-selective fertilized egg implantation: Another way to favour one sex over the other would be to determine the "sex" of a sperm before fertilizing the egg, which will then be implanted in the fallopian tube or the uterus (depending upon whether GIFT or IVF is used). All eggs carry an "X" chromosome; therefore, the sex of the baby is dependent upon the "sex" of the sperm ("X" for a girl; "Y" for a boy). This type of screening seems to be simply a question of time.

Using such techniques to tackle sex-linked diseases may be appropriate, but will it stop there? How many parents will want boys? Then tall, healthy boys? Then intelligent boys? Interestingly, the Dutch concluded that Holland's preference in favour of boys was narrow, so that the impact of sex selection, no matter why it was carried out, would be small. But global availability of sex-selection technology could well destabilize the large number of societies that prefer male children.

Infertility treatments

If you want to have children, there can be few more devastating things to be told than that you can never become a parent. Our society is structured around people settling down, at some stage, and building families. Our expectations and hopes in this area can be very powerful.

Most of us assume, however, that we can choose to delay the day. But the "biological clock" is ticking and many women do not realize how rapidly their fertility rate falls after the age of 35, nor that it plummets from the age of 40. With growing numbers of women postponing having children while developing their careers, or because marriage is happening later in life, infertility is becoming something of a modern plague. Other factors such as smoking and diet have an important effect on fertility—and there is concern that chemicals in our environment may also be a factor. The growing controversy over "gender-bender" chemicals (page 29) also indicates that there may be problems here that we have not even begun to understand.

In Canada, there are now more than 30 fertility clinics.

If you were infertile—or "barren"—in the past, you had little choice but to accept it and work out how to live a life without children. With the success of the first "test-tube" baby in 1978, however, related developments have exploded—along with ethical controversies. In the U.S. alone there are now more than 300 fertility clinics.[6] Let's look at what's on offer and at some of the problems these technologies are designed to address.

Becoming more fertile

Approximately 10 to 15 per cent of couples, or one in every seven marriages in Canada, is affected by infertility. In around 40 per cent of the cases, the problem is found in the woman's reproductive system, in another 40 percent of cases it is in the man's, and the rest of the time it is impossible to say where the root of the problem lies.

Approximately 10 to 15 per cent of couples, or one in every seven marriages in Canada, is affected by infertility.

On the male side, typical problems include low sperm production and failure to project semen into the woman's vagina, either because of impotence or ejaculation disorders. Low sperm production can have a number of causes. These include blockages in the reproductive tract, varicose veins in the testicles, undescended testicles and infections. Among the first steps for anyone suffering such problems is stopping or cutting back on smoking and alcohol. Given that stress is also often at least part of the problem, it is not surprising that a number of alternative therapies (page 268–270) have had some success in treating male infertility.

On the female side, the problems can include ovulation failures and low progesterone production, which jointly account for around 15 per cent of infertility cases. Obstructions of the fallopian tubes and the effects of pelvic inflammatory disease (PID), endometriosis and infections are sometimes to blame. In addition, polyps, fibroids, adhesions and congenital problems in the uterus may also make it difficult for the embryo to implant after fertilization.

Women with ovulation problems may be prescribed drugs such as clomiphene citrate, or human menopausal gonadotropins. Problems with progesterone production can be corrected with clomiphene citrate or progesterone supplementation. Fallopian tube disease or pelvic adhesions are treated with surgery. If this is not successful, IVF may be the best next step. Increasingly, too, women with fertility problems are responding to "alternative" or "complementary" therapies (page 268–270). Both partners will be more likely to conceive if they are well nourished, with growing evidence that many cases of lower-than-normal fertility are linked to vitamin and mineral deficiencies. Men may also be affected by estrogens in our drinking water and in some foods, such as soybeans, which may interfere with their ability to impregnate.

Ethical dilemmas

So does technology offer real hope to would-be parents? Would some of us be better off learning

Table 8.2: SOME WAYS TO BOOST HUMAN FERTILITY

Treatment	***Description***	***Reasons for Use***	***Success Rate***
Stimulated cycle	Treatment to stimulate a woman's ovaries to produce more than one egg.	A common first treatment for infertility. Also used before collecting eggs prior to IVF and for women who have "ovulation block," helping to trigger ovulation.	Average live birth rate per stimulated cycle is around 15 per cent.[7]
Artificial Insemination (AI)	Putting specially prepared sperm directly into the womb. One version of AI is Intrauterine Insemination (IUI).	Could help the infertile man and lesbian couples. But could also be used to insert screened sperm.	Once fertilization is achieved, same as for normal pregnancy.
IVF, or In Vitro Fertilization	Sperm and eggs are collected, and put together to fertilize and create an embryo outside the body.	Where male to female intercourse is impossible, unsuccessful or not desired.	Average live birth rate per stimulated cycle is around 15 per cent and around 12 per cent for unstimulated cycles.
Embryo transfer	Fertilized eggs or embryos are inserted into the uterus.	As above.	Twelve to 15 per cent.
Donor eggs	Egg production of a "donor" woman is stimulated before the eggs are removed for fertilization with sperm.	Inability of woman to conceive or produce healthy eggs of her own.	May be lower than when using woman's own eggs.
Donor sperm	Collecting sperm from another male.	Male infertility: may not have enough active (or healthy) sperm to fertilize woman's eggs.	Once fertilization is achieved, same as for normal pregnancy.

Table 8.2: SOME WAYS TO BOOST HUMAN FERTILITY *continued*

Treatment	***Description***	***Reasons for Use***	***Success Rate***
Gamete Intra-Fallopian (GIFT)	Introducing donor eggs into a woman's fallopian tubes to be fertilized inside her body.	Enabling a woman to use donor sperm and donor eggs without IVF.	Where up to three fertilized eggs are implanted at a time, success rate is obviously higher—but so is risk of multiple births.
Surrogate mothers	Another woman carries an embryo created by another mother's egg, or another father's sperm, or—potentially—by an egg and sperm from other people entirely.	Inability of woman to conceive or carry a child through pregnancy.	Once pregnancy begins, same as for normal pregnancy—except that there may be an issue with the mother not wanting to give up the baby.
Frozen embryos	Once IVF has taken place, the fertilized eggs or embryos are frozen to preserve them for use at a later date. This is effective, but the success rate falls over time.	May be used for women who have more fertilized eggs than can be inserted at one time (usually a maximum of three) and want to have another go. With permission, frozen embryos could be kept as stock by hospital for later use.	Not all embryos survive freezing and thawing, so success rate is usually lower than for fresh embryo transfers.
Intra-Cytoplasmic Sperm Injection (ICSI)	A variation of IVF, where a single sperm is injected into the inner cell of an egg.	For couples where the male partner has severely impaired—or few—sperm.	Broadly similar to standard IVF.
Pre-implantation genetic diagnosis	After IVF, one or two cells are removed from the embryo while still outside the body, and tested to detect sex or genetic make-up.	For people who want to select the sex of their baby, or check for genetic disorders.	Should not make a significant difference.
Sub Zonal Insemination (SUZI)	Variation of IVF treatment. Single sperm is helped to penetrate the outer layer of the egg.	For men whose sperm fails to penetrate the woman's eggs. Very similar to ICSI, above.	Again, similar to ICSI.

to live with the problem rather than endlessly trying for pregnancy? Would it be better to spend the same resources on other forms of health care? Will there be longer-term effects of helping some of these embryos to survive? And then there are concerns over the efficacy and cost implications, too. The most pressing ethical dilemmas include the following:

Unnatural: Some people oppose the principle of any assisted conception, arguing that it is "against nature." Is it? And, if so, does it matter?

Multiple births: Some forms of IVF, particularly stimulated cycles and the GIFT approach using multiple embryos, carry a much greater risk of multiple births. These, in turn, can raise the risks of complications during pregnancy, as well as premature birth and low birth weight, disability, stillbirth or death within 28 days of birth. In addition, multiple births can cause enormous strains for parents, including financial difficulties and physical or emotional exhaustion. But most IVF treatment centres now limit the number of eggs implanted to minimize this problem.

Age: Should older women be offered IVF? There have been cases where women in their fifties, even sixties, have undergone this treatment. Is this something we should accept—or try to ban? And would it really be possible to ban?

Quality control: Couples undergoing infertility treatment want to have some guarantees on the quality of sperms and eggs they receive. Most collection points for eggs and sperm do gather information from the donors, particularly about genetic diseases. Meanwhile, in the U.S., there is a centre that only offers sperm from people with above-average IQ. Genetic screening can already be offered as part of IVF, with the result that embryos may be excluded not simply because they will suffer from a disease but also because they may be carriers.

Payment: Men are usually paid for donor sperm, but there is some debate about whether women should be paid for donor eggs. Because producing donor eggs is more complicated, the concern is that some women may be inclined to cover up genetic and other problems if there is a financial incentive to do so.

Anonymity: Donor sperm, eggs or embryos can be given by a relation or friend, but not everyone feels comfortable about having a child that is genetically "theirs" raised by someone else.

Involuntary incest: There are guidelines on how many sperm or eggs can be used from the same anonymous donor because of the increased possibility of unintentional incest. The children of one donor might meet in later life and fall for each other.

Egg donors: On the physical front, there is a rare, but complicated, side-effect called "ovarian hyper-stimulation syndrome" (OHSS). Research is still ongoing to find out if this causes ovarian cancer. Women who have not yet had children are often advised not to act as donors because they may regret the decision in the future, if they then have infertility problems.

Change of mind: This is a particular problem with surrogate motherhood. Even if the pregnancy is a result of eggs and sperm from the couple who are using the surrogate, there can be tremendous difficulties if she changes her mind. The process of pregnancy and birth produces natural hormones designed to trigger maternal feelings, which for some people can be impossible to suppress.

Permission: Should it only be possible to remove donor eggs or sperm from people who are in a coma, or dying, with their previous written permission? A couple may have been trying to have a baby when one is fatally injured, but there have also been cases where a parent or partner wanted to remove eggs or sperm when the issue had not previously been discussed.

Organ donor cards: Should it be assumed that any woman carrying an organ donor card would agree to the removal of her eggs for use in infertility research—or should a separate card be required?

No claim: Should frozen embryos be destroyed if no one is legally claiming them or able to give permission for them to be used?

Priority needs: Infertility can be caused by medical errors or problems, but should it be possible for the treatment of healthy people to take precedence over the treatment of life-threatening diseases?

Setting limits: There are no rules to stop anyone from having children if they wish. But should the same approach be taken for fertility treatment? Should it be equally available to gay couples, single parents, couples with other children, couples who cannot afford to pay for the upkeep of their child, people with a criminal record and so on?

Embryo research: This increases our understanding of the causes of infertility and birth abnormalities and may well decrease the need for egg donation in the future, but some people want to ban it. Is this ethically acceptable?

Use of fetuses: One future possibility may be to use ovarian tissue or immature eggs from aborted fetuses for research and for impregnation. This is widely opposed, particularly by antiabortionists. They argue that: it would require the deliberate killing of a fetus; it may create psychological/identity problems for the resulting child, since it will have a "mother" who never lived; and it is a step toward "designer babies" and baby farms. Another issue is whose consent would be required to use a fetus in this way? The mother's, the mother and father's, or neither's?

Ovarian tissue: It may become possible to use ovarian tissue, rather than eggs, to produce babies—which is getting pretty close to creating a clone. But some people view it as little different than egg donation, arguing it should be treated the same. Should it?

Artificial wombs: Currently, it is possible to fertilize an egg outside a womb, but not to carry out the whole pregnancy in an "artificial womb." If this approach became possible, it would avoid the need for surrogate mothers—but would it be acceptable to society?

The complexities of these moral dilemmas are clearly such that people will draw the line in different places. Already there have been some challenging cases where it is impossible to make judgements on any "normal" basis. But society must make judgements, and governments—after thorough and open discussion—must pass new laws.

Adoption and fostering

People do not need to have gone through all the above steps and issues to decide to adopt or foster a child. But neither adoption nor fostering is an easy option, either for childless couples or for those with children of their own. In fact, in many countries it is becoming ever-harder to find babies or children for adoption. This problem, in turn, increases the pressure on would-be parents to make their own reproductive systems "produce the goods." Most of us tend to think of babies when thinking of adopting, but school-age children are more likely to be in need of a home. One difficulty here is that the early years of life are the really formative years, with our characters usually set by the age of five. Most people want a baby of the same colour, and without disabilities, which will almost certainly mean a longer wait—because of limited availability and greater competition from would-be adopters.

Interestingly, one of the impacts of the "pro-life" movement in the U.S. is a greater availability of babies for adoption. But many children offered for adoption are not good advertisements for modern family life: they may have been abused, and will almost certainly have suffered intense change and lack of security. As a result, their behaviour may be challenging, and made even more stressful by the fact that there is no genetic link between child and the adoptive parents.

Fostering, on the other hand, involves shared caring. Foster parents are not the child's legal parents, instead helping their natural parents to cope with the task of bringing them up. Fostering is an urgent need in many countries, and there are few constraints on foster parents in terms of their marital status, their age or the number of children they may have. It takes remarkable courage and self-sacrifice, however, to be able to foster children who have suffered terrible abuse or come from troubled backgrounds—and then to let them go when the time comes for them to move on.

The baby's coming

So, it's happened. The baby is on the way. But now there is a new set of issues. For example, what about prenatal screening, home versus hospital births, pain relief during birth and breastfeeding?

Health checks for the unborn

Interest in fetal-screening methods is growing rapidly. And, with increasing desire to have fewer children, it would seem certain that screening will boom in the 21st century, to ensure that those born do not suffer major disabilities. But different people think of screening in different ways: many health professionals, for example, regard the ultrasound as a way of searching for problems, while parents—and mothers in particular—tend to be looking for reassurance.

Although the vast majority of babies are born "normal," we should remember that there are still a considerable number of miscarriages. There is also a risk of babies having some form of physical or mental disability, such as Down's syndrome. This syndrome is caused by faulty chromosomes, and the risk of having an affected baby significantly increases with age. A woman of 20 would have a roughly 1 in 1500 risk, a 40-year-old a 1 in 100 risk—and a 44-year-old a 1 in 30 risk.

The idea of prenatal screening is to inform women whether they are more likely to have a baby with a particular disability. They can then choose whether they want to go on and have a diagnostic test (see below). Ultrasound has become standard practice in prenatal care—it is often used in the early stages of pregnancy as a general check-up and to confirm the estimated delivery date. The "double" and "triple test" blood tests may also be used to work out the chance of having a baby with Down's syndrome or to detect other abnormalities.

One of the concerns about prenatal ultrasound is that it may cause unnecessary fears, which in a few cases has led to women ending pregnancies when in fact there was little or nothing wrong with the baby. Conversely, women may feel reassured and then find that they are among the small group of women for whom abnormalities had not been picked up.

If you have a "high-risk" result from the ultrasound, you may be offered amniocentesis, which offers a more accurate result. It involves passing a thin needle into the uterus to remove amniotic fluid from around the fetus. But the technique carries a one per cent risk of triggering a miscarriage. Chorionic villus sampling (CVS) is an alternative method: after a local anesthetic, a needle is passed through the abdomen to sample fragments of the placenta. It has the advantage that it can be carried out earlier, so that if an abortion is needed, it can be done sooner. However, the disadvantage is that there is a higher chance of it causing a miscarriage or damaging the fetus. Whichever technique is used, it is assumed that women will want to know about potential abnormalities—and that if they are discovered, they will want an abortion. Many women share this view, but may not feel that invasive tests are worth the risk—the chance of losing the baby, for example, may be higher than the possibility of its having an abnormality. Furthermore, you have no idea how seriously the baby may be affected. Some children born with Down's syndrome have few health problems, others many. Their IQ and ability to cope with daily activities also vary widely. False positive results have led to the abortion of what would have been healthy babies.

Some women also object to the assumption that they might terminate a much-wanted baby. And this decision must be made in a very short period of time. It is also argued that such testing adds to the discrimination against disabled people, who may be viewed as "worthless." Compound all this with the extra-emotional state of pregnancy and this can be a period fraught with decision-making, rather than a relaxed time of expectation.

But noninvasive screening tests are improving all the time, so future tests of this type may make sense. On the other hand, the range of conditions that will be diagnosed in this way will expand from diseases, which anyone would accept can be a major problem (e.g., cystic fibrosis, Down's syndrome, sickle cell anemia), to conditions or tendencies that are not life-threatening but, at least in some quarters, may be viewed as socially unacceptable.

Some parents even believe they can boost the IQ of their children in the womb. One Californian research team has formed a "Prenatal University," giving parents manuals and cassette tapes to help them interact with their unborn children. It is hard to tell whether the claimed results of enhanced physical and mental development are real, given that such babies must have received extra attention after birth from the sort of parents prepared to enrol in the program. But who knows where all this will lead?

Home or hospital birth?

As with other areas of health care, trends in childbirth change with the times. For many decades, hospital births have been the norm in Canada. Now we are hearing voices arguing the virtues of home birth. The advantages of home births are that women are in familiar surroundings, have more control over what happens and enjoy greater privacy. It is also a way of avoiding things like monitoring and intravenous drips, as well as serious hospital infections, which are on the increase (page 264). Medically, there is no reason why home births should not be an option for women with uncomplicated pregnancies, as long as there is a willing and competent team or individual on hand—and an acceptance that some facilities, such as epidurals for pain relief, will not be available. Increasingly, Canadian women have access to trained midwives to facilitate home births. Mothers-to-be can coordinate with their medical doctor, who can provide back-up services if necessary, and, should an emergency develop, the mother-to-be can be transferred to a hospital. Although home births are theoretically available to any woman wanting one, in practice some doctors may not be keen to offer the service. Certainly, medical associations in Canada have tried to prevent the licensing of midwives. In some cases, a woman wishing to give birth at home may need to search around for a supportive physician. Some hospitals offer "birthing centres," with home-like surroundings and midwifery services, with full hospital back-up for emergencies.

Birthing pains

Most women give birth in an increasingly technological environment. Even during labour, when clear thinking may be difficult, there is a baffling array of choices. Obviously, women will be better able to cope if they have access to information before labour begins. For mothers preparing for their first child this may not be as easy as it sounds, since it is impossible to know what reaction they may have or what sort of birth to expect, whatever others might have experienced.

Another problem women face is that health professionals can be more sensitive than they were in the past about witnessing pain, resulting in a speedier use of pain-relief drugs. But, remember, whichever approach to pain relief is chosen there may be associated problems. Let's run through the options and see what the issues are:

Complementary techniques: These include breathing, acupuncture, massage, hypnotherapy, homeopathy, aromatherapy, reflexology and music. It is thought that some of these techniques can reduce labour time by as much as half.[8] Acupuncture is also proving popular, both during birth and in pregnancy.

Water births: Some women use baths during labour, others through the whole birth—finding that being submerged in water provides some relief.

Gas and air: You breathe a gas mixture (entonox or trilene) through a face mask, or mouthpiece. The benefits of this are that there are no reported side-effects and women can control the dose administered, by themselves. However, the actual pain relief provided is small.

TENS: Here a woman can administer tiny electrical pulses through four pads strapped to her back. These block pain messages to the brain, as well as stimulating the body's natural painkillers (endorphins). There is no evidence that this will harm the baby, but the relief may not be strong enough.

Pethidine: This narcotic drug, given by injection, often makes patients feel woozy. It is still commonly used, although some women hate the sick feeling they experience. It can also suppress a baby's breathing and the effects may even be apparent for a week or more after birth. Potentially, this may affect the mother's relationship with her baby; for example, by making the baby take to the breast more slowly.

Epidurals: These are injections into the spine, which numb the pain and relax muscles. Often effective, but there can be problems. For example:

- they do not work for all women;
- they can make it more difficult for women to adopt any posture they may wish, increasing

the risk of an assisted delivery—with forceps or a vacuum cup (ventouse) used to speed up the child's birth;
- there is a very small chance of an extreme itching reaction; and
- there is also concern that epidurals may cause long-term chronic backache, although this is unproven.

Caesarean sections: A local or general anesthetic is given, an incision is made in the abdomen and the baby is removed. This is not generally used for pain relief, but as a life-saving measure. However, some critics note that there has been a considerable rise in the number of Caesarean sections. Surveys show that U.S. obstetricians put fear of litigation at the top of their list of reasons for carrying them out, rather than medical necessity. Some suspect that doctors (and expectant mothers!) trying to keep childbirth to convenient times might also be a contributing factor. Robert G. Evans, an economist at the University of British Columbia, speculates on the interplay of economics and the adoption of new technologies. He notes that the incidence of Caesarean sections has raised the average health-care billings per delivery.

Just as controversially, it seems that some women are requesting Caesareans as their preferred option. Where maternity units have been under pressure to question the number of Caesarean births, rates have come down. Caesareans put women in the position of undergoing a major operation, which takes time to recover from. A Caesarean also increases the risk of infection and thrombosis, in addition to the possibility of the baby suffering breathing difficulties, because it has not been stimulated by a natural birth.

In the last 30 years, Caesarean births have more than tripled in the U.K., while there has been a slight downward shift in Canada.

In at the birth: There is now a widespread expectation that husbands or other partners will attend the birth of a woman's child, thereby giving support when needed—and producing an enriched experience for all. Some women find that a reluctant or uneasy supporter is more of a trial than a support, however, so we should be wary of forcing the issue. Whoever provides it, however, continuous support often means that a woman is less likely to need medical interventions in labour.

Breast is best

The benefits of breastfeeding for newborn babies are enormous. It is said to prevent, or significantly reduce, the risk of a whole range of diseases. It is well established, for example, that breastfeeding reduces the risk of gastroenteritis, ear infections, urinary tract infections and insulin-dependent diabetes. Less certain—but also debated—are the benefits in relation to sudden infant death syndrome (SIDS), measles and meningitis.

Breastfeeding not only provides a complete food for the baby but also has benefits for the mother. For example, it can help to bond mother and child, cut the risk of after-birth bleeding and help to protect the mother from ovarian and breast cancers.

Unfortunately, all women in industrialized countries have toxic contamination at levels that ensure that PCBs, DDT and other chemicals are in their milk. Most environmental health professionals still urge nursing as the best option–but toxic mother's milk is a real problem in some areas, particularly the Arctic.

Having said this, a small proportion of mothers are uncomfortable with this option. Others are put off by inappropriate advice, or more often by finding that starting breastfeeding is not as easy as they had imagined. But the evidence suggests that it is well worth persevering. A key factor is the baby's position at the breast, with midwives and breastfeeding counsellors able to advise on the best approach.

Current advice suggests that breastfeeding should continue for a year, but most mothers stop earlier—chiefly because of the difficulties of fitting it in with modern-day lifestyles. As an absolute minimum, mothers should try to breastfeed during the first few weeks, because the early stages are the most critical. A small number of mothers go on feeding until the child is several years old.

Meanwhile, manufacturers of baby formula have been the target of a number of recent boycotts because of their marketing practices in poorer countries. Given that breastfeeding is simultaneously better for the baby, the mother and the household budget, the push toward using baby formula in the Third World makes little sense. Quite apart from the cost, one problem here is that contaminated water may be used to prepare the formula.

Where hygiene is poor, bottle-fed babies have a 20 per cent higher chance of dying than those who are breastfed.[9]

Manufacturers have been criticized in developed countries too, for distributing "freebies," for example, to hospitals that bottlefeed babies without parents' prior permission. It should be pointed out, however, that while there are serious problems with the inappropriate marketing of baby milk, it does offer something that even breastfeeding mothers might want at some stage. Some mothers do not feel able to feed their baby for the whole of its first year of life. In such cases, baby formula provides essential vitamins and nutrition that cow's milk on its own does not. Longer term, too, genetic engineering offers the extraordinary prospect of cows producing human milk (page 36).

What next?

Where will all of this take us? The options beginning to open up seem to move us closer to the ominous picture conjured up by Aldous Huxley's *Brave New World*, where people came off a production line to batch specifications.

There are those who propose something like conveyor-belt Caesareans to avoid the pain of childbirth. Others suggest it may make more sense for men to be sterile throughout their lives, thereby removing the need for any other contraceptive device. Sperm would be removed early in their lives to be frozen and stored for use at a later date. The spectres of a power outage in the state sperm bank or of sperm being destroyed as a punishment are worthy of sci-fi drama.

Given the drive for fewer children, it seems even more likely that parents will try to ensure that any that they do have are "good ones." Designer babies produced by screening out bad genes and promoting good ones are on the horizon. To begin with, this will be an option for the rich, then the richer countries. But, if successful, such screening could eventually go global.

In the Beginning

✔Citizen 2000 Checklist

1. USE—AND SUPPORT—FAMILY PLANNING

On the international scene, organizations such as the U.S.-based **Zero Population Growth** campaign on population and family planning issues. In Canada, a useful source of information is the **Planned Parenthood Federation of Canada**. **Serena Canada** and many local and church organizations offer advice and support on natural family planning methods.

For those considering adopting a child, the **Adoption Council of Canada** is an umbrella organization with a library and clearing-house, newsletters, publications lists and referral resources. The **Infertility Awareness Association of Canada (IAAC)** also covers adoption in its mandate. The publisher of *Adoption Helper* and *Post-adoption Helper* magazines also has a *Family Helper* website with information about infertility, adoption, genealogy and family-member finding, and a book with country-specific information *(The Canadian Guide to Intercountry Adoption).* **Parent Finder of Canada** is the Canadian Adoption Reunion Register, assisting those over age 18 or 19 (depending on the province) to obtain background information on their families and to search for relatives.

Several infertility information sources also deal with the issue of voluntary or involuntary childlessness. Although those choosing to be childless are more organized in the U.S. than in Canada, there is a Vancouver branch of a social club for "child-free" couples and singles, called **No Kidding!**

2. Support Responsible Approaches to Fertility Treatments

The **IAAC** is a good source of information and advice, covering issues such as the success rates of *in-vitro* fertilization, other options, donor insemination, insurance, drugs to treat infertility, adoption and living "child-free." They also sell consumer journals and books. **Pen Parents of Canada** is a correspondence network for those who experience pregnancy loss or a child's death. *Baby Dancing* and *Family Helper* are Internet sources of information on infertility issues. The **Parents of Multiple Births Association** helps parents cope with twins, triplets, quads and so on, and to deal with the problems of singleton siblings.

The **New Reproductive Alternative Technology Society** is a support group for families created through donor insemination, and there is also the **Gamete Donation Advocacy and Support Group (GDASG)**.

3. Seek the Best Advice on Pregnancy and Childbirth

With more women having children at later ages, genetic screening tests are becoming more common–giving parents early warning of potential problems. The **Canadian Cystic Fibrosis Foundation** and the **Canadian Down's Syndrome Society** are among the many organizations that provide information, advocacy and resources for families affected by genetic disease.

The **Canadian Genetic Diseases Network** is a consortium of genetic researchers investigating and commercializing technologies at the leading edge. **Network** researchers have discovered genes associated with Alzheimer's disease, cell death (an important issue in aging research), and breast and ovarian cancer.

For information on other genetic support groups, ask your library for the *Canadian Directory of Genetic Support Groups* compiled by the **Canadian Association of Genetic Counsellors**. The Directory is also available on the Internet. In addition, the January 1998 issue of the U.S. magazine *Exceptional Parent* has listings of numerous Canadian and U.S. national organizations and other resources for parents of children with specific disabilities and conditions, and there is a **Canadian Clearinghouse on Disability Issues**. **AboutFace**, an international organization begun in Canada in 1985, provides information, networking and public education to assist all persons with facial differences to have a positive self-image and self-esteem.

Pregnancy, pre- and postnatal information is widely available from doctors, public health nurses and other government sources, but magazines such as *Today's Parent* and *Family Helper* also provide useful information and ideas. The **La Leche League of Canada** and the **Infant Feeding Action Coalition** provide help and contacts for breastfeeding mothers.

8.2 The Slippery Slope

How far are we prepared to go to preserve human life?

The 20th century has seen some stunning advances in medicine and human health care. Novel drugs, such as penicillin and other antibiotics (page 264) have worked near-miracles. The increase in life expectancy tells its own story: it has leapt from 49 in 1900 to 75 or more in the late 1990s.[10]

We should bear such advances in mind when thinking of the inevitable downsides of modern medical science and technology. They have already had significant effects on the way we see the world and think of our lives. Increasingly, we have a sense of near-immortality for much of our lives, with the result that death is probably feared more than it was in the past.

Now as we enter the 21st century, new biological, genetic and medical technologies are evolving, exploding the range of options and choices open to us. For example: How will we develop and test these technologies to ensure that they are both effective and safe? Should we use animals, people or alternative testing methods based on microbes, computers or something else? Should animal testing only be used on life-saving products, or is it acceptable to test anything, for any reason?

Below we look at some of the extraordinary issues that are emerging as we push medical science and technology to—and through—the limits. We also look at how genetic engineering is being used for research and for medicine, as well as for war. Potentially, too, it may be used in attempts to create a "perfect race." Eugenics, an early 20th-century curse, looks set to be back on the agenda in the 21st.

Living things

We exert every sinew to keep more people alive longer. This quest brings out the best in people, particularly the medical profession, but it can also be a slippery slope. We start out trying to do one thing, yet end up doing something altogether different. Below, we look at such areas as organ transplantation, cloning and human genetic engineering.

Human experiments

If medical pioneer Edward Jenner were still alive today, and attempted to repeat the human experiment that made him famous, he would end up in prison. He injected an eight-year-old boy with pus from a milkmaid's cowpox pustule and then, two months later, with a potentially fatal dose of smallpox. This experiment seems horrendous by modern standards, but the boy lived. In the process, Jenner helped to revolutionize medicine: this was the first vaccine.

The 20th century has seen human tests being carried out on unwilling—or unwitting—subjects in such countries as Germany, Japan and even the U.S. Nor is this a thing of the past: it is reported that Iraq recently used Iranian prisoners of war to test germ-warfare weapons. But such experiments are absolutely forbidden by international law and cause outrage when discovered.

To be fair, some doctors have tried out their new drugs on themselves before testing them on other people. In today's world, however, all new drugs must be tried out in animals first, then in small, controlled samples of patients, before finally being cleared for wider use. Any abuse of the system is likely to be picked up by an army of lawyers ready to pounce on the health-care industry for mistakes or misdemeanours. The pace of development in medical technology will be fast and furious over the next couple of decades. For example, we may even see complete organs raised for transplantation from single cells. In the process of stretching our technology in this way, we will conjure up an endless succession of taxing ethical issues.

Why animals?

We should admit that the world is a much better place, at least for people, because of animal experimentation. Almost all of the medicines and surgical techniques used on humans were first developed, improved, tested and otherwise made safer by research using animals.

Recent years, however, have seen raging controversies over whether we should use animals for research, which animals it is appropriate to use, for what purposes and in which ways. Some people argue that animals have the right not to be used in this way, while others accept that tests will be carried out and therefore focus on animal welfare issues.

Meanwhile, the statistics show that the number of experiments reported publicly on animals is not a good indicator of the number of animals killed—given that two or three times more animals may be culled because they are "unsuitable" for tests, for one reason or another.[11]

One key reason for carrying out animal research is that we can do things to animals that would not be legal to do to humans. Within the limits set by the law, we can lock them up, feed them what we want, in the conditions we want, and then kill them and cut them open to see how they have reacted. Just as importantly, because they have shorter life spans, we can see some effects in a few months or years, which would take decades in humans.

What are they used for?

Life-saving medicines or vital research into cures for cancer and other fatal diseases are something that most people feel can justify causing animal suffering. However, such experiments comprise less than half those carried out in North America.

At the other end of the scale, animal experiments are also carried out to test the safety of a huge range of products, from agrochemicals to cosmetics. Many people think that animal testing for cosmetic products and ingredients, basically to feed our vanity, is unacceptable. Increasingly, as a result, consumers are looking for products carrying labels such as "cruelty-free" or "not tested on animals."

One key problem for consumers is that there are many supposedly "animal-friendly" labels, which can mean vastly different things—a problem that campaigning organizations are trying to address.[12] New laws are in the pipeline in some countries to address such problems, but even there the issues will not vanish entirely. So here are some of the issues we face:

Product vs. ingredient: Animal testing could be carried out either on a complete product or on ingredients used in the product.

Source: "Cruelty-free" claims should mean that animal tests have not been carried out by any supplier right down the chain.

Tested elsewhere: Companies may test an ingredient on animals because that ingredient will be used for medicinal purposes. They may then use the ingredient in cosmetic products, as long as the tested ingredient does not represent more than a given percentage of the final "cruelty-free" product.

Timeframe: "No animal testing" could either mean no testing for a rolling time period of, say, five years, or it could mean no testing since a fixed date. Clearly, the fixed date is likely to mean fewer animals are used, because a company could not introduce a new animal-tested ingredient and then label it as "cruelty-free" after five years.

Hostile testing: One suggestion has been to ban companies using any ingredients that have been tested on animals by anyone. But this could open the door to so-called hostile testing, where a rival company might test a key ingredient on animals simply to prevent another company from using it in a "cruelty-free" product. Stranger things have happened.

New ingredients: Given that all new ingredients must be tested on animals, any company that commits to avoiding animal-tested ingredients will be restricted to using existing ingredients, thereby potentially stifling innovation.

Clearly, it can be hard to draw the line. There are many products that are neither "life-saving" treatments nor "frivolous" cosmetics. Ailments that reduce the quality of life, but are not usually life-threatening, include eczema, hayfever and migraines.

For scientists, one of the most troubling aspects of the animal-testing controversy is that society might try to curtail their experiments by testing the validity of their research objectives. The problem here, they argue, is that most of the revolutionary discoveries of science have been stumbled on when researching something else entirely. By enforcing strict guidelines on what products or areas of interest may justify animal research, we may be closing the door on a cure for AIDS, cancer or another killer disease.

Whatever our views, most of us would probably agree that the principles we should be aiming to apply in the near term, as a minimum, are to continue to cut the number of animals used in research, improve research methods to minimize cruelty and replace animals wherever alternative methods are available.[13]

Which animals?

The more intelligent the animal, the more pain and distress it is likely to suffer. So there is usually greater concern about experiments on chimpanzees than on mice. Our feelings about using primates are stronger because we are exploiting a species very close to our own.

Chimpanzees, our closest animal relative, share more than 97 per cent of our genetic make-up.

Despite these concerns, chimpanzees and monkeys are still being used in a variety of ways in Europe and the U.S. Monkeys have been shot up into space in rockets. Chimps have been used to develop vaccines for AIDS, malaria and neurological diseases like Parkinson's—and some scientists see them as the "experimental animals of choice" for BSE ("mad cow" disease, page 53) research.[14]

Clearly, the similarity of such nonhuman primates to humans makes them potentially useful "guinea pigs." So, for example, kidneys from genetically engineered pigs were transplanted (see opposite) into monkeys, to see whether the organs "took" in their new animal hosts. But critics argue that it is easy to exaggerate the value of such research—and thereby the importance of using primates.

Dogs, cats, horses and pigs are also widely used. Given that all are highly intelligent and the first three often kept as "companion animals," there are strong concerns over their treatment. But, again, it is hard to draw the line. Most experiments are conducted using rodents, such as mice and rats. We may feel that rats are a lower form of life, but anyone who has kept a rat as a pet will know that they, too, can be highly intelligent. If animals are to be used, the choice of species is very important in developing an effective model or test. It is quite possible, for example, that a chemical may cause a problem in mice but not in humans, or vice versa. Tests for thalidomide did not reveal any problems in rabbits, but the effect in human babies was appalling. However, the problem here was not simply the species used, but the fact that the drug was not tested on pregnant animals.

One new area of research where there is surging demand for animal research is genetic engineering. So we will now turn to some of the issues that crop up in the development and use of some of the new genetic technologies.

Gene themes

One highly controversial use of genetic engineering involved designing a mouse (the "Oncomouse," page 35) in such a way that it is more likely to develop cancer when exposed to particular substances. In effect, it has been designed to suffer. Other animals are being modified in such a way that key elements of their immune systems are more similar to those of humans, so they more closely reflect the results of drugs on human patients.

Other potentially emotive uses of animals in this area include the transfer of human genes into animals (and vice versa); "gene pharming," in which animals are used as "furry fermenters" to produce drugs in their blood or milk; and the breeding of animals as sources of organs for transplant surgery.

Let's focus on some of the issues surrounding four of these approaches: *transgenics* (transferring selected genes from one species to another); *cloning* (replicating another genetically identical being); *genetic screening* (looking for genetic defects); and *gene prospecting* (hunting for genes with a potential commercial value). We will then look at the potential role of genes in creating a "perfect race" and germ-warfare weapons.

A change of heart

The grafting of animal organs—such as hearts, lungs, kidneys, bones, bone marrow and pancreases—into humans has been tried, but has not yet been successful. Pig organs have been transferred into a monkey, although the time before rejection occurred was measured in days.

One of the most widely known failures was when an American girl, "Baby Fae," received a baboon's heart. She died. And in 1995 an American man suffering from AIDS was given bone marrow, also from a baboon, in a failed, last-gasp effort to save his life.

There is now serious work under way to develop animals, particularly pigs, as "organ factories." In what is called "xenotransplantation," human genes will be inserted into the pigs to make their organs as similar as possible to the human organs they are meant to replace, to avoid the risk of rejection by the host's immune system.

It seems that it is only a matter of time before this technology succeeds, although it is far from certain that it will be a good thing. The news that headless frog embryos had been produced raised the outlandish long-term prospect of headless humans, stored until their organs were needed.

Some scientists, however, are predicting something even more dramatic. They believe that they will eventually be able to transplant our brain into a body of our choice. Perhaps memories will be transferred onto microchips and then downloaded into a new brain, or maybe the scientists will come up with a way of slowing down aging in the brain. Perhaps even sooner we will be able to have silicon implants into our brains—scientists are already growing nerves on computer chips—enabling us to speak Japanese like a native, for example.

Whether or not such schemes come to anything, it is clear that our ethics will be tested as never before. Some of the issues now being raised include the following:

Animal welfare: Genetically altered animals used as organ sources would need to be kept in completely sterile conditions—such as stainless-steel cages. To reduce the risk of infection, it may even be "necessary" to use Caesarean section on a pregnant sow, so that her piglets can be born directly into sterile plastic "bubbles."[15]

Human epidemics: There is the very real fear that transplanting organs from one species to another could introduce uncontrollable and deadly agents—similar to HIV or the prions involved in "mad cow disease"—into the human population, giving rise to the spread of new, unknown diseases. Efforts to breed pigs that are free of viruses that infect people seem doomed to failure.[16]

Religious objections: These can work in a number of ways. Buddhists may worry that it is wrong to harm animals and many Muslims believe that it is wrong to transplant pig organs into true followers of the Prophet. Some also object to human genes being inserted into plants, particularly if the plants are then eaten. Is this a new form of cannibalism?

Subspecies: Once we have started, where will we stop? One gene or one organ from a pig will not make us into a pig, but if we managed to create a half-pig–half-human, what would it be—and what rights would it have? Far-fetched today, but one can easily imagine a day when "subhuman" workers might be created, with incredible physical strength but low intelligence.

Spare parts: Growing numbers of critics argue that this "spare parts" approach to health care is leading us up the wrong path. China, for example, has started executing criminals pretty much to order, with the extracted organs supplied to transplant hospitals outside the country. Quite apart from the hugely taxing ethical issues, however, we may well be in danger of being seduced by the exciting challenge of this technology—rather than concentrating on more cost-effective approaches to disease prevention.

Bring on the clones

No sheep in history has been photographed as many times as "Dolly." Apparently, the interest in the animal claimed to be the world's first cloned sheep was so great that she even learned to play up to the cameras. The announcement of her existence led to one of the biggest controversies in recent years, raising concerns about human cloning.

So what is cloning? Basically, it means producing genetically identical living organisms. Identical twins are naturally produced clones. The underlying thinking is that once we have managed to find, or produce, an animal with the properties we want, we can then reproduce endless identical copies. Essentially, it is little different to a factory producing identical products, except that instead of producing kettles or cars, this "factory" would produce more or less identical beings.

Scientists tend to focus on the medical benefits that this technology may bring. Future Dollies, we are told, will produce medicines to treat everything from cystic fibrosis (page 229) to leukemia—with the medicines extracted either from their blood or milk. The work may well open the way to cures for diabetes, spinal cord injuries, even cancer. And it might also provide a source of "medicine milk" or genetically altered organs for transplants (see above).

Clearly, successfully cloning one species also

inevitably opens up the possibility of cloning others. Indeed, an American team quickly followed up on the announcement on Dolly with the news that they had successfully created two cloned monkeys. Whether or not they managed the trick, the spectre of cloning humans has certainly moved closer to reality.

One eccentric American physicist even announced plans to set up a human cloning clinic in Chicago. He argued that public opposition to cloning will evaporate the minute people behold "half a dozen bouncing-baby, happy smiling clones."[17] Although he seems unlikely to succeed, science often proceeds in leaps and bounds. Things that were once declared impossible eventually become reality. So it would be wise to give ourselves a chance to decide where we want to draw the line, whether for ourselves or for society.

Meanwhile, there remains a real possibility that key advances will be achieved outside the law. If illegal human clones were to be produced, what would we do? Put them down? Lock them up? Hardly. The chances are that we would try to treat them just as we would normal people, which makes it even more likely that such clones will be produced.

Cloning embryos: There is already intense debate about the idea of cloning embryos. Some scientists point out that the medical research value is immense and propose a cut-off date beyond which the embryo should not be kept alive. This debate will run and run.

Replacements: Imagine losing a much-loved child or baby in a car accident. Might you be tempted to replicate that child if it were possible? It has been reported that a Canadian religious sect has set up secret laboratories to sponsor research into human cloning. For $350 000, it was said, customers would be offered the chance to clone themselves. Almost certainly this was hype, but it seems almost certain that human cloning will be carried out in the 21st century.

Life extension: The possibility of being able to produce replicas of ourselves could bring narcissism to new heights. We might be able to make one or more replicas that would go on living after we had died, a similar idea to cryogenics (page 275), but without the memories stored in our brain.

Old brain, new body: Alternatively, toward the extreme end of the spectrum of speculation, we might even start producing identical counterparts of ourselves so that we could replace organs—kidneys, hearts or lungs—that begin to fail. This would have the clear advantage of minimizing problems of rejection. Another long-term possibility might be to move our brain, with its memories, to a new body when the old one fails. Don't count on it happening any time soon!

Human tests: There is considerable debate over how much of our personality is dictated by our genetic make-up, and how much by environmental factors and our family background. Producing clones, some people fear, would enable unprincipled scientists to make identical people and put them in different environments to monitor how they develop and compare.

Baby farming: The Nazis tried this, albeit with low technology. With genetic engineering the possibilities open up considerably. Given the rate of progress, it is hard to know what is far-fetched and what is not. Imagine that we wanted to satisfy our taste for particular people, say Marilyn Monroe, Madonna or Michael Jackson. The time may come when we can pick up an infant replica, just as one might pick up a new pet. Perhaps, too, we would need homes for abandoned clones—once the fashion for a particular look died.

Mass-produced dictators: What would happen if a dictator, like Iraq's Saddam Hussein or Nazi Germany's Adolf Hitler, had himself (or, much less likely, herself) cloned? One possible consolation is that the resulting clones might be genetically identical to whomever they came from, but their personalities would almost certainly be different—because of their different childhood backgrounds.

Research into the cloning of animals and people could lay the foundations of hugely important new industries, potentially bringing unimaginable benefits. But the risks are equally worth considering. And we have been warned. The Nobel prize-winning scientist whose work led to the building of the atomic bomb has called for a ban on human cloning. He pointed out that he managed to deceive himself that his work would lead to the betterment of humanity. Instead, he noted it led to "hundreds of thousands of people dying in the twinkling of an eye."

Who owns your genes?

Cloning is certainly a big issue, but there are plenty of others, which we should be taking seriously. As the impact of genes for our health and quality of life becomes better understood, companies are scouring the world for genes that may help prevent or treat diseases. This activity—known as "bioprospecting"—is now increasingly common and also has the potential to bring rich rewards.

The best place to look for genes linked to human health conditions is in inbred populations like those of Iceland, Tristan da Cunha or Easter Island. Such communities tend to have narrower gene pools, making it easier to track down those responsible for particular conditions.[18] Unfortunately, as one pioneer put it, this is often "helicopter science"; companies fly in, take what they want and then fly out again.

Consider the experience of the Hagahai people of Papua New Guinea.[19] Their first contact with the outside world, in 1984, led to them being exposed to viruses and disease for which they had no resistance. Many died. The survivors contacted foreign researchers, who brought in vaccines that helped save them. So far, so good. But the researchers also took samples, which suggested that these people were resistant to leukemia and other degenerative diseases. The researchers then claimed ownership of the genetic qualities of the Hagahai people by taking out a patent. Following a massive uproar, led by Canadian campaigners, the patent was dropped.

In the Pacific region, people such as the Maori and Aborigines have also found themselves being investigated by researchers. The result has been a series of high-temperature controversies. Critics say that it took centuries to overturn the slave trade, which was based on property rights over humans, and that the implications of this new trade in human genes are very similar.

The implications of this new trade in human genes are very similar to those of the slave trade.

Nor is it just a question of the genes of indigenous tribal populations being at risk. One westerner discovered that his genes had been patented and that he had no legal right over them—or the profits that might be generated from them. John Moore, a U.S. citizen, underwent treatment for a rare and potentially fatal form of cancer. The doctor treating him discovered that he produced an unusual blood protein that might be used to develop an anticancer agent. He promptly filed a patent application. When Moore discovered this, he filed a lawsuit. Although the court found the doctor had breached his duty by not revealing his research and financial interests, it also denied Moore's claim to the cells removed from his body.

Protecting the free flow of research materials and research information among scientists is important if progress is to be made. But does it take precedence over an individual's right to his or her own genetic material, whether they live in America, Albania or Amazonia?

Gene screens

Meanwhile, scientists are compiling a map of all the genes that make up a human being and identifying which ones make each individual different from another. The figures boggle the imagination. The Human Genome Project, which began in 1990, is an international, 15-year effort designed to discover all 60 000 to 80 000 human genes (the human genome) and open them up for further research. Another goal is to work out the sequence of the three billion DNA building blocks of our genes.

The challenge has been described as equivalent to tearing up six volumes of the *Encyclopaedia Britannica* and then trying to put it all back together to read the information. As the work proceeds, and the number of genes decoded grows, we will get a much better idea of which genes cause which diseases. But the project will also open a whole series of Pandora's boxes, challenging our very understanding of what it means to be human. As a result, a huge number of new choices will invade our lives, particularly via genetic screening.[20]

Genetic screening can take place at different stages of life and, for various reasons, including preconceptual planning (page 236), looking for fetal abnormalities and testing for disease to which you may be genetically predisposed. The future promises even wider applications of genetic "screens." There are three main approaches to genetic screening to date:

Screening prospective parents: This may be done to assess the likelihood of adults passing on particular diseases to their children. They can then decide whether they want to take this risk, find their way around it in some way or choose to not have children.

Screening fetuses in the womb: This would determine whether the fetus has a particular genetically inherited disease. If it is found to have cystic fibrosis, mental illness or a disorder such as being albino, it may be aborted. Alternatively, the parents may decide to go ahead anyway.

Screen tests: Another approach is to assess the likelihood of someone contracting a particular disease in later life. Consider the following scenario. You receive promotional material from a genetic testing company, which offers a test for breast cancer genes. Do you take the test? If the result is negative, do you relax—given that the test only picks up hereditary forms of breast cancer, which account for a relatively small proportion of all breast cancers? If the result is positive, you know that one option likely to be suggested would be to have one or both of your breasts removed. How seriously should you take new treatments, such as tamoxifen? And what should you tell your life insurance company (page 220)? This is no parlour game. For many women, these issues are now a challenging reality.

More positively, our new understanding of the genetic differences between people could clearly bring huge benefits. Take the area of drug dosing. Some time in the 21st century, based on genetic tests, it will be possible to predict the response of each individual to particular forms of medication. So instead of giving every adult the same dose and waiting to see what side-effects may arise, doctors should be able to prescribe the right amount of the right drug, with minimum side-effects. Genetic screening also paves the way for "gene therapy." Having identified a "faulty" gene, scientists are working on ways to replace the gene with one that works. Research on this approach has moved furthest in relation to finding a treatment for cystic fibrosis (page 229).

Perhaps the main concern about genetic screening and gene therapy is that they take us a step closer to designing out faults from the human race, with unknown consequences. And as we have seen in the past, this opportunity is unlikely to be ignored by those most likely to abuse it.

Designer people

The idea behind "eugenics" is deceptively simple. If we can breed animals like dogs, cows or horses to improve the stock, then surely we can do the same with people? The best way to improve society, many have felt, would be to improve people. Utopia, they feel, is more likely to be achieved if we can work out how to breed people who are more intelligent, less likely to carry hereditary diseases, more hard-working and without criminal tendencies.[21]

Charles Darwin, who was himself a president of the Eugenics Society, argued that in evolution only the fittest survive. Some of his more enthusiastic supporters, however, soon concluded that only the fittest should survive—and they also wanted to define who was fit and who not.[22] Partly as a result, the 20th century saw numerous attempts to improve the human genetic stock, with terrible consequences.

In the 1930s, for example, the Australians introduced a program to try to eliminate the Aborigines by dispersing them and interbreeding them with the white population. This process of slow genocide ended as recently as 1970.

But the introduction of concentration camps by Adolf Hitler and the Nazis was the most notorious example of eugenics in practice. Driven by a desire to improve the German people, the Nazis were not content simply to destroy those they saw as unfit, but also planned to breed a new race of super-people. They began to set up baby farms where "pure Aryan" parents could produce the new generations who would inherit a world cleared of "lesser" peoples.

No one would claim that these "Aryan stud farms" were a success, not least because so much of what each of us becomes depends on our childhood environment, not simply our genes. But they symbolized a desire for human perfection that is unlikely to end with the 20th century.

China's leaders have openly pursued an active eugenic policy, declaring that "idiots breed idiots." In Singapore, too, the government has encouraged university graduates to mate with other graduates, aiming to build an "intelligent society." In Austria, forced sterilization is still legal for mentally handicapped children as young as 10 or 11 and, as in Sweden and other Scandinavian countries, it has been revealed that for much of the 20th century forced sterilization of "undesirables" was widespread.

In the 21st century, eugenics will inevitably take new forms. Some, for example, would argue that many current uses of abortion amount to a form of eugenics, as parents decide to abort children with a risk of certain diseases, such as Down's syndrome (page 236). Genetic screening, too, will produce huge volumes of information on what might be in store for each of us and, no doubt, we will see a growth in the numbers of abortions because the fetuses will have been found to be less than perfect.

Totally new choices will become available. Picture this. A couple might produce a number of embryos and then have them genetically profiled, choosing which profile they like best. The selected embryo would then be grown a bit further in the test tube, so that some cells can be snipped out to provide tissue for repairs in later life. And then, finally, the pregnancy can begin. Eugenics, in short, may become an accepted part of our daily lives, a subject of personal choice, rather than something imposed upon us.[23]

And things may go even further. A biology professor at Princeton University warns that once the genes for intelligence are identified, the better off will start to enhance the brainpower of their children.[24] This, he suggests, will lead to a genetic class system that will be much less flexible than the current class system. Within the space of a few generations, he forecasts, we may even see the evolution of different human species. To start with, there are two: the "GenRich" and the "Naturals." Then, by the 26th century, there will be more. They won't intermingle—and they won't intermarry—across the intellectual divide. We may even learn how to program ourselves so that we can experience the acute sense of smell that dogs have, the sonar abilities of bats and dolphins, or the sensitivity to magnetic fields that allows birds to navigate across continents. It is at least conceivable that future "super-beings" will have many of the powers once reserved in mythology for the gods.

Ethnic weapons

Some of the most terrifying possibilities, however, relate to the use of genetic engineering for weapons. Just as insecticide science was used by First World War and Nazi scientists to design "insecticides for people," so genetic engineering will inevitably be used to engineer new germ-warfare weapons. Japan's Aum cult, which released chemical nerve gas weapons (particularly sarin) in the Tokyo subway system, was also hard at work on biowarfare weapons.

Bacteria or viruses might be designed to resist antibiotics, or to react to treatment by producing even deadlier toxins. But perhaps most frightening of all is the idea of "ethnic weapons." It may well be possible in the future to kill off everyone with a particular gene. For example, everyone with blue eyes, fair hair, an IQ below 100 or who happens to be either male or female might be targeted. Given that many wars are fought between two different races it is not impossible to imagine selecting a particular gene that is common in the enemy. Eliminating all those who have the gene might provide a tidy, and effective, way of annihilating the opposition.

By the end of the Second World War at least six countries—the U.S.S.R., the United States, the U.K., France, Japan and Canada—are believed to have worked on the technology for large-scale use of biological warfare agents. Biological warfare research has succeeded in producing a full spectrum of agents capable of inducing a range of effects, from incapacitation to death. There have been no successful large-scale uses of biological warfare agents in modern war; however, despite U.N. attempts to control this serious threat to humanity, some countries are still undertaking research into biological warfare. Here are some of the biological weapons that people like Iraq's Saddam Hussein have been working on:[25]

Aflatoxin: This often turns up in moulds that grow on nuts, for example, peanuts. Iraq is a large producer of pistachio nuts, which could provide a useful source of such agents. Aflatoxin destroys the immune system in animals and causes cancer in humans.

Anthrax: An infectious disease of sheep, goats, cattle and humans. Causes flu-like symptoms and fatigue, followed by severe chest congestion. It is fatal in 80 per cent of cases. The spores can retain their virulence in the soil for many years. A Russian germ-warfare storage facility blew up in 1979, spreading anthrax spores and killing 64 people.

Botulinum: This bacterium is normally found in contaminated food. It produces a highly toxic substance that causes a dry mouth, blurred vision, difficulty in speaking and weakness. Paralysis and respiratory failure can follow, with a 30 per cent death rate.

Clostridium perfringens: This bacterium is a common source of food poisoning. It forms spores that can live on in the soil—and cause gas gangrene when they infect battlefield wounds. Gas gangrene can cause swelling, shock, jaundice and death.

Rotavirus: Among the other biological agents that Iraq is thought to have been investigating as potential weapons are camelpox and hemorrhagic conjunctivitis (which causes the eyes to bleed). But perhaps one of the nastiest areas of research focuses on human rotavirus, which causes the most common form of severe diarrhea among children.

Many people fear the combination of such weapons with ballistic missiles like the Russian-built Scud. But it is even more likely that they will be carried to the release site by terrorists, as was the case in the Tokyo subway.

Like it or not, the whole of modern life is now a vast, open-ended experiment with nature and the planet. At the same time, it is also an experiment with human nature. We couldn't stop these experiments, even if we wanted to. But we can do more to make sure they are planned and carried out in ways that limit the risks and provide better early warning signals when things start to go wrong.

The Slippery Slope

✔Citizen 2000 Checklist

1. Find Out More and Work Out Where You Stand

Good ways of keeping track of the issues covered in this section include reading the medical sections of the main daily newspapers, subscribing to *New Scientist* and watching the national news broadcasts and TV programs like *W5, The Health Show* and David Suzuki's *The Nature of Things*. There is also a great deal of information on the Internet, although it is often harder to be sure of its quality.

2. Support Campaigns for Responsible Practice

There are always at least two sides to every debate. Groups such as the **Animal Defense/Anti-Vivisection Society of B.C. (ADAV)**, the **Animal Alliance of Canada** and the **Animal Defense League of Canada** champion animals, while the **Canadian Association for Laboratory Animal Science (CALAS) Biosciences Animal Service** promotes "humane use of animals in research." The **Ontario Society for the Prevention of Cruelty to Animals** emphasizes that it works within the law and cooperates with research and industry representatives, the public and government "to improve conditions for animals while maintaining a balanced sensitivity toward both animal and human needs."

The **Centre for Medicine, Ethics and Law** at McGill University is one of the university centres for bioethics that examine many of the ethical issues arising from medicine.

We are not aware of any organizations campaigning specifically on chemical and biological weapons, although **Physicians for Global Survival (Canada) (PGS)**, which has professional and public membership, campaigns for limits to the free trade in arms, the abolition of nuclear weapons, the elimination of land mines and for nonviolent conflict resolution. **Vets Against Nuclear Arms**, the **Act for Disarmament Coalition** and the **Canadian Coalition for Nuclear Responsibility** are also active in this field.

3. Consider Becoming a Donor

You can give both blood and–when you die–organs, to help keep other people alive and healthy. Contact your local hospital for information on donating blood. If you want information on organ donation, **Organ Donors Canada** can help you. The **CNIB**, the **Kidney Foundation, B.C. Transplant** and Ontario's **Multiple Organ Retrieval and Exchange Program (MORE)** will give you information on anatomical gift giving.

8.3 *Hooked*

Why have addictions exploded in the 20th century?

In the western world, addictions are now among the most important causes of preventable disease and ill health. So this is an area rich in life choices, whether or not we recognize, or feel able, to make the right ones. Increasingly, we know that we can become addicted to a wide range of things, from drugs, alcohol, cigarettes and gambling to chocolate, jogging, work and even shopping. In the United States, for example, five million people—or one in nine Internet users—are now thought to be in the early stages of addiction to the Internet. In severe cases, this can lead to such problems as divorce, child neglect, job loss, debt and dropping out school.[26]

Many addictive substances are actually poisonous. But, whatever the addiction, it is likely to be bad for us and for our families because, by definition, an addict has lost control. We will look at how addiction evolves, at some of the social and environmental implications of addiction, and at ways in which these habits can be avoided or kicked.

Addictions have become a key 20th-century issue for a number of reasons. One reason is that it is easier to see big-picture patterns these days, so that we know how many people are addicted to particular substances nationally or even internationally. Another reason is that modern chemistry has produced a much wider range of substances to which we can potentially become addicted. And, third, there are now huge legal, semilegal and illegal industries dedicated to feeding our appetite for everything from cigarettes to hallucinogens.

Getting hooked

Before we begin, though, let's accept that we are all—or almost all—drug users. Our own bodies can produce addictive drugs, among them adrenaline and endorphins, which accounts for the addictive nature of stressful pursuits. We mislead ourselves if we think in terms of "them" and "us": many dependent drug users appear no different from "you" or "me."

That said, the process of addiction generally develops in four stages. In the first stage, for example, when choking on a first cigarette or spluttering through that first glass of spirits, an "alarm phase" is experienced: we feel unwell. In simple terms, the body is giving a warning that what is being done is potentially harmful.

In the second stage, a "lift" or "buzz" is felt, followed by a withdrawal reaction. In the case of alcohol, we know this withdrawal as a "hangover." The same roller-coaster is found in other areas: drug users who have been "high" start to come down. As a general rule, the higher the initial lift the bigger the subsequent crash.

The third stage arrives when the developing addict starts to get used to the "poison." The body reacts less to each dose because it has worked out how to break down the poison more rapidly. Bigger and more frequent doses must now be taken to achieve the same effect. Typically, too, addicts take further doses to delay or soften the crash—alcohol drinkers talk of the "hair of the dog."

The fourth and final stage is true addiction. Tolerance levels fall and the addict begins to feel unwell most of the time, taking his or her "poison" to alleviate the pain of the strong and persistent withdrawal systems. The standard vicious cycle has been created and will now often spin out of control. A given dose of the drug can now cause much more damage, because the body's ability to cope has been overwhelmed. The results will include profound ill health, social alienation and, ultimately, death.

The pattern of events described above largely relates to physical addictions, but many of the same symptoms and trends can be seen in mental fixations and addictions. Some of these, including extreme exercise and overwork, can trigger our internal versions of addictive drugs, in the form of substances like adrenaline and endorphins.

Why do we do it?

The process of addiction is now well understood. So why, when we can so clearly see that something is bad for us, do we still do it? Let's focus on drugs, whose use and public profile has developed rapidly over the past half-century. Obviously, some drugs can produce pleasurable effects, at least for a while. Or we may want to open what Aldous Huxley called the "doors of perception." But let's run down a list of some of the factors that are commonly understood to fuel human addictions.

Addictive genes: One theory is that addiction is genetically inherited, whether the addiction is to drugs, religion or shopping. But genes are not the only answer. To paraphrase Shakespeare, some people are born addicted, some achieve addiction—and some have it thrust upon them. The theory that addiction flows from one or more genes does not mean that those affected automatically become addicts, however. Rather, they are much more likely to get hooked if they try an addictive substance or activity. As with the idea of a "criminal gene," the "addictive gene" will continue to be a controversial idea, not least because it may eventually lead to parents being able to choose not to include the "addictive gene" when creating their designer baby (page 250).

Addictive personalities: Whether or not there is an addictive gene, most of us would accept that there are "addictive" personalities. For whatever reason, some people seem to be more susceptible than others to addictions. Once exposed to a potentially addictive substance or activity, they are also more likely to be caught "hook, line and sinker."

Peer pressure: Worryingly, most young drug users get their first drugs from a close "friend." Young people are particularly vulnerable to "peer pressure" because they are at a stage in life when it seems important not to be too different from others in their peer group—and this is the age when it also seems exciting to experiment.

Pushers: Once users become addicted to illegal drugs, they will need to find enough money to "feed" their habit. Getting other people hooked on drugs, and supplying their growing habits, provides a way of getting enough money to pay for their own.

Social background: Around the world, experience shows that a healthy and supportive social and emotional environment lessens the chance of addiction. Where addiction happens, a good environment can also speed the process of recovery. But clearly this is far from foolproof, because of the many other factors involved.

Emotional breakdown: Addictions can be triggered by emotional trauma. A family rift, the breakdown of a relationship, a death or other forms of stress might be the catalyst. Another factor may be retirement, when people may increasingly feel that they are useless.

Age: Surprisingly, perhaps, the younger and fitter you are, the less prone to irretrievable addiction you are likely to be. It's surprising only because we tend to think of addictions as being primarily a problem for teenagers and those in their early twenties, because of the high profile of illegal drugs. But drug addiction can be found in many other forms: older people, for example, may prefer coffee and alcohol—or more heavy-duty tastes like gambling, barbiturates and brand-name drugs like Valium.

Chemical hooks: Pretty much from the time of Sir Walter Raleigh, right through to the early 1960s, the world was largely ignorant of the addictive power of the nicotine in cigarettes. Even today, some would have us believe that there is no such power: in 1995, for example, the "Tobacco Seven," the major U.S. tobacco company heads, swore before Congress that they believed that cigarettes were not addictive. Since then a raft of damning documents has appeared,[27] including proof that one company, at least, saw cigarettes as "nicotine delivery devices."

Once you are addicted, the withdrawal symptoms often provide one more reason for continuing with the addiction. The effects can be felt in various ways. With alcohol we talk of a "hangover," with heroin of "cold turkey." Even ordinary hangovers can begin to shade over into delirium tremens (DTs) and hallucinations. Whatever they are called, the effects of withdrawal are usually fairly unpleasant.

A family habit

One of the worst things about addictions is that they often become afflictions for the family, not just for the addicts. Often, the addict blames other family members, and parents and siblings are put through an ordeal that can last for years as they try to help.

Family therapy is a recognized approach to dealing with addiction, where members of the addict's family attend clinics for joint therapy. This can be important given that an addict may get better, only to find that his or her family goes into decline. We need to be told not only how to help the addict, but also how to help ourselves through the process.

Addictions can be "infectious" in unexpected ways. As a way of coping, spouses or partners may take on all the habits of the addict, such as moods, secretiveness, paranoia and low self-esteem. Relationships are strained in other respects, too. Ironically, more couples break up when an addict improves than during the period of addiction. Partners have got used to the predictability of the addict's behaviour—and cannot cope when the addict wants to take back some control over his or her life. There can be few people who would willingly become addicts if they knew the pain and agony that it would cause, not just to themselves but to those people closest to them. In some cases, however, the only way in which the addiction can be broken is to break off all relations with the addict, although there is a risk that this could drive the addict over the edge.

These are terrible dilemmas, but even worse ones can surface where parents pass on addictions to their unborn children. Some children are born addicts. Some are also born with AIDS: the infected needles used by drug addicts are a frequent cause. And some acquire a taste for addiction through their early exposure to their parents' consumption of such stimulants as nicotine.

The risk of sudden infant death syndrome increases by 100 per cent for every hour a day a baby spends in a smoky atmosphere.

In some cases, there is no time to pass on the addiction. Research has shown that parents who smoke may be a major cause of sudden infant death syndrome (SIDS, or "crib death") in infants. It is thought that the risk increases by 100 per cent for every hour a day a baby spends in a smoky atmosphere.

In the U.S., meanwhile, one lobby group has been attempting to sue mothers who use drugs during pregnancy—and subsequently miscarry—for manslaughter. It wants new legislation banning the use of drugs during pregnancy. Others worry that such a law could "open the floodgates" for cases against ordinary mothers or pregnant women who smoke, drink alcohol, take medicine or even eat unhealthily.

The global ashtray

Burning tobacco is the main source of indoor pollution—worldwide. Tobacco smoke contains some 4000 chemicals, a number of them known to cause cancer. In recent years, as a result, there has been little good news for cigarette makers or smokers. Even "low-tar" cigarettes, marketed as less harmful, turn out to be linked to a new wave of lung cancer—because smokers tend to inhale more deeply and expose a larger area of lung to cancer-causing chemicals. Most victims of this form of cancer will be dead within five years.[28]

In Western Europe and North America, smoking is on the decline. Only 3 out of 10 adults now smoke, compared with around 6 out of 10 forty years ago.[29] The figure for adult smoking in Canada is even better—one in five. A disturbing trend, however, is the increased percentage of smoking among our young people. Smoking is no longer acceptable in many homes, offices and public places. Most restaurants have smoke-free areas, while most theatres, trains and planes have become smoke-free.

But the picture is different in the Southern Hemisphere, where 50 per cent of men and 8 per cent of women now smoke. Forty years ago, almost no women would have smoked, and only 20 percent of men would have done so. And tobacco companies are now focusing their attention in this direction. It is a deep irony that they are hoping to fund the health-liability payments imposed in the West, running into billions of dollars, by selling more cigarettes in new markets. China, for example, is the largest cigarette market in the world—and will see an estimated 2.5 million of its people die of cigarette-related diseases by 2020. This has been described as the "New Opium War."

The health effects of smoking, however, are only part of the picture. Check out the proportion of litter, for example, that is smoking-related as you walk down the street. Nor is that all. Tobacco production causes deforestation—often in tropical areas—with about half of the South's crop of tobacco leaf being dried by wood fires or charcoal made from wood.

The European Commission estimates that for every 300 cigarettes made in the Third World, a tree is burned to dry the tobacco. So the average smoker needs a tree every two weeks! Also, tobacco crops, which are vulnerable to all sorts of pests, are sprayed with heavy doses of pesticides and are grown in fields that might otherwise be growing food. Under food crops, the land used to grow tobacco could feed 10 to 20 million people.

The European Commission estimates that for every 300 cigarettes made in the Third World, one tree is burned to dry the tobacco.

Legal and lethal?

It's hard to argue that there is no problem with taking so-called recreational drugs. Few people, even among heavy users, would wish their children to become addicts. Unfortunately, agreement on this issue often seems to stop there.

Different countries, and different people, draw the line in different places. Indeed, the same person may draw different lines at different points in their own lives. Not surprisingly, one of the fiercest debates over this whole issue is whether some drugs—or all drugs—should be legalized.

To legalize or not?

So why are some drugs illegal? The standard answer runs along the following lines: they are dangerous, addictive and have social consequences. Fine, but if you look into these answers in any detail, there seems to be little logic in a world where drugs from cannabis to ecstasy, from cocaine to crack, remain illegal—while cigarettes and alcohol remain legal.

Consider the risks to our own health in using some of these stimulants. Cannabis has never been shown to kill anyone directly, although it must have played a role in many traffic accidents (and blood tests are now needed to check for it). Tobacco, on the other hand, kills 0.9 per cent of its users each year. Alcohol is slightly more restrained at 0.5 per cent, while, for comparison, heroin kills about 1.5 per cent. Ecstasy kills "just" 0.0002 per cent of its users, although that is no comfort for those whose children or friends die. Ironically, alcohol and nicotine are thought to be more addictive than cannabis and ecstasy, and their social consequences can be even more devastating.

The growing call for legalization of at least some drugs should therefore come as no surprise. The case "for" runs as follows:

Free society: We live in a free society and, at least in principle, should not be prevented from doing something that, in theory, does not harm others. There will be casualties, as with alcohol, but an open society will be better placed to tackle them.

Prohibition doesn't work: Draconian anti-alcohol laws in the U.S. failed to stop the alcohol economy and, more recently, it has proved impossible to stem the flow of illegal narcotics into developed countries. In Ontario in 1995, more than 40 per cent of grade 11 students said they had used cannabis at least once.

Safer products: Legalization could result in a safer product. Many drug-related problems are caused by adulterated materials. Better quality standards would save lives.

Save public money: The police and the customs and excise services could switch to other problems. Prison populations would be cut significantly. An estimated 10 per cent of the U.K. prison population is charged with drug possession or dealing.

Less crime: Drugs would be cheaper and part of the legal economy, giving less incentive to pushers, making it less likely that people would have to steal to support their habits—and less likely that young drug users would be sucked into the underworld.

Source of revenue: Most of the drug trade is illegal and therefore part of the black economy (page 200). As such, it evades tax. It is said that the illegal drug trade is worth some US$500 billion a year, but who really knows? All we know is that if it were out in the open, governments could start to make a pot of money from it.

Marijuana as medicine: A relatively new spin on the debate focuses on the potential medicinal uses of some of these drugs, particularly cannabis or marijuana. Those who see a medicinal role for marijuana have four possible uses in mind: to control glaucoma, which damages eyes; to reduce the nausea brought on by anti-cancer drugs; to relieve the pain suffered by multiple sclerosis patients; and to stimulate the appetites of those with AIDS.[30]

With so much apparently going for it, it seems surprising that legalization has not made more progress. But there is also a downside. The case "against" includes the following arguments:

Access for all: It is very likely that cheap, easily accessible drugs will boost use.[31] People who would never have considered taking drugs would find it easier to experiment. Some would become hooked.

Drugs are different: The big difference between cigarettes and most of the drugs discussed here is that, while they may be physically addictive, cigarettes do not have the same mood-altering effects—nor do they usually break up families as other drugs can.

Marijuana is not harmless: Even though marijuana is not physically addictive like "hard" drugs, it has been found to be mentally addictive. Many users come to depend upon it. In some cases, it may be a contributing factor in depression and even suicide.

Addicts ignored: It is also possible that the wider availability of drugs will make it harder for addicts to get necessary support, as society's reaction switches from "poor X has been entrapped by the drug pushers" to "well, after all, it's a free country—and it was their decision."

Whatever the government policy may be, for many people the choice of whether to use, abuse or avoid drugs will remain an important life choice.

Food junkies

The modern economy is partly built on industries that exploit our weaknesses, rather than helping us understand and address them. Much of the fashion industry, for example, builds sales by promoting ideals that leave many people feeling inadequate. Our bodies do not match those paraded on the catwalk or in advertisements. Stir those tensions in with the offerings of the diet industry and you have a powerful, volatile mixture. Then try mixing in a range of food addictions. Indeed, such addictions are much more common than we might imagine. Even people who have simply switched from ordinary coffee to decaffeinated varieties complain of withdrawal symptoms: headaches, drowsiness and fatigue.

Whether or not we think we are hooked on food, there is now a huge diet industry offering us endless ways of trimming the pounds or kilos. There's no question that average weights are rising in North America—and it is estimated that nearly a third of all adults resolve to diet as part of their New Year's resolutions, many for the umpteenth time.[32] It is also estimated that

Table 8.3: ADDICTIVE SUBSTANCES AND THEIR EFFECTS

Substance	***Effect***	***Side-Effects***
	LONG ESTABLISHED	
Alcohol	Depressive, but brings out feelings of pleasure and reward. Reduces inhibitions and social anxieties.	Addictive. Causes accidents from a reduced ability to function when drunk. Heavy drinkers are more prone to high blood pressure, heart disease, strokes and cirrhosis of the liver.
Caffeine (in coffee, tea, chocolate and some soft drinks)	Mild stimulant making the user more awake and alert.	High doses produce jitters and insomnia. Also increases heart rate and blood pressure.
Cannabis (marijuana, pot, grass, hashish, weed)	Bursts of laughter, talkativeness, distorted sense of time, relaxation and a greater appreciation of sound and colour. Positive medical effects (see previous page).	Short-term memory loss. Can induce feelings of confusion, unease or paranoia. Because drug is sometimes mixed with tobacco, the main dangers are those linked with smoking.
Inhalants (nitrous oxides, aerosol propellants, glues)	Short-lived, light-headed euphoria.	Common among teenagers, due to availability. Symptoms include watering eyes, poor muscle control, nausea and fainting. Can damage lungs, liver and kidneys. Can also trigger strokes.
Lysergic acid diethylamide (LSD)	Hallucinogen, with profound mind-altering potential. Effects begin in one hour and last 8-12 hours. Can recur over long time period.	Tolerance builds fairly rapidly. Main dangers are psychological. Can trigger latent mental illness.
Opiates (e.g., opium, heroin, morphine)	Affect the dopamine area of the brain, connected with pleasure and reward. Relief of stress and discomfort. Sense of detachment and euphoria.	Highly addictive. High risk of overdosing. Health problems partly linked to unknown substances mixed in with drugs sold on street.
Tobacco	Immediate effect on the brain in the part connected with pleasure and reward. Short-term stress and anxiety relief. Dulls appetite.	Very addictive and causes strong cravings. Causes many health problems for smoker and for "passive smokers," particularly for babies and children. Smoker's children more likely to take up the habit.

Table 8.3: ADDICTIVE SUBSTANCES AND THEIR EFFECTS *continued*

Substance	***Effect***	***Side-Effects***
Tranquillizers & barbiturates (e.g., Diazepam, Tamazepam, Valium)	Similar effects to alcohol. Effects include drowsiness, depression, slurred speech, flat personality, lack of expression.	Short-term effects include headaches and vertigo. Can also cause unpredictable emotional reactions.
	IN THE HEADLINES	
Ecstasy (MDMA)	One of the early designer drugs, combining hallucinogenic and amphetamine elements. First synthesized in 1914 as appetite suppressant. Affects brain serotonin levels. Normal doses produce mild effects, with no hallucinations. Sense of spiritual enlightenment, social understanding.	Small number of deaths have resulted from allergic reactions. Dehydration also a risk. Can produce hangover effects lasting several days. Also a real danger from unknown substances sold as "E."
Crack cocaine	Cocaine is long established, being obtained from the cocoa plant. Crack is made from cocaine and baking soda, while "freebase" crystals are made from cocaine and ammonia. Affects dopamine area of brain. Sense of euphoria, mental sharpness.	Highly addictive. Can trigger anxiety or panic attacks, leading to paranoid psychosis. Production method is very dangerous; many untrained producers have died.
Speed, Ice	Methamphetamine, widely known as a broncho-dilator, allowing asthmatics to breathe. Stimulates dopamine centres of brain. Elevates mood, heightens endurance, suppresses fatigue.	Highly addictive. Can also trigger heart attacks.

about 90 percent of diets fail: even if we manage to take weight off for a while, it soon goes back on when we resume our normal eating habits.

Some new products appear to offer us the prospect of eating as much food as we like without getting fat. One product looks like fat, tastes like fat and cooks like fat—but is not digested. Available in the U.S. after extensive review by the health authorities, it can cause stomach upsets if eaten in excess. It can also absorb some fat-soluble vitamins from other foods, so extra vitamins are now added to replace those lost. The evidence suggests that health is more likely to come from a combination of a balanced diet, regular exercise and the support, affection and interest of our families and friends. But the trend often seems to be going in the opposite direction. Let's look at some of the many ways in which we abuse our bodies.

Getting fatter: The obesity trend is most obvious in America. One American mother was even found guilty of child abuse after her 13-year-old daughter died weighing an incredible 305 kg. In this case, the cause seems to have been an insatiable appetite, coupled with an almost complete lack of exercise. There are many reasons why obesity is becoming more of a problem, but they include changes in diet, shifts in patterns of exercise and the collapse of the traditional family.

Overeating: Food junkies show many symptoms of their addictions, but the most obvious is their size. Around the world, children are getting fatter. And chubby children usually grow into overweight teenagers and adults.[33] Nor is this simply a social problem. Heavy children—and adults—run a greater risk of a wide range of health problems, including atherosclerosis, diabetes, hypertension and musculo-skeletal problems.

Diet: It's an extraordinary fact that the diet eaten by most U.S. kids contains about 40 to 45 per cent fat. Hamburgers, whether from McDonald's, Burger King or elsewhere, illustrate the problem. Health professionals suggest that a young child should eat no more than 30 per cent fat, with the result that a single cheeseburger and fries can consume two days' fat allowance. Yet how many parents are aware of this need to balance their children's fat intake? A healthier diet will typically contain fewer calories and less fat, less salt and less sugar. At the same time, it will contain more grains, more dietary fibre, more fresh vegetables and fruit.

Low-fat diets: Ironically, the focus on having too much fat has made it difficult to obtain full-fat dairy products. This may be fine for most adults, but children need these fats and some are suffering from malnutrition as a result.

Anorexia and bulimia: These are eating disorders, although the addiction is often less to food than to self-denial or to emotional turmoil. Such disorders are most likely to affect young girls, but are also found in men and women. More than two million Americans suffer from eating disorders. Those most vulnerable tend to have low self-esteem, set themselves unrealistic goals and suffer from severe anxiety. The resulting depression, shame and sense of isolation disrupts families, interrupts schooling, damages careers, destroys relationships and can cause infertility.

Antiobesity drugs: Some of the drugs used to combat obesity are now thought to cause health problems of their own. Two antifat drugs have been withdrawn from sale worldwide because of concern that they might cause heart-valve abnormalities.[34] Rather than relying on such pharmaceutical props, we should be working out ways of avoiding the problems in the first place—or of dealing with them with willpower and necessary treatment once they have surfaced.

The TV treadmill: More and more people, children and adults alike, are becoming "couch potatoes." Many people routinely log six or more hours a day watching TV and videos, or tapping away at the computer. "We don't tell our young patients they must give up TV," said the medical director of one U.S. weight loss clinic. "Just reduce their TV time to three hours daily. Or, we ask them to ride a stationary bike or walk on a treadmill while watching television."

Snackers: Equally important, there are the less obvious changes in the way we live as families. One cause of overeating is that more children are now "home alone" after school, and can snack as often as they want, on whatever happens to be in the fridge. More children than ever before eat in front of the TV, "grazing" on snacks.

The key to curing individuals is to use therapy, sometimes together with medication, to restore—or even build—their inner resources. They need to be helped to look forward to normal, balanced lives. Curing society as a whole, whether in terms of its dedication to overeating or its overconsumption of natural resources generally, looks set to be an even tougher task.

Indeed, doctors believe that one of the main causes of obesity may simply be that families are less likely today to sit down to formal meals as they would have done in the past. Families, the subject of Chapter 4, eat less when they eat together because they talk. Conversation, it turns out, slows down the speed of eating, giving the brain time to register that the stomach is full.

Hooked

✔Citizen 2000 Checklist

1. Be Aware of the Early Signs of Addiction

Addictions are all around us, so it pays to be alert to the early symptoms. Support campaigning groups that are trying to turn the tide of addiction. An important source of information on substance abuse and problem gambling is the **Canadian Centre on Substance Abuse (CCSA)**. Subjects include statistics, youth, women, cannabis issues, Fetal Alcohol Syndrome/Fetal Alcohol Effects, and workplace and health enforcement. The **Centre** has databases on substance abuse and addictions, organizations, treatment services available, education programs offered by postsecondary institutions, and *Employee Assistance Programs*. They also provide details on resources related to problem gambling. Governments deserve kudos for effective commercials fighting drinking and driving, but the introduction of gambling casinos onto the Canadian scene in recent years has brought another addiction to the forefront.

The **Canadian Council for Tobacco Control** was created to ensure concerted action against tobacco use, Canada's leading cause of preventable death and disease. The Council runs a National Clearinghouse resource on Tobacco and Health (NCTH) and, along with 130 Canadian organizations, is part of the *Tobacco OR Kids* campaign.

Two organizations at opposite ends of the age spectrum are the **Fetal Alcohol Support Network** and the **Canadian Coalition on Medication Use and Seniors**.

Concerns Canada promotes a drug- and tobacco-free lifestyle and is active with young people through their *"Toc Alpha"* program. **MediaWatch** has been reporting on beer commercials, which seem to be appealing to younger and younger audiences these days. In the U.S., the **Center for Science in the Public Interest (CSPI)** has challenged the alcohol industry to put in place a voluntary ban on broadcast advertising for alcohol–and is particularly asking for an end to ads that might appeal to young people. **CSPI** argues that alcohol is "a deadly drug in children's hands."

2. Know Where to Turn for Help

The first port of call is your local doctor. Schools, hospitals, libraries, community health centres and public health departments are other good sources of information. **Kids Help Line** provides non-judgmental telephone counselling and referrals for young people, and **The Kaiser Youth**

Foundation in B.C. is active in discouraging substance abuse.

Provincial contacts include the **Addictions Foundation Manitoba** and **Centre for Addiction and Mental Health** (formerly Addiction Research Foundation) in Ontario.

In addition, there is now a virtual A-to-Z of organizations offering different types of help. Many are based on the Alcoholics Anonymous formula, as follows: **Cocaine Anonymous**, **Gamblers Anonymous**, **Narcotics Anonymous**, **Overeaters Anonymous**, **Sex and Love Addicts Anonymous**, **Spenders Anonymous**, **Alateen** and so on. There seems to be no central reference point for these organizations, so check at your local library for their contact details.

3. Don't Dismiss Drug Legalization Out of Hand

Given the damage that drugs can cause, it is no surprise that many people, the police and the government believe that criminalization and prosecution are key parts of the answer to drug abuse. But there are also strong arguments for legalization. The **Canadian Foundation for Drug Policy** is a source of information concerning the issue and, interestingly, a number of right-of-centre politicians and commentators are coming out in favour of legalization. **The Fraser Institute** recently held a one-day conference on *Sensible Solutions to the Urban Drug Problem*, and delegates considered legalization, decriminalization and harm reduction. Some of the arguments for and against legalization are briefly explained on pages 257–258.

8.4 Doctors' Dilemmas

What keeps the medical profession awake at night?

When we become ill, most of us turn to our doctor. Generally, we want a cure, fast. As more health issues arise, doctors are having to become walking encyclopedias on an extraordinary range of subjects. Not an easy life, but one that has a critical influence on the quality of our own lives. Nor is it simply a question of medical issues. Doctors obviously need to understand their patients and how to treat their various ailments, real or imagined. They need to encourage more preventive measures, help us understand different options and have at least a working knowledge of alternative therapies. And finally, and perhaps most tricky of all, they have a growing range of ethical issues to wrestle with.

So what do we do? Do we turn to doctors only when we want pills? Do we begin to take more responsibility for our health ourselves? Or do we expect them to play some of the roles that the clergy used to play? In the end, inevitably, it will be some mixture of all these options. Below, we briefly review some of the pressing issues likely to tax the medical profession in the early decades of the 21st century.

Taking the medicine

In the past, doctors had enormous authority. Previous generations took what they were told by doctors pretty much as the "gospel" truth. Nowadays, by contrast, most of us have at least a smattering of medical knowledge—and plenty of ways of finding out more. Reference books on diseases, cures, drugs and therapies abound, while for those people plugged into the cyberworld (page 165) there is a profusion of health resources on the Internet. As a result, we are far more likely to question the advice we are given.

Treating patients

At the same time, patients' rights have been extended to include good-quality medical care, choice, information, health education, confidentiality, dignity, respect of any wishes on treatment and religious assistance. The idea is for doctors to treat their patients as customers, an approach that has many benefits. However, it also puts an onus on each of us to try to understand what we can do to improve our own health.

This new approach may well bring about positive changes that are overdue. So, for example, it has become standard practice to treat patients in hospital. Organizing treatments at home, in familiar and comfortable surroundings, can be difficult—and, it has to be said, stretches health-care resources. On the other hand, hospital environments tend to be sterile, impersonal and run to a timetable that suits medical resources more than patients. Some new types of organization are being set up to try to alleviate this problem. They aim to turn hospitals into "healing environments" by offering support and nurture on all levels: physical, mental, emotional and spiritual. This might include home-like decor, low noise levels, massages and an uninterrupted sleep schedule. The potential benefits are considered to include improved job satisfaction for the carers, making them more likely to stay in their profession, and happier patients who are more likely to make lifestyle changes that will make them better. The approach also decreases postoperative infections.

This last point is important. Most of us tend to think of hospitals as ultraclean places, but the real picture can be very different. Hospital infections are rife, impossible to eradicate completely and seem to be getting worse as antibiotic resistance spreads (see below). Some 10 per cent of all patients suffer from infections acquired in hospital, with U.S. evidence suggesting that up to a third of these cases could be prevented.

Some 10 per cent of all patients suffer from infections acquired in hospital.

Antibiotic resistance

Among the most valuable "miracle" medicines of modern times are antibiotics. We use them to kill the harmful bacteria that cause infection and disease, and they can be very effective, saving huge numbers of lives. However, the vital role that antibiotics play in combating disease is being threatened by the way we use (and overuse) them.

Resistance to antibiotics is spreading. There are some diseases for which there are only one or two antibiotics left that can treat them, suggesting that we may be on the brink of modern plagues. Action is long overdue. Below we look at some of the many ways in which antibiotics are being abused—and at some of the issues.

Misuse: For antibiotics to work, they need to be applied to the right problems. They do not kill viruses, yet many doctors still prescribe them for viral diseases—often simply to keep patients quiet. Many patients wrongly insist that antibiotics are what they need and some doctors who have tried to be sensible about prescribing them have found that patients have gone elsewhere. Equally, the correct dose needs to be applied. If patients forget doses—or do not finish the course—the risks grow that the bacteria will become resistant and spread.

Allergies: Some people are allergic to particular antibiotics. Allergies to penicillin are relatively common, requiring substitutes to be used. Growing resistance narrows the range of available substitutes.

Animal and fish use: Antibiotics are being used to treat farm animals, particularly pigs and cows, and can boost their growth rates (page 58). Sometimes antibiotics are put in animal or fish feed, thereby dosing whole populations rather than individuals. Clearly, this practice increases the risk of antibiotic-resistance and, in the case of fish, there is the added concern that the resistance may spread to wild fish populations (page 74). Bacteria that are resistant to antibiotics can be passed on to humans—and become impossible to treat.

Marker genes: Antibiotic resistance may be spread by using antibiotic-resistant genes as "marker genes" to identify plants or animals that have been successfully engineered.

Shotgun effects: Most antibiotics are not specific to a single organism, killing more than one type of bug. As a result, they can also spread resistance in different types of bug and kill off healthy bugs (bacteria) that might aid recovery.

Over the counter: In some countries, there is no need to even consult a doctor—because antibiotics can be bought over the counter.

Big money: Some pharmaceutical companies, not surprisingly given the big money to be made, have been promoting antibiotic remedies, regardless of whether they are appropriate or safe, further encouraging the spread of resistance.

This issue is potentially one of the most serious we face. As more people travel and come into contact with each other, the risk of new infectious diseases grows. We simply must wake up to this risk and learn to conserve and manage antibiotics as the extraordinary medical treasures that they undoubtedly are. So-called phage medicine is being developed by one of the old Soviet states, Georgia, and has been taken up by the Americans. The idea is that for each bacterium that comes up, there is a "phage" virus that will attack and destroy it. This has been shown to be very effective, but there is a long way to go before it is a treatment routinely offered in the West.

Nor are the concerns confined to antibiotics. Steroids may be catching up with antibiotics as "the most abused class of drugs in your doctor's black bag."[35] As with antibiotics, products once reserved for emergencies are now being used on the most trivial of conditions. Steroids may even be used to treat babies for gripe, and hydrocortisone is included in over-the-counter medicine for hemorrhoids. They are also included as ingredients in medicines for such problems as asthma, eczema, arthritis, back pain, bowel problems and a range of inflammatory conditions. Yet steroids are not a cure. They work by suppressing your body's ability to express a normal response. Sometimes this can give the body a chance to heal itself, but there can also be very real risks. Doctors maintain that it can be years before steroids damage your health, while campaigners allege that damage can occur in a shorter timeframe.[36] There are conditions where steroids are tremendously helpful, even life-saving, but this is another area where it is just as well to double-check before accepting the doctor's prescription.

Even simple painkillers such as aspirin are coming under fire. A condition known as Medication Misuse Headache (MMH) is believed to affect one in 50 people. Experts believe that taking drugs three times a week or more can cause headaches, once the effects start to wear off. The patient mistakes this for a normal headache or migraine, takes another painkiller and the cycle is repeated.[37]

Drug pushers?

Whatever the truth about the damage caused by such drugs, the fact remains that they should be prescribed with caution—and with the best long-term interest of patients in mind. Yet the world pharmaceutical industry is among the wealthiest and most powerful. Its advertising and marketing budgets are huge. Doctors may argue that advertising does not work, but why then does the industry spend thousands of dollars per doctor each year on advertising?

A number of factors are pushing us toward the pill culture. Doctors are busy. The drug industry is promoting new wonder cures. And patients expect pills. Not infrequently, however, such cures turn out to cause problems of their own. Half of the drugs introduced in the U.S. between 1976 and 1985 had to be relabelled to indicate the possibility of severe adverse reactions. Partly as a result we are seeing growing interest in traditional, alternative and complementary medicine.

Alternatives take time

Although drugs are expensive, it is quite possible that alternative therapies would be even more costly, at least to begin with. An ideal health system would provide doctors with more time to get to know their patients and to practise "holistic" medicine—treating the whole patient, and focusing on the causes of problems rather than just the symptoms. Where necessary, holistic doctors would provide close, long-term support for patients. Yet doctors' time is expensive.

One way of squaring this circle might be to use computers. If your medical records were stored in an "expert system" that also had access to the world's on-line medical knowledge, you might get much of the help you needed without ever seeing a doctor.

In fact, if current trends continue, computers might eventually provide a more understanding and comforting service than the average, harried doctor. Able to carry out a number of consultations simultaneously, future computers will have more time to let patients explain their full range of symptoms—and to draw from the world's knowledge on what may be going on and how it might best be handled.

Certainly, one of the biggest benefits offered by many alternative therapists is that they give the patient more time—and try to understand the whole person. In these fast-paced, over-stressed times, this style of treatment can bring enormous benefits. Apart from anything else, the patient is encouraged to take greater responsibility for his or her own health.

Complementary therapies take longer to work because they encourage our bodies to do the job, rather than relying on drugs to do it for them. In the long run, this is a much healthier approach to treatment, as the root cause of illness is addressed rather than the symptoms simply being suppressed.

Different people and different diseases may respond very differently to conventional medicine and to the growing range of alternative approaches. On occasion, however, the two approaches may be used in parallel. This approach is known as "complementary medicine." Table 8.4 explains this and other alternative approaches.

Prevention or cure?

Most doctors spend most of their formative years learning how to cure ill health. And most medical systems are set up on the same basis. But there is another strong strand in medicine, based on preventing disease or ill health occurring in the first place. Let's look at prevention.

Clearly a good diet, exercise and a positive frame of mind are key factors in living a healthier lifestyle. One theory is that humans, like other animals, have a "natural" diet and "natural" forms of behaviour. Modern living, it is argued, has moved us a long way from this ideal state. There are lengthy and vociferous debates in this area, of course, but there are some areas of agreement. It is important to remember, though, that whatever measures are taken, they can be done to excess—and this can be at least as damaging as not doing them at all. For example, how many of us know people who have damaged their bodies by overexercising?

More positively, preventive medicine is moving into the medical mainstream. Some doctors even have arrangements with the local fitness centre whereby they can "prescribe" attendance. It has been found that this approach can reduce illnesses in the patient, saving the doctor's limited resources.

In some countries, innovative approaches are also being tried in the private health-care sector. The idea here is that you should not be paying when you are ill, only when you are well. On this basis, our health advisors would have a very strong and direct financial interest in our having a long and healthy life. If this meant healthy lifestyles rather than more drugs, these would be prescribed and encouraged.

Campaigning prescriptions

Clearly, the medical profession gets involved in campaigns, like those against AIDS or for healthier diets. But most doctors simply do not have the time to get involved in tackling some of the much deeper issues that, increasingly, lie behind the symptoms surfacing in their clinics.

So, for example, any doctor worth his or her salt will advise us to take care in exposing our skins to the sun and recommend using sunblocks and other forms of protection. But how many also tell us that the rise in the number of skin cancers is being accelerated by the depletion of the ozone layer (page 21)—and that the best way to prevent this would be to prescribe a membership to organizations campaigning to slow ozone destruction?

Or, how much advice do we get on the use of such highly toxic compounds as organophosphates (page 41) in ordinary household products? These chemicals turn up in such products as fly sprays, ant killers and even head-lice treatments. Side-effects appear to be surfacing, yet inadequate information is given on most packets. So, are most doctors lobbying for nontoxic ways of dealing with head lice? Hardly.

An even more pressing set of problems relates to the growing numbers of people—particularly children—suffering from allergies. Many of these are caused by environmental factors. Possible causes range from an increasing susceptibility, as more children are kept alive by modern medicine to dietary factors; worsening air pollution in cities and towns, where most of us now live; immunization; and poor air quality in homes and offices, particularly with improved energy efficiency.

We certainly live in a different chemical environment than our grandparents were used to. The use of chemically based products and pesticides has increased exponentially. New clothing, carpeting, cleaning products, cosmetics, computer printers, copy machines, mothballs, particle board, plywood, agrochemicals, perfumes, deodorizers, cigarettes, food additives, cars and paint—the list of products that incorporate and exude synthetic chemicals goes on and on.[38]

Chemical levels can be two to five times higher inside our homes than outside.

Nor is this simply a matter of individual allergies. Growing numbers of people appear to be suffering from what is variously called "multiple chemical sensitivity (MCS)," "total allergy syndrome," "chemical AIDS" or even "20th-century disease." The fact that these sorts of reactions are showing up in some parts of the population, coupled with early signs that our very ability to reproduce may be affected by everyday chemicals, suggests that too little is being done to limit our exposure to pollutants.

Table 8.4: ALTERNATIVE MEDICINE AND HEALTH

Method	*Description*
Absent healing	Healers use the "healing forces of nature," which are then channelled to patients (who may not be aware of this), activating their power to heal themselves.
Acupressure	Oriental medicine has developed a system of special massage points as a healing art. Thought to be a forerunner of acupuncture.
Acupuncture	Patients are treated by applying needles at particular points that lie along invisible "energy channels," believed to be linked to internal organs.
Alexander technique	This technique teaches you to improve your posture, so that your body can work in a more natural, relaxed and efficient manner.
Aromatherapy	Ill health is treated with concentrated oils, extracted from plants, through massage, inhalation or by adding them to compresses or baths.
Bach flower remedies	A series of 38 preparations made from wild flowers and plants designed to treat "negative emotions," which may be manifesting themselves as illness.
Bates method	Simple eyesight exercises to keep your eyesight strong and healthy.
Charismatic healing	Treatment of disease based on Christian faith and prayer.
Chiropractic	Correcting disorders of the joints and muscles, particularly of the spine, by skillful use of the hands.
Colour therapy	Practitioners believe that specific ailments can be cured by adjusting the colour input to the eyes and brain.
Cranial osteopathy	Detecting and correcting displacements in the skull and facial bones, using a delicate form of manipulation.
Cymatics	Using the healing effects of sound waves.
Faith healing	A belief in positive or "right" thinking, particularly when practised within a Christian system.
Feldenkrais method	Method used to improve patterns of movement.

Table 8.4: ALTERNATIVE MEDICINE AND HEALTH *continued*

Method	***Description***
Herbalism	Using plants and their healing properties.
Homeopathy	Natural remedies, diluted to an extreme degree, are used to boost the body's own healing ability.
Hydrotherapy	Water is used to stimulate the body into curing itself.
Hypnotherapy	The use of hypnosis to improve a person's health.
Kinesiology	Practitioners believe that each group of muscles is related to other parts of the body, so they work on relaxing and thereby improving their health.
Massage	One of the longest-established forms of healing.
Meditation	Seen as a way of shedding your cares and strains, reaching a tranquil state without the use of drugs.
Megavitamin therapy	Using large doses of vitamins to improve health.
Moxibustion	A method of applying heat locally to regulate tone and supplement the body's vital energy.
Naturopathy	Helping the body to cure itself by use of various herbal therapies.
Nutritional therapy	Using food and supplements to address any deficiencies that might be causing illness or imbalance.
Osteopathy	Aims to diagnose and treat mechanical problems in the body's skeletal framework.
Polarity therapy	Based on the belief that most illness is caused by "blockages" of the body's energy system, aiming to unblock them.
Psychotherapy	Helping people to talk through their problems.
Reflexology	Treating illness with foot and hand massage, based on the belief that the feet and hands mirror the body.
Shiatsu	Using pressure on surface points along body's energy paths to stimulate flow of life forces.

Table 8.4: ALTERNATIVE MEDICINE AND HEALTH *continued*

Method	***Description***
Sound therapy	Relieving conditions by directing sound waves at affected parts of the body.
Tai Chi Chuan	Slow-moving, circular, dance-like movements designed to get people to focus on their mental and emotional state as well as their body.
Traditional medicine	Use of folk remedies and country cures.
Visualization therapy	Patients are taught imaginative techniques to reinforce positive feelings, behaviour and images of themselves.
Yoga	A system of highly focused spiritual, mental and physical training.

Source: Family Guide to Alternative Medicine, Reader's Digest, 1994.

Vaccination

Preventive medicine is not without its own problems, however. Let's focus on some of the issues around vaccinations. The idea behind vaccination is to introduce a small amount of an infectious agent (usually in a neutralized form) into your body to enable it to build up its defences. If, and when, you encounter the real infective agent in the future, your immune system should swing into action faster and more effectively.

The overall objective is to control and even eradicate infectious diseases—and vaccines have been amazingly successful in some areas. To date, the diseases brought under control, at least in some regions, include smallpox, diphtheria, polio and tuberculosis.

However, as some of these diseases disappear from our lives, the balance is shifting. There has been growing concern, for example, about the side-effects that a small percentage of people suffer as a result of being vaccinated. In some cases, these may even result in serious disability or death. Most medical advice would suggest that immunization provides the most effective protection against a range of diseases, but responsible parents need to know about some of the issues that can arise.

Herd immunity: Vaccines are most effective when everyone—or almost everyone—is treated. In Canada, for example, there is generally an 80 to 95 per cent take-up of the common childhood vaccinations. The result is a form of "herd immunity," which means that the targeted infections find it much harder to get a foothold. But the benefits to the population as a whole are offset, to some degree, by the risks to individuals being vaccinated. Ironically, by achieving "herd immunity" through vaccination programs, doctors are making it easier for some individuals to refuse vaccines for diseases with a lower risk of being caught.

Vaccines as sources of disease: For some diseases, there are more cases caused now through vaccinations than occur naturally. It works like this. Routine immunization virtually eliminates the disease, except for an odd case, which turns out to have been contracted from someone who has recently been treated with a "live" vaccine. There is a risk of polio, for example, being transmitted for up to six weeks after vaccination—perhaps by something as simple as changing a recently immunized child's diaper.

Multiple vaccines: Multiple vaccines, such as the MMR (Measles, Mumps, Rubella) have been introduced because having one needle is seen to be less of an ordeal than having three. They are also more cost-efficient. However, there are serious concerns that, by exposing very young children to a number of infections simultaneously, we may be overloading their immune systems. As a result, a number of lobby groups have been set up by parents of children who have had severe reactions to vaccinations.

Targeting: Rubella, also known as German measles, is usually mild in children, but can be very harmful to unborn babies if contracted by pregnant women. Some people argue that rather than vaccinating every child against the disease before they are two, it would be more appropriate to vaccinate only girls, and to do so at the age of puberty.

Alternatives: There are limited alternatives to some vaccines, such as homeopathic approaches, but even most homeopaths admit that they have not been entirely effective.

Response time: One of the most difficult aspects of vaccination programs is that the health profession seems to take a long time before it reacts to fears of serious problems. Concerns over the risk of increased number of cases of sudden infant death syndrome after vaccination, and of possible reactions to triple or multiple vaccines and the malaria vaccine (mefloquine, brand name Larium), have all been met with strong denials and placatory statements. Usually, the authorities state that there is no cause for concern because the risk of developing side-effects is far less than the risk of acquiring the disease. Meanwhile, more problems often come to light, and it is essentially left to the public to try to understand the issues, balance the arguments and work out whom to trust. Despite the issues outlined above, vaccines have a bright future. There are many difficult-to-treat diseases for which vaccines could be an effective preventive approach. AIDS and cervical cancer are two leading candidates.

Quality or quantity?

Although most people now have a longer life expectancy than previous generations, for many the added years are not of a quality that they consider worth living. Old age can be very debilitating, as your body slowly packs up—and more and more assistance is needed to do even mundane tasks.

Flashpoint: At What Cost HRT?

- **One of the trickiest choices that we are likely to face–indeed, that some already face–is whether we want to live longer or live better. Hormone replacement therapy (HRT) potentially offers such a choice. HRT is designed to relieve hot flashes and other symptoms of menopause in women, as well as reducing the risk of osteoporosis (brittle bone syndrome) and heart disease. Most women who take the therapy find themselves feeling rejuvenated as they are dosed with estrogen and/or progesterone.**
- **Research has shown that HRT does reduce–and very effectively–the**

mortality rate of women in the first 10 years of taking it. But the advantages of a significantly reduced chance of suffering a heart attack and of developing osteoporosis are in part offset by the somewhat increased chance of getting breast cancer in the following 10 years. For most women, HRT is more likely to extend than shorten their lives. The exceptions are those who are not likely to be at risk of heart disease or hip fractures, but who have two or more close relatives who have–or had–breast cancer.[39] This risk is well understood, and the breasts of women on HRT are regularly checked, so the disease is likely to be caught early. Although the long-term risks of taking HRT may be relatively small in statistical terms, this is an issue that may well tax women for generations to come. Inevitably, opinion will swing both for and against in this time.

- **Most of the estrogen used in HRT has been extracted from pigs' ovaries or pregnant mares' urine, a substance particularly high in estrogen (hence the name Premarin). There has been concern over the treatment of mares. After they become pregnant, mares are brought into barns and housed in individual stalls. A harness-type device is attached to their rear quarters so that their urine can be collected. The horses spend most of the next six months in these stalls, which are often too small to allow the animals to lie down comfortably. In most cases, tethers are too short to allow the horses to lay their head on the ground, and water is restricted to ensure a higher concentration of estrogen in the urine. Since inspections started, changes have been made at certain farms and veterinary supervision has been stepped up. However, in many cases, inspectors have been refused re-entry to the farms. Adult horses are not the only ones to suffer in the production of Premarin. Each year thousands of foals are born, sold off cheaply, fattened up and then slaughtered for pet food.**

A suitable case for treatment?

Around the world, one of the thorniest problems for doctors is the lack of resources. There is potentially no limit to the demand for health-care and related services, yet there are very real limits to what can be offered as a public service. Even for those people who can afford to pay what it costs to go private, there are real limits imposed by virtue of how much suffering they, or their relatives, may be prepared to put up with, or, in the case of organ transplants, by the availability of donor organs. We now look at the difficulties of allocating resources and deciding when to call it a day.

Who to treat

With medical resources scarce, and the cost of many treatments soaring, how should we ration health-care resources? How do we decide who should get treatment and who not? Should we even try to steer resources to those with more "social worth"? In short, do we all have an equal right to life, or do some people deserve a lower place on the list? Doctors already have to prioritize, whether they—or we—like it or not. Let's look at what criteria might be used:

Wealth: If you have enough money to pay, you can usually get whatever treatment is on offer. But is this approach really appropriate when it comes to medical care, to life-and-death situations? Should we able to buy life when others are dying?

Value to society: Should a former world leader or a superstar opera singer, for example, take priority over a tramp or an addict? And should we favour someone who is more likely to achieve something valuable—a young doctor or scientist, say, over a middle-aged football player?

Responsibilities: If someone is the sole breadwinner in the family, or has young children, should they be picked out from the crowd and treated ahead of others?

Age: Should we be prioritizing the young over the old? Even if the old have paid taxes for years? Should we be setting criteria limiting the sort of operations or treatment on offer to older people, given that they have less time left to appreciate the improved health—and the chances of success may be lower?

Past abuse: Should we look at the causes of illness? If someone is dying of cirrhosis of the liver caused by alcohol abuse, should they take a lower priority than someone else who has consciously lived a healthier lifestyle?

Appreciation: Some people apparently receive donor organs and then refuse to take the appropriate medication, living a lifestyle that lowers their chances of survival. Should we assess past compliance with medical advice, and the level of appreciation of what is being offered, before allocating new resources?

Cost: Some medical treatments are exorbitantly expensive. Should these treatments be available when the same resources might be used to treat many more people with less expensive ailments?

As the sophistication of medical technologies grows, and the complexity of the conditions needing treatment also evolves, the number of such ethical issues facing doctors will soar. The rest of us need to think whether we are content to leave it all up to the medical profession, as we once left spiritual matters up to the clergy, or whether we want to take an informed part in the key discussions about our lives and health.

Should we fight on?

We all admire fighters. We love stories of people beating the odds and pulling through life-threatening situations. Indeed, it has now been shown that a positive attitude in relation to diseases, particularly those—like cancer—where the health of our immune system is critical, can often significantly increase the chances of survival. But, it is also important to be able to accept the idea of death and, once it is inevitable, to make the process of dying as comfortable as possible.

Pain, it is often forgotten, can be even more frightening than dying. So one doctor's dilemma can involve striking the right balance between the use of painkillers and allowing the patient the best chance of recovery. There are concerns about addiction to some painkillers, which are often based on drugs of abuse (see Table 8.3), but too much pain can also slow the healing process. One of the most agonizing decisions is to decide when to stop fighting for the life of a child. Few of us could expect to be totally logical in this situation. But at some point we may decide that the suffering caused by the fight, through operations and hospitalization, are no longer worth the potential benefits of going ahead.

For those not as closely involved it may be easier to recognize when the time has come to stop fighting. Indeed, guidelines are being developed that indicate the circumstances under which doctors might stop curative medical treatment. These are labelled as follows: the "Brain Dead Child," the "Permanent Vegetative State," the "No Chance" Situation, the "No Purpose" Situation and the "Unbearable" Situation."[40] In such cases the doctor may do more to help by managing the process of dying rather than fighting interminably to keep a child alive.

In the end, we need to begin to think about life and death in new ways. We cannot expect our doctors to sort out all our problems for us. So, in the concluding section of this chapter, we turn from life to death, from the process of living to the process of dying. In doing so, we argue that a good death is an inseparable part of a good life.

Doctors' Dilemmas

✔Citizen 2000 Checklist

1. Don't Leave It All Up to the Doctor

Be prepared to debate the dilemmas and issues. Keep abreast of the latest developments. One source of information is *What Doctors Don't Tell You*. And an excellent publication on medical ethics for the seriously interested is the U.K.-based *Bulletin of Medical Ethics*. This may be something to inquire about at your library. The University of Alberta has an on-line *Bioethics Bulletin* for health-care professionals. You may also want to investigate whether the teaching hospital near you has a medical ethics centre–the universities of Alberta, British Columbia, Montreal and Toronto, and McGill and Dalhousie universities all have such centres.

To educate yourself on vaccination, you may wish to call the **Vaccination Risk Awareness Network (VRAN)**. The **Association for Vaccine Damaged Children** is predominantly concerned with the pertussis (whooping cough) vaccine.

2. Be Prepared for "Cures" that Take Time

Exercise and eat a healthy diet. Call for and support preventive medicine. If you become ill, don't insist on "miracle cure" drugs like antibiotics, which may not be appropriate–and may sometimes carry other risks. Be prepared to explore some of the alternative therapies outlined on pages 268–270. But remember that even the most successful will almost certainly take longer to work their effect. Numerous Canadian companies, including major health insurers, are providing exercise, yoga or Tai Chi classes and massage therapy and other health services in their office buildings, as well as membership discounts in local health and fitness clubs. Such companies want the benefits of decreased absenteeism and increased productivity of their employees.

3. Support People-Friendly Health Care

However careful we may be, we will all get ill at some point. Indeed, as the population ages, the demands on our health services look set to explode. But that shouldn't mean that we merely accept a poor health service. We should call for the services to be as people-friendly as possible. If we want to give birth–or to die–at home, this should be a real option. **Planetree** in the U.S. is an organization aiming to create people-friendly healing environments. And again, don't expect the medical profession to do it all on its own. If new equipment or new facilities are needed, see what you can do to help raise the funds.

4. Think of Wider Impacts

The **World Society for the Protection of Animals (WSPA)** has campaigned to raise awareness about the treatment of mares used to produce Premarin. Another organization concerned about this is **PETA (People for the Ethical Treatment of Animals)**.

8.5 Till Death Do Us Part

Are there better ways of dying?

Most of us choose to ignore the Grim Reaper—in the forlorn hope that he may never come, or at least, not just yet. This is neither healthy nor sensible. If death is inevitable, surely we should plan for it. Yet most people never even complete a will.

Even those who are happy to look death in the face generally do not look forward to it. Indeed, we try to camouflage the aging process in a variety of ways, from cosmetics through to facelifts. A few people take this to extremes, re-sculpting their faces and bodies, like you might remodel a house, and sometimes to such an extent that they are almost unrecognizable. An oddity today, perhaps, but will we see it taken for granted in the future?

Such is the desire for life that anyone who finds a genuine cure for aging—or some means of extending healthy life for several decades—may well end up richer than the Rockefellers with their oil, the Fords with their cars or Bill Gates with his software.

One current candidate for a "youth serum" is the prescription drug Deprenyl, used in the treatment of Parkinson's disease. The drug has helped animals live to the human equivalent of 120 to 150 years, maintaining a youthful appearance and remaining active for much of their extended lives. But this drug has not been shown to work on humans—and taken in large doses does have side-effects. The intense interest in such serums and elixirs will almost certainly produce dramatic results in the 21st century. Meanwhile, growing numbers of people dream of cryogenic technology (which involves freezing the body), helping them survive in suspended animation until a cure has been found for the disease that killed them. In some cases, people cannot afford the preservation of the whole body, so they have their head sawn off and frozen. Their chances of recovery, let alone seeing value for their money, seem remote.

The art of dying

Choices about how we die are not new: even the ancient Greeks debated the issue of euthanasia. But today decisions over whether to die at home or in hospital, and over the role doctors might play in helping us into the other world, have created strongly opposed opinions. Before looking at some of the more pressing issues, let's begin by asking whether it is possible to consciously make death a part of life.

DIY obituary

Alexander the Great's father, Philip of Macedonia, asked one of his retainers to perform a single, simple duty: to approach him every day and say: "Philip of Macedonia, thou too shalt die."[41] The job was a dangerous one: reminded of his mortality, the king often flew into a violent rage, but he continued to keep the man in his employ.

A simpler way to rehearse for death—and one available to all—is to prepare a "do-it-yourself" obituary. Throughout history, many have expressed regret as they lay dying about things they wished they had done or not done. Almost universally, when people look back on their lives, they wish that at least some of their life choices and priorities had been different.[42] So how do we prepare a DIY obituary?[43] A good first step would be to write down what your main achievements have been, what you are most—and least—proud of, what lessons you have learned, whom you have been closest to, and what you would have liked to have done. What would those close to you say stood out in their minds about you—and about your life. The purpose of the exercise is to see how we might change our lives a long time before our death is imminent.

Where to die

During wars, most people have little choice about where—or how—they die. Living in more peaceful times, we increasingly have to think about these issues and make choices. Furthermore, medical science has developed technologies and approaches that can keep many people alive much longer.

Most people would prefer to die at home, but many end up dying in some form of institution. This sort of environment may be fine for as long as you want to fight for life, but can be less acceptable once you decide that death is inevitable. Obviously, hospitals specialize in trying to make people better by medical means: once they have failed on this front, they tend to have less to offer. Medical staff may even treat death as a failure of their medical skills, potentially leading to rejection of the dying. At the same time, the logistics of caring for incapacitated patients on a large scale often lead to an impersonalized, undignified approach, where the patient can feel rather like a product on a conveyor belt. Although hospital staff are increasingly aware of these issues, resources are generally strained. Inevitably, staff become over-stretched and incapable of doing everything. One excellent idea for tackling this problem is that, just as we have midwives to attend births, there should be a new profession of "midwives for the dying."[44]

Hospices are another humane approach to the problem of caring for the dying. Instead of dedicating themselves to saving the patient, whatever the cost, they are committed to ensuring that death happens with as much dignity as possible. Hospices in Canada care for people dying of all types of illnesses. Some, like Toronto's Casey House for people with AIDS, specialize in one type of illness.

The right to die

These days, there is a fine line between dying naturally and being assisted in dying. Pain relief, for example, can speed death. So a key life choice issue, paradoxically, focuses on what is sometimes called the "right to die," or euthanasia. This movement is still hugely controversial.

Among the most prominent supporters of euthanasia has been American Dr. Jack Kevorkian, nicknamed "Dr. Death." He has assisted in the suicides of more than 20 people with chronic or terminal illnesses, regularly being tried for manslaughter or murder—and just as regularly being acquitted. Unfortunately, these issues have split both juries and the medical profession. Doctors practising euthanasia are not prosecuted in the Netherlands if certain guidelines are followed. Among the requirements that need to be met before a suicide is assisted are the following: the patient must make a voluntary request; the request must be well considered; the wish for death should be sustained; the patient is in unacceptable suffering; and the physician has consulted a colleague, who has agreed with the proposed course of action.

In Australia's Northern Territories, a law permitting assisted suicide for terminally ill patients was introduced in 1996, but was overturned less than a year later. During the time the law operated, four people died using the system of dosing themselves with a lethal amount of a drug, by pressing a button on a computer.

Elsewhere, doctors can legally practise "passive" euthanasia, withdrawing treatment or providing pain relief in such doses that death is hastened. It is known that some doctors in Canada have helped patients to die, despite the risk of prosecution. In 1998, Dr. Nancy Morrison was prosecuted for first-degree murder in the death of a cancer patient at Victoria General Hospital in Halifax. She was acquitted and, despite much public protest,

Crown attorneys appealed the acquittal. The Crown subsequently decided to drop the case. Whatever the true facts of the Morrison case, taking any active role in helping a person to die remains very controversial both inside and outside the medical profession. Sue Rodriguez, before her death from ALS (amyotrophic lateral sclerosis or Lou Gehrig's disease) in 1994, made an eloquent plea to the Supreme Court of Canada to change the law to allow assisted suicide. The MPs turned down her request, though in the end Rodriguez got her wish for a good death, thanks to an unknown doctor.

It is known that some doctors in Canada have helped patients to die.

One difficulty with debates of this sort is that there are always exceptions, people who, for example, might argue that if a law had been in place they would be dead—and yet they would much rather not be. So, first, let's run through some of the arguments for euthanasia:

Right to choose: Surely we have the right to choose how long we should live, particularly when in great pain or distress?

Unnecessary suffering: Patients may be put through lengthy and unnecessary suffering. Many patients are kept alive well beyond their natural span. Most welcome the medical profession's efforts, but at some stage many people will find that they simply do not want to go on. About five per cent of terminal pain is uncontrollable, even in hospices. Many other distressing symptoms cannot be relieved.

Hospital makes it harder: As medical technology advances, more of us are likely to die of long, drawn-out degenerative diseases. However, much as we may want to "die well," the choice may not be ours to make. Once in hospital, we may find it much harder to end our life, even if we want to.

Now, some of the arguments against:

Slippery Slope: The main argument is that what starts out as a voluntary option might eventually begin to become more of a requirement.

Abuse by doctors: There is a fear that some doctors may encourage patients toward euthanasia for reasons that may have more to with cutting costs or freeing up bed space. Patients and relatives may also fear that "euthanasia" might be applied without their agreement.

Abuse by relatives: Relatives may want to hurry death, so that they can get an inheritance, or stop having to pay high costs of care.

Guilt of patient: On the other side of the coin, patients may feel obliged to agree to die, so as "not to be a burden."

Change of mind or mistakes: People may think that they would want euthanasia when they were in a hopeless situation, but could feel different when the time came. Or, again, patients may be misdiagnosed as being in a persistent vegetative state, yet later recover.

Of course, there is usually the option of fasting to death, long practised in countries like India—but it is far from an easy option. Common sense, as well as compassion, suggests that both "passive" euthanasia (letting a patient die by withholding treatment) and "active" euthanasia (helping a patient who wants to die to do so) should be more widely available in the future. When a U.S. survey asked doctors and the public for their views, 56 per cent of the doctors supported medically assisted suicide—as did 66 per cent of the public.[45] The challenge will be to frame legislation and operate a system that does not cause more suffering than it alleviates—and where mistakes are rare.

Now you are dead

Clearly, once you are dead, things are pretty much out of your hands. But there is a great deal you can do while still alive to determine what happens after you have gone. In drafting a will you can outline not only what you would like to happen to your worldly goods, but also to your mortal remains.

A sad undertaking

Relatives organizing a funeral rarely feel in the mood to make, let alone to consider in any depth, the choices they face. In particular, it can be difficult if they want to do things differently from normal. Religions, for example, give great comfort to many people, but they are not for everybody. The funeral business has been slow to adapt to these new needs, although there are some signs of progress.

Most churches, perhaps not surprisingly, tend to balk when asked for permission to hold nonreligious funerals or celebrations in their buildings, but some—among them the Unitarians—do not. Other possibilities include a humanist service. The main objective is to break out of the "assembly-line" approach to funerals, allowing natural feelings about both the dead and the living to be expressed. Whether religious or not, a successful funeral ceremony is a celebration of life. It reminds mourners of the better sides of the departed's character and of the challenges he or she confronted. It should also be a comfort to the friends and relatives, helping them adjust to their loss and preparing them to make the best of their own lives.

Buried or burned?

And what about your mortal remains? It is increasingly common for people to choose cremation, which was originally marketed in the U.S. and Europe on the basis of "keeping the land for the living."[46] There was concern that burial sites were taking up too much land and were in danger of spreading across the country. In some over-crowded places, such as Hong Kong, burial sites offer short stays, rather like parking lots. After a few years, the bodies are removed and cremated, with other bodies then slotted into the available space.

Today, cremation begins to look a bit less attractive, given the possibility of toxic emissions and contributions to global warming. Although emissions from crematoria are tightly controlled, it would be difficult to get the levels down very low without having fewer—but bigger—crematoria.

The necessary equipment takes up a large amount of space and is very costly. It has even been suggested that large crematoria could be used as power stations. But this would require a continuous supply of bodies, day and night—and critics argue that it would be disrespectful. Interestingly, most crematoria are currently designed so that they need a rigid object put into them. This makes it impossible to do without a coffin, or the equivalent. About five per cent of the ashes that are returned to relatives are actually the ashes from the coffin.

Again, the environmental impact of coffins cannot be ignored. A considerable amount of wood and other materials, including tropical hardwoods, can go into coffins. Greener alternatives to virgin wood include woollen shrouds, cardboard, and wicker and chipboard coffins. The greenest option would be no coffin at all. The Tibetans traditionally leave their dead on the rocks to be eaten by vultures, which must be one of the fastest ways to become part of the natural world, although it is hard to picture this going down well in suburbia.

One of the most energy-intensive ways of disposing of our bodies is now to blast our ashes into space. For example, a Spanish rocket was used to send the ashes of LSD guru Timothy Leary and 23 other people into space. The capsules are only the size of a lipstick, but if we made this option available to everyone on Earth the impacts would be mind-boggling. Nor is the service permanent. After circling the planet for about 10 years, the capsules are expected to re-enter the atmosphere, burning up in a flash of light.

In the really long term, one alternative "cremation" option that might come into play would be a form of composting—a "biological cremator." Advances in genetic engineering could create bacteria and enzymes that could entirely digest a body quite rapidly.[47] If such a system were introduced, and the composted remains put back on the land, this might well be the most ecologically sound approach of all. However, it is hard to see this approach winning the popularity stakes in the near future. In the meantime, some form of burial probably offers the greenest option. Conservationists recognize that burial sites can actually protect the land from the living, acting as nature reserves. In some cases this has been unintentional: burial grounds simply were not obvious places to develop. Increasingly, however, sites are being identified where people can be buried and trees planted instead of headstones. The bodies and coffins will eventually enrich the soil and the burial site help to preserve the woodland.

It is also possible to be buried on your own ground, as was the case with Princess Diana. Surprisingly, perhaps, getting buried in your garden or grounds is relatively simple, but you do need to get permission. But, particularly if you have a small garden, it is worth thinking about what the resale value of your property might be with a less famous body buried in it. Whatever changes the future may bring, funerals are ritual occasions where we say goodbye to those we love. This may curtail innovation, but there is a value to having living ceremonies that are not simply an equivalent of an annual general meeting for the funeral trade.

Remembering the dead

The traditional symbols used for remembering people have been gravestones, with larger memorials and statues for the famous. Increasingly, trees and wilderness areas are being used. But virtual alternatives have also been introduced on the Internet, with electronic "Gardens of Remembrance." Now, anyone and everyone can potentially be remembered "forever." The advantages include a smaller environmental footprint and global accessibility. A memorial website could include photos, clips of favourite music, video and tributes from family and friends.

Some people also argue that we should set aside at least one day a year to remember the dead. The first—and hugely successful—"English Day of the Dead" was held in 1993. It was modelled on the Mexican Day of the Dead, which is as big an event as Christmas or Easter. Mexican families have street parades, fireworks and feasting, making elaborate altars with photographs of dead relatives. The English event was more sober, but the aim was the same: "It was a day for remembering those who have died and for acknowledging one's own mortality."[48] As far as the afterlife is concerned, there are many and various views. But the people of the third millennium may come to think of the "afterworld" as Planet Earth, which will live on long after we have gone—and of "afterlives" in terms of future generations of humans (and other species) going on without being overburdened by the problems we have left them.

Till Death Do Us Part

✔Citizen 2000 Checklist

1. FIND THE BEST WAYS OF HELPING THE ILL, DYING OR BEREAVED

With time becoming ever more pressured, this greatest gift that we can give becomes even more valuable. Be prepared, however, to spend time with the ill, the dying or the bereaved. If you need help, your municipal community and social services department can put you in touch with an appropriate organization. **Caregiver Network Inc.** is also a good source of information. To find a local hospice for someone who is dying, contact the **Canadian Palliative Care Association** or your provincial or local associations.

2. WORK OUT WHERE YOUR STAND ON EUTHANASIA

This issue could come around sooner than you might imagine, if not for you then for a relative or friend. Decide where you stand on the issue. If you want to ensure that your life is not extended beyond the point where you would prefer to die, ask for and sign a living will (available from your lawyer). The **Right to Die Network of Canada** lobbies for the legalization of physician-assisted suicide and voluntary euthanasia. It provides information and support to those who are trying to have as good a death as possible. It endorses the living will in **Penguin Books Canada Limited's** *Let Me Decide* and the Canadian Medical Association-approved will available from the **University of Toronto Centre for Bioethics**. **Dying with Dignity** is an information organization whose mission is to improve the quality of dying for all Canadians in accordance with their own wishes, values and beliefs. In addition to living wills, the group provides enduring powers of attorney for personal care and other advance health-care directives. It provides counselling and advocacy services to those who request them.

3. THINK ABOUT WHAT YOU WANT TO HAPPEN AFTER YOUR DEATH

Prepare a DIY obituary (page 275). In addition to traditional funeral homes, **Aftercare–Funeral Alternatives**, **Basic Funeral Services** and the memorial societies in your area can offer information to help you plan for after your death.

For anyone looking for a nonreligious funeral service, **The Humanist Association** can provide an "officiate" for nonreligious funerals. You might also check with a local **Unitarian Church**.

Part III

9 Citizen 2000 action plan

You must be the change you want to see in the world.
–Mahatma Gandhi

Manual 2000 lays out many of the issues with which we will have to wrestle in the 21st century. The Citizen 2000 checklists throughout the book explain some of the actions that can be taken to promote change. Some will be for individuals, but others will be for businesses or governments. In this final, brief chapter, we outline how to make the most of your influence and go through the practical steps we can all take. Remember, optimism flows from action. Those who simply think and worry about great issues often find themselves becoming increasingly pessimistic. This helps no one. By contrast, those who take a stand on the issues—and act—usually find their optimism and energy boosted both by the cause and by those around them. It's time to draw up our resolutions for the new millennium. So here is the 10-step *Citizen 2000 Action Plan* to help you use people power to shape the future you want.

1. Draw Up Your Own Action Plan

This is the crucial first step. When we focus on the bigger picture, we risk drowning in issues. So decide what's really important to you. List your priorities. Work out what you are going to do, which organizations you plan to join, what your targets will be. Share your plan and targets with family and friends. Maybe encourage them to make an action plan too.

2. Start the Buzz

Why do people suddenly start talking about new issues? Every time, it's because of a few individuals. Once you know your issues, start your own buzz. Use your social networks. Talk about the issues in the mall, and on the bus or train. Get people interested. Accept that other people will often draw the line in different places. This is part of the challenge–and interest.

3. Make Your Views Known

When faced with problems, don't just grin and bear it. React. Write letters to those responsible for causing–or managing–the problems. Start petitions. Write to your local newspaper, local authorities, the police, your MP or MPP/MLA, government departments and companies. Take part in phone-in programs on the issue. Let people know if you like what they are doing, too.

4. Act Locally

Get actively involved in your community. Help organize and develop local events and

groups. Protect the local environment, celebrate local traditions. See what you can do to get your local library, community volunteer groups, businesses, schools, community college or university actively involved in your campaign.

5. Join Up

Ask organizations campaigning on your priority issues to send you information packs. Join at least one–and it makes it more interesting and effective to join several. This helps them, both financially and because every new member boosts their influence with the outside world. When choosing organizations to contact, use the Citizen 2000 Checklists in Part II as a starting point.

6. Be a Conscious Consumer

We can vote for change every day by using our consumer power. Think about the social, ethical, environmental and fair trade issues associated with each product or service you buy. Challenge retailers, manufacturers and growers–and compliment them when they try to do the right thing. Use the same principles when saving money or investing.

7. Live Your Values

See if you can change your lifestyle to make it easier to live your values. You might consider changing your shopping habits to cut down on the amount of waste you produce, or how far you travel. When buying a new house, you could include the nearest bus stop as part of the "location, location, location" advantage. You could take account of how good public transport facilities are before deciding to move house. Or you may switch your bank on the basis of their environmental and social activities.

8. Engage the Young

Don't rely on the young to save the world on their own. Recognize how important these issues might be for them. Take care not to overwhelm them. Help them understand what is going on. Encourage them to think positive. Explain what they can do to shape the future. And help their schools and teachers to cover environmental and ethical issues in their teaching.

9. Do It Yourself

Don't just wait for the rest of the world to sort out problems. Accept that we all have responsibility. If no one else is campaigning on your priority issues, either suggest a new campaign to an appropriate organization–or take the bull by the horns and set up your own.

10. Vote, Vote, Vote

The opportunities to vote are few and far between, but in a democracy voting is one of the most powerful ways of communicating our views. Vote locally, provincially and nationally. Support those who support your causes. But don't just take their word for it. Challenge them when they seek your vote–and monitor what they do once in power. Show that you are interested, and let them know what you think.

The future is not simply something that happens to us and over which we have no control. If enough of us care and are prepared to act, the world can move in a very different direction. *Manual 2000* is designed to help readers to understand the issues, to get a grasp of some of the emerging solutions, and to identify other individuals and organizations interested in driving things forward. Many people have been working on these issues for years, as earlier chapters make clear, but to succeed they need our support. Indeed, there is no time like the present for us all to start building the future we want. Good luck, and keep us posted on your progress, using the contact details provided on page 13.

Directory

AA (see Al-Anon)

Aboriginal Tourism Authority, PO Box 1240, Stn. M, Calgary, AB T2P 2L2/Tel: 403-261-3022/Fax: 403-261-5676/Internet: www.aboriginalnet.com

AboutFace, 123 Edward St., Ste. 1003, Toronto, ON M5G 1E2/Tel: 416-597-2229/Toll free: 1-800-665-3223/Fax: 416-597-8494/Internet: www.aboutfaceinternational.org

Act for Disarmament Coalition, 602 Markham St., Toronto, ON M6G 2L8/Tel: 905-849-5501

Addictions Foundation of Manitoba (AFM), 1031 Portage Ave., Winnipeg, MB R3G 0R8 Tel: 204-944-6233/Outside Winnipeg Toll Free 1-800-463-1554/Internet: www.mbnet.mb.ca/crm/health/afm.html

Adoption Council of Canada, PO Box 8442, Stn. T, Ottawa, ON K1G 3H8/Tel: 613-235-1566

Aftercare—Funeral Alternatives, 327 Eglinton Ave. E., Toronto, ON M4P 1L7/Tel: 416-440-8878/Toll free: 1-800-316-3231/Fax: 416-440-8964/Internet: www.interlog.com/~after/care

Against Drunk Driving (ADD) Canada, PO Box 397, Stn. A, Brampton, ON L6V 2L3/Tel: 905-793-4233/Fax: 905-793-7035/Internet: www.add.ca

Agriculture and Agri-Food Canada, Sir John Carling Bldg., Carling Ave., Ottawa, ON K1A 0C5 Tel: 613-759-1000/Internet: www.agr.ca

Al-Anon Family Groups, 1711 Avenue Rd., PO Box 54533, Toronto, ON M5M 4N5 Tel: 416-366-4072/Toll free: 1-800-443-4524

Amnesty International, Canadian National Office, 214 Montreal Rd., 4th Floor, Vanier, ON K1L 1A4/Tel: 613-744-2411/Toll free: 1-800-AMNESTY/Fax: 613-746-2411/ Internet: www.amnesty.ca

Animal Alliance of Canada, #101 – 221 Broadview Ave., Toronto, ON M4M 2G3/Tel: 416-462-9541/Fax: 416-462-9647/Internet: www.inforamp.net/~aac/

Animal Defence League of Canada, PO Box 3880, Stn. C, Ottawa, ON K1Y 4M5/Tel: 613-233-6117

Animal Defence/Anti-Vivisection Society of British Columbia (ADAV), PO Box 391, Stn. A, Vancouver, BC V6C 2N2 Tel: 604-733-3486

Association for Vaccine Damaged Children, 56 Briscoe St., Brampton, ON L6V 1W8 Tel: 905-454-2237

Association of Parent Support Groups in Ontario, PO Box 27581, Yorkdale Postal Outlet, Toronto, ON M6A 3B8/Tel: 416-223-7444/Toll free: 1-800-488-5666

Other parent support contacts:

Kitchener: **Parents Are People Too, Inc.**, Tel: 519-745-8128/Toll free: 1-800-263-1070

Montreal: **Information and Referral Centre of Greater Montreal**, Tel: 514-527-1375/Fax: 514-527-9712/Internet: www.info.reference.qc.ca

Thunder Bay: **Catholic Family Development Centre**, Tel: 807-623-2218/Fax: 807-345-7323

Vancouver: **Parents Together**, Parentline: 604-325-0511/Office: 604-588-1621

Victoria: **Parents Together**, Tel: 250-474-6468

Atlantic Canada Cycling, PO Box 1555, Station Central, NS B3J 2Y3/Tel: 902-423-2453/Fax: 902-423-2452/Internet: http://atlcanadacycling.com http://home.istar.ca/~cycling

Auto Free Ottawa, PO Box 56007, Ottawa, ON K1R 1A1 Tel: 613-237-1549/Internet: www.flora.org/afo

B.C. Automobile Association (see British Columbia Automobile Association)

B.C. Cycling, Internet: www.cycling.bc.ca

B.C. Healthy Communities Network, Internet: www.bchealthycommunities.com

Back Association of Canada, 83 Cottingham St., Toronto, ON M4V 1B9/Tel: 416-967-4670/ Fax: 416-967-0945

Basic Funeral Alternatives Inc., 6026 Yonge St., North York, ON M2N 3W5/Tel: 416-226-2480/ Fax: 416-226-3689

Biosciences Animal Service, University of Alberta, CW 401, Biological Science Building, Edmonton, AB T6G 2E9/Tel: 403-492-5193/Fax: 403-492-7237

British Columbia Automobile Association (BCAA), 4567 Canada Way, Burnaby, BC V5G 4T1/Tel: 268-5000/Toll free: 1-800-719-2224/Internet: www.bcaa.ca

Campaign for Food Safety (formerly Pure Food Campaign), 860 Highway 61, Little Marais, MN 55614 USA/Tel. 218-726-1443/Fax: 218-226-4157/Internet: www.purefood.org

Campaign for Pesticide Reduction (CPR!), 1 Nicholas St., Ste. 412, Ottawa, ON K1N 7B7 Tel: 613-241-4611/Fax: 613-241-2292

Canada Mortgage and Housing Corporation (CMHC), 700 Montreal Rd., Ottawa, ON K1A 0P7/Tel: 613-748-2520/Internet: www.cmhc-schl.gc.ca

Canada Trust—Friends of the Environment (Community Fund and Canada Fund), Internet: www.fef.ca (or check with local branch)

Canadian Advanced Technology Association, 2nd Floor, 388 Albert St., Ottawa, ON K1R 5B2/Tel: 613-236-6550/Fax: 613-236-8189/Internet: www.cata.ca

Canadian Association for Home-Based Businesses, 3510 – 1200 E. Prince of Wales Dr., Ottawa, ON K2C 3Y4/Tel: 613-724-2949

Canadian Association of Financial Planners, 439 University Ave., Ste. 1710, Toronto, ON M5G 1Y8/Tel: 416-593-6592/Toll free: 1-800-346-2237/Fax: 416-593-8459/Internet: www.cafp.org

Canadian Association of Genetic Counsellors, Internet: http://is.dal.ca/~jbeis/fact.html

Canadian Association of Retired Persons (CARP), 27 Queen St. E., Ste. 702, Toronto, ON M5C 2M6/Tel: 416-363-5562/Fax: 416-363-7394/Internet: www.fifty-plus.net (also offices in Montreal, Vancouver, Victoria)

Canadian Association of Volunteer Bureaux and Centres, Internet: www.volunteers.ca

Canadian Automobile Association, 1145 Hunt Club Rd., Ste. 200, Ottawa, ON K1V 0Y3 Tel: 613-247-0117/Fax: 613-247-0118/ Internet: www.caa.ca

Canadian Cancer Society, 10 Alcorn Ave., Ste. 200, Toronto, ON M4V 3B1/Tel: 416-961-7223/Fax: 416-961-4189/Internet: www.cancer.ca

Canadian Centre for Business in the Community, 255 Smyth Rd., Ottawa, ON K1H 8M7/Tel: 613-526-3280/Fax: 613-526-1747/Internet: www.conferenceboard.ca/ccbc

Canadian Centre for Philanthropy/IMAGINE, 425 University Ave., Ste. 700, Toronto, ON M5G 1T6/Tel: 416-597-2293/Fax: 416-597-2294/Internet: www.ccp.ca

Canadian Centre for Policy Alternatives, 251 Laurier Ave. W., Ste. 804, Ottawa, ON K1P 5J6/Tel: 613-563-1341/Fax: 613-233-1458/ BC Office Tel: 604-801-5121/Fax: 604-801-5122/Manitoba Office Tel: 204-943-9962 Fax: 204-943-9978/Internet: www.policyalternatives.ca

Canadian Centre on Minority Affairs, Internet: www.interlog.com/~ccma

Canadian Centre on Substance Abuse, 75 Albert St., Ste. 300, Ottawa, ON K1P 5E7/Tel: 613-235-4048/Fax: 613-235-8101

Canadian Clearinghouse on Disability Issues, Toll free: 1-800-665-9017

Canadian Coalition for Nuclear Responsibility, PO Box 236, Stn. Snowdon, Montreal, QC H3X 3T4/Tel and Fax: 514-489-5118

Canadian Coalition on Medication Use and Seniors, 350 Sparks St., Ste. 1005, Ottawa, ON K1R 7S8/Tel: 613-238-7624/Fax: 613-235-9744

Canadian Community Investment Website, www.web.net/~invest/

Canadian Council for Multicultural and Intercultural Education (CCMIE), 124 O'Connor St., Ste. 200, Ottawa, ON K1P 5M9/Tel: 613-233-4916/Fax: 613-233-4735/Internet: www.ccmie.com

Canadian Council on Social Development, 441 MacLaren St., 4th Floor, Ottawa, ON K2P 2H3/Tel: 613-236-8977/Fax: 613-236-2750/Social Indicators Site: www.ccsd.ca/soc_ind.html

Canadian Council for Tobacco Control (CCTC), 170 Laurier Ave. W., Ste. 1000, Ottawa, ON K1P 5V5/Tel: 613-567-3050/Fax: 613-567-2730

Canadian Council of Christians and Jews, 2 Carlton St., Ste. 820, Toronto, ON M5B 1J3 Tel: 416-597-9693/Toll free: 1-800-663-1848/Fax: 416-597-9775/Internet: www.interlog.com/~cccj/contentv3.html

Canadian Cycling Association, 212A – 1600 James Naismith Dr., Gloucester, ON K1B 5N4 Tel: 613-748-9149/Toll free: 1-800-378-2233/ Fax: 613-485-0960/Internet: www.ccff.ca/~cfwww/index.html

Canadian Cystic Fibrosis Foundation, 2221 Yonge St., Ste. 601, Toronto, ON M4S 2B4 Tel: 416-485-9149/Toll free: 1-800-378-2233/ Fax: 416-485-0960

Canadian Day Care Registry, Internet: www.canadiandaycare.com

Canadian Direct Marketing Association 1 Concorde Gate, Ste. 607, Don Mills, ON M3C 3N6/Tel: 416-391-2362 Internet: www.cdma.org.

Canadian Directory of Genetic Support Groups, London Health Sciences Centre, Victoria Campus, 800 Commissioners Rd. E., London, ON N6C 2V5/Tel: 519-685-8453/ Toll free: 1-800-243-8416/Fax: 519-685-8214/ Internet: www.lhsc.on.ca/programs/ medgenet/-support.htm

Canadian Down Syndrome Society, 811 – 14 St. N.W., Calgary, AB T2N 2A4/Tel: 403-270-8500/Toll free: 1-800-883-5608/Fax: 403-270-8291/Internet: http://home.ican.net/~cdss

Canadian Environmental Law Association (CELA), 517 College St., Ste. 401, Toronto, ON M6G 4A2/Tel: 416-960-2284/Fax: 416-960-9392/Internet: www.web.net/cela

Canadian Environmental Network, 300 – 945 Wellington St., Ottawa, ON K1Y 2X5/Tel: 613-728-9810/Fax: 613-728-2963/Internet: www.cen.web.net

Canadian Ethical Environmental and Social Funds (Plus Banks & Credit Unions) Internet: www.goodmoney.com/candfunds.htm

Canadian Ethnocultural Council (CEC), 251 Laurier Ave. W., Ste. 1100, Ottawa, ON K1P 5J6, Tel: 613-230-3867/Fax: 613-230-8051/Internet: www.web.net/~cec

Canadian Foodgrains Bank (Head Office), 280 Smith St., Ste. 400, PO Box 767, Winnipeg, MB R3C 2L4/Tel: 204-944-1993/Toll-free: 1-800-665-0377/Fax: 204-943-2597/Internet: www.foodgrainsbank.ca/

Canadian Foundation for Drug Policy, 70 MacDonald St., Ottawa, ON K2P 1H6/Tel: 613-236-1027/Fax: 613-238-2891/Internet: http://fox.nstn.ca/~eoscapel/cfdp/cfdp.html

Canadian Foundation for World Development, 2441 Bayview Ave., Willowdale, ON M2L 1A5/Tel: 416-445-4740

Canadian Genetic Diseases Network, 348 – 2125 East Mall, Vancouver, BC V6T 1Z4/Tel: 604-822-7886/Fax: 604-822-7945/Internet: www.cgdn.generes.ca

Canadian Health Food Association, 550 Alden Rd., Ste. 205, Markham, ON L3R 6A8/Tel: 416-479-6939/Toll free: 1-800-661-4510/Fax: 416-479-1516

Canadian Industrial Hemp Council, Internet: www.cinevision.com/cihc/

Canadian Institute for Environmental Law and Policy (CIELAP), 517 College St., Ste. 400, Toronto, ON M6G 4A2/Tel: 416-923-3529/ Fax: 416-923-5949/Internet: www.web.net/~cielap

Canadian Marketing Association (CMA), Communications, One Concord Gate, Ste. 607, Toronto, ON M3C 3N6/Tel: 416-391-2362/ Fax: 416-441-4062/Internet: www.thecma.org

Canadian National Institute for the Blind (CNIB), 1929 Bayview Ave., Toronto, ON M4G 3E8/Regional Offices Across Canada/ Internet: www.cnib.ca

Canadian Nature Federation, 1 Nicholas St., Ste. 606, Ottawa, ON K1N 7B7/Tel: 613-562-3447/Toll free: 1-800-267-4088/Fax: 613-562-3371/Internet: www.cnf.ca

Affiliates:

Ecology North, Ste. 4 – 4807 49th St., Yellowknife NT X1A 3T5/Tel: 867-873-6019/Fax: 867-873-3654

Yukon Conservation Society, PO Box 4163, Whitehorse, YT Y1A 3T3/Tel: 867-668-5678/Fax: 867-668-6637

Federation of British Columbia Naturalists, Ste. 425 – 1367 West Broadway, Vancouver, BC V6H 4A9/Tel: 604-737-3057/Fax: 604-738-7173

Federation of Alberta Naturalists, PO Box 1472, Edmonton, AB T5J 2N5/Tel: 403-453-8629/Fax: 403-453-8553

Nature Saskatchewan, Room 206 – 1860 Lorne St., Regina, SK S4P 2L7/Tel: 306-780-9273/Fax: 306-543-1894

Federation of Nova Scotia Naturalists, c/o NS Museum of Natural History, 1747 Summer St., Halifax, NS B3H 3A6/Tel: 902-585-1469/Fax: 902-585-1059

Federation of Ontario Naturalists, 335 Lesmill Rd., Don Mills, ON M3B 2W8/Tel: 416-444-8419/Fax: 416-444-9866

Manitoba Naturalists Society, Ste. 401 – 63 Albert St., Winnipeg, MB R3B 1G4/Tel: 204-943-9029/Fax: 204-943-9029

Natural History Society of P.E.I., PO Box 2346, Charlottetown, PEI C1A 8C1

Natural History Society of Newfoundland and Labrador, PO Box 1013, St. John's, NF A1C 5M3

New Brunswick Federation of Naturalists, R.R.#1, Site #2, PO Box 22, Shediac, NB E0A 3G0/Tel: 506-532-3482

Union québécoise pour la conservation de la nature, 690 Grand Allee Est, Quebec, QC G1R 2K5/Tel: 418-648-2104/Fax: 418-648-0991

Canadian Organic Advisory Board (COAB), Ste. 506, 206 7th Ave. S.W., Calgary, AB T2P 0W7/Tel: 403-262-4640/Fax: 403-262-4630/Internet: www.coab.ca/

Canadian Organic Growers, PO Box 6408, Stn. J, Ottawa, ON K2A 3Y6/Tel: 613-231-9047/Fax: 613-256-4453/Internet: www.gks.com/cog (See also COG listings, Canadian Health Food Association, Nova Scotia Organic Growers Association, OPIS, and Pro Organics Marketing Inc.)

Canadian Organization of Small Businesses Inc., PO BOX 11246, Stn. Main, Edmonton, AB T5H 3J5/Tel: 403-423-2672/Fax: 403-423-2751

Canadian Palliative Care Association, 43 Bruyere St., Ottawa, ON K1N 5C8/Tel: 613-241-3663/Toll free: 1-800-668-2785/Fax: 613-562-4226

Canadian Petroleum Products Institute, 275 Slater St., Ste. 1000, Ottawa, ON K1P 5H9/Tel: 613-232-3709/Fax: 613-236-4280/Internet: www.cppi.ca

Canadian Renewable Fuels Association, 90 Woodlawn Rd. W., Guelph, ON N1H 1B2/Tel: 519-767-0431/Fax: 519-837-1674/Eastern Office: 555 boul. Roland-

Therrien, Longueuil, QC J4H 3Y9 Tel: 514-679-0530/Fax: 519-679-6372/Western Office: 212 - 111 Research Drive, Saskatoon, SK S7N 3R2/Tel: 306-975-0262/Fax: 306-975-0136/Internet: www.greenfuels.org/

Canadian Research Committee on Taxation, PO Box 913, Stn. B, Ottawa, ON K1P 5P9 /Tel: 613-594-5881/Fax: 613-594-3952 Internet: www.crctaxation.org

Canadian Senior Citizens Information and Services Center, Internet: www.infoseniors.com

Canadian Society for the Prevention of Cruelty to Children, 356 First St., Box 700, Midland, ON L4R 4P4/Internet: http://cnet.unb.ca/orgs/prevention_cruelty

Canadian/Telework Association (CTA), Internet: www.ivc.ca/part 12.html

Canadian Vehicle Manufacturers Association, 25 Adelaide St. E., Toronto, ON M5C 3A1/Tel: 416-364-9333

Canadian Wildlife Federation, 2740 Queensview Dr., Ottawa, ON K2B 1A2/Tel: 1-800-563-WILD/613-721-2286 (Ottawa Area)/Fax: 613-721-2902/Internet: www.cwf-fcf.org

Canadian Wood Council, 1400 Blair Pl., Ste. 210, Ottawa, ON K1J 9B8/Tel: 613-747-5544/ 1-800-463-5091/Fax: 613-747-6264/Internet: www.cwc.ca

Canadian Y2K, Internet: www.albertaweb.com/year2000/

Canadians for Ethical Treatment of Food Animals (CETFA), PO Box 18024, 2225 W. 41st Ave., Vancouver, BC V6M 4L3/Tel: 604-261-3801

Caregiver Network Inc., 561 Avenue Rd., Ste. 206, Toronto, ON M4V 2J8/Tel: 416-323-1090/ Fax: 416-966-2341/Internet: www.caregiver.on.ca

Center for Neighborhood Technology, 2125 W. North Ave., Chicago, IL 60647 USA/Internet: www.cnt.org

Center for a New American Dream, 6930 Carroll Ave., Ste. 900, Takoma Park, MD 20912 USA/Tel: 301-891-ENUF (3683)/Fax: 301-891-3684/Internet: www.newdream.org

Centre for Addiction and Mental Health (Ontario), 33 Russell St., Toronto, ON M5S 2S1/Tel: 416-595-6000/Toll free: 1-800-463-6273, Infoline: 416-595-6111/Fax: 416-595-5017/Internet: www.arf.org

Centre for Medicine, Ethics and Law, McGill University, 1110, av Pine oest, Montreal, QC H3A 1A3/Tel: 514-398-7400/Internet: ircm.umontreal.ca/bioethiqu/english.index.html

Centre for Science in the Public Interest (CSPI), PO Box 70373, Stn. A, Toronto, ON M5W 2X5/Tel: (Washington DC) 202-332-9110/ Fax: 202-265-4954/Internet: www.cspinet.org/canada

Child and Family Canada, Internet: www.cfcefc.ca

Child Care Advocacy Association of Canada (CCAAC), 323 Chapel St., Ottawa, ON K1N 7Z2/Tel: 613-594-3196/Fax: 613-594-9375 E-mail: ccac@web.apc.org

Child Welfare League of Canada, 180 Argyle Ave., Ste. 312, Ottawa, ON K2P 1B7/Tel: 613-235-4412/Fax: 613-788-5075/Internet: www.magi.com/~cwlc

Childnet International, Internet: www.childnet-int.org/edu.html

Citizens Bank of Canada, Internet: www.citizensbank.ca

Citizens for Local Democracy, 50 Baldwin St., Ste. 304, Toronto, ON M5T 1L4/Tel: 416-977-8736/Internet: http://community.web.net/citizens

City Farmer, 801 – 318 Homer St., Vancouver, BC V6B 2V3/Tel: 604-685-5832/Fax: 604-685-0431/Internet: www.cityfarmer.org

Clean Air Commute (see Pollution Probe, Commuter Challenge listings and Auto Free Ottawa)

Clean Environment Mutual Funds Ltd., 65 Queen St. W., Ste. 1800, Toronto, ON M5H 2M5/Tel: 1-800-461-4570 Internet: www.cleanenvironment.com/

Coalition on the Niagara Escarpment, 517 College St., Ste. 204, Toronto, ON M6G 4A2 Tel: 416-960-9606

Coastal Communities Network, RR 5, New Glasgow, NS B2H 5C8/Tel/Fax: 902-922-2283/e-mail: coastal.network@north.nsis.com

COG Alberta, 1124 – 4th Ave. N.E., Calgary, AB T2E 0K5/Tel: 403-263-9941/Fax: 403-291-9049

COG B.C. Islands, 171 Vesuvius Bay Rd., Salt Spring Island, BC V8K 1K3/Tel: 250-537-2616/Fax: 250-537-2681

COG Durham, R.R. 1, 4636 – #2, Newtonville, ON L0A 1J0/Tel: 905-786-2089/Fax: 905-434-4608

COG Essex Kent, 26933 Winterline Rd., R.R. 6, Wallaceburg, ON N8A 4L3/Tel: 519-354-7675/Fax: 519-687-3745

COG Kawartha, 1910/Television Rd., Peterborough, ON K9L 1E9/Tel: 705-748-0046/Fax: 705-745-4413

COG Niagara, 3403 – 11th St. S., R.R. 1, St. Catharines, ON L2R 6P7/Tel: 905-562-0151/Fax: 905-562-0152

COG Perth-Waterloo-Wellington, R.R. 2, Drayton, ON N0G 1P0/Tel: 519-669-3700

COG South Island, PO Box 807, Sooke, BC V0S 1N0/Tel: 250-642-3671

COG Toronto, 18 Grenville St., #1502, Toronto, ON M4Y 3B3/Tel: 416-922-5523/Internet: www.gks.com/cog/toronto

COG Wentworth-Burlington, 845 Collinson Rd., R.R. 2, Dundas, ON L9H 5E2/Tel: 905-627-7651

Community Resource Centre, Internet: www.community.web.net

Commuter Challenge (Calgary), PO Box 64229, 5512 – 4th St. N.W., Calgary, AB T2K 6J0/Tel: 403-230-9395/Fax: 403-230-1496/Internet: www.telusplanet.net/public/commuter

Commuter Challenge (Edmonton), Alberta Environmental Network, 10511 Saskatchewan Dr., Edmonton, AB T6E 4S1/Tel: 403-433-9302/Fax: 403-433-9305/ E-mail: aen@web.net

Commuter Challenge (London), 1017 Western, London, ON N6C 5B2/Tel: 519-645-2845/ Fax: 519-645-0981/Internet: www.wwdc.com/trea/bikefest.html

Commuter Challenge (Vancouver), Better Environmentally Sound Transportation (BEST), 822 – 510 W. Hastings, Vancouver, BC V6B 1L8/Tel: 604-669-2860/Internet: www.sustainability.com/best

Commuter Challenge (Victoria), BC Environment, Air Resources Branch, Tel: 250-387-6851/Fax: 250-356-7197/Internet: www.env.gov.bc.ca/epd

Compassion in World Farming, 5a Charles St., Petersfield, Hampshire, GU23 3EH UK/Tel: 011-44-1730-264-208/Fax: 011-44-1730-260-791

Computers for Schools, 515 Superior St., Victoria, BC/Tel: 250-360-1490/Fax: 250-380-1442

Concerns, Canada, 112H – 4500 Sheppard Ave. E., Willowdale, ON M1S 3RL/Tel: 416-293-3400/Fax: 416-293-1142

Connexions, PO Box 158, Stn. D, Toronto, ON M6P 3J8/Tel: 416-537-3949/Internet: www.connexions.org

Consumers International, 24 Highbury Crescent, London N5 1RX UK/Tel: 011-44-171-226-6663/Fax: 011-44-171-354-0607/ Internet: www.consumersinternational.org

Consumers' Association of Canada, PO Box 9300, Ottawa, ON K1G 3T9/Tel: 613-238-2533/Fax: 613-563-2254

Co-operative Auto Network (CAN-VAN)/Tel: 604-660-9725

Council (THE COUNCIL [CLAW]), 32739 McRae Ave., Mission, BC V2V 2L8/Tel: 604-826-7344/Fax: 604-820-4255 (See also Wholesome & Humane Program 2000)

Council for Business and the Arts in Canada, 165 University Ave., Ste. 705, Toronto, ON M5H 3B8/Tel: 416-869-3016/Fax: 416-869-0435

Council for Responsible Genetics, 5 Upland Rd., Ste. 3, Cambridge, MA USA 02140/Tel: 617-868-0870/Fax: 617-491-5344/Internet: www.essential.org/crg

Council of Canadians, 151 Slater St., Ottawa, ON K1P 5H3/Tel: 613-233-2773/Fax: 613-233-6776/Internet: www.canadians.org

Crop Protection Institute, 21 Four Seasons Place, Ste. 627, Etobicoke, ON M9B 6J8/Tel: 416-622-9771/Fax: 416-622-6764/Internet: www.cropro.org

CUSO, 2255 Carling Ave., Ste. 400, Ottawa, ON K2B 1A6/Internet: www.cuso.org

David Suzuki Foundation, 219 West 4th Ave., Vancouver, BC V6K 4S2/Tel: 604-732-4228/Fax: 604-732-0752/Internet: www.vkool.com/suzuki/index.html

Department of Fisheries and Oceans, 200 Kent St., Ottawa, ON K1A 0E6/Tel: 613-993-0999

Diaper Club, 1246 Lorimar Rd., Unit #1, Mississauga, ON L5S 1R2/Tel: 905-564-1737/ Toll free: 1-800-566-9278/Fax: 905-564-4987

Ducks Unlimited Canada, PO Box 1160, Oak Hammock Marsh, MB R0C 2Z0/Tel:1-800-665-DUCK (3825)/Fax: 204-467-9028/Internet: www.ducks.ca

Dying With Dignity, 55 Eglinton Ave. E., Ste. 705, Toronto, ON M4P 1G8/Tel: 416-486-3998/Toll free: 1-800-495-6156/Fax: 416-489-9010/Internet: www.web.net/~dwdca

Earth to Table, 201 – 917 18th Ave. S.W., Calgary, AB T2T 0H2/Tel: 403-244-6071/Fax: 403-266-4055

Earthwatch International, 680 Mt. Auburn St., PO Box 9104, Watertown, MA 02272 USA Toll free: 1-800-776-0188/Fax: 617-926-8532/Internet: http://gaia.earthwatch.org

EcoAction 2000 (Formerly Action 21) Environment Canada (see Environment Canada Green Lane)

Eco-Travel Services, 5699 Miles Ave., Oakland, CA 94618 USA/Tel: 510-655-4054/Toll free: 1-800-655-4054/Fax: 510-655-4566/Internet: www.life.ca/nl/43/travel.html

Electric Vehicle Association of the Americas, 601 California St., Ste 502, San Francisco, CA 94108/Fax: 415-249-2699/Internet: www.evaa.org/

Environment Canada Green Lane, Internet: www.doe.ca

Environment Canada, 10 Wellington St., 28th Floor, Hull, QC K1A 0H3/Tel: 819-997-2800/ Fax: 819-953-2225/Internet: www.ec.gc.ca

Environmental Choice Program (see TerraChoice)

Environmental Protection Agency (EPA) USA, Internet: www. epa.gove/energystar.html/ appdstar/esoe/products.html

Environmentally Sound Packaging (ESP) Coalition of Canada, 605 –198 West Hastings St., Vancouver, BC V6B 1H2/Tel: 604-689-3770/Fax: 604-689-3779

Ethical Funds, Internet: www.ethicalfunds.com

Ethical Funds Inc., Toll-free 1-800-267-5019

Ethical Investment Research Service (EIRiS), 504 Bondway Business Centre, 71 Bondway, London SW8 1SQ UK/Tel: 011-44-171-735-1351/Fax: 011-44-171-735-5323

EthicScan Canada, Lawrence Plaza Postal Outlet, PO Box 54034, Toronto, ON/Tel: 416-783-6776/Fax: 416-783-7386/Internet: www.ethicscan.on.ca

Fair TradeMark Canada (TransFair Canada), 323 Chapel St., 2nd Floor, Ottawa, ON K1N 7Z2/Tel: 613-563-3351/Fax 1-613-237-5969/Internet: www.web.net/fairtrade

Fair TradeMark Canada, 797 Somerset St. W., PO Box 57052, Ottawa, Ontario, K1P 6P0/Tel: 613-563-3351/Fax: 613-567-3351

Family Helper, 185 Panoramic Dr., Sault Ste. Marie, ON P6B 6E3/Internet: www.helping.com

FarmFolk/CityFolk, 208 – 2211 W. 4th Ave., Vancouver, BC V6K 1S2/Tel: 604-730-0450/Internet: www.alternatives.com/ffcf

Fathers' Resources International, PO Box 114, Stn. A, Toronto, ON M5A 1A2/Tel: 416-861-0626/Fax: 416-861-1932

Fetal Alcohol Support Network, 614 Arbor Rd., Mississauga, ON L5J 2J9/Tel: 416-274-7700

Fiducie Desjardins Inc., Tel: 1-800-361-2680

Field to Table, 200 Eastern Ave., Toronto, ON M5A 1J1/Tel: 416-363-6441/Fax: 416-392-6650/E-mail: fdshare@web.net

Fly Fishing Canada (FFC), 7171 Torbram Rd., Unit 50, Mississauga, ON L4T 3W4/Tel: 905-678-0422/Fax: 905-678-0424

Forest Stewardship Council, Avenisa Hidalgo 502, 68000 Oaxaca, México Tel:++ 52 951 46905, 63244/Fax & Tel:++ 52951 62110/Internet: www.fscoax.org/

Forum for the Future, 227a City Rd., London EC1V 1JT UK/Tel: 011-44-171-251-6070/Fax: 011-44-171-251-6268

Fraser Institute, 626 Bute St., 2nd Floor, Vancouver, BC V6E 3M1/Tel: 604-688-0221/ Fax: 604-688-8539/Internet: www.fraserinstitute.ca

Friends of the Earth (FOE), 251 Laurier Ave. W., Ste. 701, Ottawa, ON K1P 5J6/Tel: 613-230-3352/Fax: 613-232-4354

Georgia Strait Alliance, 201 – 195 Commercial St., Nanaimo, BC V9R 5G5/Tel: (250-753-3459)/ Internet: http://onenw.org/~gsa/index.html

Goodwill Toronto, 234 Adelaide St. E., Toronto, ON M5A 1M9/Tel: 416-362-4711/Fax: 416-362-0720

Green Building Information Council, Internet: www.greenbuilding.ca/

Green Canada, Internet: www.greencanada.org

Green Communities Association, 4 Knox St., Peterborough, ON K9H 2A8/Tel: 705-745-7479/Fax: 705-745-7294/Internet: www.ptbo.igs.net/~gca

Green Lane (see Environment Canada Green Lane)

GreenDisk, 16398 N.E. 85th St., Ste. 100, Redmond, WA 98052 USA, Toll Free: 1-800-305-DISK (3475) Fax: 425-883-0425

Greenpeace, 250 Dundas St. W., Ste 605, Toronto, ON M5T 2Z5/Tel: 416-597-8408/Fax: 416-597-8422/Internet: www.greenpeacecanada.org

Greenpeace USA, 1436 U St., N.W., Washington, DC 28009/Tel: 202-462-1177/Fax: 202-462-4507/Internet: www.greenpeaceusa.org

Hike Ontario, 1185 Eglinton Ave. E., Ste. 411, North York, ON M3C 3C6/Tel: 416-426-7362/Fax: 416-426-7045/Internet: www.sympatico.ca/hikers.net/hikeont.htm

Human HiTec Assist Computer Recycling, 45 Granville St., Vancouver, BC V6Z 1L4/Tel and Fax: 604-214-9276

Humanist Association of Canada, PO Box 3736, Stn. C, Ottawa, ON K1Y 4J8/Tel: 613-739-9569/Fax: 613-738-1462/Internet: www.magi.com/~hac

Huntington Society of Canada, 13 Water St. N., Ste. 3, PO Box 1269, Cambridge, ON N1R 7G6/Tel: 519-622-1002/Fax: 519-622-7370/Internet: www.hsc-ca.org/

Infant Feeding Action Coalition, 10 Trinity Square, Toronto, ON M5G 1B1/Tel: 416-595-9819/Fax: 416-598-0292/E-mail: infact@ftn.net

Infertility Awareness Association of Canada (IAAC), 396 Cooper St., Ste. 201, Ottawa, ON K2P 2H7/Tel: 613-234-8585/Toll free: 1-800-263-2929/Fax: 613-234-7718/Internet: http://fox.nstn.ca/~iaac

Institute for Social Inventions, 20 Heber Rd., London NW2 6AA UK/Tel: 011-44-181-208-2853/Internet: www.newciv.org/GIB

Institute for Work & Health, 250 Bloor St. E., Ste. 702, Toronto, ON M4W 1E6/Tel: 416-927-2027/Fax: 416-927-4167/Internet: www.iwh.on.ca/home.htm

Interfaith Center on Corporate Responsibility, 475 Riverside Dr., Room 566, New York, NY 10115/Tel: 212-870-2295/Fax: 212-870-2023/Internet: www.domini.com/ICCR.html

Intermediate Technology Development Group, Schumacher Centre for Technology & Development, Bourton Hall, Bourton on Dunsmore, Warwickshire CV23 9QZ UK/Tel: 011-44-178-866-1100

International Council for Local Environmental Initiatives (ICLEI), World Secretariat, 8th Floor, East Tower, City Hall, Toronto, ON M5H 2N2/Fax: 416-392-1478/Internet: www.iclei.org

International Federation of Organic Agriculture Movements (IFOAM), c/o Okozentrum Imsbach, D-66636 Tholey-Theley, Germany/Tel: 011-49-6853-5190/Fax: 011-49-6853-30110/Internet: http://ecoweb.dk/ifoam

Investors Group, Tel: 1-800-361-2680/Internet: www.investorsgroup.com/

Jane Jacobs: Ideas That Matter, 170 Bloor St. W., Ste. 804, Toronto, ON M5S 1T9/Tel: 416-944-1303/Fax: 416-944-8915/Internet: www.jacobs97.com

Johnny's Selected Seeds, Foss Hill Road, Albion, ME 04910 USA/Tel: 207-437-4301/Fax: 207-437-2165/Internet: www.johnnyseeds.com

Kaiser Youth Foundation, 1500 Georgia St. W., 19th Floor, Vancouver, BC V6G 2Z8/Tel: 608-681-9211/Fax: 604-685-9406/Internet: www.tether.com/kyf

Kids Help Phone, 439 University Ave., Ste. 300, Toronto, ON M5G 1Y8/Tel: 416-586-5437/ Fax: 416-586-0651/Internet: http://kidshelp.sympatico.ca

Knives and Forks, 1 Cadorna Ave., Toronto, ON M4J 3W7/Tel: 416-422-1944/Toll free: 1-800-719-9108

La Leche League Canada, 18C Industrial Dr., Chesterville, ON K0C 1HO/Tel: 613-448-1842/Fax: 613-448-1845

LETS Toronto, Internet: www.web.net/~lets/tor-lets.html

Manitoba Child Care Association, 364 McGregor St., Winnipeg, MB R2W 4X3/Tel: 204-586-8587/Fax: 204-589-5613/Internet: http://cfc-efc.ca/mcca

Manitoba Healthy Communities Network,/Tel: 204-638-2149 or 204-627-8236/Internet: www.pangea.ca/~healthy

Marriage Encounter,/Tel: 1-800-795-LOVE (795-5683)/Internet: **www.wwme.org**

Media Awareness Network, 1500 Merivale Rd., 3rd Floor, Nepean, ON K2E 6Z5/Tel: 613-224-7721/Toll free: 1-800-896-3342/Fax: 613-224-1958/Internet: www.media-awareness.ca

Media Foundation, 1243 W. 7th Ave., Vancouver, BC V6H 1B7/Tel: 604-736-9401/Toll-free (USA & Canada only): 1-800-663-1243/Fax: 604-737-6021/Internet: www.adbusters.org/

MediaWatch, 517 Wellington St. W., Ste. 204, Toronto, ON M5V 1G1/Tel: 416-408-2065/Internet: www.mediawatch.ca

Michael Jantzi Research Associates, 372 Bay St., Ste. 1906, Toronto, ON M5H 2W9/Tel: 416-861-0403/Fax: 416-861-0183

MORE Toronto, 10NU-166, 200 Elizabeth St., Toronto, ON M5G 2C4/Tel: 416-340-3587/ Toll free: 1-800-387-6673/Fax: 416-340-4539

Motherisk Program, Helplines: Nausea and vomiting in pregnancy, Toll free: 1-800-436-8477 (Greater Toronto Area: 416-813-7809);

Exposures to drugs, chemicals, radiation, infectious diseases etc. during pregnancy: 416-873-6780; Alcohol and substance use, Toll free: 1-877-587-8953 (Greater Toronto Area: 416-813-8738); HIV drugs & treatments & pregnancy: Toll free: 1-888-246-5840/Internet: www.motherisk.org

Mothers Against Drunk Driving (MADD) Canada, 6507 Mississauga Rd., Mississauga, ON L5N 1A6/Tel: 905-813-6233/Toll free: 1-800-813-6233/Fax: 905-813-8920/Internet: www.madd.ca

Multi Organ Transplant Program, Victoria General Hospital, 1278 Tower Rd., Halifax, NS B3H 2Y9/Tel: 902-473-5500

Multiple Organ Retrieval and Exchange Program of Ontario (MORE), 250 Dundas St. W., Ste. 406, Toronto, ON M5T 2Z5/Tel: 416-351-7328/Toll free: 1-800-263-2833/Internet: www.transplant-ontario.org

Multiple Sclerosis Society of Canada, 250 Bloor St. E., Ste. 1000, Toronto, ON M4W 3P9/Tel: 416-922-6065/Fax: 416-922-7538/Internet: www.mssoc.ca/

National Coalition Against the Misuse of Pesticides (NCAMP), 701 E St. S.E., Washington, DC 20003/Tel: 202-543-5450/ Fax: 202-543-4791/Internet: www.ncamp.org

National Family Planning Association, 3050 Yonge St., Ste. 205, Toronto, ON M4N 2K4/Tel: 416-481-5465

National Farmers Union, 250C 2nd Ave. S., Saskatoon, SK S7K 2M1/Tel: 306 652-9465/ Fax: 306 664-6226/Internet: www.nfu.ca

National Foundation for Family Research and Education, 605 5th Ave. S.W., Ste. 1250, PO Box 31, Calgary, AB T2P 3H5/Tel: 403-263-4696/Fax: 403-263-4699

National Institute of Nutrition, 265 Carling Ave., Ste. 302, Ottawa, ON K1S 2E1/Tel: 613-235-3355/Fax: 613-235-7032/Internet: www.nin.ca

National Shared Parenting Association, PO Box 114, Stn. A, Toronto, ON M5A 1A2/Tel: 416-861-0626/Fax: 416-861-1932

Natural Resources Canada, 580 Booth St., Ottawa, ON K1A 0E4/Tel: 613-995-0947/Fax: 613-992-7211/Internet: www.nrcan.gc.ca

Nature Conservancy of Canada, 110 Eglinton Ave. W., Ste. 400, Toronto, ON M4R 1A3/Tel: 416-932-3202/Fax: 416-932-3208

Neighbourhood Watch, Internet: http://neighbourhoodwatch.ottawa.com

New Economics Foundation, Vine Court, 112 Whitechapel Rd., London E1 1JE UK/Tel: 011-44-171-377-5696/Fax: 011-44-171-377-5720/Internet: sosig.ac.uk/neweconomics/-newecon.html

New Reproductive Alternative Technology Society,/Tel: 604-754-3900

No Kidding! Box 27001, Vancouver, BC V5R 6A8/Tel 604-538-7736/Internet: www.nokidding.bc.ca

North American Vegetarian Society (NAVS), PO Box 72Q, Dolgeville, NY 13329 USA/Tel: 518-568-7970/Internet: www.cyberveg.org/navs

Nova Scotia Organic Growers Association, PO Box 16, Annapolis Royal, NS B0S 1A0/Tel: 902-825-6209/Internet: www.gks.com/nsoga

Office for Disability Issues, Human Resources Development Canada, Internet: www.indie.ca/odi

One Parent Families Association of Canada, 6979 Yonge St., Ste. 203, Willowdale, ON M2M 3X9/Tel: 416-226-0062/Fax: 416-226-3089/Internet: www.tcn.net/~oneparent

Ontario Farm Animal Council, 7195 Millcreek Dr., Mississauga, ON L5N 4H1/Tel: 905-821-3880/Fax 905-858-1589/Internet: http://info.sources.com/listings/1890.htm

Ontario Healthy Communities Coalition, 180 Dundas St. W., Ste. 1900 Toronto, ON M5G 1Z8/Tel: 416-408-4841/Toll free: 1-800-

766-3418/Fax: 416-408-4843/Internet: www.opc.on.ca/ohcc/

Ontario Heritage Foundation, 10 Adelaide St. E., Toronto, ON M5C 1J3/Tel: 416-325-5000/ Fax: 416-325-5071

OPIS—Organic Product Information Service, 15 Innovation Blvd., Saskatoon, SK S7N 2X8/Tel: 306-933-5449/Fax: 306-933-7896

Organ Donors Canada, 5326 Ada Blvd., Edmonton, AB T5W 4N7

Oxfam Canada, 294 Albert St., Ste. 300, Ottawa, ON K1P 6E6/Tel: 613-237-5236/Fax: 613-237-0524/Internet: www.oxfam.ca

Pacific Salmon Alliance, PO Box 1086, 101 – 1001 W. Broadway Ave., Vancouver, BC V6H 4G4/Tel: 604-255-3161/Fax: 604-939-3940/Internet: http://diane.island.net/~psa/

Parent Finders of Canada, 3998 Bayview Ave., Vancouver, BC V7V 3J5/Tel: 604-980-6005/ Fax: 604-926-2037/Internet: www.ltinc.net/reunion

Parents and Friends of Lesbians and Gays (PFLAG), Internet: www.cglbrd.com/ categories/pflag.htm (or see your phone directory)

Parents of Multiple Births Association of Canada, 240 Graff Ave., PO Box 22005, Stratford, ON N5A 7V6/Tel: 519-272-2203/ Fax: 519-272-1926/Internet: www.pomba.org

Parents of Multiple Births Association of Canada, PO Box 234, Gormley, ON L0H 1G0/Tel: 905-888-0725/Fax: 905-888-0727/ Internet: www.pomba.org

Partnership on Sustainable Coastal Communities in Nfld. & Labrador, contact: Newfoundland & Labrador Environment Network, PO Box 944, Cornerbrook, NF A2H 6J2/Tel: 709-634-2520

Pembina Institute for Appropriate Development, PO Box 7558, Drayton Valley, AB T0E 0M0/Tel: 403-542-6272/Fax: 403-542-6464

PEN Canada, 24 Ryerson Ave., Ste. 309, Toronto, ON M5T 2P3/Tel: 416-703-8448/Fax: 416-703-3870/Internet: www.pencanada.ca

Pen Parents of Canada, PO Box 52548, RPO Coquitlam Centre, Coquitlam, BC V3B 7J4

People for the Ethical Treatment of Animals (PETA), 501 Front St., Norfolk, VA 23510 USA/Tel: 757-622-PETA (7382)/Fax: 757-622-0457/Internet: www.peta-online.org/

Pesticide Action Network North America (PANNA), 49 Powell St., Ste. 500, San Francisco, CA 94102 USA/Tel: 415-981-1771/Fax: 415-981-1991/Internet: www.panna.org/panna

Physicians for Global Survival (PGS Canada), 145 Spruce St., Ste. 208, Ottawa, ON K1R 6P1/Tel: 613-233-1982/Fax: 613-233-9028/Internet: www.web.net/~pgs

PITCH-IN CANADA, Box 45011, Ocean Park RPO, White Rock, BC V4A 9L1/Tel: 604-290-0498/Fax: 604-535-4653/Internet: www.pitch-in.ca

Planned Parenthood Federation of Canada, 1 Nicholas St., Ste. 430, Ottawa, ON K1N 7B7/Tel: 613-241-4474/Fax: 613-241-7550/Internet: www.ppfc.ca

Pollution Probe, 12 Madison Ave., Toronto, ON M5R 2S1/Tel: 416-926-1907/Fax: 416-926-1601/Internet: www.pollutionprobe.org

Preservation of Agricultural Lands Society (PALS), PO Box 1090, St. Catharines, ON L2R 7A3/Tel: 905-468-2814/Fax: 905-468-7614

Pro Organics Marketing Inc., 3454 Loughheed Hwy., Vancouver, BC V5M 2A4/Tel: 604-253-6549/Fax: 604-253-0439/E-mail: prosales@proorganics.com/ Unit #3-5, Bldg. 709, 433 Horner Ave, Etobicoke, ON M8W 4Y4/Tel: 416-252-3386/Fax: 416-252-3142/e-mail: mfronte@proorganics.com

Progeni Computers, 3281 Yonge St., Toronto, ON M4N 2L8/Tel: 416-322-6512

Public Interest Advocacy Group (PIAC), 1 Nicholas St., Ste. 1204, Ottawa, ON K1N 7B7/Tel: 613-562-4002/Fax: 613-452-007

Quebec Transplant, 4200 St. Laurent Blvd., Ste. 1111, Montreal, PQ H2W 2R2/Tel: 514-286-1414

Rails to Greenways, #306, 1600 James Naismith Drive, Gloucester, ON K1B 5N4/Tel: 613-748-5651

Rare Breeds Canada, Dan Price-Jones, Trent University, Environmental and Resource Study Program, Peterborough, ON K9J 7B8/Tel: 613-473-1395/Fax: 613-473-1396

Reboot Canada, 1179A King St. W., Ste. 016, Toronto, ON M6K 3J6/Tel: 416-534-6017/ Fax: 416-534-6083/E-mail: infor@reboot.on.ca

Rechargeable Battery Recycling Corporation, Tel: 1-800-8BATTERY/www.rbrc.com

Recycling Council of Alberta, Tel: 403-287-1477 Fax: 403-287-1942 / Internet: www.recycle.ab.ca

Recycling Council of British Columbia, In Greater Vancouver Tel: RECYCLE 732-9253/Outside Lower Mainland Toll-free: 1-800-667-4321 / Internet: www.rcbc.bc.ca

Recycling Council of Ontario, 489 College St., Ste. 504, Toronto, ON M6G 1A5/Tel: 416-960-1025/Fax: 416-960-8053 / Internet: www.rco.on.ca/

Recyc-Québec, Internet: www.recyc-quebec.gouv.qc.ca

Resource Conservation Manitoba, 70 Albert St., Ste. 2, Winnipeg, MB R3B 1E7/Tel: 204-925-3777/Fax: 204-942-4207/Internet: www.escape.ca/~rcm

Rein*CAR*nate Vehicle Recycling Program, Toll free in Ontario: 1-888-CAR-DIED 227-3433; in Greater Toronto Area: 416-960-1025 Ext. 23/Internet: www.rco.on.ca/reincarnate.html

Right to Die Network of Canada, 532 Montreal Rd., Ste. 200, Ottawa, ON K1K 4R4/Toll free: 1-888-736-6660/Greater Toronto Area: 416-535-0690/Internet: www.rights.org/deathnet

Saskatchewan Waste Reduction Council, 115 2nd Ave. N., Ste. 203, Saskatoon, SK S7K 2B1/Tel: 306-931-3242/Fax: 306-665-2128/Internet: www.link.ca/~swrc

Scambusters, Internet: www.scambusters.com

SCRAP-IT Program, British Columbia Ministry of Environment, Lands and Parks, Tel: 604-294-8330/Toll free: 1-888-655-1000

Seeds of Change, PO Box 15700, Sante Fe, NM 87506 USA/Tel: 1-888-762-7333/Internet: www.seedsofchange.com

Seeds of Diversity Canada, PO Box 36, Stn. Q, Toronto, ON M4T 2L7/Tel: 905 623-0353/ Internet: www.interlog.com/~sodc

Serena Canada, 151 Holland Ave., Ste. 201, Ottawa, ON K1Y 0Y2/Tel: 613-728-6536/Toll free: 1-888-3SERENA (1-888-373-7362)/Fax: 613-724-116

Shepherd's Garden Seeds, 30 Irene St., Torrington, CT 06790 USA/Tel: 860-482-3638/Fax: 860-482-0532/Internet: www.shepherdseeds.com

Shorter Work Time Network of Canada, Internet: www.vcn.bc.ca/timework

Sierra Club of Canada, 1 Nicholas St., Ste. 412, Ottawa, ON K1N 7B7/Tel: 613-241-4611/Fax: 613-241-2292/Internet: www.sierraclub.ca

Simple Living Network, Internet: www.simpleliving.net

Social Investment Organization (SIO), 366 Adelaide St. E., Ste. 443, Toronto, ON M5A 3X9/Tel: 416-360-6047/Fax: 416-360-6380/Internet: www.web.net/~sio

SOHO Business Group, 2255B Queen St. E., Ste. 3261, Toronto, ON M4E 1G3/Tel: 416-973-7646/Toll free: 1-800-693-7646/Fax: 416-693-2103/Internet: www.soho.ca

Solar Energy Society of Canada Inc. (SESCI), 116 Lisgar St., Ste. 702, Ottawa, ON K2P 0C2/Tel: 613-234-4151/Fax: 613-234-2988/Internet: www.solarenergysociety.ca

Sustainable Communities Info Service Databank, Nova Scotia Environment & Development Coalition, 1657 Barrington St., Ste. 133, Halifax, NS B3J 2A1/Tel: 902-422-4276/Fax: 902-423-9736/Internet: www.cfn.cs.dal.ca/Environment/SCN/SCN_home.html

Syrotech Industries, 242 Main St., Winnipeg, MB R3C 1A9/Tel: 204-942-7900/Internet: www.syrotech.mb.ca/recycle.html

Taskforce on Churches and Corporate Responsibility, 129 St. Clair Ave. W., Toronto, ON M4V 1N5/Tel: 416-923-1758/Fax: 416-927-7554/e-mail: tccr@web.apc.org

Ten Days for Global Justice, 947 Queen St. E., Ste. 201, Toronto ON M4M 1J9/Tel: 416-463-5312/Fax: 416-463-5569/Internet: www.web.net/~tendays

TerraChoice Environmental Services Inc., 2197 Riverside Drive, Ste. 300, Ottawa, ON K1H 7X3/Tel: 613-247-1900/Fax: 613-247-2228/Internet: www.terrachoice.ca

TLC, 169 Eastern Ave., Toronto, ON M5A 1H7 Tel: 416-955-1551/Fax: 416-955-0796

Today's Parent Online, Internet: www.todaysparent.com

Trans Canada Trail Foundation, Toll free: 1-800-465-3636/Internet: www.tctrail.ca

Transport 2000 Canada, PO Box 858, Stn. B, 111 Sparks St., Ste. 102, Ottawa, ON K1P 5P9/Tel: 613-594-3290

Unitarian Churches, Canadian Unitarian Council, 55 Eglinton Ave. E., Ste. 705, Toronto, ON M4P 1G8/Tel: 416-489-4121/Toll free: 1-888-568-5723/Fax: 416-489-9010/Internet: www.web.net/~cuc

University of Alberta Bioethics Centre, Tel: 403-492-6676/Fax: 403-492-6673/Internet: www.ualberta.ca/~ethics/bio-bull.htm

University of Alberta Computing and Network Services Security, Internet: www.ualberta.ca

University of Toronto Joint Centre for Bioethics, 88 College St., Toronto, ON M5G 1L4/Tel: 416-978-2709/Fax: 416-978-1911/Internet: www.utoronto.ca/jcb/

Vaccination Risk Awareness Network (VRAN), 439 Wellington St. West, Ste. 5, Toronto, ON M5V 1E9/Tel: 416-280-6035

Vancouver City Savings Credit Union (VanCity), Internet: www.citizensbank.ca

Vancouver Community Network, 411 Dunsmuir St., 2nd Floor, Vancouver, BC V6B 1X4/Tel: 604-257-3811/Internet: www.vcn.bc.ca

Vancouver Co-operative Auto Network (CAN-VAN), Tel: 604-660-9725

Vanier Institute of the Family, 94 Centrepointe Dr., Ste. 300, Nepean, ON K2G 6B1/Tel: 613-228-8500/Fax: 613-228-8007/Internet: http://familyforum.com/vanier

Vets Against Nuclear Arms, 240 Holyrood Rd. N., Vancouver, BC V7N 2R5

Victoria Car Share Co-op, Tel: 250-995-0265

Volunteer Canada, 1 Nicholas St., Ste.302, Ottawa, ON K1N 7B7/Tel: 613-241-4371/Toll free: 1-800-670-0401/Fax: 613-0241-6725 /Internet: www.volunteer.ca

WestHemp Canada, Internet: www.westhemp.com

WFD Canada, 155 Gordon Baker Rd., Ste. 212, North York, ON M2H 3N5/Tel: 416-492-3475/Fax: 416-496-8258/Internet: www.wfdcanada.com

Wholesome & Humane Program 2000, 314 – 6577 Royal Oak Ave., Burnaby, BC/Tel: 604-435-9032/Fax: 604-433-5569/E-mail: dknowles@dowco.com

Wildlife Habitat Canada, 7 Hinton Ave. N., Ste. 200, Ottawa, ON K1Y 4P1/Tel: 613-722-2090/Fax: 613-722-3318

Women Business Owners of Canada, 20 York Mills Rd., Ste. 100, North York, ON M2P 2C2/Internet: www.wboc.ca/index.htm

Work-Life Harmony Enterprises, 207 Shaughnessy Blvd., Ste 601, North York, ON M2J 1J9/Tel: 416-497-8942/Fax: 416-492-8799

Working Well CHC, 1599 Hurontario St., Ste. 300, Mississauga, ON L5G 4S1/Tel: 905-278-6065/Toll free: 1-800-463-1189/Fax: 905-278-5950

World Society for the Protection of Animals, Internet: www.wspa.org.uk

World Wildlife Fund Canada (WWF Canada), 90 Eglinton Ave. E., Ste. 504, Toronto, ON M4P 2Z7/Tel: 416-489-8800/Toll free: 1-800-26-PANDA (267-2632)/Fax: 416-489-3611/Internet: www.wwfcanada.org

Worldwide Fund for Nature (WWF), Panda House, Weyside Park, Godalming, Surrey GU7 1XR UK/Tel: 011-44-1483-426-444/Fax: 011-44-1483-426-409/Internet: www.wwfuk.org

Y2K Citizen's Action Guide, Internet: www.utne.com/y2k

Y2K Watch, Internet: www.globetechnology.com/summary/Y2K.html

Year 2000 Support Centre, Internet: www.support2000.com

Zero Population Growth, 1400 16th St. N.W., Ste. 320, Washington, DC 20036/Tel. Toll-free: 1-800-767-1956/Internet: www.zpg.org

Endnotes

Chapter 1

1 Jo Knowsley, "Timetable Set for the Brave New World," *Daily Telegraph*, 6 July 1997

2 Martin Jacques, "The Floral Revolution," *The Observer*, 7 September 1997

Chapter 2

1 William Greider, *One World, Ready or Not: The Manic Logic of Global Capitalism*, Simon & Schuster, 1997

2 Nicholas Schoon, "Good News: World Population Boom Is Ending," *The Independent*, 12 January 1998

3 Alan Thein-Durning, "How Much Is Enough?" Worldwatch Institute, Washington, D.C., 1996

4 Lester Brown et al., *Vital Signs*, W.W. Norton, 1997

5 Centre for Alternative Technology, "Water Conservation in the Home," www.foe.co.uk/CAT/publicat/watercon, March 1997

6 Nicholas Schoon, "World Is Running Out of Water," *The Independent*, 25 January 1997

7 *One Thousand Days: A Special Report on How to Live in the New Millennium, The Guardian* in association with WWF U.K., 1997

8 Claude Fussler with Peter James, *Driving Eco-Innovation: A Breakthrough Discipline for Innovation and Sustainability*, Pitman Publishing, 1996

9 Ernst von Weizäcker, Amory B. Lovins and L. Hunter Lovins, *Factor Four: Doubling Wealth, Halving Resource Use*, Earthscan, 1997

10 Estimate by Paul Hawken, President of the U.S. end of The Natural Step.

11 Andrew Goudie, *The Future of Climate*, Phoenix, 1997

12 Theo Colborn et al., *Our Stolen Future*, Dutton Books, 1996

13 Deborah Cadbury, *The Feminization of Nature*, Hamish Hamilton, London, 1997

14 Nick Nuttall, "Scientists Alarmed by Extent of Fish Mutations, *The Times*, 22 January 1998

15 Robin Maynard, "Sperm Alert," *Living Earth Magazine*, Soil Association, October 1995

16 "Packaging Chemical is Oestrogenic," research from University of Missouri-Columbia, *ENDS Daily*, 27 March 1997

17 German EPA, 1994

18 Nigel Hawkes, "Mice Given Green Light to Assist Scientists," *The Times*, 13 June 1997

19 Francis Crick

20 Neil Spiller, Visionary, BBC Online, "Tomorrow's World," 25 March 1998

21 Frequently asked questions about biodiversity, Union of Concerned Scientists, www.ucusa.org/global/biofaq

Chapter 3

1 World Cancer Research Fund, 1997

2 Michael Hornsby, "Parents Told to Peel 'Pesticide' Fruit," *The Times*, 15 March 1997

3 U.S. Environmental Protection Agency, as reported in *Pesticide News* 35, March 1997

4 World Wildlife Fund Canada

5 *Food and Pesticides*, Food Safety Directorate, Ministry of Agriculture, Fisheries and Food, London, 1992

6 Dr. Robert Repetto and Sanjay Baliga, "Pesticides and the Immune System: Public Health Risks," World Resources Institute, Washington, 1994

7 Peter Beaumont, "Where Have All the Birds Gone?" *Pesticides News* 36, June 1997

8 Canadian Diabetes Association, www.banting.com/wn/new2.html

9 "Packaging Chemical Is Oestrogenic," *ENDS Daily*, 27 March 1997

10 Lois Rogers, "Bad Food Really Does Make You Bilious," *The Times*, 4 January 1997
11 Many of the items in this section are based on: Peter Cox and Peggy Brusseau, *Secret Ingredients*, Bantam Books, 1997
12 Christine Gorman, "Vitamin Overload?" *Business Week*, 10 November 1997
13 "High Levels of Dioxins Found in Fish Oils," *The Food Magazine*, February 1998
14 Joanna Blythman, *The Food We Eat*, Michael Joseph, 1996
15 Peter Cox and Peggy Brusseau, *The Complete Fat Counter*, Telegraph Books Direct, 1998
16 Betty Martin, Mission Impossible, 5950-H State Bridge Road, Suite 215, Duluth, GA 30155 USA, www.dorway.com/possible or www.tiac.net/users/mgold/aspartame/
17 Jane Bradbury, "Shiny Red Apples Are Not for Veggies," *The Food Magazine*, April-June 1996
18 "Food Irradiation: Solution or Threat?" International Organization of Consumers Unions, London, Briefing paper no. 3, September 1994
19 Joanna Blythman
20 "Food Irradiation: Solution or Threat?" op. cit.
21 Tim Lobstein, Food Commission
22 Anna Kohn, "Natural Growth: Organic Produce Is Becoming Part of the Mainstream Food Chain," *The Financial Post Magazine*, 1 March 1998
23 Anne Marshall, *The Complete Vegetarian Cookbook*, Landsdowne, Sydney, 1993
24 World Cancer Research Paper, 1997
25 Brian Cole, "BST Review Fuels Worry," *Winnipeg Free Press*, 6 January 1998
26 The Canadian Agri-Food Research Council, www.carc-crac.ca, Voluntary Codes of Practice (Veal)
27 Ibid.
28 David Fraser and Marty L. Leonard, "Farm Animal Welfare," in J. Martin, R.M. Hudson and B.A. Young (editors), *Animal Production in Canada*, University of Alberta, Faculty of Extension, Edmonton
29 Sarah Boseley, "How the Truth Was Butchered," *The Guardian*, 24 March 1996.
30 Charles Leadbeater, "Why the Beef Industry Has Led Itself to Slaughter," *The Observer*, 22 December 1996
31 Sharon Lem, "How Now Mad Cow? Millions of Dollars at Risk If European Union Members Ban Some Canadian Animal Products," *The Ottawa Sun*, 25 May 1998
32 Douglas Powell and William Leiss, *Mad Cows and Mother's Milk*, McGill-Queens University Press, 1997
33 Ibid.
34 Nahlah Ayed, "Chicken, Pork, Beef Taken from Stores Across Canada," *Winnipeg Free Press*, 7 March 1998
35 Ibid.
36 Oliver Walston, "Swept Away on a Tide of Hysteria," *The Times*, 23 March 1996
37 Philip Lymbery, *The Welfare of Pigs*, CIWF Trust, 1993
38 Anthony Bevins, "Plan Is Hatched to Phase out Battery Hens," *The Independent*, 25 July 1997
39 Review of "Report on the Welfare of Laying Hens," a report by the Farm Animal Welfare Committee (FWAC)
40 *Food for Thought: Facts about Food and Farming in Canada*, Ontario Farm Animal Council (OFAC), 1996 (booklet)
41 David Fraser and Marty L. Leonard, op. cit.
42 David Fraser, "A Canadian Perspective on Farm Animal Welfare," in K.B. Beesley, S. Burns, M. Campbell and P. Sanger, (editors), *Decision Making and Agriculture: The Role of Ethics*, Truro, Canada, Research Centre, 1995

43 Ibid.

44 Personal conversation with David Fraser, Faculty of Agricultural Sciences and Centre for Applied Ethics, The University of British Columbia

45 *Ostrich Farming*, CIWF Trust, 1996

46 Peter Stevenson, *Factory Farming and the Myth of Cheap Food*, CIWF Trust, Fact Sheet, 1997

47 Cindy Deachman, "A Feast on the Fringe of the Valley," *The Globe and Mail*, 30 May 1998

48 Tim O'Brien, *Factory Farming and World Health*, CIWF Trust, July 1997

49 *Where to Buy Organic Food*, The Soil Association, March 1997; July 1998

50 Consumer Alert, Council for Responsible Genetics, www.essential.org/crg/crg6, 12 June 1997

51 "Spilling the Genes: What We Should Know about Genetically Engineered Foods," *The Genetics Forum*, London, 1996

52 Steve Connor, "New Tomato Keeps Men Healthy—With a Bit of Sauce on the Side," *Sunday Times*, 8 February 1998

53 Peter Geigen-Miller, "The Labelling Debate Pits Practicality Against the Consumer's Right to Know," *The London Free Press*, 17 September 1998

54 Andy Coghlan, "Tubby Tubers," *New Scientist*, 2 August 1997

55 *Food for Our Future: A Guide to Modern Biotechnology*, The Food and Drink Federation, London

56 Michael Durham, "Children Refuse to Eat up Chocolate-Flavour Greens," *The Observer*, 28 December 1997

57 Peter Geigen-Miller, op. cit.

58 Food & Agriculture Organisation (FAO)

59 FAO, *State of the World—Fisheries and Aquaculture*

60 Where prawns are mentioned the same issues apply to shrimp

61 Mark Kurlansky, *Cod: A Biography of the Fish that Changed the World*, Walker and Company, 1997

62 Ibid.

63 Ibid.

64 Georgia Strait Alliance, onenw.org/~gsa/index.html

65 Ibid.

66 Ibid.

67 Ibid.

68 *Canadian Press Newswire*, 29 July 1997

69 Margaret Philp, "As the Salmon Disappear, So Does a Way of Life in B.C.," *The Globe and Mail*, 1 August 1998

70 Greenpeace International, *Industrial Fisheries: From Fish to Fodder*

71 Richard Beeston, "Rise of the Caviar Mafia," *The Times*, 20 June 1997

72 Michael L. Weber, "So You Say You Want a Blue Revolution?" *The Amicus Journal*, Fall 1996

73 Linda Jackson, "Salmon Leaps over Haddock to Top Sales League," *The Sunday Telegraph*, 6 July 1997

74 Georgia Strait Alliance, op. cit.

75 Ibid.

76 Tom Fort, "Loathsome Louse of the Lochs," *Financial Times*, 11 January 1998

77 David Brown, "Ranching Will Mean Cheaper Lobster," *Daily Telegraph*, 24 February 1997

78 Natural Resources Defense Council, "Shrimp Cocktail—Recipe for disaster," NRDC website, www.nrdc.org/status/ocshrsr

79 Greenpeace, *North Sea Fish Crisis: Our Shrinking Future.*

80 "The Fish Crisis," *Time*, 11 August 1997

81 Greenpeace, *North Sea Fish Crisis: Our Shrinking Future*, op. cit.

82 Ibid.

83 Ibid.
84 Charles Clover, *The Fisheries Effect*, WWF International, Gland, Switzerland, 1996
85 Greenpeace, *North Sea Fish Crisis: Our Shrinking Future*, op. cit.
86 "Marine Fishes in the Wild—Wanted Alive," WWF
87 Greenpeace, *North Sea Fish Crisis: Our Shrinking Future*, op. cit.
88 Michael Harris, "Rotten State of Our Fishery," *The Toronto Sun*, 12 April 1998
89 "Bananas: Picking the Best of the Bunch, Shopping for a Better World," a project of NEAD/Third World Centre
90 Christopher Hirst, "Dry It and They'll Buy It," *Weekend Telegraph*, 23 December 1995
91 Madelaine Drohan, "Western Trend to Treat World as Its Larder Concerns Environmentalists," *The Globe and Mail*, 9 December 1997
92 Wupperal Institute, Germany
93 SAFE Alliance, *Food Miles: A Guide to Thinking Globally and Eating Locally*, London, 1996
94 Vilmorin's "The Vegetable Garden," first printed in 1885; reprinted in 1997 by Ten Speed Press, California

Chapter 4

1 Mary Nemeth, "The Family: Canadians See Tradition in Crisis Even as a New Poll Uncovers Enduring Strength," *Maclean's*, 20 June 1994
2 Louise Brown, "Number of Kids Growing but Families Are Smaller," *The Toronto Star*, 6 February 1996
3 Andrew Bolger, "Segregated by Sex," *Financial Times*, 11 December 1997
4 Louise Brown, op. cit.
5 Alanna Mitchell, "Work in Progress: Women Take Laborious Road to Work for Pay," *The Globe and Mail*, 2 January 1997
6 Andrew Bolger, op. cit.
7 Stephen McGinty, "Fear of Flirting Kills off the Office Romance," *Sunday Times*, 30 November 1997
8 Reuters, "Happiness Widens the Age Gap," *The Times*, 27 November 1997
9 Geoff Mulgan and Ivan Briscoe, "The Society of Networks," in Geoff Mulgan (editor), *Life After Politics*, Fontana Press, 1997
10 Lawrence Wright, "Twins Prove Life's a Script," *The Times*, 3 November 1997
11 Denis Staunton, "Germans Rush to Rent a Granny," *The Guardian*, 22 November 1997
12 Robert Nurden, "Grey Generation Seizes its Second Chance," *The European*, 11 September 1997
13 Guy Crittenden, "Front-Porch Challenge," *The Globe and Mail*, 20 June 1998
14 William Thorsell, "Canada Is a Country of Fences that Make Good Citizens," *The Globe and Mail*, 19 July 1997
15 Lorrayne Anthony, "Safe and Sound Behind the Gate," *Maclean's*, 21 July 1997
16 Charles Leadbeater, *Civic Spirit: The Big Idea for a New Political Era*, Demos, 1997
17 Michael Valpy, "Citystate: Rusting Mill Scars Face of Gutted Mountain," *The Globe and Mail*, 11 February 1991
18 Mike Funston, "Gravel Pits a 'blight,' Councillors Say," *The Toronto Star*, 25 August 1994
19 William J. Mitchell, "Do We Still Need Skyscrapers?" *Scientific American*, December 1997
20 Brian Bergman, "The Island's New Link: Confederation Bridge Still Inflames Passions," *Maclean's*, 2 June 1997
21 "Eco Lightbulbs," *Ethical Consumer*, November/December 1995
22 Anthony Barnett, "The Deadly Secret of DIY's Dream Material." *The Observer*, 21 September, 1997

23 Frequently Asked Questions, Water, Rocky Mountain Institute website, September 1997
24 "Ultra Low Flush Toilet RAQ," Natural Resources Defense Council, NRDC website, June 1997
25 Haya El Nasser, "As Predicted, Dalmatians Are Being Dumped at Pounds," *USA Today*, 8 September 1997
26 Manfred Jager, "We'll Soon Cotton to Hemp: Insider Predicts Crop Will Sweep Clothing Biz," *Winnipeg Free Press*, 19 October 1998
27 "Clothes Code Campaign," *Ethical Consumer*, July/August 1997
28 CAFOD, *Ethical Consumer*, October/ November 1997

Chapter 5

1 Birna Helgadottir, "A Great Idea, But Please, Not Yet," *The European*, 18–24 September 1997
2 Peter Martin, "The Anatomy of a Traffic Jam," *The Observer Review*, 20 April 1997
3 Paul Marston, *Daily Telegraph*, 14 January 1998
4 Jim Boothroyd, "Driving Ourselves Sane," *Canadian Geographic*, May/June 1998
5 Russell Ash, *The World in One Day*, Dorling Kindersley, 1997
6 Michael Valpy, "An Antidote to the Car Drive to School," *The Globe and Mail*, 19 September 1997
7 Cathy Stepells, "Time to Get Back in the Saddle: 66% of Adult Canadians Are Not Active Enough to Maintain Good Health," *The Toronto Sun*, 21 September 1998
8 Study by French Railways
9 "Air Canada: It Seems Like Only Yesterday," *Canada NewsWire*, 5 September 1997
10 Steve Keenan, "Strewth, We've Come a Long Way," *The Times*, 6 December 1997
11 Russell Ash, op. cit.
12 Farrol Kahn, "The American Love of Flying," *Financial Times*, 19 April 1997
13 Ian Brodie, "US Faces Weekly Air Crash After 2000," *The Times*, 24 March 1997
14 British Airways Holidays
15 Russell Ash, op. cit.
16 Adbusters website, www.adbusters.org/pop/autosaurus
17 Jim Boothroyd, op. cit.
17 William Underhill, "Europe's Traffic Trauma," *Newsweek*, 25 August 1997
19 Worldwatch Institute
20 Kevin Eason, "Most Popular Cars Found to Be Least Safe," *The Times*, 18 April 1997
21 Tunk Varadarajan, "Trigger-Happy Americans Add Increasing Danger to Road Rage," *The Times*, 29 May 1997
22 Automobile Association of America
23 "Road Rage Like 'World War III'," *The Toronto Sun*, 27 January 1998
24 "Rage Spurs Shooting," *Winnipeg Free Press*, 22 September 1998
25 Jerry Adler, "Road Rage: We're Driven to Destruction," *Newsweek*, 16 June 1997
26 Mick Hamer, "Curb the Cars, Cure the City," *Tomorrow*, January/February 1996
27 Jane Armstrong, "Commuters Maintain Love Affair with Car," *The Globe and Mail*, 18 March 1998
28 Marcia D. Lowe, "Reinventing Transport," *State of The World 1994*, Worldwatch Institute, W.W. Norton & Co., 1994
29 Recycling Council of Ontario, www.rco.on.ca/reincarnate.html
30 Keith Allott, Environmental Data Services
31 Environmental Data Services, "Cleaner Europe Means Dirtier Russia" *ENDS Daily*, 11 September 1997
32 Paul Brown, "25 Deaths a Day Hastened by Exhaust Dust," *The Guardian*, 9 November 1997

33 Eve Edmonds, "Stats to Keep You Bicycling," *Ottawa Sun*, 10 October 1998
34 "Cooler Cars Increase Global Warming Threat," *ENDS Daily*, 14 August 1997
35 Ibid.
36 Mark Porter and David Brierley, "Has the Car Reached the End of the Road?" *The European*, 18–24 September 1997
37 NSCA, *Choosing and Using a Cleaner Car*, National Society for Cleaner Air, 1997
38 Recycling Council of Ontario, op. cit.
39 Ibid.
40 David Crane, "Made-in-Canada Fuel Cell Will Change Auto Industry," *The Toronto Star*, 9 January, 1999
41 Jason Lothian, "Part of a Cutting-Edge Car-Safety System which Automatically Calls for Help Following an Accident Is Being Manufactured in Lethbridge," *Lethbridge Herald*, 20 May 1998
42 Nick Nuttall, "Free with Petrol: A Chance to Help Save the World," *The Times*, 4 February 1998

Chapter 6

1 Andy Grove, "Man of the Year Issue," *Time*, 29 December 1997, Vol. 150, No. 27
2 Philip Ball, "Take It to the Limit," *New Scientist*, 2 August 1997
3 Raymond Snoddy, "Internet Boom Is Threat to Future of TV," *The Times*, 20 September 1997
4 Bill Gates, with Nathan Mynrvold and Peter Rirearson, *The Road Ahead*, Viking, 1995
5 Jon Katz, "The Digital Citizen," *Wired*, December 1997
6 Kathy Marks, "The 24-Hour Society Edges Nearer," *The Independent*, 29 September 1997
7 Peter Cochrane, *Tips for Time Travellers*, Orion Business Books, 1997
8 Nicholas Negroponte, *Being Digital*, Hodder & Stoughton, 1995
9 Ian Burrell, "Roboshops Show the Convenient Way Forward," *The Independent*, 2 January 1998
10 Germaine Greer, "Let's Catch Cads on the Internet," *Daily Mail*, 29 January 1998
11 Chris Partridge, "Simulations Show the Way to Find Mr Right," *Interface*, 9 April 1997
12 Philip Elmer-Dewitt, "The Great Green Network," *Time*, November 1997
13 Michael Schrage, MIT Researcher
14 Edward Welsh, "Information Fatigue Saps the E-Mail Set," *Sunday Times*, 20 April 1997
15 Henley Group, *Dying for Information? An Investigation Into the Effects of Information Overload in the UK and Worldwide*, 1997
16 Jonathan Leake, "Mobile Phones Are a Forgettable Experience," *Sunday Times*, 21 September 1997
17 Tom Utley, "Mobile Phonies Join the Ranks of Social Outcasts," *Daily Telegraph*, 22 October 1997
18 Karen O'Byrne, "Tower Infernal: What Goes Up Must Come Down," *The Globe and Mail*, 12 September 1998
19 "The Gloom Boom," *Benefits Canada*, January 1997
20 Russell Jenkins, "Video Games 'Teach Sexism and Violence'," *The Times*, 19 September 1997
21 Michael Medved, "Hollywood's Addiction to Violence," *Sunday Times*, 14 February 1993
22 "The Idle Generation," *Daily Mail*, 2 January 1998
23 Roberto Verzola, "Racing along the Information Highways," *The Month*, July/August 1997
24 Gavin Hainsworth, "The Darkening Mirror: Fighting the Effects of TV Violence on Our Children," *Teacher Newsmagazine*

25 Mike Yardley, "Video Nasties?" *Police Review*, 31 May 1996
26 Nicci Gerrard, "Fun with Mummy," *The Observer*, 30 March 1997
27 Mark Griffiths, "Friendship and Social Development in Children and Adolescents: The Impact of Electronic Technology," *Educational and Child Psychology*, Vol. 14 (3), 1997
28 Peppe Engberg, "Off the Record," *Scanorama*, July/August 1997
29 Consumers International, World Consumer Rights Day website, 15 March 1997
30 Julia Finch, "WPP Says No to Ads for Lads," *The Guardian*, 15 November 1997
31 *The Oxford Dictionary of New Words*, Oxford University Press, 1997
32 Barrie Clement, "Flying Pickets on the Superhighway," *The Independent*, 8 February 1997
33 Nicholas Rufford, "Electronic ID Cards to Go on Trial," *Sunday Times*, 24 August 1997
34 Audrey Magee, "Sweet-Toothed Teenager Is Dublin's First Internet Thief," *The Times*, 14 July 1997
35 David Lee Taylor, "Cyberscams and Digital Theft," *Internet Business*, September 1997
36 Thomas McCarroll, "Next for the CIA: Business Spying," *Time*, February 1993
37 Andrew Wyckoff, "Imagining the Impact of Electronic Commerce," *The OECD Observer*, No. 208, Oct./Nov. 1997
38 Wayne Ellwood, "Seduced by Technology," *New Internationalist*, December 1996
39 Madeleine Acey, "Snail Mail to 'Die Within a Decade,'" *Interface*, 3 September 1997
40 IBM
41 Esther Dyson, "Mirror, Mirror on the Wall," *Harvard Business Review*, September/ October 1997
42 Joshua Quittner, "Invasion of Privacy," *Time*, 25 August 1997
43 Steve Connor, "Brain Chip Signals Arrival of Bionic Man," *Sunday Times*, 16 November 1997
44 Alexander Goldsmith, "Old Chips for New," *Green Futures*, December 1996

Chapter 7

1 "Global Business Outlook," *Financial Times* Survey, 13 January 1998
2 Pam Woodall, "Thriving in the Shadows: The World in 1998," *The Economist*, 1997
3 Frances Russell, "They're After Our Water," *Winnipeg Free Press*, 23 December 1998
4 Matthew Valencia, "Money's Electronic Future, The World in 1998," *The Economist*, 1997
5 Jubilee 2000 Coalition, "Take Action Today to Cancel Third World Debt," www.oneworld.org/jubilee2000/ action_today
6 Paul Ekins, *Wealth Beyond Measure: An Atlas of New Economics*, Gaia Books, 1992
7 Center for a New American Dream, "Why Consumption Matters," www.newdream.org/main/index
8 Paul Ekins, op. cit.
9 Michael Chossudovsky, "The Global Financial Crisis," TFF Features, www.transnational. org/features/ global_finance_crisis.
10 Michael Thompson-Noel, "The Sly Lesson Taught by Lottoland," *Financial Times*, 17 January 1998
11 "RRSPs Not the Ticket for Everyone," *Winnipeg Free Press*, 16 January 1999
12 Ross Howard, "Is B.C.'s Economic Backbone History?" *The Globe and Mail*, 11 December 1998
13 Polly Ghazi and Judy Jones, "The Future of Work Revealed," *Independent on Sunday*, 28 September 1997

14 Lina Saigol, "Women Wear the Trousers Now," *The Guardian*, 19 April 1997
15 Paul Ekins, Mayer Hillman and Robert Hutchinson, op. cit.
16 Fraser Nelson, "Big Companies Change Emphasis in the Business of Giving to Charity," *Daily Telegraph*, 8 September 1997
17 Friends Provident, a guide written by Frank Blighe, www.moneyworld.co.uk
18 Sandra Gordon, Canadian Press, "Ethical Investing Takes Off." *The Toronto Sun*, 12 October 1998
19 Birna Helgadottir, "Norway Seeks a Clean Home for Oil Money," *The European*, February 1998
20 Melanie Bien, "Still Planning Our Retirement," *The European*, 24–30 July 1997
21 John Elkington, "The Life-Cycle of Money," *Tomorrow*, July/August 1996
22 Martin Wright, "God, Mammon and the Markets," *Tomorrow*, May/June 1996

Chapter 8

1 John Guillebaud, quoted in *Sex, Genes and All That*, by Anthony Smith, Macmillan, 1997
2 University Diagnostics Ltd.
3 Canadian Wire Stories, "Sex-Selection Method Gives Birth to Controversy," *Winnipeg Free Press*, 6 December 1998
4 "Sex Selection for Non-Medical Reasons," *Bulletin of Medical Ethics*, June 1996, pp. 8–10
5 David Fletcher, "Doctor Offers Parents a Choice of Baby's Sex," *Daily Telegraph*, 26 February 1997
6 Michael D. Lemonick, "The New Revolution in Making Babies," *Time*, 1 December 1997
7 Success rate information taken from: Human Fertilisation & Embryology Authority, *The Patients Guide to DI and IVF Clinics*, 3rd Edition, 1997
8 Sonia Gent, Maternity Unit, Peterborough (U.K.) Hospital
9 Anthony Smith, *Sex Genes and All That*, Macmillan 1997
10 Hans Koning, "Notes on the Twentieth Century," *Atlantic Monthly*, September 1997
11 David Harrison, "Secret Slaughter of Eight Million Animals Not Suitable for Tests," *The Observer*, 1 February 1998
12 BUAV, *Working towards new standards on animal testing*
13 FRAME—Fund for Replacement of Animals in Medical Research
14 D.M. Van Bekkum and P.V. Heldt, "BSE and Risk to Humans," *Nature*, 15 August 1996
15 Susan Greenfield, *Tomorrow's World*, www.bbc.co.uk/tw/9798/9801vision
16 Michael Day, "Tainted Transplants," *New Scientist*, 18 October 1997
17 J. Madeleine Nash, "Cloning's Kevorkian," *Time*, 19 January 1998
18 Robin Mckie, "Iceland's Gene Pool Holds the Key to Curing Diseases," *The Observer*, 9 November 1997
19 Aroha Te Pareake Mead, "Resisting the Gene Raiders," *New Internationalist*, August 1997
20 Catherine Baker, "Your Genes, Your Choices," *American Association for the Advancement of Science*, 1997
21 John Casey, "Eugenics: The Sinister Subplot to the Search for Social Utopia," *Daily Mail*, 30 August 1997
22 Jeremy Laurance, "A Short Step from Different to Undesirable," *The Independent*, 30 August 1997
23 Oliver Morton, "Overcoming Yuk," *Wired*, January 1998
24 Lee M. Silver, *Remaking Eden: Cloning and Beyond in a Brave New World*, Avon Books, 1997

25 David Fairhall, Richard Norton-Taylor and Tim Radford, "Saddam's Deadly Armoury," *The Guardian*, 11 February 1998
26 Tunku Varadarajan, "http://www.help-I-am-hopelessly-addicted," *The Times*, 16 March 1998
27 Patricia Sellers, "Team Tobacco Goes up in Smoke," *Fortune*, 9 September 1996
28 Lois Rogers, "Mild Cigarettes Cause New Wave of Cancer," *Sunday Times*, 16 November 1997
29 *Tobacco: The Smoke Blows South*, Panos Media Briefing, 1994/1997
30 "A Subtle Syllogism," *The Economist*, 16 August 1997
31 Ibid.
32 Lisa Buckingham, "Fat Is a Financial Issue," *The Guardian*, 27 December 1997
33 Charles Downey, "A Weighty Problem: Obesity in Children," Lycos Cityguide, www.healthgate.com, 1997
34 Tracy Corrigan, "Two Anti-Fat Drugs To Be Withdrawn," *Financial Times*, 16 September 1997
35 *What Doctors Don't Tell You*, Internet site "Steroids," www.smallpla.net/galleria/wallace/leadv7n2
36 Ibid.
37 Dr. Steiner, Princess Margaret Pain Migraine Clinic, London, "Headaches Are Caused by Too Many Tablets," *Sunday Telegraph*, January 1998
38 Peter Radetsky, *Allergic to the Twentieth Century*, Little, Brown, 1997
39 Jane E. Brody, "Estrogen Therapy? A Dilemma," *International Herald Tribune*, 21 August 1997
40 *Withholding or Withdrawing Life-Saving Treatment in Children*, Royal College of Paediatrics and Child Health, September 1997
41 Nicholas Alberry, *The Natural Death Handbook*, Rider/The Natural Death Centre, 1997
42 Richard Carlson, *Don't Sweat the Small Stuff ... And It's All Small Stuff*, Hyperion, 1997
43 Nicholas Alberry, op. cit.
44 The Natural Death Centre
45 "Dr Death Again," *Bulletin of Medical Ethics*, January 1996. See also *New England Journal of Medicine*, No. 334, 1996
46 Kirsty McGee, "Letting Go and Taking Control," *Ethical Consumer*, April/May 1997

Index

Page numbers in italic refer to listings found in tables